OCTOBER 7
THE WARS OVER WORDS AND DEEDS

OCTOBER 7
THE WARS OVER WORDS AND DEEDS

Edited by Donna Robinson Divine
and Asaf Romirowsky

ACADEMIC STUDIES PRESS
BOSTON
2025

Print LCCN 2025033522

Copyright © Academic Studies Press, 2025

ISBN 9798897830756 (hardback)
ISBN 9798897830763 (Adobe PDF)
ISBN 9798897830770 (ePub)

Book design by PHi Business Solutions
Cover design by Ivan Grave

The map on p. ii was provided by the Spokesperson's Unit of the Israel Defense Forces (IDF) with their permission

Published by Academic Studies Press
1007 Chestnut Street
Newton, MA 02464, USA
press@academicstudiespress.com
www.academicstudiespress.com

Contents

Introduction: October 7: The Wars Over Words and Deeds   1
Asaf Romirowsky

Part 1: The Violence and the Myths   7

1. The IDF: Handling Strategic and Operational Criticism in Gaza   9
Andrew Fox

2. Tragedy and Responsibility: The Debate over Casualties in Gaza   29
David Adesnik

3. Antisemitism Is about Semites like Dolichocephaly Is about Language   56
Franck Salameh

4. What Hamas Really Wants: The Ideology of the Islamic Resistance Movement   77
Cole Bunzel

Part 2: The Global Delusions   107

5. Does Terrorism Succeed? New Lessons from Hamas, the Global Intifada, and Antisemitism in America   109
Max Abrahms

6. Deterrence after October 7   126
Ben Fishman

7. US-Israel Relations in the Wake of October 7   146
Jonathan Rynhold

8   See No Evil, Hear No Evil, Speak No Evil: The Erasure of Hamas in
    UN Human Rights Narratives, and the Implications after October 7   168
    Anne Herzberg

Part 3: The Campus and the Land of Make-Believe   197

9   Higher Education Responds to October 7   199
    KC Johnson

10 The Political Economy of Antisemitism and Israel Hatred in
    Twenty-First-Century America   222
    Alex Joffe and Asaf Romirowsky

11 Fruit of the Land   245
    Aviya Cammy and Justin Cammy

12 Locating Sexual Violence: October 7 and Its Aftermath, Historically
    Conceptualized   265
    Skylar Ball

13 From the Cold War to University Campuses Today: The USSR,
    the Third World, and Contemporary Antizionist Discourse   277
    Izabella Tabarovsky

Part 4: The Social Contract and the Elected Government   299

14 Consensus and Polarization in the Israeli Party System in the
    Aftermath of October 7   301
    Csaba Nikolenyi

Conclusion: October 7—The Wars over Words and Deeds—Taking Stock   322
Donna Robinson Divine

Introduction:
October 7: The Wars Over Words and Deeds

Asaf Romirowsky

Lenin famously said that "there are decades where nothing happens; and there are weeks where decades happen." This is a fitting observation regarding the world after October 7 where an avalanche of antisemitism and cultural toxicity have attempted to reshape American society, impacting politics, media, and academia, all at lightning speed. These spheres function as interacting feedback loops, where small inputs and manipulations have wide-ranging effects. This volume gives many good illustrations of such effects because the October 7 atrocities have triggered worldwide changes that reach beyond the Middle East. To capture these dynamics, the book has been divided into four sections: the origins of the war, its ideologies and fallacies; the international institutions and relations that have augmented the regional war; the campus battleground for the hearts and mind of the West through an echo chamber of fallacies; and the changes within Israeli society brought about by the war and the potential long-term effects.

October 7 cast a destructive shadow not only on the men, women, and children caught on the battlefields or in the crossfire but also on the professionals—educators, journalists—expected to describe and explain what was happening. Notwithstanding the extreme brutality of its attacks—normally eliciting absolute condemnations by most democracies, Hamas's strategy of extreme violence won it substantial sympathy, if not outright backing in many of these rightly ruled societies. Consider the jubilant joy of faculty and students erupting at universities across the globe who spread the call for a global Intifada to make "Palestine free (or Arab) from the river to the sea." The message was transmitted from the precincts of the campuses to public roads, bridges, rail stations, penetrating government offices, municipal council meetings, and even delivered to the front doors of museums, hospitals, synagogues, and churches. Protests disrupted traffic, classes, and lectures. Buildings were occupied and defaced, and Jewish students were harassed and attacked, asphyxiating almost all attempts to examine the wars erupting on land, air, and sea with the analytic tools once taken for granted by scholars. The emotional pitch seemed to eradicate the desire, if not the possibility of probing the latest manifestation of this century-long conflict by diving deeply into its history and politics or by grounding all interpretations in carefully assembled data. Instead of examining October 7 for what was done, it was distilled as part of the larger culture wars, thereby totally unmooring it from what was unfolding on the ground. That so many in the media and in the universities projected these atrocities as the path to liberation not only for Palestinians but also for the oppressed all over the world defies not only logic but also everything known about human history on every continent.

It should be said clearly at the outset that this is a volume put together by people who are convinced these terrible events reinforce rather than eliminate the need for a meticulous examination of what happened on October 7 and for what motivated such savagery. Not only does this book belong in the classroom, it is the classroom that has shaped its contents. That view is illustrated best by the essay written by Skylar Ball, an undergraduate, who was assigned to write about the sexual violence perpetrated against women on October 7. Her essay demonstrates that this topic can be examined without the constraints of having to express unbridled faith in a righteous cause.

The October 7 assaults were astonishing acts, and the ambitions behind them can only be properly understood by examining words and deeds. For that reason, each section offers a mixture of data-driven analysis with a careful account of narratives and ideology. Thus, Franck Salameh's essay on how Muslims view Jews and Cole Bunzel's chapter on Hamas ideology in Part 1 serve as counterpoints to Andrew Fox and David Adesnik's investigations of what is known about IDF military strategy and what can be said about the terrible toll of these actions on the people living in the Gaza Strip.

The same mixture applies to Part 2, which focuses on the relationship of the Israel-Hamas War to world politics. Max Abrahms gathers data to examine what "globalizing the Intifada" actually means for the chances of fulfilling the near and distant goals set by terrorist movements. Jonathan Rynhold probes Israel's critical relationship with the United States. Ben Fishman supplies background on how both countries see the restoration of deterrence for Israel and for securing some sort of quiet for the region. Anne Herzberg unravels the web of connections between Palestinian terrorist movements and international organizations deemed guardians of peace and human rights.

Part 3 interrogates how the war catalyzed campus protests. KC Johnson surveys the protests that have been filtered through the legal system. Justin and Aviya Cammy examine the ritualized performative aspects of protests through a focus on the watermelon as symbol and icon. Alex Joffe and Asaf Romirowsky disclose, for the first time, the sources of funding for various movements promoting the October 7 barbarism as the beginning of liberation for Palestinians. Izabella Tabarovsky uncovers the ideological roots of the dominant narrative embraced by faculty and students. Finally, Part 4, which contains the remarkable essay by Csaba Nikolenyi, rooted in recent survey data, explains how the Israeli coalition in office on that terrible day of death and destruction has retained its hold on power.

We began by noting the shadow this war has cast on so much of what we take for granted about life, values, expertise. We end by declaring this volume as the standard to measure how much of a footprint October 7 leaves on war and peace in the world going forward. Furthermore, the echo chamber of the last decade has only tightened, and its political and social dynamics worsened by the events of October 7. Hamas's mass murder and kidnapping generated an intellectual and physical high from advocates of post-colonialism. The placement of "Palestine" at the center of the Islamic-leftist alliance against the West and capitalism—exemplified by the phrase "globalize the Intifada"—has also turned Palestinians into symbols of broader rebellions. "Palestine" is "intersectionally" used to promote a slew of other causes, such as climate rebellion, decolonization, and anti-racism.

With the breakthrough achieved through hyper-violence, Palestinians reclaimed the world's attention, but foreign movements hurried to hijack the brand. Intifada and the keffiyeh (the iconic symbol that was ironically mandated by the British as a means of social control over the West and East Banks of the Jordan River) are now "culturally expropriated" as trademarks by Western enthusiasts who also wave Hezbollah and Houthi flags and throw soup on masterpieces of Western art, and by hipsters making coffee.

The current project to reclaim language related to the Arab-Israeli conflict has another bloody dimension. Too many intellectuals since October have been frank in their celebration of Hamas's violence, a reflection of a longstanding deep addiction to terror. The French revolutionaries of the late eighteenth century, who invoked Jean-Jacques Rousseau, and the physician ideologues of ISIS like Ayman al-Zawahiri have been joined by figures such as Walaa Alqaisiya, a research fellow at Columbia University, who wrote: "Academics like to decolonize through discourse and land acknowledgments. Time to understand that

Decolonization is NOT a metaphor. includes armed struggle to LITERALLY get our lands and lives back!"[1] The notion of decolonization, which along with "settler-colonialism" dominates academic discourse on Israel, provides moral justification for violence. Decolonial theorists Eve Tuck and K. Wayne Yang expounded at length on the "entangled triad structure of settler-native-slave" and the "the real and symbolic violence of settler colonialism" but argued "decolonization is not obliged to answer" what methods are involved or what the future looks like for anyone. Faced with the evidence that decolonization looks like rape, kidnapping, and torture, academics have been quick to deny the facts and to accuse Israel of 'genocide'—albeit by expand the definition to include unspecified harm to civilians.

Both inside and outside of academia, normal people with normal morality are confronted with a profound problem—how to respond to academics who advocate terror. One way is to identify, repudiate, and isolate intellectuals who espouse these views. The shield of academic freedom to defend such hateful views may prevent individuals from losing their jobs but not from the contempt they deserve. Such views should be publicized and condemned widely. Society, which already holds negative opinions of academia for its nearly unvarnished hatred of normal values and behaviors, and its bizarre abstractions and conceits, must challenge the idea of decolonization and its immorality as well as question the fitness of those who promote it as teachers and thinkers.

But what can be done institutionally? Condemning universities and think tanks that employ bigots who salivate over murder may cause embarrassment but offers no path to change. Refusing to engage with these institutions might. They rely on their social reputations for their very existence—reputations that should already be in tatters for countless other reasons, exorbitant costs, nonsensical course offerings, and lying about taking billions from unfree states such as Qatar, to name just a few. Moral obscenities like cheering mass murder in the name of decolonization should be the final straw.

Shattering the reputations of academics who support murder and repudiating their influence and roles in society are critical. Without it, murder will find high-sounding advocates who sway students, akin to those thirty student groups at Harvard who "hold the Israeli regime entirely responsible for all unfolding

---

1 Asaf Romirowsky and Alex Joffe, "Hamas and the Immorality of the 'Decolonial' Intellectuals," National Interest, October 13, 2023, https://nationalinterest.org/feature/hamas-and-immorality-decolonial-intellectuals-206933.

violence."² Those students, too, should be identified, questioned regarding their support for violence, and if necessary, shunned. But without addressing the intellectual foundations that support—in this case, Islamic antisemitic terrorism—academia will become irredeemable. Hence this latest collection of essays.

Historical revisionism and intellectual dishonesty have been festering for decades inside academia and its supporting structures but have exploded since October 7. As a result, this volume has been conceived to dissect the reverberating impact of the Gaza War, which has established 'Palestine'—at once the quintessential bloody shirt and mythical abstraction—as the only global cause the world should rally behind.

Antisemitism has frequently been called the "world's oldest hatred," but this anodyne formula obscures how ideas are recycled with innovations to fit the times, created, then transmitted, and supported. The political economy of anti Israel bias and antisemitism in America, which has only been sketched here, provides a portrait of how individual beliefs and movement scale ideologies are reproduced and disseminated. Though "timeless" in the sense of Jews being the perennial target of shifting forms of hatred, there is nothing organic about antisemitism.

This book assembles a group of scholars committed to the rigors of the scholarly enterprise—to ground explanations of developments and narratives on concrete evidence and logic and not on ideology or fidelity to one or another presumed righteous cause or crusade. We are fully aware that we are writing about a war that continues to cause casualties and massive destruction as well as the possibility for radical political change.

Those paying attention to the essays will see differences among them. Rigorous analysis is bound to generate interpretations that do not necessarily align perfectly with one another. What unites this volume is not a uniformity of view. Rather, it is a faith that even in the midst of such uncertainty, there are some things that can be said with confidence.

---

2   Madeline Halpert, "Growing Backlash over Harvard Students' Pro-Palestine Letter," BBC, October 10, 2023, https://www.bbc.com/news/world-us-canada-67067565.

Part 1

THE VIOLENCE AND THE MYTHS

CHAPTER 1

The IDF: Handling Strategic and Operational Criticism in Gaza

Andrew Fox

From the beginning of Operation Swords of Iron in Gaza, Western commentators have lined up to criticize the Israel Defense Forces (IDF) and their chosen approach. This chapter will provide a summary of this criticism at the strategic and operational levels. It will focus specifically on military critique, putting aside broad objections to the morality of the war, such as the anonymous letter published by CNN in February 2024, in which a broad spread of government officials object to the entire premise of the war.[1]

The chapter will also examine Western failures in Iraq, using the story of the British Army in Basra as a case study to understand how lessons learned from these conflicts might be applicable to the IDF—and, most critically, why IDF operational design has avoided many of these errors already. It will analyze Israel's strategy and operational plan to understand the strengths and weaknesses of Israel's approach, and whether parallels with the Global War on Terror are valid. The chapter will then conclude on the effectiveness of Operation Swords of Iron and the extent to which any criticism is justified.

Doctrinally, there are three levels of military decision-making: the strategic, the operational, and the tactical. Strategy gives the "ends": the desired conclusion for which military force is being applied. The operational level gives the "ways": the sequencing of tactical engagements. The tactical level provides the

---

1 Mick Craver, "More Than 800 Western Officials Sign Scathing Criticism of Gaza Policy," CNN, February 2, 2024, https://edition.cnn.com/2024/02/02/middleeast/western-officials-criticism-gaza-policy-israel-intl/index.html.

"means": the physical actions to be carried out. These "means" at the tactical level are the actions carried out to achieve desired strategic aims. The operational level coordinates these actions along lines of operation. For example, the tactical level can involve deploying a division to carry out missions, coordinated at the operational level, which cumulatively achieve strategic objectives. This notion of tactics as a framework is not to be confused with low-level, small-unit tactics (for example, fire and movement or satellite patrolling).

These three levels of military decision-making should stem from a set political aim: policy. The calculation of a joined-up plan for arriving at a policy end-state, articulated as "the capacity . . . to devise and sustain a continuing process which can promote our national interest,"[2] has been known in the past as "Grand Strategy," although the preferred modern term is "National Strategy" (not to be confused with military strategy). In his autobiography, Major General Chip Chapman gives the timely reminder: "Strategy is not policy and policy is not strategy. Policy states what is to be done, or sometimes what is not to be done."[3] He goes on to quote Viscount Alanbrooke's definition of military strategy:

> Determine the aim, which is political: to derive from that aim a series of objectives to be achieved; to assess these objectives as to the requirements they create and the preconditions which the achievement of each is likely to necessitate; to measure available and potential resources against the requirements, and to derive from this process a coherent pattern of priorities and a rational course of action.[4]

At the strategic level, criticism of Israel broadly focuses on the "end state," or how the operation will conclude in a manner that achieves political goals. Israeli strategy has been articulated by Prime Minister Netanyahu in October 2023 as "destroying Hamas's military and governing capabilities and bringing the captives back home."[5] He expanded on this in November 2023: "We have clearly

---

2   *Who Does UK National Strategy?*, First Report of 2010–11, Public Administration Select Committee (October 12, 2010), 3.
3   Chip Chapman, *Notes from a Small Military* (London: John Blake Publishing, 2013), 310.
4   Ibid.
5   "Israel-Hamas War: 'We will fight and we will win,' Says Benjamin Netanyahu," *Sky News*, October 28, 2023.

defined the goals of the war: Eliminate Hamas, free our hostages and ensure that on the day after Hamas, Gaza will no longer constitute a threat to Israel."[6]

The statements represent an articulation for the war in Gaza, but at every stage to date they lack specificity. There is a fair and accurate criticism that this is a military goal, not a political goal. Another criticism has been over the lack of articulation of what the "day after" looks like and who will replace Hamas. Until this question is answered, the IDF might find themselves having to plan operations to set the conditions for Hamas's removal and eventual replacement, but with no concept of what that replacement will be.

That said, operational security usually demands that a military does not reveal every detail of their plans. A rebuttal to this criticism of a lack of strategy is that Israel is perfectly within reason not to broadcast their plans to the world, including their enemies. This key detail appears to have passed by many critics.

There is also an issue in terms of lexicon and semantics. "Destroy" is a term used by Netanyahu in a political context. We must be careful in making assessments of strategy from press conferences. There is value in making threatening rhetorical speeches during wartime, both to bolster the will of one's domestic audience and to intimidate one's enemy. Where Netanyahu said "destroy," a far better summary of Israel's strategic goals is *the dismantling of Hamas's administrative and strategic warfighting capabilities* (i.e., Hamas's ability to attack Israel).

It is here that we see the challenges of articulating a coherent policy in a chaotic domestic and international context. The situation in October 2023 saw the aftermath of a terror attack within Israel's borders, an immediate counterattack campaign in Gaza, rocket attacks from Hezbollah in Lebanon displacing more than 60,000 Israelis in the north of Israel, threats from other Iranian regime proxies, and from Iran itself.

October 7 demanded a credible response, but this most complex of scenarios represented a significant challenge. At the political level, tensions in the War Cabinet between Netanyahu, Defense Minister Yoav Gallant, and Benny Gantz led to a fluid and iterative strategy, incorporating the Gaza Strip, Lebanon, and the West Bank as immediate and competing priorities. In Gaza, this has forced the IDF to devise a military plan coherent to a vague political outcome. As Sun Tzu wrote: "Strategy without tactics is the slowest route to victory. Tactics without strategy is the noise before defeat."

Therefore, objections to Israel's political strategy are entirely valid, at this point, but only because there is no viable long-term solution to the broader

---

6 "Statement by PM Netanyahu," November 23, 2024, https://www.gov.il/en/pages/event-press-conference221123.

issue of Israel-Palestine relations. As Anchal Vohra wrote, "How would Netanyahu eliminate the idea of armed resistance without a political solution on the horizon?"[7] Netanyahu himself said at the UN General Assembly three weeks before October 7, "For peace to prevail, the Palestinians must stop spewing Jew hatred, finally reconcile themselves to the Jewish state. By that I mean not only to the existence of the Jewish state, but to the right of the Jewish people to have a state of their own in their historic homeland—the land of Israel."[8]

Rajan Menon sums up the situation:

> When the guns eventually fall silent in Gaza, Israelis and Palestinians will confront a decades-old reality that cannot be overcome by violence and political half-measures. Both Jews and Palestinians will continue to assert privileged ownership of Palestine, citing centuries of history, the merits of which will never be settled conclusively by historians, let alone by the two principals. The question, therefore, is not whether Jews and Palestinians will continue living cheek by jowl, but how. Will they do so amid endless spasms of bloodletting or a coexistence created by a negotiated settlement that reconciles Israel's need for security with Palestinians' desire for statehood?[9]

The Israeli war cabinet therefore found and continue to find themselves with an impossible task: articulating a coherent regional policy whilst under attack on multiple fronts, with the other actors involved unwilling to compromise on the issue of Israel's very existence. There is no middle ground in these two positions. A political solution to the Israel-Palestine conundrum has escaped statesmen for seven decades. It is both unreasonable and unrealistic to expect the Israeli government to articulate the answer to this problem in the immediate aftermath

---

7   David Petraeus, Meghan L. O'Sullivan, and Richard Fontaine, "Israel's War of Regime Change Is Repeating America's Mistakes," *Foreign Affairs*, June 17, 2024, https://www.foreignaffairs.com/israel/israel-war-regime-change-repeating-americas-mistakes-david-petraeus.

8   "Prime Minister Benjamin Netanyahu's 2023 UN General Assembly Speech," September 22, 2023, *Haaretz*, https://www.haaretz.com/israel-news/2023-09-22/ty-article/full-text-benjamin-netanyahus-2023-un-general-assembly-speech/0000018a-bd3c-d490-adca-fdff21270000.

9   Rajan Menon, "The No-State Solution: Could a Ceasefire Deal Ever Appease Both Sides?," UnHerd, August 19, 2024, https://unherd.com/2024/08/the-no-state-solution/.

of the worst massacre of Jews since the Holocaust, at a time when war has been declared on Israel by Iran, their proxies, and their allies in Gaza, the West Bank, Lebanon, Yemen, and Iraq.

Given this paradox, political goals have been, and could only ever have been, reactive to events—and, in Gaza, finding an alternative solution to Hamas's governance has no straightforward and reasonable answer. Muddling through has always been the best option. At least from what could be discerned from the options before leaders, securing Israel's borders and citizens from attack in the short- to medium-term horizon is the best and most realistic political outcome to aim for. That aim is set, and who governs next in Gaza is an end state that will evolve over time when as an understanding of what is possible develops.

Below political-strategic criticism, the objection to IDF military strategy in Gaza could be summarized by the comments of Kurt Campbell, US Deputy Secretary of State. Addressing the NATO Youth Summit, he said the United States was "struggling over what the theory of victory is . . . Sometimes when we listen closely to Israeli leaders, they talked about mostly the idea of some sort of sweeping victory on the battlefield, total victory. . . . I don't think we believe that that is likely or possible."[10]

"Victory" is an unhelpful term in this context. A positive result for Israel is better expressed in terms of achieving strategic goals. If we examine Israel's strategy through Alanbrooke's lens, the IDF's strategy is clearly a rational course of action to achieve those set political strategic goals.

The IDF articulate their strategy clearly. Their strategic objectives are:

1. dismantling Hamas and PIJ administrative and military capabilities in the Gaza Strip.
2. removing threat posed to Israel from the Gaza Strip in the long term.
3. restoring security to the residents of the border communities.
4. strengthening the personal security and national resilience of Israeli citizens.
5. creating conditions that will enable the return of hostages to Israel.
6. restoring deterrence and projecting power in all arenas, with immediate readiness for any development in the northern arena.[11]

---

10 Matt Berg and Alexander Ward, "Israel's 'Total Victory' in Gaza Is Unlikely, Top U.S. Official Says," Politico, May 13, 2024, https://www.politico.com/news/2024/05/13/israel-total-victory-gaza-unlikely-00157678.
11 Interview with IDF Chief of Staff, April 2024.

At the time of writing, we have seen unprecedented developments in the northern arena in the fight against Hezbollah.

Whilst all Israel's current military efforts interconnected at the strategic level, this chapter focuses on the Gaza Strip. In Gaza, the operational design to support IDF's objectives as listed above is also clearly articulated. This design can be split into several phases. It is worth noting that these phases are not necessarily sequential. Some are conditions-based and some run concurrently.

- Phase A: defense on October 7 and in its aftermath; air strikes in Gaza; population evacuation.
- Phase B1&2: North Gaza City maneuver; maximizing achievements where targets present; destroying underground capabilities.
- Phase B3: ceasefire and hostage return.
- Phase B4: Khan Younis, north Gaza, target Central Battalions, Rafah.
- Phase C: continuous efforts to dismantle Hamas administrative and military capabilities; raids and concentrated operations; create the conditions for alternatives to Hamas.
- Phase D: stabilizing alternative to Hamas in Gaza; maintaining freedom of operation.[12]

If we measure this against Alanbrooke's definition of strategy, the IDF has clearly analyzed the preconditions necessary for the achievement of each of their war aims. Resources have been measured against these requirements, and it has been found that the aims are achievable with the assets the IDF has. The "coherent pattern of priorities and a rational course of action" are clear. The IDF operational design is therefore logical, even where the alternative governance solution to Hamas is still an evolving strategic solution.

Western critique is not limited to strategic criticism, however. In May 2024, General CQ Brown, chair of the US Joint Chiefs of Staff, gave a stern critique of Israel's operational design: "Not only do you have to actually go in and clear out whatever adversary you are up against, you have to go in, hold the territory and then you've got to stabilize it. . . . [Israel] cleared they didn't hold, and so that allows your adversary then to repopulate in areas if you're not there."[13] This was echoed in June 2024 by retired US general David Petraeus, who wrote of

---

12 Ibid.
13 Paul Mcleary and Laura Seligman, "Biden's Top Military Adviser Chides Israel for Losing Ground to Hamas," Politico, May 20, 2024, https://www.politico.com/news/2024/05/20/biden-adviser-critiques-israel-strategy-00158978.

Israel's proposed "regime change" in Gaza.[14] He drew comparisons with Iraq, Afghanistan, and Syria, describing these experiences as "bloody, costly, and humbling." Petraeus's criticisms can be summarized as follows: firstly, no plan to create a post-war governance structure; secondly, failure to retain terrain in Gaza once cleared of Hamas fighters; and thirdly, excessive civilian casualties. He goes on to laud America's successes in these campaigns and urges Israel to copy his own "surge" strategy from Iraq in 2007, where US troops flooded the most violent areas of Iraq to pacify them.

Petraeus's first criticism has already been addressed above. Let us address the second point, however. Western counterinsurgency doctrine requires a military force ratio of 20 to 25 security force personnel per 1,000 head of population.[15] This equates to a soldier to civilian ratio of 1:40–1:50. For the Gaza Strip, with a population of 2.1 million, this would require between 42,000 and 52,500 combat soldiers in permanent occupation of the territory for the duration of the operation. Going by the example of Iraq or Afghanistan, this means for at least a decade. This does not include the enabling support arms of logistics, medical, engineers, and others required, which would number many tens of thousands more IDF soldiers to be mobilized.

Petraeus effectively argues for the entirety of the IDF's regular strength to be deployed to Gaza on an enduring basis. This would be unsustainable and therefore is an unrealistic recommendation. The IDF is designed as a raiding force, based around mobilization of reserves. They are not designed for enduring expeditionary operations. To undertake the solution suggested by Petraeus would come at an impossible cost to Israel's economy, both in terms of the conflict and in having to mobilize tens of thousands of reservists indefinitely, away from their civilian employment.

Petraeus places an emphasis on the need to prevent an enemy from regrouping once rendered incapable. He draws the parallel between US forces in Iraq, launching missions to clear various areas of insurgent groups such as Al Qaeda and Iranian regime-backed Shiite militias. Once the Americans concluded these missions and withdrew, insurgents would reinfiltrate those areas. Petraeus suggests that this is what Hamas and their allies are doing in Gaza. He misses the fact that in the areas in which they operate the IDF is degrading Hamas infrastructure and strategic capability—Hamas's ability to project force into Israel. The IDF is destroying tunnels, cohesive fighting formations, and rocket manufacture

---

14 Petraeus, O'Sullivan, and Fontaine, "Israel's War of Regime Change."
15 Bill Rollo, "Campaigning and Generalship: Iraq 2008," in *British Generals in Blair's Wars*, ed. Jonathan Bailey, Richard Iron, and Hew Strachan (Farnham, Surrey: Ashgate, 2013), 185.

and launch sites. This is the entire purpose of the mission: not to seize territory the IDF has no hope of holding indefinitely. Of course, the IDF has been slowed down at the tactical level by the need to learn how to fight effectively in tunnels. This strategy has also seen the IDF incurring casualties in areas they have already fought in. However, Petraeus's alternate solution is no better. What is proposed in his criticism, as an alternative to current Israeli action, is a repeat of Western counterinsurgency tactics in Iraq and Afghanistan—but done better, in unspecified ways.

Petraeus suggests that, in Gaza, the IDF should pledge security to the people of Gaza as well as economic development. His third criticism suggests that Israel has not done enough to minimize civilian casualties, despite unprecedented measures such as the Civilian Harm Mitigation Cell (CHMC). The CHMC is the product of eight years of research and technological development. It is a team of twenty-five officers and soldiers, commanded by a one-star brigadier general. CHMC produces a map of Gaza, updated hourly, split into 620 cells based around Palestinian municipal life to show the population density in each. Each cell can be individually interrogated for data. Every IDF operations center, both army and air force, has access to this map, but content is centrally controlled only by the CHMC. This map contains granular detail of the strike history in each cell, and the percentage of current civilian occupation compared to the original population. This can be cross-checked with real-time air photography to verify civilian presence. Furthermore, drones are used as a tool to predict civilian casualties. Targets are observed for at least an hour to ascertain the pattern of life and minimize civilian collateral damage. Strikes, using a targeting process entirely analogous to NATO militaries, are aborted where numbers of civilians disproportionate to the value of the target are identified.[16]

Petraeus further suggests that Israeli operations are creating more fighters than they kill, as civilian deaths provoke hitherto undecided Gazans to join Hamas as retribution for family losses. This is a broad assumption that is unsubstantiated by current evidence. Indeed, opinion polls in show a continuing decline in support for both Hamas and armed struggle as a means of resistance.[17]

Whilst Petraeus notes that "Iraq in 2007 and Gaza today differ in clear and significant ways," he does not articulate precisely how he believes the situations are different, or why the tactics he recommends would work in Gaza where they

---

16 *Amicus Curiae Observation of High-Level Military Group Pursuant of Rule 103*, International Criminal Court, No. ICC-01/18–267, August 5, 2024.
17 *Public Opinion Polls No. 93*, Palestinian Center for Policy and Survey Research, September 17, 2024, https://www.pcpsr.org/en/node/991.

did not in Iraq. He also claims as "beyond dispute" that Hamas will continue to reconstitute itself until such time as an armed force, be it the IDF or an outside military, is able to "clear Hamas fighters, hold territory, and build basic infrastructure and governing mechanisms."

This work contends the opposite: this point is highly disputed. Preventing Hamas from reconstituting is the entire purpose of the operation. So far, we have seen up to 20,000 Hamas fighters killed, hundreds of miles of tunnels destroyed, and the destruction of Hamas's strategic capabilities in terms of rockets that can strike Israeli territory, and the ability to repeat a October 7-style attack. At this point, it is irrelevant to IDF strategy if Hamas reconstitutes as a guerilla fighting force if that force does not have the ability to project into Israeli territory.

Petraeus lauds the success of his own "surge" strategy:

> Eighteen months after the surge began, violence in Iraq had declined by nearly 90%, and it declined further until the last U.S. combat troops withdrew from the country in 2011, some three and a half years later. By that point, economic life had returned, and extremist and insurgent recruiting had faltered. Over time, U.S. forces managed to hand security and other responsibilities over to local authorities, allowing American troops to thin out and then withdraw. The situation deteriorated only when the U.S. troop presence vanished completely, and Iraq's prime minister at the time, the Shiite leader Nouri al-Maliki, pursued a highly sectarian agenda.[18]

This is a bewildering observation. Any short-term successes of the surge in Iraq are surely negated by the immediate total collapse of security following American withdrawal. Petraeus's surge demonstrably failed to achieve any of the US government's strategic goals in Iraq and led directly to the formation of ISIS.

Petraeus slopes his shoulders at the lack of Iraqi political embrace of his own military genius and loads the blame for the surge's failure onto the sectarian policies of the Iraqi prime minister. However, in counterinsurgency operations, any military effort will be a failure if not aligned with the political strategy of the host nation.

---

18 Petraeus, O'Sullivan, and Fontaine, "Israel's War of Regime Change."

As Clausewitz wrote, "War is nothing but a continuation of politics with the admixture of other means."[19] There is no sense in lauding the success of a military operation at the tactical level if everything that directly follows does not achieve a single strategic objective. Petraeus's surge was an abject failure in the long term because his military operational design did not align with Iraqi political strategy. This is the true lesson for Israel from American operations in Iraq. Petraeus criticizes Israel's tactics whilst failing to understand that those tactics are in perfect alignment with the Israeli government's desired goals of dismantling Hamas's strategic capabilities and securing Israel's borders.

Petraeus's criticism then disappears into a fantasy of peaceful Gazans rallying together under direct IDF military rule and occupation providing security; the IDF co-opting Hamas's police force to maintain law and order; and the incorporation of "trustworthy" Palestinian administrators to run the Gaza Strip. This naively represents a total failure to understand the situation in Gaza, the history of the conflict, or the nature of the enemy the IDF are fighting within Gaza itself.

It is also possible that Petraeus's mindset is one that could only be advanced by someone whose experiences are framed by citizenship of a global superpower with all the concomitant resources. Israel and the IDF could never hope to achieve the physical mass or the twenty-year economic commitment that was needed just to hold Afghanistan in balance without a decisive result, for example. The Afghanistan and Iraq campaigns show that rebuilding military capabilities in countries utterly torn apart by one's own forces is simply a means of opening the door to corrupt sectarian influences. Israel will never persuade Gazans that they are not occupiers, just as NATO coalitions could not in both Afghanistan and Iraq.

In Western criticism, then, typified by Petraeus's observations, we may observe a clear drumbeat: the IDF must hold the ground they fight over. The IDF must provide security for Gazans. The IDF must conduct reconstruction in Gaza. The implication is that, if they do not, then the mission must inevitably fail as it did for NATO in Iraq and Afghanistan.

The overarching worldview of this commentary and criticism is that Israel is fighting an insurgency in Gaza, and that the issue can be resolved through a US-style counterinsurgency strategy. This shows not only a misunderstanding of Operation Swords of Iron, but also a continued misunderstanding of the wars in which these critics themselves commanded. Despite their confident

---

19   Carl von Clausewitz, *On War* (Ware, Hertfordshire: Wordsworth Editions Limited, 1997), bk. 1, ch. 7.

recommendations to the IDF, these generals still do not understand why they lost—or even that they were defeated at all.

The conflict Israel fights in Gaza, however, is not a counterinsurgency. British doctrine gives a definition of insurgency as "an organised, violent subversion used to effect or prevent political control, as a challenge to established authority."[20] The American definition is "an organized movement aimed at the overthrow of a constituted government through the use of subversion and armed conflict."[21]

Hamas clearly do not fit into this categorization. They are not challenging established authority or trying to overthrow a constituted government. In the Gaza Strip, Hamas themselves *are* the constituted authority. As part of Area A under the Oslo II Accord, Gaza was considered an area in which the Palestinian authority had full civil and security control. Since 2007, Gaza has been, in effect, a separate political entity from the West Bank. After that year's Fatah-Hamas clashes and the expulsion of Fatah, Hamas has been the sole *de facto* government of the Gaza Strip. They cannot therefore be classified as an insurgency. What Israel is attempting in Gaza is regime change.

Counterinsurgency and regime change are different things, and only loosely connected. As Petraeus correctly identifies, the root cause of insurgency in Iraq was the initial decapitation of the Iraqi governance system as part of a regime change operation. It is this failure that demands closer examination to correctly draw lessons for the IDF in Gaza. As part of this wider campaign, the failure of the British in Basra gives an excellent example of how the disaster unfolded. It demonstrates how misclassifying the nature of any given conflict, as Petraeus does in his criticism of IDF operations in Gaza, can lead to mission failure at the first hurdle. It is replete with genuine lessons for the IDF.

The crucial moment of failure in Iraq was decision to remove all Ba'ath Party members from government institutions. This included the machinery of state and the Iraqi Army,[22] replacing them with the American-led Office of Reconstruction and Humanitarian Assistance. This is turn was quickly replaced by the Coalition Provisional Authority led by Paul Bremer, which led to a vacuum at the heart of Iraq's government system. Thousands of angry, armed, unemployed Iraqi ex-soldiers dispersed amongst the general population.

---

20 *Army Field Manual—Countering Insurgency*, vol. 1, part 10 (AC71876, January 2010), 1–4.
21 *U.S. Army/Marine Corps Field Manual 3–24, Counterinsurgency*, 2.
22 Tim Cross, "Rebuilding Iraq 2003: Humanitarian Assistance and Reconstruction," in *British Generals in Blair's Wars*, ed. Jonathan Bailey, Richard Iron, and Hew Strachan (Farnham, Surrey: Ashgate, 2013), 77.

In the aftermath of the invasion of Iraq in March 2003, the British plan was to hand over control of Basra to Iraqis at the earliest opportunity. However, because they had not properly analyzed the nuances of Shi'a versus Sunni factionalism within southern Iraq in their planning, they failed to understand exactly whom they were empowering in Basra. They made a litany of governmental errors that worked directly against their desired strategic end state.

For example, shortly after the invasion, on April 11, 2003, British divisional commander Major General Binns appointed Muzahim al-Tamimi to lead a new local council. Al-Tamimi was a Sunni who had been on Saddam Hussein's payroll. His appointment in a majority Shi'a city sparked protests the next day involving "several hundred" of the local populace.[23] Right from the beginning of their stabilization operations in Basra, the British failed to gain the consent of the people—the main goal of a counterinsurgency operation.

Whilst Gaza is not a counterinsurgency, this clearly highlights the dangers of appointing alternative governance in an area where governance is contested along tribal lines, as it is within the Gaza Strip outside of Hamas's control. It is a recipe for unrest and further conflict. In the proposed regime change, it is vital that any administration in Gaza after Hamas has the consent of the population from the offset—no matter how unpalatable that might be to Israel.

A further example: the British were prevented from employing former Hussein forces in a policing role. For instance, they were ordered by the Coalition Provisional Authority (CPA) to disband a fledgling port police force based around elements of the Iraqi Navy. In attempting to hand over policing to local forces, the British trained and supported units such as the Serious Crimes Unit (SCU)—which Ledwidge terms a "gang of rapists, torturers and murderers who took orders no from the governor but from Muktada Al-Sadr."[24] In September 2005, the SCU abducted two members of the Special Air Service, deeply exposing British lack of control in the city.[25]

If the IDF are serious about removing Hamas from power, it is therefore vital that any subsequent governance is not merely making placatory noises but is genuinely free from Hamas influence, which represents an enormous challenge. In Gaza this will be more easily said than done—and it is arguably impossible, which gives a further clear indicator of what the likely end state will look like.

---

23 Jack Fairweather, *A War of Choice: The British in Iraq 2003–09* (London: Jonathan Cape, 2011), 31.
24 Frank Ledwidge, *Losing Small Wars* (New Haven, CT: Yale University Press, 2011), 33.
25 David H. Ucko and Robert Egnell, *Counterinsurgency in Crisis* (New York: Columbia University Press, 2013), 59.

This British lesson from Basra suggests that Israel cannot afford to be complicit in the inevitable violent power struggle that will follow Hamas vacating their governmental role or fighting to keep it.

The British in Basra, with their strategy to hand over political control in a hurry, were grossly exposed by the failure of the CPA to deliver governance. Other groups rushed to fill the void and won appointments across the board in the 2004 Interim Government. It is no coincidence that the violence in Basra escalated soon after these appointments. In the largely Shi'a South, these groups were dominated by the Iranian-backed Supreme Council for Islamic Revolution in Iraq (SCIRI). Their armed wing was the Badr Brigade and the Jaish al-Madhi (JAM) militia, led by vocal anti-occupation cleric Moqtada al-Sadr with his subordinate in Basra, Ahmed al-Fartosi. According to Ucko and Egnell, SCIRI members filled provincial governorships, council seats, and senior police posts, and members of the Badr Brigade became heads of intelligence and customs police in Basra.[26]

For example, Ahmed al-Maliki was appointed director general of education: a follower of al-Sadr, he proceeded to purge Sunni teachers from the education system in favor of his own Shi'a followers, and he applied a conservative Shi'a ideology, removing women from positions of authority, splitting classes by gender, and questioning the education of girls over the age of twelve.[27]

This system of questionable appointments and democratic legitimacy was further brought into question by the nature of Arab loyalty in the Shi'a South. Major General Shaw quoted the Basra Police Chief, Maj Gen Jalil, when he stated, "Whatever abstract appeals the Coalition might have offered in terms of democracy and development, they were powerless set against the blood loyalties of family, tribe, religion, and ethnicity."[28] In essence, whatever the Coalition sought to achieve, the "consent of the people" would always have to be measured and weighed against their religious and ethnic delineations.

This is plainly the case in Gaza, where any alternative governance to Hamas must be measured against their existing loyalties to family, tribe, Palestinian Authority, Hamas, or even wider Sunni religious affiliations in the region such as the Muslim Brotherhood—not to mention the requirement to ensure that any replacement for Hamas governance is not simply a proxy for Hamas themselves.

---

26 Ibid., 56–57.
27 Fairweather, *A War of Choice*, 68.
28 Jonathan Shaw, "Basra 2007: The Requirements of a Modern Major General," in *British Generals in Blair's Wars*, ed. Jonathan Bailey, Richard Iron, and Hew Strachan (Farnham, Surrey: Ashgate, 2013), 177.

This is underpinned by the requirement for any governance to have legitimacy in the eyes of the population, which almost certainly precludes any Israeli attempt at appointing "puppet governance."

Furthermore, the political delineations in Basra were tested to the extreme by the actions of a small number of Coalition soldiers. A series of public relations catastrophes occurred which received Iraq-wide, and indeed worldwide, publicity. The American scandal at Abu Ghraib prison (which raised memories of the very worst atrocities of Saddam's reign in that prison, and thus associated Coalition occupation with the Saddam Regime in the minds of many Iraqis); British abuse of prisoners at Camp Breadbasket; fake pictures of prisoner abuse in the British *Daily Mirror* newspaper; the death in British custody of hotel receptionist Baha Moussa; the extreme violence with which the US military razed the city of Fallujah fighting against al-Sadr's forces in 2004; and the Yusufiyah rape and murder.

These events, of which any one alone would have raised doubts about the Coalition occupation, in combination destroyed any moral legitimacy the Coalition might have had to continue to run Iraq.[29] These events were a disaster at the strategic level: with a British objective of "the endorsement of an interim administration leading to representative government for the Iraqi people," any appointed interim administration would now be tainted by the moral failings of the Coalition, making any perception of representative government (in a country where tribal and religious affiliations trumped institutional loyalty at every level) almost impossible.

Here we see a vital and challenging lesson for the IDF. Already in this campaign, IDF soldiers have put on social media a variety of reputationally damaging videos. They show themselves looting, taking a cavalier attitude to damage within Gaza, mishandling prisoners of war, and committing open sedition against the government and chain of command. Whilst these are a tiny minority of the 300,000 IDF soldiers who have rotated through Gaza, they have nevertheless done tremendous strategic damage to the Israeli cause. This damage cannot be understated. These images will haunt IDF operations in Gaza forever; they have had lasting international impact and will further reinforce Israeli illegitimacy in the eyes of Gazan civilians. This will make a significant impact on the chances of a successful Israeli-backed interim governance in Gaza under IDF security control.

Additionally, Israel's international legitimacy for operations in Gaza has been undermined by the allegations of prisoner abuse, including sexual assault, at the

---

29 Fairweather, *A War of Choice*, 113.

Sde Teiman detention facility. Unquestionably this is a sordid incident. There are broader concerns about IDF conduct in Sde Teiman more generally. There is a case before Israel's High Court of Justice to shut down this facility completely due to concerns over prisoner maltreatment and abuse. The scenes of right-wing activists protesting the arrests and court proceedings were unsavory. There is an overarching principle here that—no matter how vile the prisoner's crimes, no matter to what extent the prisoner has forfeited claim to humanity, no matter the offense charged—what separates the righteous from the obscene is maintenance of the moral high ground. Retaining humanity in the face of obscenity is what underpins the moral case to destroy Hamas in Gaza. Incidents like this, if proven true, undermine the moral basis for the whole war.

To once more draw the British parallel holistically, there was a near-perfect storm in Basra that must be avoided by Israel in Gaza at all costs. A soft military approach lacked operational direction, combined with a rapid draw-down of troops against a background of rising violence, as well as catastrophic violations of the Geneva Convention by British soldiers which totally undermined the moral legitimacy of the occupation. Basra saw the appointment into positions of real power of controversial Sunni leaders and extreme, Iranian-backed Shi'a leaders by the Coalition Provisional Authority as they handed over control to the Iraqi Interim Government on June 28, 2004. They failed to provide a police force with any validity in the eyes of the local populace. Shi'a ties of loyalty were stronger to tribe and religion than they were to institutions, and there was a failure to deliver basic civic requirements such as sewerage, clean water, and electricity. This potent combination saw a rapid deterioration in the security situation in Basra and the surrounding area.

The parallels are obvious. Alternative governance to Hamas must be acceptable to the people of Gaza, as well as not being broadly and resentfully perceived as Israeli puppets. Even a tacitly supported alternative governance must receive aid to re-establish critical civic infrastructure, and that aid must not be a cover for malign influence from China or Iran. Most importantly, Israel must maintain a clear operational military plan and avoid permanently committing troops to occupy Gaza. To do so would be a recipe to instigate the kind of asymmetric insurgency faced by British and American forces in Iraq and Afghanistan.

Any violence in Basra was classified as an insurgency from the outset, in the way that Western commentators have tried to do with Gaza.[30] As a result,

---

30 Andrew Stewart, "Southern Iraq 2003–2004: Multi-National Command," in *British Generals in Blair's Wars*, ed. Jonathan Bailey, Richard Iron, and Hew Strachan (Farnham, Surrey: Ashgate, 2013), 80.

counterinsurgency tactics were espoused theatre-wide, as Petraeus and others espouse in Gaza. In Iraq, this led to significant doctrinal changes by both British and American forces, pioneered by Petraeus himself and formally articulated with the publication of Field Manual 3–24 in December 2006.

The British persisted with counterinsurgency doctrine at the tactical level. Efforts continued to be made to establish governance. In January 2005, Shi'a Islamists won provincial elections; however, this only exacerbated the situation by formalizing extremist control of the city. The Iranian-backed Supreme Council for the Islamic Revolution in Iraq (SCIRI) and Dawa parties combined as "Islamic Basra" with fellow Islamists of the Fadhila party and ran a slate for the elections. Islamic Basra won 33% of the vote, and Fadhila won just over 20%. The British congratulated themselves on an incident-free election, but the true reason for the peaceful period was that the extreme Islamists did not want to interfere in an election in which they were going to be voted into power. Violence in Basra and against the British swiftly escalated after the election as Islamic Basra politicians used their influence and power to create militias, which in turn created no-go areas in Basra and became the real power brokers in the city. As newspaper reports at the time noted,

> While the British Army's strategy of appeasement has brought quiet to the Shiite-dominated south for some time, it has allowed militias such as Sadr's Mahdi Army to quietly regroup and flourish. Consequently, Sadr's followers—who have close ties to the city police—have more control of Basra's streets than British troops.[31]

British tactics backfired: by attempting to reconcile with extremist Shi'a leaders to keep the peace, they simply stored up violence for later once these leaders consolidated their power bases using the Coalition's own democratic means against them. They began to challenge each other and the British Army for overall control of Basra. Tactical failure made strategic success impossible. In Gaza, the situation is the opposite: overwhelming tactical success faces strategic defeat if the Israeli government are unsuccessful in articulating an end state to operations that satisfies their political-strategic goals. The critical challenge in finding alternative governance is the establishment of an authority that is palatable to both Israel and the people of Gaza.

---

31 Jill Carroll, "Sadr Militia's New Muscle in South," *Christian Science Monitor*, September 21, 2005.

The IDF's operational design is markedly different from the counterinsurgency approaches used by Western powers in Iraq and Afghanistan. Rather than attempting to occupy or control Gaza, the IDF aim to degrade Hamas's strategic military capabilities over time without becoming entangled in governance or prolonged conflicts. This pragmatic strategy is based on destruction of strategic infrastructure and cohesive battalions of Hamas-formed units, precision strikes, the use of intelligence, and avoiding the ground-holding mistakes made by Western forces that led to prolonged and costly engagements in the Middle East.

Western counterinsurgency models espoused by critics of Israel, which center around holding territory and nation-building, have a proven inefficiency. Iraq and Afghanistan proved their lack of sustainability. In contrast, Israel acknowledges that a full military victory in the traditional sense, or stable political settlement, is not feasible while Hamas retain governance in the Gaza Strip. Israel's aim is more modest: to manage the conflict by continually degrading Hamas's ability to threaten its security. This operational design allows Israel to maintain its military and political objectives without overcommitting its resources or becoming embroiled in long-term governance challenges.

The IDF's approach has been more aligned with Israel's strategic goals than a full-scale invasion would have been. Israel has learned from the experiences of Iraq and Afghanistan, where Western powers became stuck in quagmires trying to win hearts and minds while governing volatile regions. Israel, on the other hand, is focused solely on security, allowing the IDF to conduct targeted operations aimed at minimizing Hamas's capabilities without assuming the full burden of nation-building.

Israel's intelligence infrastructure is a critical factor in the success of this operational design. Western powers often lacked this degree of intelligence capability, contributing to their struggles in insurgent environments. Basra once again gives us an excellent example.

The population in Southern Iraq is even more split than the rest of the country, comprising some 80% Shi'a.[32] In the region for which the United Kingdom was responsible, Multi-National Division (South-East), therefore, the majority of the population were recently liberated practitioners of a religious affiliation prone to extremism, faced with both foreign forces seen as occupiers, and aggressive remnants of the minority that had oppressed them for decades. They also maintained strong links to their fellow Shi'a in Iran—a theocratic Shi'a-led

---

32 *Basra: Post-Saddam Governance*, Defence Intelligence Analysis Staff, March 11, 2003, 6.

state, hostile to the United States and its allies, with a disputed maritime border with Iraq and the desire for regional hegemony.[33]

Even a cursory analysis would suggest that this would be a highly volatile situation. British pre-invasion planning, however, brushed over the pitfalls inherent in the region, recording that, "We have very little information on religious life in Basra,"[34] even whilst identifying the likelihood of Iranian-backed Shi'a military activity and the likelihood of such groupings basing their political power on their control of armed elements.[35] It was a gaping oversight and a clear failure to draw second-order conclusions from the intelligence available in the planning process.

The IDF has developed a sophisticated intelligence network that allows it to precisely target Hamas leaders, weapons caches, and infrastructure. Israel has tried to reduce collateral damage, mitigates civilian casualties, and maintains the legitimacy of Israel's military actions both domestically and internationally in the face of fierce and often misguided international criticism. This has been a challenge. Hamas's strategy has been to maximize civilian casualties by embedding civilian infrastructure. Attacks on Hamas locations embedded in civil infrastructure and the destruction of the tunnels has inevitably damaged the superstructure above, and this has caused widespread international condemnation. Israel has not explained this well: their information campaign has been poor. A vital lesson from the war in Gaza is the need for future information operations to support such destructive maneuver and shore up international backing.

Israel's military operations in Gaza are designed to be repeatable and sustainable. Unlike the Western approach of large-scale operations followed by long-term occupations, Israel's tactic is to strike hard, withdraw, and prepare for the next intelligence-driven mission. This reflects a recognition that the conflict with Hamas is long term and that, in the short term, Israel can only hope to degrade, dismantle, and neuter strategic capabilities rather than fully resolve the threat posed by Hamas and broader Palestinian extremism.

As established, this approach is not without criticism, especially from those who argue that Israel's repeated military operations have not yet provided a lasting solution. However, Israel's strategy is more realistic considering the geopolitical situation and the nature of its adversary. Hamas is deeply entrenched in Gaza, both militarily and politically, and any attempt by Israel to remove Hamas entirely would likely result in a costly and prolonged occupation. Instead, Israel's

---

33 *CIA World Factbook*, https://www.cia.gov/library/publications/the-world-factbook/geos/ir.html.
34 *Basra: Post-Saddam Governance*, 6.
35 Ibid., 11.

strategy involves striking a balance between dismantling Hamas's strategic capabilities, maintaining security, and avoiding unnecessary entanglements.

Israel's strategy relies heavily on its domestic consensus. Whilst the Netanyahu government remains controversial and heavily criticized domestically, it is broadly accepted that a long-term political settlement with Hamas is impossible, given the group's ideological commitment to Israel's destruction. Israeli society itself has been attacked by Hamas, who have repeatedly used the execution of hostages as a psychological weapon to try and put pressure on the Israeli government. This will continue whilst the hostages remain in Gaza. The complication of the hostages presents the Israeli government with two conundrums: how to retain support for the war under this psychological onslaught; and how to balance the lives of the remaining hostages with the need for security for Israel's wider population.

In conclusion, the strategic and operational dynamics of Operation Swords of Iron have demonstrated the complexities Israel faces in its conflict with Hamas. While criticisms from Western commentators, particularly regarding Israel's lack of a long-term governance plan post-Hamas, are valid, they often overlook the unique geopolitical and military realities that Israel must navigate as well as the requirement for operational security. Unlike the Western counterinsurgency efforts in Iraq and Afghanistan, which sought to impose governance and nation building, Israel's focus has been more pragmatic.

Israel's strategy in Gaza has broader implications for how Western militaries might learn from Israel's focus on sustainable conflict management, rather than attempting to impose political solutions in regions with complex, deep-rooted conflicts. The Western obsession with resolving conflicts through governance and nation-building, de-escalation and diplomacy, often ignores the reality that some conflicts can only be managed, not solved. Israel's approach in Gaza is an alternative model for dealing with intractable conflicts in other parts of the world.

The lessons from Western military operations in Basra and the broader Middle East provide cautionary tales for Israel, but they also highlight the distinctiveness of the conflict in Gaza. Israel's military operations are designed to be sustainable and repeatable, targeting Hamas's infrastructure and military assets without the need for prolonged occupation, with the exception of the Netzarim and Philadelphi Corridors. This strategy reflects Israel's understanding that it cannot impose a political solution where none is feasible, especially when dealing with an adversary like Hamas, which is deeply entrenched both militarily and politically.

By focusing on degrading Hamas's capabilities, preventing future attacks, and safeguarding Israeli citizens, the IDF's strategy is aligned with the country's long-term security goals. While some critics argue that Israel's operations will not lead to a lasting peace, the Israeli government and military seem to recognize that a definitive resolution to the decades-old conflict with Palestine is unattainable at this moment in time. Instead, the goal is to manage the threat to ensure that Hamas remains too weakened to pose a significant danger to Israeli security.

The broader implications of this approach may offer lessons for other nations dealing with insurgencies and entrenched political adversaries. Rather than pursuing unrealistic goals of governance and nation-building, Israel has adopted a model that prioritizes security and deterrence. This strategy may offer a more sustainable path for managing intractable conflicts, particularly in regions where deep-rooted political solutions remain elusive.

While Operation Swords of Iron has faced significant criticism, much of it overlooks the specific challenges Israel faces in Gaza and ignores the failures of such recommended approaches in the past. The IDF's strategy, grounded in military pragmatism rather than Western-style counterinsurgency doctrine, reflects a realistic approach to a conflict that is likely to persist for the foreseeable future. Israel's focus on security, deterrence, and the degradation of Hamas's military capabilities provides a model for managing, rather than attempting to solve, long-term conflicts in complex geopolitical landscapes.

At the time of writing, however, this chapter must end on a note of caution. Whilst IDF operations continue, the danger of strategic drift remains ever-present. Former Defense Minister Yoav Gallant reportedly declared in November 2024 that the IDF had achieved all its operational goals in Gaza.[36] Prior to that, in October 2024, he said, "Hamas as a military formation no longer exists. Hamas is engaged in guerrilla warfare and we are still fighting Hamas terrorists and pursuing Hamas leadership."[37]

The IDF has so far avoided NATO's mistakes of ground-holding and attempted nation-building. The IDF's superb operational design has allowed them to present their government with a menu of options as to how this campaign ends. In the face of this continued unclear strategic end state, the government of Israel must now choose an option. They must ensure that the perceived lack of political strategy does not lead the IDF into seizing defeat from the jaws of victory. It is now for the politicians to decide how this ends. Sun Tzu looms large over the Netanyahu government: "Tactics without strategy is the noise before defeat."

---

36 "Yoav Gallant: 'Israel Army Has Nothing Left to Do in Gaza,'" *Guardian*, November 7, 2024, https://www.theguardian.com/world/2024/nov/07/yoav-gallant-israel-army-nothing-left-to-do-in-gaza.

37 "Gallant: Hamas as Military Formation in Gaza Is Gone, Now Only Guerrilla Warfare," *Times of Israel*, https://www.timesofisrael.com/gallant-hamas-as-military-formation-in-gaza-is-gone-now-only-guerrilla-warfare/.

CHAPTER 2

Tragedy and Responsibility: The Debate over Casualties in Gaza

David Adesnik

On the evening of March 7, 2024, President Joe Biden delivered his final State of the Union address. While discussing the war in Gaza, he observed, "More than 30,000 Palestinians have been killed."[1] Biden presented this as a simple fact, never mentioning that the source of his information was the Gaza Ministry of Health, an entity under the control of Hamas. Yet only days earlier, the Health Ministry itself acknowledged its reliance on unidentified "media sources" to determine that 13,000 of the deaths in question had in fact taken place.[2] The ministry would never identify these sources, nor would Western journalists press it for answers.

This episode illustrates how claims that lent themselves to assertions of Israel's inhumanity achieved the status of accepted fact despite their uncertain origins. While the Israeli military quickly demonstrated that Hamas's armaments and extensive tunnel networks could not prevent it from seizing key terrain in Gaza, neither the Israel Defense Forces (IDF) nor the country's civilian government has found a way to counter hostile narratives that portray Israel's conduct toward Palestinians as criminal in its brutality. Hamas's military operations

---

1 "Remarks of President Joe Biden—State of the Union Address as Prepared for Delivery," White House, March 7, 2024, https://www.whitehouse.gov/briefing-room/speeches-remarks/2024/03/07/remarks-of-president-joe-biden-state-of-the-union-address-as-prepared-for-delivery-2/.
2 "Health Sector Emergency Report for Day 149 of the Aggression," Health Emergency Operations Center, Palestinian Ministry of Health—Gaza Strip (@MOHMediaGaza), Telegram, March 3, 2024, 8, https://t.me/MOHMediaGaza/5122.

barely limited Israel's freedom of action, yet accusations of inhumanity often tied Israel's hands, even threatening to terminate the IDF's campaign to destroy Hamas. Most importantly, these accusations led Washington to threaten it would suspend the delivery of weapons if Israel did not accept specific restraints.

This chapter will examine how the US government, American journalists, the United Nations, and others came to trust the casualty figures announced by the Gaza Ministry of Health and another Hamas-run entity, Gaza's Government Media Office (GMO). Even though the Health Ministry spread misinformation in the first weeks of the war, both Western journalists and UN observers chose to treat its casualty figures as credible and did not revisit this decision even after additional evidence of statistical manipulation emerged.

Neither the IDF nor the Israeli government effectively challenged the status of the Gaza Health Ministry as the arbiter of casualty figures. The Israelis reminded foreign audiences that Hamas exercised control of the ministry and that the ministry's figures included thousands of Hamas fighters along with civilian casualties. Yet Israel never directly disputed the data or methodology underlying the Health Ministry's figures or related claims by the GMO. Israeli representatives did not seem to grasp that US journalists would treat their claims as little more than politically motivated assertions in the absence of supporting data. Meanwhile, the Gaza Health Ministry invested substantial effort in producing data that substantiated some of its claims, especially lists of the deceased that included names and official identification numbers. Satisfied by this effort, neither journalists nor the UN probed much further. Their confidence in the ministry's figures bolstered that of the Biden administration. While there is ample evidence of both journalists and UN officials proving credulous with regard to Health Ministry claims, the Israelis had no reason to expect even-handed treatment and should have been prepared to resist the Health Ministry narrative with the same vigor as they conducted military operations.

Broadly speaking, the Israelis appreciated the necessity of waging an information war in concert with military operations. In particular, they placed consistent emphasis on how Hamas deliberately embedded its military assets within civilian structures, turning their occupants into human shields—a war crime. The IDF conducted tours for journalists of the tunnels that Hamas built under hospitals and even under the headquarters of the UN Relief and Works Agency (UNRWA), the chief provider of aid to Palestinians. The IDF also released combat footage showing fighters in mosques, schools, hospitals. While the Biden administration concurred fully with the Israeli view that Hamas employed human shields in a pervasive and systematic way, the Israeli effort did not change the way that journalists approached the question of casualty figures.

While the Biden administration became increasingly critical of Israeli conduct with regard to Palestinian civilians, it rarely delayed shipments of arms despite repeated threats to do so. This pattern of behavior suggested to Israel's critics in Washington that the White House lacked the courage of its convictions. Meanwhile, friends of the Jewish state resented the damage done to the legitimacy of Israel's war effort. As American opinion toward Israel became more polarized, the middle ground became elusive.

With the war in Gaza still under way, one cannot assess the long-term impact of the damage to Israel's reputation over the past year. Perhaps it will gradually fade, as did the intense vitriol that spread during Israel's war in Lebanon in 1982–1983. But there remains the risk of enduring harm to Israel's relationship with the United States if the first draft of history portrays the war against Hamas as the moral equivalent of the October 7 massacre. Israel's military capabilities remain extraordinary for a country of its size, yet this war has also demonstrated that Jerusalem's partnership with Washington is indispensable to the security of the Jewish state. Even if this war produces an outcome that Israelis consider a victory, its end will only mark the beginning of a new struggle to define how the war is remembered.

Counting the Dead

On the night of October 17, a lethal explosion rocked al-Ahli Arab Hospital in northern Gaza. A headline spanning the breadth of the *New York Times*'s website reported, "Israeli strike kills hundreds at Gaza hospital, Palestinians say."[3] The next version of the headline specified 500 fatalities but no longer described the alleged airstrike as "Israeli," suggesting uncertainty. Then, in the absence of evidence that an airstrike had taken place at all, a third version of the headline changed the word "strike" to "blast." Questions also began to emerge about the death toll. On the morning of October 18, the print edition of the paper carried a banner headline reading, "Blast kills hundreds at Gaza hospital."[4] It would quickly become clear than an errant rocket fired by Palestinian fighters had been

---

3   "Israeli Airstrike Hits Gaza Hospital, Killing 500, Palestinian Health Ministry Says," *New York Times*, October 17, 2023, archived October 17, 2023, 15:43, https://web.archive.org/web/20231017194544/ https://www.nytimes.com/live/2023/10/17/world/gaza-news-israel-hamas-war.

4   Patrick Kingsley, Aaron Boxerman, and Hiba Yazbek, "Blast Kills Hundreds at Gaza Hospital," *New York Times*, October 18, 2023, https://static01.nyt.com/images/2023/10/18/nyt-frontpage/scan.pdf.

responsible for the carnage. Scores died, possibly hundreds, but the number 500 had no basis in fact.

The *Times* was far from alone in its rush to report a version of events based on claims by the Gaza Ministry of Health and its representatives. Just hours after the blast, the IDF told reporters that rockets fired by Palestinian Islamic Jihad (PIJ), an ally of Hamas, had been close to the hospital at the time of the explosion. Yet, across the globe, headlines reported an Israeli strike. A correspondent for the BBC said his experience in Gaza showed that no Palestinian rocket could cause such a massive explosion.[5] But after the break of dawn it became clear that the crater in the hospital parking lot was far too small for an Israeli bomb to have made.[6]

In the days after the attack, some news outlets reflected on why they had promoted the fiction of Israeli responsibility for an atrocity committed by Palestinians. The *Times* conceded that it "relied too heavily on claims by Hamas and did not make clear that those claims could not immediately be verified."[7] Yet this self-awareness proved to be fleeting. Even though the Health Ministry had deceived the press, journalists soon accepted it as an authoritative source on the extent of Palestinian casualties.

The Health Ministry's Reliance on Unidentified "Media Sources"

Nine days after the blast at al-Ahli Hospital, the Health Ministry released a list of 6,747 individuals it said had been killed since the war began. Each entry on the list included the individual's name, date of birth, age at death, and the ID number assigned to Gaza residents by the Israeli Ministry of the Interior. The day before the ministry released its list, President Biden said he had "no confidence in the number that the Palestinians are using."[8] The press corps sought to adjudicate, firmly assessing the ministry to be a trustworthy source for two principal reasons.

---

5   "Corrections and Clarifications Archive—2023," BBC, October 19, 2023, amended October 23, 2023, https://www.bbc.co.uk/helpandfeedback/corrections_clarifications/archive-2023#:~:text=23/10/2023%20amended%20with%20apology.

6   "Identifying Possible Crater from Gaza Hospital Blast," Bellingcat, October 18, 2023, https://www.bellingcat.com/news/2023/10/18/identifying-possible-crater-from-gaza-hospital-blast/.

7   "Editors' Note: Gaza Hospital Coverage," *New York Times*, October 23, 2023, https://www.nytimes.com/2023/10/23/pageoneplus/editors-note-gaza-hospital-coverage.html.

8   "Biden Says He Has 'No Confidence' in Palestinian Death Count," Reuters, October 25, 2024, https://www.reuters.com/world/middle-east/biden-says-he-has-no-confidence-palestinian-death-count-2023-10-26/.

First, as the *Washington Post* noted, "The Gaza Health Ministry has had a pretty good track record with its death estimates over the years, notwithstanding that it is part of the Hamas-run government."[9] Second, the ministry could collect its data directly from the facilities that handle the bodies. "Hospital administrators say they keep records of every wounded person occupying a bed and every dead body arriving at a morgue," the Associated Press reported.[10]

These were reasonable arguments, yet journalists seemed to discount that, only days earlier, the ministry had misled them about the cause and impact of the explosion at al-Ahli Hospital. Nor did the ministry ever report the actual number of fatalities caused by the blast. Its list of names did not resolve this question, since it omitted the date of death for the individuals it included—thus, it was not clear who died on October 17, let alone which of them had been at al-Ahli. While the ministry held press conferences and its officials made themselves available for interviews, Western media did not press them on their omissions.[11] Meanwhile, the ministry's statistics gained further validation when UN officials in Gaza began to include them in UN publications shortly after the blast at al-Ahli.

In late October, the entry of Israeli forces into Gaza disrupted the ministry's system for collecting data. Moving from north to south, the IDF wrested control of hospitals away from Hamas fighters. As a result of the turmoil, the ministry released no statistics from November 10 through November 30. During that time, however, Gaza's Government Media Office (GMO) began to release its own casualty figures, notable for the extremely high proportion of women and children among the dead.

Soon, the ministry appeared to recover from the disruptions. On December 12, it released the first of its statistical digests, which included data ranging from hospital bed occupancy rates to the number of operations performed in Gaza hospitals. Regarding casualties, the December 12 digest put the death toll at 18,412 but divided that figure into two parts. The first consisted of individuals "registered through the central information system," meaning that hospitals

---

9   Glenn Kessler, "Biden's Dismissal of the Reported Palestinian Death Toll," *Washington Post*, November 1, 2023, https://www.washingtonpost.com/politics/2023/11/01/bidens-dismissal-reported-palestinian-death-toll/.
10 Isabel Debre, "What Is Gaza's Ministry of Health and How Does It Calculate the War's Death Toll?," Associated Press, November 6, 2023, https://apnews.com/article/israel-hamas-war-gaza-health-ministry-health-death-toll-59470820308b31f1faf73c703400b033.
11 The ministry posted footage of many of its press conferences on its Telegram channel, @MOHMediaGaza. See, for example, the conference from October 23, 2023, posted at https://t.me/MOHMediaGaza/4187.

recorded their deaths. But 4,143 deaths (22.7%) were attributed to information from "reliable media sources" as a result of the "interruption of communication with hospitals in Gaza [City] and the north." The report identified neither the media sources on which it relied nor how it verified those sources' information. This should have been a flashing red light for reporters and UN officials.

The person who did notice the problem was Gabriel Epstein, an analyst at the Washington Institute for Near East Policy. In a January 2024 paper, Epstein flagged the Health Ministry's reliance on unidentified sources, which undercut one of the two principal arguments for its trustworthiness, namely that it collected data directly from facilities that handle the remains of the dead. Epstein also called attention to how the health ministry's numbers undercut claims made by the GMO. For example, the latter reported on December 11 that there were 8,000 children and 6,200 women among the dead, or 77% of the total. Since the GMO reported a total of 18,412 fatalities, if 14,200 were women and children, then no more than 4,212 could be adult men. Yet the Health Ministry's first statistical digest reported that Gaza medical facilities had identified 5,577 adult male cadavers. Thus, the GMO figures for women and children violated the laws of simple arithmetic. Notably, the Health Ministry's own figures for women and children were also far below what the GMO reported: 4,327 children, not 8,000; and 4,349 women, not 6,200.[12]

Nevertheless, the claim that 70% of the dead were women and children became a fixture of media coverage. Initially, the UN demonstrated a measure of skepticism. Regarding the GMO figures, the UN's Office for the Coordination of Humanitarian Affairs (OCHA) cautioned on December 21 that "their methodology is unknown."[13] By mid-January, OCHA had stopped using the GMO figures, although it continued to employ Health Ministry data.

As Hamas lost control of more hospitals in the first months of 2024, the Health Ministry began to rely more heavily on its "reliable media sources" to count the number of deaths. In its statistical digest for February 13, the ministry reported that media sources constituted the evidence for 11,558 fatalities. According to the ministry's March 31 digest, the figure had risen to 15,070, or 46% of all deaths reported. Despite the absence of pressure from journalists to explain its methods, the ministry soon shifted its terminology to obscure its

---

12 Gabriel Epstein, "How Hamas Manipulates Gaza Fatality Numbers," The Washington Institute for Near East Policy, Policy Notes 144, January 2024, https://www.washingtoninstitute.org/sites/default/files/pdf/PolicyNote144Epsteinv2.pdf.

13 "Hostilities in the Gaza Strip and Israel | Flash Update #75," United Nations Office for the Coordination of Humanitarian Affairs (UN OCHA), December 21, 2023, https://www.ochaopt.org/content/hostilities-gaza-strip-and-israel-flash-update-75.

reliance on unidentified sources. Beginning on April 1, the ministry's statistical digests employed a new approach to categorizing the data. For the majority of cases, the ministry said it had "complete data," which consisted of a full name, ID number, gender, date of birth, and "date of martyrdom." For the remainder, the ministry had "incomplete data," implying that it maintained rigorous standards for data quality and was presenting a conservative estimate of fatality figures. In fact, the ministry had simply relabeled as "incomplete" the records it previously described as being based on "reliable media sources."

Meanwhile, the ministry periodically updated the lists in which it identified the deceased by name. The list dated March 29 included 21,323 entries. On April 30, there were 24,682 names. The ministry said these included only those individuals for whom it had "complete data," yet thousands of entries were missing information. Michael Spagat, an economist who studies civilian casualty data, reported that 2,278 entries had invalid ID numbers, 470 were missing ID numbers, and 440 of the valid numbers were duplicates of other entries. All in all, Spagat found about one in seven entries was missing at least one of the four data points necessary for a complete entry. Moreover, he noted that the lists did not resolve the uncertainty surrounding the entries with incomplete data, which amount, in Spagat's words, to "roughly 13,000 deaths that have, apparently, been entered into an unavailable database using an unknown methodology."[14] Still, journalists displayed little interest in these anomalies, despite featuring the ministry's casualty figures in numerous dispatches from Gaza each day.

A Brief Moment of Scrutiny from the Media

Despite its initial concern that the GMO employed an "unknown" methodology to produce casualty data, OCHA resumed its use of GMO figures in the spring of 2024. On May 6, OCHA's daily update on events in Gaza indicated that more than 9,500 women and 14,500 children had died in the war.[15] Two days later, OCHA's daily update cut those numbers nearly in half, reporting that 4,959 women and 7,797 children had actually lost their lives—a

---

14 Mike Spagat, "Analysis of New Death Data from Gaza's Health Ministry Reveals Several Concerns," Action on Armed Violence, April 17, 2024, https://aoav.org.uk/2024/analysis-of-new-death-data-from-gazas-health-ministry-reveals-several-concerns/.

15 "Hostilities in the Gaza Strip and Israel—Reported Impact | Day 213," UN OCHA, May 6, 2024, https://www.ochaopt.org/content/hostilities-gaza-strip-and-israel-reported-impact-day-213.

combined reduction of more than 11,000.[16] The anomaly quickly caught the attention of right-of-center publications, such as Fox News, the *Washington Examiner*, and *Washington Free Beacon*, which often challenged mainstream reporting about the war in Gaza. Soon, more prominent outlets weighed in on the controversy, including the *New York Times*, the *Washington Post*, and the BBC. Their coverage demonstrated reporters' lack of familiarity with the Health Ministry's evolving process and terminology for counting fatalities. Correspondents grasped that OCHA had shifted from reporting GMO figures to using Health Ministry data, but stumbled when it came to explaining their divergence.

A UN spokesperson insisted that the two diverged because the GMO tally included information about the number of women and children among the war's "unidentified" casualties, while the Health Ministry only reported the death of women and children whose records contained "complete data."[17] Reporters accepted this explanation. Yet the GMO had no means of determining which of the unidentified casualties were male, female, or younger than eighteen. Nor could it get that information from the Health Ministry, which never claimed to have it. After all, it documented the death of unidentified casualties by relying on unidentified media sources, so the age and gender of the deceased was likely unknown.

These critical details eluded correspondents for all of the top publications. They did not report the ministry's reliance on unidentified sources, let alone challenge the ministry to be more transparent. Nevertheless, once the UN stopped using the GMO figures, so did almost all of the top media outlets, underscoring the UN's ability to determine what information journalists considered to be credible. With its numbers in doubt, the GMO's claim that 70% of the dead were women and children began disappearing from US media. That represented a step forward, but journalists never made clear to their readers that the GMO had been spreading fabricated numbers which the media had treated as credible.

---

16 "Hostilities in the Gaza Strip and Israel—Reported Impact | Day 215," UN OCHA, May 8, 2024, https://www.ochaopt.org/content/hostilities-gaza-strip-and-israel-reported-impact-day-215.

17 David Adesnik, "How the UN Got Away with Wildly Inflating the Casualty Numbers in Gaza—and the Media Bought It," *Newsweek*, June 3, 2024, https://www.newsweek.com/how-un-got-away-wildly-inflating-casualty-numbers-gaza-media-bought-it-opinion-1907436.

Identifying the Dead

As the spring of 2024 progressed, there were increasing signs that the Gaza Health Ministry considered its reliance on unidentified media sources as a liability. The first indication, described above, was the relabeling of deaths reported by the media as entries with incomplete data. Next, after the commotion that followed OCHA's disavowal of GMO figures, the ministry began releasing far less data. It also began to whittle away at the list of unidentified casualties with creative bookkeeping. Shortly after the first anniversary of the war's outbreak, the ministry indicated that only 1,293 unidentified victims remained, down from 12,263 on April 1.[18] Ministry officials also began to deny that they had ever relied on media sources to document any deaths. It was all a misunderstanding, they said, even though those words appeared again and again in official publications.

In late May, the ministry's statistical digests contracted from forty-plus pages per edition to just seven or eight. The data concerning fatalities also became far less specific. Previously, each digest included a chart with a demographic breakdown of the deceased into four categories: children, adult men, adult women, and the elderly. The chart also indicated how many deaths in each category had been reported by each of the major hospitals in Gaza. As of May 28, this disappeared. Instead, updates indicated only three things: first, the total number of deaths; second, the number of records with complete versus incomplete data; and third, the number of complete records generated by hospitals and family members, respectively. This last category would be the key to reducing the number of unidentified fatalities.

Disagreements about the number of fatalities in Gaza extend to questions about how many individuals are missing and are presumed to be dead. Gaza health officials and civil defense workers often tell journalists that the true death toll greatly exceeds the number reported by the Health Ministry, "since many bodies remain buried under the rubble of buildings destroyed in airstrikes."[19] Amb. Barbara Leaf, the State Department official in charge of Middle East policy, made the same point in testimony before Congress.[20] The GMO claims there are

---

18 Palestinian Ministry of Health—Gaza Strip (@MOHMediaGaza), Telegram, October 20, 2024, 08:55, https://t.me/MOHMediaGaza/5948.
19 Wafaa Shurafa and Julia Frankel, "More Than 40,000 Palestinians Have Been Killed in Gaza, the Territory's Health Ministry Says," Associated Press, August 15, 2024, https://apnews.com/article/gaza-death-toll-hamas-war-israel-40000-32a79e03c8eb62669412dab23d03219e.
20 Laura Kelly, "Death Toll in Gaza Likely 'higher than is being reported': U.S. Official," The Hill, November 11, 2023, https://thehill.com/policy/international/4301551-gaza-deaths-likely-higher-than-cited-us-official/.

10,000 individuals missing, and it adds them to the Health Ministry's casualty figures to produce its estimate of the total number of "martyrs and missing."[21] Yet the ministry has been taking a very different approach. In early 2024, the ministry created a system for families to document deaths for which the ministry had no record. This included an online portal "to report martyrs and missing persons." Rather than treating these reports as an addition to its casualty figures, it reduces by one the number of "incomplete records" for each report filed by families of the deceased. From a bookkeeping perspective, this is problematic. The families are not actually completing an incomplete record—they are creating new ones. As of September 16, families had filed 6,187 reports via the ministry's portal, enough to bring the count of incomplete records down to 7,200.[22] When the ministry releases updated lists of the deceased, it now indicates which records are hospital-generated and which reflect family reports. On October 20, the ministry released a graphic indicating 1,293 incomplete records remain. The reduction from roughly 7,200 to 1,293 in just over a month is remarkable, but the project appears to be a priority for the ministry. All in all, the ministry has integrated about 12,000 of the missing into its casualty figures. This effort has two major implications. First, in Michael Spagat's words, "we should dismiss the common claim that, because many of the dead are trapped under rubble or are missing for other reasons, the announced totals are undercounts."[23] Rather, the ministry has counted them despite the GMO's claims to the contrary. Second, the ministry's overall casualty figures may now be considerably more accurate. As noted above, in late March, unidentified media sources constituted the only evidence for 46% of the reported deaths in Gaza. The ministry appears to have brought that number down to single digits. Bit by bit, it appears to have replaced phantom reports with more substantive ones, although little is known about the process by which family reports are verified.

As matters now stand, the debate over casualty reporting may have reached an unlikely resting place. During the first several months of the war, the Health Ministry employed opaque methods to nearly double its death toll. Then, by quietly folding in reports from the families of the missing, it assembled a more

---

21 Government Media Office (@mediagovps), Telegram, October 30, 2024, 09:43, https://t.me/mediagovps/3263.

22 "Health Sector Emergency Report for Day 347 of the Aggression," Health Emergency Operations Center, Palestinian Ministry of Health—Gaza Strip (@MOHMediaGaza), Telegram, September 16, 2024, 2, https://t.me/MOHMediaGaza/5828.

23 Mike Spagat, "Analysis of New Death Data from Gaza's Health Ministry Reveals Several Concerns," Action on Armed Violence, April 17, 2024, https://aoav.org.uk/2024/analysis-of-new-death-data-from-gazas-health-ministry-reveals-several-concerns/.

tangible basis for claims once based on unidentified media sources. This brings us to the present, in which the ministry's figures appear to be more accurate, but its methods remain far from transparent, and it refuses to acknowledge that it ever employed deceptive techniques to raise the casualty count. Tellingly, the ministry now denies it ever relied on unidentified media sources as the basis for its fatality figures.

Initially, this was not a point of embarrassment. In April, Britain's Sky News published a lengthy and sympathetic account of the ministry's struggle to record fatalities. SkyNews secured the first published interview since the beginning of the war with Zaher al-Wahaidi, head of the ministry's Health Information Center. Wahaidi explained that he and "his team rely on reports from journalists and first responders to collate reports of deaths not recorded by hospitals."[24] In August, the same Sky News correspondent returned to Gaza to speak with Wahaidi again. Regarding the provenance of the ministry's data, Wahaidi said, "It's not from journalists. We don't depend on any press sources for data—this is the policy of the Ministry of Health." Foreign critics claimed that the ministry relied on media sources because they mistranslated its reports. Rather, the phrase in question refers to the hospital's public relations staff.[25] But this is simply false. The Arabic phrase *masadir al-alamiat al-mawthuqa* means "reliable media sources." None of the three words is ambiguous. If the ministry were referring to its public relations staff, there are common words it could use to convey that meaning. More importantly, the ministry's denial that it ever relied on media sources underscores the extent to which its credibility remains compromised. Extreme caution is necessary when addressing any of its factual claims.

What the Numbers Mean: US and Israeli Responses

By itself, the number of lives lost in Gaza is a sterile figure. The judgment of political actors is necessary to endow it with moral significance. One may see the number as *prima facie* evidence of contempt for civilian well-being, either on the part of Hamas gunmen who fight from inside hospitals, or Israeli troops

---

24 Ben van der Merwe, "Israel-Hamas War: Gaza's Morgue Network Has Effectively Collapsed—How Are They Recording Their Dead?," Sky News, April 4, 2024, https://news.sky.com/story/israel-hamas-war-health-system-collapse-in-gaza-leaves-authorities-struggling-to-count-the-dead-13107279.

25 Ben van der Merwe, "Gaza Conflict: Thousands Remain Unidentified as Death Toll Reaches 40,000," Sky News, August 15, 2024, https://news.sky.com/story/gaza-conflict-thousands-remain-unidentified-as-death-toll-reaches-40-000-13197287.

and their tremendous firepower. Alternatively, one may see the number as little more than a reminder that urban battles inevitably claim the lives of numerous civilians if they cannot escape the battlefield. From a military and diplomatic perspective, the judgement of the Biden administration had the greatest significance since it could delay or suspend the delivery of weapons essential for the Israeli war effort. Buffeted by pressure from both supporters and antagonists of the Jewish state, the administration sought a middle path by criticizing Israel sharply while taking only the mildest of punitive actions. For its part, Israel maintained that Hamas employed the people of Gaza as a human shield, sacrificing them to generate sympathy abroad. Despite making this point consistently, Israeli arguments lacked depth. At least in public statements, neither the IDF nor the Israeli government demonstrated familiarity with the methods employed by the Gaza Ministry of Health. Accordingly, Israeli challenges to the ministry's credibility had a negligible impact. In contrast, the ministry satisfied the desire of both UN agencies and journalists for tranches of data that added an apparent heft to its claims. In turn, these UN agencies and journalists exerted a substantial influence on the Biden administration's view of the death toll.

The White House Searches for a Middle Ground

Despite the president's initial skepticism toward Health Ministry figures, the Biden administration began to treat them as credible and launched a coordinated campaign in late 2023 to pressure Israel to do more to prevent harm to civilians. On November 30, Secretary of State Antony Blinken met with Benjamin Netanyahu in Jerusalem as a temporary ceasefire in Gaza approached its expiration date. As Blinken prepared to depart the country, he told the press corps that, when he met the prime minister, he conveyed a requirement that, before Israel resumed operations, "it must put in place humanitarian civilian protection plans that minimize further casualties of innocent Palestinians." Blinken also emphasized the "imperative that Israel act in accordance with international humanitarian law and the laws of war."[26] The secretary framed his language in a way that strongly suggested but never explicitly stated that Israel was taking insufficient measures to protect civilians and comply with the laws of war. Secretary of Defense Lloyd Austin and Vice President Kamala Harris would adopt the same approach. On December 2, Austin told a California audience,

---

26 "Secretary Antony J. Blinken at a Press Availability," U.S. Department of State, November 30, 2023, https://www.state.gov/secretary-antony-j-blinken-at-a-press-availability-43/.

"I have repeatedly made clear to Israel's leaders that protecting Palestinian civilians in Gaza is both a moral responsibility and a strategic imperative," adding, "I have personally pushed Israeli leaders to avoid civilian casualties."[27] The same day, Harris declared in Dubai, "Too many innocent Palestinians have been killed," and "we believe Israel must do more to protect innocent civilians."[28]

For friends of Israel, these remarks seemed to entail grave accusations presented without evidence or even much specificity as to what the IDF had done wrong. To critics, the remarks seemed to reflect a deficit of the courage necessary to speak plainly about Israeli violations, let alone take meaningful action to hold Jerusalem accountable. In addition to navigating this political minefield, the administration had to be wary of the legal implications of what it said. The White House was preparing to release National Security Memorandum 20 (NSM-20), a new policy on the provision of weapons to foreign partners, which made their delivery contingent "credible and written assurances . . . that the recipient country will use any such defense articles in accordance with international humanitarian law."[29] If senior officials directly stated that Israel was violating the laws of war, it could force the administration to cut off the supply of weapons. Despite the caution exercised by the vice president and cabinet, Biden himself stated on December 12 that Israel's "indiscriminate bombing" was undermining support for its cause.[30] Much like those instances in which Biden pledged unconditionally to defend Taiwan from a Chinese invasion, the president appeared to be contradicting his own administration's policy. If, in fact, Israel's bombing was indiscriminate, there would be little choice but to invoke NSM-20's prohibition on the provision of weapons to those who violate the laws of war, which require belligerents to take all appropriate precautions to protect civilians.

---

27 "'A Time for American Leadership': Remarks by Secretary of Defense Lloyd J. Austin III at the Reagan National Defense Forum (As Delivered)," U.S. Department of Defense, December 2, 2023, https://www.defense.gov/News/Speeches/Speech/Article/3604755/a-time-for-american-leadership-remarks-by-secretary-of-defense-lloyd-j-austin-i/.
28 "Remarks by Vice President Harris on the Conflict Between Israel and Hamas," White House, December 2, 2023, https://www.whitehouse.gov/briefing-room/speeches-remarks/2023/12/02/remarks-by-vice-president-harris-on-the-conflict-between-israel-and-hamas/.
29 "National Security Memorandum on Safeguards and Accountability With Respect to Transferred Defense Articles and Defense Services," White House, February 8, 2024, https://www.whitehouse.gov/briefing-room/presidential-actions/2024/02/08/national-security-memorandum-on-safeguards-and-accountability-with-respect-to-transferred-defense-articles-and-defense-services/.
30 Trevor Hunnicutt and Steve Holland, "Biden Says Netanyahu Must Change, Israel Losing Global Support," Reuters, December 12, 2023, https://www.reuters.com/world/middle-east/biden-israel-starting-lose-support-over-indiscriminate-bombing-gaza-2023-12-12/.

The official promulgation of NSM-20 on February 8, 2024 initiated a ninety day countdown at the end of which the administration would have to deliver a report to Congress addressing whether Israel and other recipients of US arms were abiding by the laws of war. Prominent NGOs, including Human Rights Watch and Refugees International, pressed the administration to conclude that NSM-20 required the suspension of military sales and assistance.[31] The administration, as it had previously, sought to navigate conflicting pressures by condemning Israel without taking punitive action. The magnitude of the Gaza health ministry's figures played a central role in the administration's report to Congress in early May. "The reported rate of civilian harm in the conflict also raises serious questions about the efficacy of Israeli precautionary measures," the report observed, "notwithstanding Hamas's deliberate embedding within and use of civilian and humanitarian infrastructure as shelter." On the fundamental question of whether the IDF was misusing American arms, the administration said it could not reach conclusive findings with regard to specific incidents, yet "it is reasonable to assess that defense articles covered under NSM-20 have been used by Israeli forces since October 7 in instances inconsistent with its IHL obligations." In effect, the administration did not have proof of misconduct but still assessed that misconduct had taken place. To supporters of Israel, this amounted once again to condemnation without evidence. To critics, it constituted another instance of the administration lacking the courage to act on what it knew to be true.

To those with a specific interest in casualty figures, the NSM-20 report revealed that the administration accepted the Gaza Health Ministry's figures because they were good enough for the UN. While noting the ministry was under Hamas control, the report said it produced figures "which international organizations generally deem credible." Neither the State Department nor any other agency appears to have examined the figures with a critical eye, instead assuming that the UN's approval was sufficient.

Concurrent with the debate over NSM-20, the Gaza casualty figures played a prominent role in arguments about the Israeli plan to launch a major ground offensive in Rafah, Hamas's last major stronghold in Gaza, perched at the southern end of the coastal strip. Two days after the State of the Union address in which he used the health ministry's figures without identifying their source, Biden told an interviewer that an assault on Rafah was his "red line" for

---

31 "Israeli Forces Conduct in Gaza: Human Rights Watch and Oxfam Submission to Biden Administration's NSM-20 Process," Human Rights Watch, March 19, 2024, https://www.hrw.org/news/2024/03/19/israeli-forces-conduct-gaza.

Netanyahu. An all-out offensive was unconscionable because "they cannot have 30,000 more Palestinians dead."[32] Two weeks later, the vice president delivered a similar message. "We've been very clear," she said, "that far too many innocent Palestinians have been killed," and an invasion of Rafah posed far too great a risk to its civilian population. "I have studied the maps," Harris said, "There's nowhere for those folks to go." When asked if moving into Rafah would cross a red line, she avoided the question but refused to rule out "consequences" for Israel.[33] The resolution of the disagreement over Rafah was another awkward compromise. Instead of delivering a hammer blow, the IDF moved into Rafah gradually. The White House said this approach was consistent with its demands. To Israel's critics, it once again seemed that Biden had said the right things but failed to restrain Netanyahu. On the other hand, forecasts of heavy civilian casualties proved mistaken.

In the summer of 2024, the salience of the debate over casualty figures began to diminish along with the intensity of the fighting in Gaza. According to the health ministry's figures, the number of fatalities per month had fallen to 1,000–1,500, in contrast to more than 10,000 in the first month of the war. Meanwhile, a war of attrition on Israel's northern border escalated into a full-blown conflict with Hezbollah. Also, as the war entered its second year, the question of humanitarian aid moved to the fore, with the White House alleging that Israel was obstructing shipments of relief to Gaza. An October 13 letter to Israel from the secretaries of state and defense threatened to suspend military sales and assistance if the situation did not improve.[34] Yet, in Gaza, access to food continually improved in the spring and summer of 2024, according to assessments by an authoritative UN-backed food security monitor.[35] For its part, Israel emphasized that more than 55,000 trucks had delivered nearly 1.1 million tons

---

32   "Biden Makes Contradictory Comments on Gaza 'Red Line' in MSNBC Interview," Reuters, March 9, 2024, https://www.reuters.com/world/us/biden-makes-contradictory-comments-gaza-red-line-msnbc-interview-2024-03-09/.
33   Rachel Scott, Fritz Farrow, Benjamin Siegel, and Arthur Jones II, "Harris Says U.S. Has Not Ruled Out 'Consequences' if Israel Invades Rafah," ABC News, March 24, 2024, https://abcnews.go.com/Politics/harris-us-ruled-consequences-israel-invades-rafah/story?id=108431225.
34   Barak Ravid, "U.S. Demands Israel Improve Humanitarian Conditions in Gaza or Risk Military Aid," Axios, October 15, 2024, https://www.axios.com/2024/10/15/us-israel-gaza-humanitarian-conditions-military-aid-letter.
35   David Adesnik, "UN-Backed Monitors Say Access to Food Improves in Gaza," Foundation for Defense of Democracies, October 22, 2024, https://www.fdd.org/analysis/2024/10/22/un-backed-monitors-say-access-to-food-improves-in-gaza/.

of goods to Gaza since the war began.[36] In response to the October 13 letter, the Israeli government took several measures to facilitate the flow of aid, including the re-opening of the Kissufim crossing from Israel into central Gaza. By the time the new crossing opened, Donald Trump had defeated Kamala Harris in the US presidential election. The outgoing administration accepted the Israeli measures as sufficient to avoid a suspension of military aid, a decision that aid groups condemned vociferously.

Israel Defends Its Record

In mid-May, at a time when the Gaza Ministry of Health was reporting just over 35,000 fatalities, Benjamin Netanyahu told an American interviewer that Israeli believed the death toll was about 30,000, consisting of 14,000 combatants and roughly 16,000 civilians.[37] Netanyahu's comments were a rare exception to Israel's continuing aversion to discussing the number of civilian deaths in Gaza. Despite offering an estimate of civilian casualties, Netanyahu gave no indication of how the Israeli government arrived at that number. His comments generated a modicum of press coverage but had no lasting impact. This is not surprising. Journalists have demonstrated a growing appetite for data to support numerical estimates of all kinds. The Health Ministry provided them with its frequent statistical updates as well as lists that are purported to identify most of the dead by name. The IDF and Israeli government either do not appreciate that this is the standard to which they are being held, or do not consider it important to compete with Hamas in that arena.

Netanyahu's estimate that 14,000 Hamas fighters had been killed did not come as a surprise. Since the first days of the war, the IDF had been offering estimates of enemy personnel killed in action. The IDF always reported numbers rounded to the nearest thousand, never claiming to have sufficiently precise data to give an exact count. The estimate rose gradually over time, reaching 17,000 by the first anniversary of the October 7 massacre. The media did report these estimates with some regularity, but often warned explicitly that Israel provided

---

36 "Humanitarian Affairs Israel," last modified December 16, 2024, https://gaza-aid-data.gov.il/main/.

37 "Israel's Netanyahu Says Militants Make Up About Half of Gaza Deaths," CBS News, May 14, 2024, https://www.cbsnews.com/news/israel-hamas-war-gaza-death-toll-netanyahu-un-civilians-women-children/.

no indication of how it arrived at these estimates, which was true.[38] Estimating the number of enemy losses is always difficult, so one would not expect the IDF to arrive at an exact number, yet identifying no methodology at all ensured that journalists would often present the Israeli number with the caveat that it had no clear basis—a warning they did not attach to data from the Gaza Health Ministry.

Underscoring the number of fighters among the dead has value, since many who cite the Health Ministry's numbers fail to mention that the ministry never distinguishes between combatants and civilians. Still, the question remains: If roughly half of the dead are civilians, does that show that Israel has been reckless or that it has taken proper care to avoid unnecessary harm? Answering this question is extremely difficult since there is no clear benchmark against which to measure the IDF's performance. The laws of war are intentionally silent on the question of how much aggregate harm to civilians is acceptable. Rather, the notion of proportionality applies to commanders' decisions whether to proceed with particular attacks. What may be possible is to compare the ratio of civilian to military casualties in different wars. Thus, in his July 25 address to a joint session of Congress, Netanyahu asserted, "the war in Gaza has one of the lowest ratios of combatants to non-combatant casualties in the history of urban warfare."[39] He did not indicate which other conflicts served as his benchmarks, nor have Israeli spokespersons elaborated on this point. American and British commentators have debated the issue, however, often comparing the numbers from Gaza to those from the battle of Mosul in 2017, which pitted the US-led anti-ISIS coalition against the Islamic State insurgents who had captured the city three years earlier. Broadly, the comparison is reasonable since both US and Israeli forces profess to uphold the laws of war and faced a similar challenge, in the form of extremists in urban terrain who employ civilians as shields. However, in the absence of reliable data from Mosul, it is hard to draw firm conclusions.

Those who have compared the campaigns against Hamas and ISIS have reached diametrically opposed conclusions about whether US or Israeli forces did more to prevent civilian harm. One expert on urban warfare contends that there were 2.5 civilian fatalities in Mosul for each ISIS fighter who died, whereas the ratio in Gaza is roughly 1:1 if the Israeli estimate of 17,000 Hamas fighters killed in

---

38 Merlyn Thomas, Jake Horton, and Benedict Garman, "Israel Gaza: Checking Israel's Claim to Have Killed 10,000 Hamas Fighters," BBC, February 29, 2024, https://www.bbc.com/news/world-middle-east-68387864.
39 "We're Protecting You: Full Text of Netanyahu's Address to Congress," *Times of Israel*, July 25, 2024, https://www.timesofisrael.com/were-protecting-you-full-text-of-netanyahus-address-to-congress/.

action proves correct.[40] In contrast, an advocate of civilian rights denounced the IDF's "tolerance for civilian casualties which is orders of magnitude greater than that that was used by, say, the U.S. Air Force in the war against ISIS."[41] Yet a broad range of estimates is possible. The US Army convened a study group after the battle of Mosul which reported there had been 3,000–5,000 fighters defending the city.[42] Precisely how many died is unknown. On the civilian side of the ledger, an investigation by the Associated Press found that 9,000–11,000 civilians had died. The authors estimated that each side was responsible for the death of 3,000 civilians, with the party responsible for the remainder unknown.[43] These numbers yield ratios ranging from 1.5 dead fighters per civilian to 5 dead civilians per fighter, all depending on the underlying assumptions. The ratio from Gaza very likely falls within that range, yet it is sufficiently broad to frustrate any rigorous comparison between the American and Israeli records on preventing civilian harm.

Perhaps the most surprising IDF response to the Health Ministry's casualty numbers was the concurrence of some Israeli figures that the numbers were probably accurate. When the Health Ministry's fatality figures passed 30,000 in March, Adm. Daniel Hagari, the IDF's top spokesperson, told reporters, "I don't push back. I don't question the number 30,000." Hagari said this at a time when the Health Ministry was relying heavily on unidentified media sources to drive up its numbers. His words demonstrated the IDF failure to examine

---

40   John Spencer, "Israel Has Created a New Standard for Urban Warfare. Why Will No One Admit It? | Opinion," Newsweek, March 25, 2024, https://www.newsweek.com/israel-has-created-new-standard-urban-warfare-why-will-no-one-admit-it-opinion-1883286.

41   Louisa Loveluck, Susannah George, and Michael Birnbaum, "As Gaza Death Toll Soars, Secrecy Shrouds Israel's Targeting Process," Washington Post, November 5, 2023, https://www.washingtonpost.com/world/2023/11/05/israel-strike-targets-gaza-civilians-hamas; Wes J. Bryant, "We Must Face the Hard Truth in Gaza: Israel Has Lost Its Moral Authority," The Hill, July 18, 2024, https://thehill.com/opinion/international/4777940-idf-gaza-civilian-harm/.

42   "Mosul Study Group: What the Battle for Mosul Teaches the Force," U.S. Army, September 2024, https://www.armyupress.army.mil/Portals/7/Primer-on-Urban-Operation/Documents/Mosul-Public-Release1.pdf; Mason W. Watson, "'We Are Coming, Nineveh': The Liberation of Mosul, 2016–2017," Army History 129 (Fall 2023): 8, https://www.jstor.org/stable/e48514763. See also: Jeffrey Martini and others, "Operation Inherent Resolve: U.S. Ground Force Contributions," RAND, October 17, 2022, https://www.rand.org/pubs/research_reports/RRA719-1.html.

43   Susannah George, Qassim Abdul-Zahra, Maggie Michael, and Lori Hinnant, "Mosul Is a Graveyard: Final IS Battle Kills 9,000 Civilians," Associated Press, December 20, 2017, https://apnews.com/article/middle-east-only-on-ap-islamic-state-group-bbea7094f-b954838a2fdc11278d65460; Stephen J. Townsend, "Reports of Civilian Casualties in the War Against ISIS Are Vastly Inflated," Foreign Policy, September 15, 2017, https://foreignpolicy.com/2017/09/15/reports-of-civilian-casualties-from-coalition-strikes-on-isis-are-vastly-inflated-lt-gen-townsend-cjtf-oir/.

evidence in the public domain despite constant pressure from both the US government and the media to account for the civilian death toll. Hagari's statement also signaled to the media that there was no need to treat the Health Ministry's numbers as controversial—if the IDF's chief advocate conceded the point, there was little reason to pay attention to the scattered critics of the ministry's numbers in either Israel or Washington. On background, other Israeli officials echoed Hagari's statement, further cementing journalists' view that they could safely rely on the Health Ministry's figures. Likewise, one senior Israel official, a hawk in most regards, told me in late 2023 that he had no reason to disbelieve the ministry's numbers.

One area in which the IDF did push back more vigorously was Hamas's exploitation of civilian structures—such as schools, mosques, hospitals, and UN facilities—to camouflage its military activities. In addition to asserting this point consistently, Israel produced evidence to substantiate its claims. Among the IDF's most effective tactics was conducting tours of Hamas tunnels, such as the ones beneath Al Shifa Hospital and the headquarters of the United Nations Relief and Works Agency (UNRWA), the main provider of humanitarian assistance. These tours resulted in extensive media coverage, with almost every top outlet treating the revelations as major stories.[44] That said, the media did not incorporate Hamas's use of civilian shields into its boilerplate language about casualty figures. While dispatches from Gaza included standard language about the number of fatalities according to the Health Ministry, they did not include a caveat indicating that Hamas deliberately put civilians in harm's way—a war crime—thus adding to the carnage. Israel was more successful in persuading Washington that Hamas constantly employed civilians to shield its fighters. The Biden administration's report to Congress regarding NSM-20 included a lengthy passage on this subject:

> Israel has had to confront an extraordinary military challenge: Hamas has embedded itself deliberately within and underneath the civilian population to use civilians as human shields. Hamas intentionally uses schools, hospitals, residential buildings, and international organization facilities for military purposes. It has

---

44 Matthew Rosenberg and others, "A Tunnel Offers Clues to How Hamas Uses Gaza's Hospitals," *New York Times*, February 12, 2024, https://www.nytimes.com/interactive/2024/02/12/world/middleeast/gaza-tunnel-israel-hamas.html; Dov Lieber and David Luhnow, "Hamas Military Compound Found beneath U.N. Agency Headquarters in Gaza," *Wall Street Journal*, February 10, 2024, https://www.wsj.com/world/middle-east/hamas-military-compound-found-beneath-u-n-agency-headquarters-in-gaza-7e29c758.

constructed a vast tunnel network beneath this civilian infrastructure not to protect civilians, but to hide its leaders and fighters and from which it stages and launches attacks.[45]

Senior officials and spokespersons often made similar points. Nevertheless, the administration asserted the magnitude of the death toll amounted to evidence that Israel must not be doing enough to protect civilians. In the words of the NSM-20 report, "The reported rate of civilian harm in the conflict also raises serious questions about the efficacy of Israeli precautionary measures, notwithstanding Hamas's deliberate embedding within and use of civilian and humanitarian infrastructure as shelter." The reasoning behind this statement remains unclear. If Hamas systematically employs human shields, how can it be clear that Israel's conduct "raises serious questions"? The best answer may be that such language was part of the White House's efforts to navigate between opposing pressures from Israel's friends and antagonists in Washington.

The Media Search for Proof of Israel's Culpability

By emphasizing the Health Ministry's casualty figures and framing civilian harm as the result of Israeli attacks rather than Hamas's use of human shields, the media created and reinforced the impression that the IDF was waging war indiscriminately. Yet this implicit attribution of guilt was insufficient for certain reporters at leading outlets, who sought to prove that the sheer number of civilian fatalities in Gaza amounted to evidence of Israeli culpability regardless of Hamas's (mis)conduct. There were two especially prominent approaches to making this argument. The first sought to show that the IDF inflicted greater harm on civilians than even Russian forces under Vladimir Putin or the Syrians under Bashar al-Assad. If the Israelis were more dangerous than these war criminals, then, the thinking goes, Israel must be committing war crimes of a similar magnitude. The second approach sought to show that one could trace the civilian death toll directly to the IDF's reliance on inherently indiscriminate weapons. Neither approach holds water.

Six weeks into the war, in late November 2023, the *New York Times* published a 3,000-word front-page story beneath the headline, "Gaza civilians, under Israeli

---

45 "Report to Congress under Section 2 of the National Security Memorandum on Safeguards and Accountability with Respect to Transferred Defense Articles and Defense Services (NSM-20)," 2024, archived at https://www.scribd.com/document/731299664/Report-to-Congress-under-Section-2-of-the-National-Security-Memorandum-on-Safeguards-and-Accountability-with-Respect-to-Transferred-Defense-Articles-a.

barrage, are being killed at historic pace." A sub-headline indicated, "In less than two months, more than twice as many women and children have been reported killed in Gaza than in Ukraine after two years of war."[46] Yet the comparison to Russian conduct in Ukraine floundered because the *Times* had its facts wrong. For Ukraine, the *Times* drew its casualty figures from a UN data set that has a very high bar for including deaths and even warns its users that the agency compiling the data "believes that the actual figures are considerably higher."[47] The UN data indicated that 2,756 women and 531 children had been killed in Ukraine. The *Times* compared those numbers to the Gaza GMO figures of 4,000 women and 6,150 children. Yet within 48 hours, the *Times* quietly made substantial changes to its story. Instead of identifying them as corrections, it simply marked the story as "updated." The old sub-headline was gone, along with any claim that more women and children had died in Gaza than Ukraine. The story now informed readers that "Ukrainian officials have estimated that more than 20,000 civilians died in the port city of Mariupol," which Russian forces besieged for months before its eventual capture.[48] Mariupol had a pre-war population of 400,000, about a fifth of the number in Gaza, and it is only one of the Ukrainian cities the Russians subjected to such intense bombardment. The *Times* might also have added that Kyiv actively seeks to minimize civilian casualties, building bomb shelters underground by converting metro stations and garages. The Hamas approach was very different. When an interviewer asked a top Hamas official why the organization had built 500 kilometers of tunnels for its fighters, but none to protect civilians, he answered, "It is the responsibility of the United Nations to protect them."[49] But the thrust of the *Times* story remained the same, even after the editors' stealth corrections.

---

46 Lauren Leatherby, "Gaza Civilians, Under Israeli Barrage, Are Being Killed at Historic Pace," *New York Times*, November 25, 2023, archived November 25 at https://web.archive.org/web/20231125101220/www.nytimes.com/2023/11/25/world/middleeast/israel-gaza-death-toll.html.

47 "Ukraine: Civilian Casualty Update," United Nations Human Rights Office of the High Commissioner, October 9, 2023, https://ukraine.un.org/sites/default/files/2023-10/Ukraine%20-%20civilian%20casualty%20update%20as%20of%208%20October%202023%20ENG.pdf.

48 Lauren Leatherby, "Gaza Civilians, Under Israeli Barrage, Are Being Killed at Historic Pace," *New York Times*, November 25, 2023, archived November 26 at https://web.archive.org/web/20231126105436/https://www.nytimes.com/2023/11/25/world/middleeast/israel-gaza-death-toll.html.

49 David Adesnik, "The Gray Lady Quietly Retracts Yet Another Slander against Israel," Washington Free Beacon, November 30, 2023, https://freebeacon.com/columns/the-gray-lady-quietly-retracts-yet-another-slander-against-israel/.

The print version of the *Times* story ran at the top of the front page on Sunday, November 26, beneath the headline, "Big Bombs in Urban Areas Raise Civilian Toll in Gaza."[50] It alleged that Israel's use of bombs weighing 2,000 pounds, rather than those with a payload of 500 or 1,000 pounds, was inherently indiscriminate because each one caused so much damage in densely populated urban settings. A month later, CNN and *The Washington Post* also published major stories that portrayed 2,000-pound bombs as inherently indiscriminate, while the *Times* ran a second piece on the subject.[51] Yet the basis for all of these stories was a flawed understanding of the actual impact of a 2,000-pound bomb on the battlefield. Detonated in an open space, such a bomb can reportedly kill individuals standing within a radius of 1,200 feet, or almost a quarter mile.[52] Detonated inside a building or under the ground, the same munition may affect a much smaller area. In 2016, the US Air Force received an order to destroy a hoard of cash the Islamic State was holding in a bank in Mosul, Iraq. The bills were in a vault in the basement of a nine-story building in a neighborhood full of civilians. To reach the target, US warplanes dropped three smaller bombs with fuses that detonated on successive floors of the building to kill ISIS personnel and open a path to the basement. Next came a pair of 2,000-pound bombs that penetrated the vault and incinerated the stockpile of cash.[53] A CNN dispatch at the time indicated that there were several civilian fatalities, yet by striking at dawn on a Sunday, the Air Force had minimized the death toll.[54] This degree of precision may require extensive planning, yet it shows the extent to which context determines the effect of munitions.

Nevertheless, CNN's story on Gaza repeatedly emphasized that 2,000-pound bombs "can cause high casualty events and can have a lethal fragmentation radius—an area of exposure to injury or death around the target—of up

---

50   Patrick Kingsley and Aaron Boxerman, "Dilemma Awaits Israel: What to Do When the Cease-Fire Ends," *New York Times*, November 26, 2023.
51   Tamara Qiblawi and others, "'Not Seen Since Vietnam': Israel Dropped Hundreds of 2,000-Pound Bombs on Gaza, Analysis Shows," CNN, December 22, 2023, https://www.cnn.com/gaza-israel-big-bombs/index.html.
52   "Explosive Weapons with Large Destructive Radius: Air-Dropped Bombs (the Mark 80 Series and Paveway Attachments)," Action on Armed Violence, March 1, 2016, https://aoav.org.uk/2016/large-destructive-radius-air-dropped-bombs-the-mark-80-series-and-paveway-attachments/.
53   Becca Wasser et al., *The Air War against the Islamic State* (Santa Monica, CA: RAND Corporation, 2021), https://www.rand.org/content/dam/rand/pubs/research_reports/RRA300/RRA388-1/RAND_RRA388-1.pdf.
54   Barbara Starr, "First on CNN: U.S. Bombs 'Millions' in ISIS Currency Holdings," CNN, January 13, 2016, https://www.cnn.com/2016/01/11/politics/us-bombs-millions-isis-currency-supply/index.html.

to 365 meters (about 1,198 feet)." The story did not include a single reference to contextual factors that shape the bomb's impact. Rather, it built its accusations against Israel on the assumption that all 2,000-pound bombs have a 1,200-foot blast radius. The video component of CNN's report displayed a satellite image of a neighborhood north of Gaza's Shati refugee camp. Nine small circles indicate the presence of craters associated with the use of 2,000-pound bombs. Red circles then expand out of the craters, covering the map, while the narrator reports that "the potential kill zone could encompass this entire area." She adds, "in an area this densely populated, and using these bombs, it's inherently indiscriminate." Put simply, CNN accused Israel of extensive war crimes in the absence of appropriate weapons forensics, and all based on misleading assumptions about the impact of 2,000-pound bombs.

A video investigation by the *Times* employed a similarly problematic approach. "When a 2,000-pound bomb detonates, it unleashes a blast wave and metal fragments thousands of feet in every direction," the narrator observes in the *Times's* video. The investigation notes in passing that the figure it provides is for "open areas," but never tells readers that the actual radius may be far smaller as a result of factors ranging from the height (or depth) of the detonation to the properties of nearby buildings.[55] Only the *Washington Post* acknowledged the importance of context for assessing a bomb's effects, yet its caveat appeared in an appendix that ran in minuscule text beneath the main body of its article. The caveat reads, "Damage depends on nearby structures, building materials, the soil, whether a bomb has been set to explode above or below ground, and other factors. Experts also noted that even the largest munitions can be employed to ensure that nearby civilian infrastructure is not damaged or is minimally affected when they explode."

These discussions of 2,000-pound bombs also argued that Israel's use of such weapons was clearly irresponsible since American forces refrained almost entirely from using them in the campaign against the Islamic State. According to the *Times*, the US military even hesitated to use 500-pound bombs in urban terrain. CNN reported, "The U.S. dropped a 2,000-pound bomb only once during its fight against ISIS—the most recent Western war on a militant group in the Middle East. It fell on the so-called caliphate's self-declared capital of Raqqa in Syria." This is an invented fact contradicted by CNN's own contemporary coverage of the war against the Islamic State. As noted above, the network reported the use of two 2,000-pound

---

55 Robin Stein, "Visual Evidence Shows Israel Dropped 2,000-Pound Bombs Where It Ordered Gaza's Civilians to Move for Safety," *New York Times*, December 21, 2023, https://www.nytimes.com/video/world/100000009208814/israel-gaza-bomb-civilians.html.

bombs in the US airstrike that incinerated an ISIS cash hoard in Mosul. US Air Force officers have also recounted how they used 2,000-pound bombs to destroy select parts of buildings in Raqqa without bringing down the entire structure or endangering nearby troops. The pilots employed the tactic often enough for it to acquire a nickname—"kneecapping." By delivering the bomb at an angle of thirty to forty-five degrees to the base of a building, the upper stories—where snipers often positioned themselves—would topple over, like a person struck in the knee.[56]

A Missed Opportunity to Save Palestinian Lives

When one's home is about to become a battlefield, the safest course of action is to relocate, at least temporarily. The Additional Protocols to the Geneva Conventions even recommends that the parties to a conflict "endeavour to remove the civilian population, individual civilians and civilian objects under their control from the vicinity of military objectives."[57] In most cases, the population can leave the zone of active hostilities without crossing an international border, but not in Gaza. It would not have been safe for Israel to open its border, but Egypt could have worked with the UN and other concerned parties to create a haven for Gaza residents in Sinai. Instead, Cairo categorically refused to accept displaced Palestinians, and Washington did not pressure it to do so.

Eight days into the war, my Foundation for Defense of Democracies colleagues Mark Dubowitz and Jonathan Schanzer published an essay in which they wrote, "With nowhere else to go, Egypt is the only possible escape route for Palestinians hoping to find refuge by land."[58] On October 18, Egyptian President Abdel Fattah al-Sisi sought to end any discussion of such a possibility, calling it "forced displacement" and suggesting Israel should take in those who wanted to leave the coastal strip. Senior Hamas official Osama Hamdan called for "rallying around [the Egyptian] position."[59] The departure

---

56 Aaron Stein, *The U.S. War Against ISIS: How America and Its Allies Defeated the Caliphate* (London: I. B. Tauris, 2021).

57 "Article 58—Precautions Against the Effects of Attacks," ICRC International Humanitarian Law Databases, https://ihl-databases.icrc.org/en/ihl-treaties/api-1977/article-58?activeTab=1949GCs-APs-and-commentaries.

58 Mark Dubowitz and Jonathan Schanzer, "Hamas's Enablers Should Take Gaza Refugees," *Wall Street Journal*, October 15, 2023, https://www.wsj.com/articles/enablers-of-hamas-should-take-gaza-refugees-c7c4b44c.

59 Nayera Abdallah, Nadine Awadella, and Mohamed Wali, "Egypt's Sisi Rejects Transfer of Gazans, Discusses Aid with Biden," Reuters, October 18, 2024, https://www.reuters.com/world/egypt-rejects-any-displacement-palestinians-into-sinai-says-sisi-2023-10-18/.

of Gaza residents would have been a major liability for Hamas, which would have found itself facing Israeli forces without its human shields. Hamas even instructed Gaza residents to ignore the Israeli call to relocate from the northern part of the enclave to the south ahead of the IDF ground offensive that began in late October.[60]

One of the principal justifications Egypt offered for its refusal was the contention that Israel would never allow those who sought refuge in Sinai to return to Gaza. Any departure from Gaza seemed to portend a repetition of the first Arab Israeli war in 1948–1949, when those who sought safety away from the front lines were never able to return.[61] The Egyptian president declared, "This is the cause of all causes, the cause of all Arabs. It is important that the [Palestinian] people remain steadfast and present on their land."[62] In the name of Arab nationalism, Sisi decided on the Palestinians' behalf that enduring the privations of war was preferable to finding safety abroad. Other Arab leaders concurred in the prioritization of principle over well-being. Their actual concerns may have been more prosaic. "No refugees in Jordan, no refugees in Egypt," said King Abdullah of Jordan. Given the uncertainty regarding postwar arrangements, Cairo especially had reason to eliminate the risk of becoming responsible for a sizable refugee population. In the first weeks of the war, the *Economist* reported that the Arab Gulf States had offered Sisi billions of dollars if he would offer sanctuary to those seeking an escape from Gaza. He refused.[63]

Neither Washington nor Jerusalem was inclined to challenge the Arab consensus. Three days into the war, US National Security Adviser Jake Sullivan said there had been discussions with Egypt about safe passage for civilians.[64]

---

60 "Hamas Tells Gaza Residents to Stay Put as Israel Ground Offensive Looms," Reuters, October 13, 2023, https://www.reuters.com/world/middle-east/hamas-tells-gaza-residents-stay-home-israel-ground-offensive-looms-2023-10-13/.
61 Greg Myre and Ava Batrawy, "Why Egypt Won't Allow Vulnerable Palestinians across Its Border," NPR, February 26, 2024, https://www.npr.org/2024/02/26/1232826942/rafah-gaza-palestinians-egypt-border.
62 "Hamas Tells Gaza Residents to Stay Put as Israel Ground Offensive Looms," Reuters, October 13, 2023, https://www.reuters.com/world/middle-east/hamas-tells-gaza-residents-stay-home-israel-ground-offensive-looms-2023-10-13/.
63 "Can Egypt Be Persuaded to Accept Gazan Refugees?," *Economist*, October 14, 2023, https://www.economist.com/finance-and-economics/2023/10/14/can-egypt-be-persuaded-to-accept-gazan-refugees.
64 "Press Briefing by Press Secretary Karine Jean-Pierre and National Security Advisor Jake Sullivan," White House, October 10, 2023, https://www.whitehouse.gov/briefing-room/press-briefings/2023/10/10/press-briefing-by-press-secretary-karine-jean-pierre-and-national-security-advisor-jake-sullivan-9/.

According to the *Washington Post*, Netanyahu asked Biden if he could persuade Sisi to welcome Gaza residents seeking refuge from the war, but Biden indicated that Cairo was categorically opposed.[65] In public, the Israeli government did not urge Cairo to take in refugees, likely because it understood that any association with the idea would contribute to suspicions that Israel wanted to depopulate Gaza permanently. Ultimately, the idea died quietly.

Conclusion

In America's public square, casualty figures from the Gaza Ministry of Health have become shorthand for the argument that Palestinian suffering is the result of Israeli callousness or even criminality. Yet the journalists and government officials who place faith in these numbers have willfully ignored both problems with the figures themselves as well as contextual factors that underscore the role of Hamas in condemning Gaza's population to misery. Whereas other embattled populations could seek refuge outside the war zone, Palestinians were denied that opportunity. Instead, they had to remain in Gaza, where their homes and places of study and worship were threaded with Hamas infrastructure. Hamas also built a fighting force of unusual size for an outlaw organization. Once the October 7 massacre ignited the conflict, these contextual factors ensured that Gaza residents would have to endure an intense and protracted battle in a confined, densely populated space where distance from Hamas fighters could be hard to achieve. It is impossible to say how many civilian casualties might have been avoided if the conditions did not apply. Nevertheless, their pervasiveness points to the folly of convenient assumptions that Israel's alleged negligence or malice must be responsible for the tragic scale of death and destruction in Gaza.

When the war ends, the debate over casualties is likely to continue. The Gaza Ministry of Health has already shown its determination to produce a complete listing of fatalities. There is likely to be a continuing effort to brand the Israeli war effort as a criminal enterprise. Just as narratives of displacement from 1948–1949 remain integral to claims against the legitimacy of the Jewish state, the death toll from this war is likely to figure prominently for decades in arguments about Israel's right to exist. Accordingly, the IDF

---

65 Yasmeen Abutaleb, John Hudson, and William Booth, "Biden and Netanyahu Heading for a Collision on Postwar Agenda," *Washington Post*, December 21, 2023, https://www.washingtonpost.com/politics/2023/12/21/biden-netanyahu-dispute-palestinian-state/.

and the government should immediately initiate a comprehensive effort to determine the number of lives lost in Gaza and whether the individuals in question were Hamas fighters, auxiliaries of various kinds, or actual civilians. The IDF and government should also assemble a comprehensive dossier, including declassified evidence, that documents Hamas's use of civilian facilities as military assets, especially hospitals. Israel cannot prevent a debate from taking place or false claims from being made, but it can provide open-minded observers with the material necessary to make informed judgements rather than relying on media that are unlikely to convey the full story. Above all, Israel should be prepared to demonstrate to sympathetic but increasingly skeptical Americans—especially elected and appointed leaders—that it upheld the two countries' liberal democratic values even after suffering a historic atrocity. The US-Israel relationship remains indispensable to Israeli national security since the implements of war are no less essential than the readiness and skill to use them, and use them in a manner consistent with the values the two countries share.

CHAPTER 3

Antisemitism Is about Semites like Dolichocephaly Is about Language[1]

Franck Salameh

Introduction

The grand narratives that once held our human societies, our national communities, our academies, and our families together—which is to say, shared histories, values, ethics, religions, languages, cultural accretions, intellectual traditions, the fact that there aren't seventy-two genders on earth or seventy-two virgins in heaven, that men cannot get pregnant, that antisemitism is vile, that totalitarian "group-think" is not an academic virtue, that at university we share and transmit knowledge, not feelings, slogans, agendas, and certitudes, and so on—all these "meta-narratives" have eroded in favor of a nihilistic view of the world; a conception of humans as rootless, anchor-less, denatured "social constructs" that ought to be deconstructed and remade. Challenging these modern norms of righteousness, disagreeing with someone on, say, questions of "gender identity," "critical race theory," "white privilege," "pronouns," "what is antisemitism and why Arabs are not Semites and *may* in fact be antisemites," along with a bevy of other fads dismissive of science, history, nature, and fact—challenging these new

---

[1] In a 2004 lecture delivered at Brandeis University, Bernard Lewis noted that the term "'Semitic' was first used as a linguistic, not as an ethnic or racial term. Like 'Aryan,' it was coined by philologists to designate a group of related languages . . . Already in 1872 the great German philologist Max Müller pointed out that 'Aryan' and 'Semitic' were philological, not ethnological terms, that to speak of an Aryan or Semitic race was as absurd as to speak of a dolichocephalic (long-headed) language," https://tremendouspatrolpanda.tumblr.com/post/643807166813323264/bernard-lewis-pdf.

"norms" of *bien-pensance*—is often viewed as "hate crimes," "Islamophobia," or "racist micro-aggressions" earning "perpetrators" punishment, tarring them as bigots meriting public humiliation and cancelation.

Already in 1998, Alan Sokal and Jean Bricmont had a name for our modern mental habits, the age of smug nihilism living in our present days; they called it "fashionable nonsense," "superficial erudition," and "incoherent pseudo-scientific gibberish."[2] In 2024 newspeak this is simply called wokeism, righteous pomposity hiding intellectual indigence. It is in this context, where a new "inclusive" language is being enforced, where antisemitism is changing its name, losing its inhibitions, "switching sidewalks,"[3] getting rehabilitated, normalized as a woke progressive virtue, that this paper will approach Arabist and Islamist antisemitism, a new faddish cause célèbre of a "Global South," taking by storm a timorous, disoriented "Global North" that has loosened its intellectual, historical, and moral moorings. In this schema, argued recently French historian and Arabist Gilles Kepel, a weaponized "Global South" is rising, meting out "the ultimate revenge" humbling an arrogant "Global North" represented by an international Jew—a term often couched in "Zionist" and "Israel" codenames—deserving of the frenzied orgies of "pillage, rapes, mutilations, and murders visited on [October 7, 2023, . . . deeming them] edifying heroic deeds honoring Muslims and their... sympathizers around the globe."[4]

And so, it is not enough to say that antisemitism is no longer a Western (Christian) malady and that it has finally infected an Islam and an Arab world otherwise immune to antisemitism—because, as the claim goes, "Arabs are Semites" and by definition a Semite cannot be an antisemite.[5] Rather, this paper will suggest that, even if, theologically grounded, Muslim Jew-hatred might have traditionally been more so a form of "social snobbery" as Bernard Lewis called it, a form of contempt as opposed to hatred for the "inferior Jew," Muslim antisemitism has long since espoused the themes, the sentiments, the iconography, and the aims of classic European (Christian) antisemitism,

---

2   See Alan Sokal and Jean Bricmont's *Fashionable Nonsense; Postmodern Intellectuals' Abuse of Science* (New York: Picador, 1998).
3   "Antisemitism has crossed the street and switched sidewalks" is an image I borrow from Franco-Israeli jurist, essayist, and public intellectual Gilles-William Goldnadel and his 2024 book/diary *Journal de guerre; C'est l'Occident qu'on assiassine* (Paris: Fayard, 2024).
4   Gilles Kepel, *Holocaustes; Israël, Gaza et la guerre contre l'Occident* (Paris: Éditions Plon, 2024), 18–20.
5   In 2024, behavioral psychologist and public intellectual Gad Saad lampooned this claim, arguing that, since he's a homo sapiens, he cannot possibly be a homophobe. Gad Saad (@GadSaad), X (formerly Twitter), October 15, 2024, https://x.com/GadSaad/status/1846004880948760706.

attributing to Jews an element of an immutable "cosmic evil."⁶ Furthermore, and contrary to their claims otherwise, Arabs are not Semites and may in fact be antisemites. To this point, and for the sake of bringing some discipline to taxonomies used loosely in the age of wokeness, it ought to be said from the outset that, save for the racist and the racialist thinker, there are no "Semitic peoples" as such, to the same extent that there are no "Aryan peoples." There are *only* languages and language families classified as Semitic or Aryan. Indeed, the term "Semite," like its Aryan cousin, was borrowed from the discipline of linguistics by nineteenth-century racialist German thinkers to stigmatize Jews with an immutable biological imprint. Thus, "Semite," in its original (racist) connotation, never applied to Arabs or any non-Jewish user of Semitic languages, who remained "users of Semitic languages" and not "Semites" or "Semitic peoples," when only Jews were deemed Semites. That is how, for racialist theorists, Jews morphed into Semites, and antisemitism into the term denoting prejudice against *them*, not Arabs. Therefore, the apocryphal term "Semite" would be a flimsy defense when brandished by Arabs as evidence of their inability to be antisemites because, again, they are *not* Semites and are quite capable of being antisemites.

The Road to October 7

In a 1947 conversation with Charles de Gaulle, Claude Guy, his former aide de camps, reported the General having relayed to him a confidence in the following terms: "Relative to this business of Palestine," said de Gaulle,

> I must admit that my preference goes to the Jews. You see, the Arabs are not worthy or our help. They are too skittish. In 1930, during my first visit to Palestine, I remember having seen the orange groves tended by the Arabs; they produced a fruit that was all shriveled, bitter, tiny. The Jews on the other hand grew their oranges remarkably successfully. These committed individualists, doubtlessly due to the fact that they were imbued in the sentiment that they were tilling their own ancestral lands . . . were eager to work in the most punishing of conditions, on the most inhospitable of fields. During the [Second

---

6 Bernard Lewis, "The New Anti-Semitism," *The American Scholar*, December 1, 2005, https://theamericanscholar.org/the-new-anti-semitism/.

World] War, when I returned to Palestine, I was stunned by the progress that the Jews had made [barely a decade following my first visit]; it was nothing short of amazing. Here is in brief why we must help the Jews, and why we ought to make haste helping them; because antisemitism, in its most virulent form, will doubtlessly rear its ugly head again, and it will do so rather quickly.[7]

Obviously, when denuded of its historical context, one may point to a number of "cringe" issues (to use a woke expression) arising from an eighty-year-old fragment of text like the above. Indeed, from a contemporary woke vantage point, one may wish to dismiss de Gaulle's confidence as part of the racist rantings of an old White-supremacist, fascist Frenchman speaking a language brimming with classic Orientalist stereotypes. One may wish to "cancel" Charles de Gaulle as a result of this statement; rename his airport, perhaps; enact a virtuous *auto-da-fé* of the hundreds of biographies written about him; remove him from French history books or the thousands of French localities, streets, or public squares bearing his name; dismantle thousands more of the monuments and statues dotting the French countryside decorating and commemorating the man—and, while we're at it, in the universe of virtue signaling fashionistas, enact the righteous act of desecrating (digging up and dismantling) de Gaulle's gravesite.[8]

After all, in the late 1950s, Charles de Gaulle had the audacity to make more similarly combustive statements that would be considered anathema today. So, one might say "de Gaulle had it coming," didn't he? When a newly elected Gaullist deputy (Alain Peyrefitte) met de Gaulle for the first time in 1959, he noted being told by the general—by then the eighteenth president of the French Republic—that French practitioners of the phony virtue of "integration" were "certified asses." "Let us not bullshit one another," said de Gaulle, "the French are a White European nation issuing from a Greco-Roman Christian civilization . . . and if we are to try to integrate tens of millions of Muslims into the French nation, France would cease being France, and my

---

7   Claude Guy, *En écoutant De Gaulle* (Paris: Grasset, 1996), 254.
8   In his monumental 2018 biography, *A Certain Idea of France; The Life of Charles de Gaulle* (London: Allen Lane, 2018), Julian Jackson writes how in today's France "Charles de Gaulle is everywhere: in memories, in street names, in monuments, in bookshops. At the most recent count over 3,600 localities had a public space—street, avenue, square, roundabout—named after him" (xxix).

[de Gaulle's] village would cease being called Colombey-les-deux-Églises to become Colombey-les-Deux-Mosquées."⁹

Scandalous as language like this may be to the righteous presentists of our time, it carries honesty and irreverence, perhaps untaintedness, that seem appropriate for our age. Indeed, de Gaulle's words from sixty years ago are an eloquent statement on the maladies plaguing our times. Because in our woke universe of inverted realities, of misinformation, of newspeak, of mind-muzzling, of historical indigence and linguistic distortions, an average Frenchman like de Gaulle can easily become a racist; and if de Gaulle is a racist, then every Frenchman must be a racist; and if every Frenchman is a racist, then no Frenchman can be racist. In fact, one never knows nowadays whether using the demonym "Frenchman" in a classroom, or in polite company, risks tarring the user with the "toxic masculinity" badge of the hated male chauvinistic phallocrat.

I deem it necessary to digress and stress the significance of bringing de Gaulle into a conversation on post-October 7 Israel and Arab social and intellectual life—to drive the point that loving one's culture, one's traditions, one's history, one's language, and wishing to preserve them, advance them, brag about them, and transmit them, is a norm of the human condition, and *ought not* be deemed a vice, certainly not a form of racism. But de Gaulle's "outspokenness" (in this age of "language policing") was not the only reason I opted to open this chapter with fragments from his intellectual legacy. The main reason was obviously de Gaulle's caution about the re-emergence of antisemitism. It was his ominous

---

9   Alain Peyrefitte, *C'était De Gaulle* (Paris: Gallimard, 2000), 65–66. See also Jackson, *A Certain Idea of France*, 511–512: "De Gaulle never believed in 'integration,' nor did he welcome it. When the recently elected Gaullist député Alain Peyrefitte met de Gaulle for the first time in March 1959, he was startled to be told that those who supported integration were 'certified asses' (*Jean-Foutre*)."

Here is the original of de Gaulle's quote that is given, in shortened form, in the text of my chapter: "C'est très bien qu'il y ait des Français jaunes, des Français noirs, des Français bruns... Ils montrent que la France est ouverte à toutes les races et qu'elle a une vocation universelle. Mais à condition qu'ils restent une petite minorité. Sinon, La France ne serait plus la France. Nous sommes quand même avant tout un peuple européen de race blanche, de culture grecque et latine et de religion chrétienne. Qu'on ne se raconte pas d'histoires ! Les musulmans, vous êtes allés les voir ? Vous les avez regardés avec leurs turbans et leurs djellabas? Vous voyez bien que ce ne sont pas des Français! Ceux qui prônent l'intégration ont une cervelle de colibri. Essayez d'intégrer de l'huile et du vinaigre. Agitez la bouteille. Au bout d'un moment ils se sépareront de nouveau. Les Arabes sont des Arabes, les Français sont des Français. Vous croyez que le corps Français peut absorber dix millions de Musulmans qui demain seront vingt millions, et après-demain quarante? Si nous faisons l'intégration, si tous les Arabes et Berbers d'Algérie étaient considérés comme Français, comment les empêcher de venir s'installer en métropole, alors que le niveau de vie y est tellement plus élevé? Mon village ne s'appellerait plus Colombey-les-deux-Eglises, mais Colombey-les-deux-Mosquées."

prescient certitude that antisemitism was coming back.[10] And so, I began sketching outlines for what became this chapter while in France in December 2023. I was reading through French sources for a different project then, and I was struck by this quote *not only* because—in 1947, months before the birth of the State of Israel—it was eerily premonitory, but *also* because in late 2023 I was witnessing first-hand its prophecies coming to pass; the re-emergence of the antisemitism that de Gaulle warned about; virulent, vile, violent, but somehow tolerated, condoned, justified, intellectualized, endorsed—in France of all places; the home of the French Revolution, which gave us the famous Jewish Emancipation Declaration at the French National Assembly (1789): "to the Jews as a nation nothing shall be given; to the Jews as individuals everything will be given."[11]

But this new antisemitism is also taking America and the American academy by storm. In the "safe spaces" of our young smart, literate, college-educated or college-bound, progressive woke fashionistas, not only is antisemitism accepted nowadays, but it is also deemed righteous, liberating. Higher education has become a veritable "train wreck," wrote Dara Horn in a February 2024 *Atlantic* article.[12] Indeed, the American university has become a safe space for unhinged and uninhibited American antisemitism; a main breeding ground of a learned, cultured, "polite society" antisemitism. Few need reminding of the disaster that was the December 2023 congressional hearing on antisemitism. Probing the presidents of Harvard, UPenn, and MIT on the topic, US representatives got the impression that "calling for the genocide of Jews [on a university campus] would violate university policies *only* depending on the context" of such calls.[13]

So, there it is. And the new antisemitism of today does not seem much different from the old antisemitism of yesterday; it has simply "crossed the street, switching sidewalks," as noted French essayist Gilles-William Goldnadel in a "war diary" he published in early 2024.[14] It is the old antisemitism repackaged, rebranded, renamed, given a good reputation, and remerchandised in smart

---

10 De Gaulle was a lot like that—obsessively pompous and sententious in his certitudes, but *always* insufferably on the money.
11 Stanislas de Clermont-Tonnerre, "Speech on Religious Minorities and Questionable Professions," delivered at the French National Assembly on December 23, 1789, considered the opening act of "Jewish emancipation."
12 Dara Horn, "Why the Most Educated People in America Fall for Anti-Semitic Lies," *Atlantic*, February 15, 2024, https://www.theatlantic.com/ideas/archive/2024/02/jewish-anti-semitism-harvard-claudine-gay-zionism/677454/.
13 Ibid.
14 Azilia le Corre, "Gilles-William Goldnadel dans le JDD: 'L'ennemi du Juif a changé de trottoir,'" *Journal du Dimanche*, January 21, 2024, https://www.lejdd.fr/societe/gilles-william-goldnadel-dans-le-jdd-lennemi-du-juif-change-de-trottoir-141359.

appealing progressive anti-colonialist wokeist labels, with "Palestinianism"[15] as its poster child. Note that what is meant by "Palestinianism" here is *not* sympathy for a "Palestinian cause," nor support for the right of the "Palestinian people" to a state of their own, nor even the love that one might have for "Palestinians" as a people. Those are all sentiments that may be justified and fair. But "Palestinianism," a term and a temperament coined by Edward Said, is something else entirely. "Palestinianism" today, especially after October 7, is an ideology, a political device mobilizing and normalizing, even exalting, antisemitism as a virtue. And in this sense antisemitism becomes synonymous with righteousness, Palestinianism as its galvanizer. Indeed, the wokist fad of "intersectionality," whereby "all oppressions intersect," the idealization of nihilistic gender fluidity, misandry, the glorification of rootlessness and multiculturalism, and the criminalization of national identities ("white people's" identities in particular) all coalesce in a righteous, justified antisemitism represented by a righteous Palestinianism.

With this in mind, Palestinianism becomes beatific no matter what the Palestinian does, and Jew-hatred, the hatred of the Palestinian's oppressor, becomes righteous no matter what the Jew does or does not do. Thus, the emaciated Jew in filthy striped pajamas behind electrified barbed wire fences is equally abhorred for his vulnerability as is his self-reliant headstrong Sabra modern counterpart in green military fatigues.[16] Likewise the homeless diasporic Jew is impugned for his rootlessness, just as the defiant Sabra in his restituted homeland is resented for his rootedness—and, indeed, deemed a settler colonial practitioner of apartheid. In other words, if in an ideal society

> piety was a given, Jews [are] impious blasphemers; if secularism was an ideal, Jews [are] backward pietists; [if] capitalism was evil, Jews [are] capitalists; if communism was evil, Jews [are] communists; [if] nationalism was glorified, Jews [are] rootless cosmopolitans; if nationalism was vilified, Jews [are] chauvinistic nationalists.[17]

---

15 The term "Palestinianism" was coined by Edward Said to connote an ideology of open-ended opposition to Zionism. See Adam Shatz, "Palestinianism," *London Review of Books* 43, no. 9 (May 6, 2021), https://www.lrb.co.uk/the-paper/v43/n09/adam-shatz/palestinianism.

16 Quitterie Desjobert, "L'antisémitisme a changé de trottoir : Gilles-William Goldnadel livre un récit personnel dans son nouvel ouvrage *Journal de guerre*," C-News, January 24, 2024, https://www.cnews.fr/culture/2024-01-24/lantisemitisme-change-de-trottoir-gilles-william-goldnadel-livre-un-recit.

17 Horn, "Why the Most Educated People."

Thus, antisemitism becomes a fight against injustice; "a righteous act of resistance against evil, because Jews are collectively evil and have no right to exist."[18] And rather than being the preserve of the vile right of yore, the standard bearer of today's antisemitism becomes the anti-racist anti-patriarchal anti-heterosexual anti-phallocratic anti-identity gender-fluid socially and intellectually hedonistic left. Thus, in a reconfigured "political geography," the new antisemitism becomes a virtuous leftist antisemitism wedded to Islamist ideologies subsumed into a so-called "Global South" darling of the "Global Left." At worst, there is no antisemitism from this perspective, there is only antizionism; at best, one cannot decry antisemitic acts and attitudes without decrying a non-extant invented Islamophobia (or, better yet, claiming Palestinians are Arabs, and Arabs are Semites, and therefore, as Semites, cannot possibly be antisemites).

But as mentioned earlier, Arabs are not Semites, and are indeed not only prone to being antisemites, with many being in fact today's posterchildren of the Islamic-leftist Third-Worldist Global South antisemitism. When the left is no longer able to pronounce Israel's name without a sense of unease; when in the manner of Arabs and Muslims of the Middle East Western leftists refer to Israel as "the Zionist entity" (rather than a member-state of the United Nations and signatory to the Universal Declaration of Human Rights); when Israel is deemed an alien allogenic "settler colonialist" cancer meriting excision because a malignant growth on indigenous beatific Palestinian Arabs (who are incidentally themselves descendants of settler colonial Muslim conquerors), antisemitism becomes a righteous leftist virtue. In this sense, a new language is emerging, a new *1984* in a 2024 newspeak version of historical inversions.

Thus, war becomes genocide; Islamist Razzia-style orgies of rape, plunder, and collection of war spoils become resistance (or, better yet, "the events of October 7");[19] civilian war spoils and hostages become "prisoners of war";[20] national borders become apartheid; statehood becomes land theft, occupation, colonialism; and antisemitism becomes impossible because, again, Arabs are supposedly Semites, and Semites cannot possibly be antisemites. Yet, October 7, 2023, which, again, in most Arabic-language media is still referred to by the innocuous euphemistic "events of October 7," had at least one origin story grounded in Arab-Muslim Jew-hatred.

---

18   Ibid.
19   Kepel, *Holocaustes*, 26.
20   Arab satellite TV described the hostages as *asra* (prisoners of war), not as *rahaa'in* (hostages).

Arab Antisemitism?

Arab-Muslim Jew-hatred may not have had its beginnings in the classic Christian versions of Jew-hatred—rebranded as "antisemitism" in the nineteenth century. But from the earliest days of Islam, there has certainly been an Arab iteration of Jew-hatred, which, in the twentieth century, seems to have proudly acquired the same "racialist" overtones of European antisemitism. Indeed, it is not a trivial matter that the Arabs of British Mandate Palestine fought the Zionist project throughout the early half of the twentieth century under bona fide Muslim banners, sometimes "Arab" banners. But Arabism and Islam are interchangeable if not indistinguishable. The literature of Arab nationalism is replete with evidence confirming this axiom. To wit, a leading Iraqi writer, Abdel Rahman al-Bazzaz, noted Islam being *par excellence* the Arabic religion of the Arabs, crafted by Arabs; "there is no contradiction between Islam and Arabism," stressed Bazzaz.[21] Another ideologue from the same school chimed in noting that "Islam is the other face of Arabism."[22] Munah al-Sulh, a Lebanese university professor and eloquent Arab-nationalist theorist, confirmed his cohorts' assertions, stressing that "Islam is another name for Arab nationalism."[23] Even Michel Aflaq himself, the Christian founder of the "secular" Arab Socialist Baath party, is noted to have claimed repeatedly that "Islam is to Arabism what bones are to the flesh."[24] But perhaps most significantly, the logo of the Arab League itself—mind you, an "Arab" and not a "Muslim" league—is emblazoned with a fragment of a verse from the Quranic Surat al-Imran, which reads: "You are the finest nation (*umma*) that has been brought forth to mankind."[25] Finally, and as regards the main theatre of "Arab antisemitism," British-Mandate Palestine, and what was spawned in its aftermath, the Palestinian Arabs' most prominent "national" leaders were

---

21 Sylvia G. Haim, *Arab Nationalism: An Anthology* (Berkeley, CA: University of California Press, 1964), 174.

22 Abu-Musa al-Hariri, *A-'Arabiyyun Huwa? Bahthun fii 'Uruubat al-Islam* [Was He an Arab? A Study Relative to the Arabness of Islam] (Beirut: The Hard Truth Series, 1984), 16. See also "On Adel Hussein's Impressions of Arabism," in Al-Tayyib Ayt Hammuda, "Arabism and Islam: Unity or Repulsion?," The Center for the Study and Research of Secularism in the Arab World, December 28, 2010, http://ssrcaw.org/ar/print.art.asp?aid=239812&ac=1.

23 See James Jankowski and Israel Gershoni, *Rethinking Nationalism in the Arab Middle East* (New York: Columbia University Press, 1997), 219. See also Kamal Salibi, *A House of Many Mansions: The History of Lebanon Reconsidered* (Berkeley, CA: University of California Press, 1988), 50.

24 Michel Aflaq, *Fī Sabīl al-Ba'ath* [For the Sake of the Ba'ath] (Beirut: Dār al-Ṭalī'ah, 1959), 43, 68. Another version of this adage is "Arabism is a body whose soul is Islam." See also Olivier Carré, *Le Nationalisme Arabe* (Paris: Petite Bibliothèque Payot, 1993), 52–53.

25 Qur'an 3:110, *kuntum khayru ummatin ukhrijat li'l-nās*.

Mufti Hajj Amin al-Husseini of Jerusalem (an admirer of the Führer himself) and a Damascene petty cleric named ʿIzz al-Din al-Qassam (a fiery antisemite and an anti-Christian Islamist preacher who would come to bequeath his name onto two of this conflict's most recognizable actors: Hamas's military wing, the ʿIzz al-Din al-Qassam Brigades, and the organization's infamous "Qassam Rockets"). Incidentally, one model of the ICBMs that Iran launched on Israel on April 13, 2024 is aptly named "Khaybar," after the Arabian Jewish oasis town that the Prophet Muhammad's army marched upon and decimated in 628 AD, and which many friends of the Palestinians today recall with the ominous rhyming chant: "Khaybar Khaybar ya Yahud, Jayshu Muhammad sa-yaʿud" (Khaybar, Khaybar, O Jews, Muhammad's army is coming back for you).[26]

In a February 2024 Sada al-Balad interview on Egyptian television, Fatah official Yasser Abu Sido noted that "the crimes perpetrated by Israel in Gaza [were] no less genocidal than the Holocaust itself." He further stressed that "a clarification" needed be made, and a question that nobody asks ought to be asked: "Why did the Holocaust take place?" He continued:

> I'm not a fan of Hitler. Hitler is not my beloved; but when Hitler perpetrated the Holocaust, he did so for valid reasons; because Jews and World Zionism . . . were planning the takeover of Germany; and they had begun decaying Germany economically, and in terms of moral disintegration toward that end, which instigated Hitler's reaction, dragging the Jews down into the streets. . . . The Jews distorted many verses in the Torah to make themselves look good. I'm not going to provide examples because some may accuse me of being an antisemite for that, in spite of the fact that we, the Arabs, are the real Semites, not the Jews . . .[27]

Again, this is not a one-off, knee-jerk emotive under-duress reaction in especially challenging circumstances. This is a symptom of a deeper malady ingrained in the Muslim and Arab psyches. To this point, former Druze Lebanese MP Fady al-Aʿwar noted on Hezbollah's al-Manar television that

---

26 Kepel, *Holocaustes*, 24–27.
27 See MEMRI TV, February 23, 2024, https://www.memri.org/tv/fatah-official-yasser-abu-sido-no-fan-hitler-holocaust-reasons-jews-control-germany.

this entity [Israel] is in dire mental disarray.... This is going to drive a great number of them [Jews] to abandon the settlements and begin a migration in the opposite direction [out of Israel . . . and] back to where they came from. Europe solved its [Jewish problem] by rounding the Jews up and cramming them onto our lands. They are now in the process of returning [to where they came from.] That may be the reason why Europeans and others are helping Israel today; to prevent [the Jews] from returning to Europe; because they are a people incapable of integration into other societies. Their entire history, and the totality of their human relations are a dark stain [on humanity].... Anyone who reads the Jewish mentality, their Talmudic mentality, will realize the extent to which [their evil is prevalent] and [the level of evil] they are capable of. Their faith makes it licit for them to murder children. [Interviewer's interjection]: Exactly! And that is precisely what is going on in Gaza. And this is what they did to Europeans [murdering European children] before they expelled them and corralled them in our direction.[28]

Worth mentioning in this regard is that this sort of discourse, and Palestinianism's, Arabism's, and Islamism's religiously grounded antisemitic tropes responding to Israel and the Zionist national project are *not* limited to the demagogue, the uncouth, the pious, or the half-literate Muslim peasant affronted by the arrogance of a recalcitrant *dhimmi* overstepping his bounds. Anti-Jewish sentiments are prevalent in enlightened, modernizing, secular, Arab nationalist literature, where "Jews" (*Yahud*) is the term of choice referring to Israel, Israelis, Zionists, *and* of course Jews *tout court*. "Jewish" and "Jews" are also terms of abuse, used by many Arabs and Arabophones as an accusation, an insult. To wit, an Arabophone non-Jew, who may not exhibit the de rigueur Arabist hostility to Zionism, is often referred to as a *'amiil* (collaborator), or a member of *"Yahud al-daakhel"* (a Jew of the interior, or an inside Jew), meaning "a fifth-column Jew," which is the Arabist/Islamist version of the Uncle Tom-type "native informer." The "power of *Takhwin* (the power to declare other men traitors)" is an awesome weapon of the Islamist and Arabist,

---

28 See MEMRI TV, February 18, 2024, https://www.memri.org/tv/former-lebanese-mp-fadi-al-awar-jews-are-fleeing-israel-and-going-back-where-they-came-jews-were.

wrote Fouad Ajami—a terrifying weapon that endows them with the power of deciding what is permissible and what is not, branding those who dissent from orthodoxy "immoral," "collaborators," "traitors."²⁹

Again, such labels are not the preserve of the uncultured. They are prevalent in Arabic language public debates, in political discourse, in journalistic treatments of the Arab-Israeli conflict, in Arabic literature, and in major widely read publications of prominent literati like Mahmood Darwish, Ghassan Kanafani, and Nizar Qabbani, all adulated by Western audiences. A few samples may suffice to illustrate the disturbing pervasiveness of this phenomenon and the level of its "normalization." In his 1967 iconic longform poem *Marginalia on the Notebook of Defeat*, in which he excoriates Arabs for collecting yet another defeat at the hands of the inferior Jew, Nizar Qabbani wrote:

ما دخل اليهود من حدودنا، انّما تسرّبوا كالنمل من عيوننا

the Jews [*not* the Zionists, *not* the Israelis, but **the Jews**] did not merely breach our borders; indeed, they crawled in like ants through the cracks of our flaws [emphasis mine].³⁰

What ought to give pause in this snippet is not merely the use of "Jews" instead of Israelis, but in fact *also* the classic antisemitic trope of the "insidious duplicitous Jew" (taken straight out of one of the most widely read "history books" in the Arab world, *The Protocols of the Elders of Zion*): The Jew stealthily "crawling through the cracks of [the Arabs' inattention, or their] weaknesses," and into the lands that ought to forever remain a Muslim preserve, is an image popularized in the *Protocols*, and one that pervades the reality of Arab intellectuals, popular culture icons, and commoners alike.

This is nowhere better illustrated than in a 2016 interview with Lebanese diva—and, since 2001, UN Food and Agriculture Organization Goodwill Ambassador, Majida el-Roumi. An activist humanitarian with an angelic voice, and a tender-hearted UN representative working indefatigably to combat world hunger, Roumi is also a proud antisemite. She would not bat an eye telling an adoring audience at a Beirut Arab University press conference that

---

29 Fouad Ajami, "The End of Arab Nationalism: A Personal and Political Odyssey," *New Republic*, July 12, 1991, https://newrepublic.com/article/91635/the-end-arab-nationalism.
30 See Franck Salameh, *The Other Middle East; An Anthology of Modern Levantine Literature* (New Haven, CT: Yale University Press, 2017), 83.

> What is ailing our world today—and I take full responsibility for what I am about to tell you here—what is ailing our world today is intrinsically related to something [presumably a cosmic truth] we read in my parents' home when we were little kids. My dad—may God rest his soul—brought home one day a book titled *The Protocols of the Elders of Zion*. He told us: "*Tolle lege*, take this and read it, and until the day you die you are **not** to forget a single word you will read in this book." That is how I learned that World Zionism had a plan to fragment the whole of the Arab World . . . They [the Elders of Zion, who are Jews, not Buddhist monks] have a cosmic plan, through which they intend to instate a single world-government, on a planetary scale, through which they would enslave the rest of us . . . In their mind [that is to say, in the minds of the Elders of Zion, who, again, are Jews, not Buddhist monks,] the whole of humanity (all of us) were created and placed on earth to live in bondage at their service. This idea is the uppermost in my mind. Not a bullet gets fired in the world; not a single explosion takes place; whether here, there, in France, or elsewhere in the world, nothing happens that is not commanded and directed by them [meaning the Elders of Zion, who are Jews, not Buddhist monks]. [Emphasis mine.][31]

This is all to reiterate that Arab antisemitism is not a random or inadvertent slip of the tongue. Rather, it is a longstanding time-honored societal—not to say cultural—malady. The same illustrious, otherwise secular Arab nationalist poet mentioned earlier, Nizar Qabbani, dreamt all his life of—and imbued much of his poetry with—one day redeeming Arabs and restituting them to Muslim Spain.[32] In a 1966 poem titled "Granada," Qabbani sneered at his Spanish tour-guide deigning to describe herself to him as a Spaniard. "How sweet," he wrote "to meet by chance, without prior plans, two brown eyes glaring, glittering from my past":

---

31 Sarcastic square brackets mine. Majida el-Roumi, press conference at Beirut Arab University, YouTube, May 16, 2016, https://www.youtube.com/watch?v=XPK8Y3xGKiM.

32 See, for instance, Efraim Karsh, *Islamic Imperialism; A History* (New Haven, CT: Yale University Press, 2006), 230. In Qabbani's vein, Karsh writes that, to this day, "many Arabs and Muslims unabashedly pine for the restoration of Spain and consider their 1492 expulsion from the country a grave historical injustice, as if they were Spain's rightful owners and not former colonial occupiers of a remote foreign land, thousands of miles from their ancestral homeland. Edward Said applauded Andalusia's colonialist legacy as 'the ideal that should be moving our efforts now. . . .'"

Centuries of my history, dripping from those two eyes;
"Are you a Spaniard?" I asked.
"Why, of course I am," she proudly blared, "Granadan, born and bred!"
"Granadan?" I snickered under my breath . . .
Suddenly seven centuries of my history began arising from deep slumbers,
Seven centuries of me, coming to life in those two brown eyes . . .
Umayyads with flags unfurled, horses neighing, galloping my way.
How ironic, history, returning me to this dark-skinned brown eyed descendant of my people . . .
Soon I was gazing at our old house in her eyes;
my mother's eyes.
Damascus.
Its rivers flowing, fluttering like my beautiful Granadan's hair.
Her face Arab.
Her lips Arab.
Squeezing in them seven centuries worth of my homeland's golden sunshine . . .
My heart bleeding as she bragged about the glory of her Granadan forefathers.
Her forefathers?
How ironic.
Hands in pockets, I search in vain for my old house keys . . . In Granada . . .[33]

"Old house keys"? Sound familiar?

Months before his passing in April 1998, Qabbani would excoriate Oslo and the prospects of peace with the Jews in another one of his trademark poems, beautifully saturated not only with antisemitic tropes and yearnings for a Muslim Golden Age, but also expropriating pre-Muslim history, claiming it to the Arabs, and making as if Islam had spread in a vacuum. "For the fiftieth time, Granada is being wrested from our hands," he wrote:

---

33 Is this innocuous nostalgia? Or is it conceit? Negationism? Appropriation? See Nizar Qabbani, "Granada," 1966, https://www.nizariat.com/poetry.php?id=79.

> For the fiftieth time History has fallen from our hands...
> Our heroics have fallen from our hands...
> Seville has fallen from our hands...
> Antioch has fallen from our hands...
> And not a single Andalusia has remained within our grasp...
> They stripped us of our doorways and our walls,
> They stripped us of our wives and our children.
> They stripped us of our olive trees and olive presses and the paving stones of our roadways...
> They ripped baby Jesus, Son of Mary, from his mother's bosom
> ...
> And they drove their so-called reconciliation into us like a dagger,
> In an act of rape...[34]

But, aside from Qabbani's mood swings and irredentist antics, Ghassan Kanafani takes the cake. A prominent intellectual of the Popular Front for the Liberation of Palestine and a pioneer of the Arabic short story, Kanafani is perhaps the most widely read Arab novelist of his generation. In his magnum opus, *Men in the Sun*, Kanafani uses the words "Jewish" and "Jews" throughout the narrative to mean "Zionists" or "Israelis" without taking the pain to nuance differences. But that is not unusual. Some time ago, in one of my classes at university, I screened *The Dupes*—a Youssef Saleh Egyptian adaptation of Kanafani's *Men in the Sun*, which students were assigned to read in English beforehand. The film was a black and white iteration of the "art cinema" genre, a decent production for its time. Its English subtitles, however, were neither "artsy" nor honest, for each time the actors uttered the words "Jewish" or "Jews" (as appeared in Kanafani's original Arabic text) the English subtitles "Westsplained" them into "Zionist" and "Zionism," therefore covering up the Arabic language's intuitive antisemitic foundations—a hallmark not only of Kanafani's work, but, as mentioned earlier, an impulse prevalent in normative journalistic, *belles lettres*, or popular treatments of the Arab-Israeli (or Arab-Jewish) dispute. I used this instance as a teaching moment, exposing my students to the dishonesty and moral cowardice—"political correctness" in today's parlance—that often accompanies Western attempts at "discernment" relative to the Middle East in general and the Arab-Israeli conflict in particular.

---

34 Nizar Qabbani, "The Gallopers," 1998, https://www.aldiwan.net/poem6511.html.

Conclusion

And so, Israel is under assault today—and antisemites are leading the charge uninhibited, with abandon—*not* because Israel is an apartheid state, not because it is committing a genocide of the Palestinian people, not because it is a settler colonial entity, and not because it is a Zionist entity, although all the preceding help. Simply put, Israel is being assaulted (and this, since its birth) because it is Jewish sovereignty in what is deemed *dar al-Islam*; it is an illustration of a *dhimmi* people rejecting *dhimmitude*; it is the last remaining "Crusader bastion" in a place where Islam must rule. From its inception, writes Bernard Lewis, Islam has been

> a religion of power, and in the Muslim worldview it is right and proper that power should be wielded by Muslims and Muslims alone. Others may receive the tolerance, even the benevolence, of the Muslim state, provided that they clearly recognize Muslim supremacy. That Muslims should rule over non-Muslims is right and normal. That non-Muslims should rule over Muslims is an offence against the laws of God and nature, and this is true whether in Kashmir, Palestine, Lebanon, or Cyprus.[35]

That is why Israel is an anomaly (from an Islamist and Arabist perspective). Before Israel, *Lebanon* was the anomaly until that anomaly was corrected, stripping it of its sovereign Christian content. Yet, noted the newly elected president of Lebanon in 1982, shortly before his assassination, our demands as indigenous Near Eastern Christians are fairly modest:

> On this very spot of our planet, as a society that has been living under the threat of dissolution for the past fourteen centuries ... it is high time for us to spell out our demands without fear and without compunctions.... Freedom and security are all that we are asking for. Freedom for our society to prosper; freedom for our society to live, teach, preserve, perpetuate, and transmit our millennial traditions, our beliefs, our cultural accretions, and our values without fear of uncertainty, and without threats of dissolution hanging over our heads.... Our second demand is security

---

35 Bernard Lewis, "The Return of Islam," *Commentary*, January 1976, https://www.commentary.org/articles/bernard-lewis/the-return-of-islam/.

> for our society; security in all that that term entails; security in the sense that we no longer be subjected every ten years or so to the onslaught of neighbors unhappy with our presence, unhappy with our freedom, unhappy with our prerogatives as a sovereign, distinct society; security in the sense that the adage "all it takes is five Palestinians to throw you into the sea" [a precursor of today's "from the river to the sea Palestine will be free"?] will no longer be our neighbors' slogan of choice, and will no longer be brandished to be hung over our heads...[36]

What happened on October 7, 2023, was a chapter in a centuries-long saga that can no longer be contemplated while giving short shrift to what some still refuse to call Arab-Muslim antisemitism. Because, beyond the usual platitudes about land, refugees, justice, Jerusalem, there are deeper cultural, intellectual, and religious questions to be pondered. And, whether secular or not, it remains the case that the more influential (and more widely read) of Arab intellectuals persist in their unwillingness to tolerate non-Muslim sovereignty (to boot, Jewish sovereignty) in what is deemed the world of Islam. Some readers may remember some of the iconography of the early anti-Israel demonstrations—especially around Christmas time 2023—replete with pictorial and linguistic elements de-Judaizing Jewish history and the history of Israel. Even if still not yet brazenly, or only mildly, antisemitic, anti-Israel slogans then were often displayed in Fraktur fonts reminiscent of Nazi iconography; Israel was depicted as a blood-soaked executioner; and the old antisemitic tropes of the "greedy money changer," the "duplicitous hook-nosed" ugly swarthy male, the "blood sucker," the "Christ-killer," the "plague bringer" were omnipresent in banners and other visual effects on display at public demonstrations. Likewise, depictions of the crucified Jesus with the grieving Madonna at his feet, always clad in PLO-style keffiyeh, completed this *Judenrein* de-Judaizing of history, memory, geography, and iconography of a Near East divested of its pre-Arab and pre-Muslim past.

How to reclaim social and intellectual equilibrium in a daily life ransacked by rampant intellectual vandalism and totalitarianism at the highest levels—from universities mandating *bien-pensance* rather than inspiring humanistic love of

---

[36] John Gotti (@The_Dapper_Don1), "Bachir Gemayel speech, ca. 1982," X (formerly Twitter), October 5, 2023, https://x.com/The_Dapper_Don1/status/1761345563482538154.

learning[37] to mediocre journalism indoctrinating consensus orthodoxies rather than transmitting information? The abject nihilism into which our societies have descended is mind blowing.[38] How then to resolve this conundrum?

One does not resolve a civilizational problem of this magnitude by submitting to the creeping ambient orthodoxies. One counters such a problem by opposing decline with clarity and dignity, by presenting cheap jingles and soundbites and memes with a civilizational project; "one needs a spiritual supplement to wrest the human spirit from the irrelevance, the subordination, the degeneracy into which it has fallen," writes French philosopher Michel Onfray. In other words, one needs a new kind of spirituality, a civilizational reawakening transcending the current stuntedness and pettiness of our current days.[39]

French novelist and former minister of cultural affairs André Malraux (1901–1976) famously noted "civilization" to be, before anything else, a form of spirituality connecting those of sharing a kindred history and a set of shared values. The essence of a civilization, he wrote, is all that which gathers around a religious text; and when a civilization shirks its spiritual bearings, when it is no longer capable of erecting a religious shrine, or building a burial site, which is to say,

---

37 It is fashionable to think of universities as "safe spaces" for teaching and encouraging critical thinking rather than mandating fashionable orthodoxies. That is fair. But only partially so. I prefer universities that transmit humanism and humanistic values; teaching and appreciating humanism rather than "critical thinking" *tout court*. France's Ministry of Education was once known by another more beautiful, more expressive name capturing what I'm referring to here; the Ministère de l'Instruction Publique et des Beaux Arts (the Ministry of Public Education and Fine Arts). It is perhaps preferable to have educational systems that teach appreciation for mankind, valorization of our human history, our human epopee. Loving one's history, culture, and literature ought to be at the heart of teaching. That, to my sense, is the role of a university—teaching the story of humanity and humanism, how we traveled through the millennia as a species on this tiny spaceship in a small corner of an immense universe. Our story (our literary traditions) ought to be at the heart of our teaching. That is the story of humanism. How can we possibly understand the world about us—and, in a sense, "think critically"—if we don't reflect on the deposits of culture, art, philosophy, technology, literature, religion, and architecture strewn on our paths by our predecessors? I am following a Ricœurian way of thinking by saying this: that we are human, and that we ought not think of ourselves as "smart" or "progressive" or "liberal" or "woke" (to use a fashionable term) by overcoming (or, to use another fashionable word, by "canceling") our humanity and the legacies left us by our human elders and predecessors. Being a humanist in the Ricœurian sense is celebrating and defending the dignity and freedom of the human self.
38 Michel Onfray, "Les abeilles de Spengler; De Gaulle, penseur tragique de la civlisation," *Front Populaire*, 4th out-of-series issue, *Quoi de neuf? De Gaulle! Une Politique de Civilisation* (2023): 4.
39 Ibid., 5.

when it shrinks from the hearth of its foundational values, it shrivels and dies.⁴⁰ As Malraux argued,

> That is the reality of our times, and this phenomenon is nowhere better explained than in the violent rise of Islam, a rise that continues to be underestimated—not to say dismissed—by our contemporaries; a rise only comparable and potentially as devastating as the Communism of Lenin's times. The consequences of this resurging Islam are still anyone's guess, shrouded in the same uncertainties that once surrounded the Marxist revolution. . . . [Yet] today, the West seems ill-prepared to confront the problem of Islam. . . . [Indeed] it may be already too late to stem the rising tides of this surging Islam. . . . We have too Western a conception of Islam and Muslims if we dare think things may turn otherwise. . . . All we might do at this point, is accept the reality and gravity of this phenomenon, and attempt to slow down its progress.⁴¹

In plain English, "civilization" is a "good book"; a book of values from which unfurls all that which characterizes the energy, the life, the history of a people—a book that may be a Torah, a Bible, a Quran, and so on, from which cultural rituals and accretions will accrue.

I will conclude with words from the same man that this chapter opened with. In December 1968, Charles de Gaulle's annual address to the French people⁴² closed with the following parting words:

> We must overcome our moral malaise. We must overcome it because, in our individualistic civilization of today, this malaise seems inherent to the modern mechanized materialist society that we have become. And should we fail to overcome this malaise, the fanatics of destruction, the deconstructionists, the doctrinaires of negationism, the specialists of demagoguery, will

---

40 André Malraux, "Note sur l'Islam," *Valeurs Actuelles*, no. 3395, June 3, 1956, https://malraux.org/islam1956-2/. "La nature d'une civilisation c'est ce qui s'agrège autour d'une religion. [Et quand] notre civilisation est incapable de construire un temple ou un tombeau, [quand elle ne sera plus] contrainte de se trouver sa valeur fondamentale, . . . elle se décomposera."

41 Ibid.

42 This is the equivalent of the American "State of the Union" speech. The December 1968 address was to be de Gaulle's last. He would step down in April of the 1969 and pass away less than two years later, in November 1970.

have a field day exploiting the bitterness we live, in order to provoke more turmoil and more unrest, despite the fact that their intellectual sterility offers no alternative to our culture except calling for its dissolution, driving it under the teeth of the totalitarian grinder of humanity and humanism.[43]

This we must do, despite it being a daunting task, fraught with challenges and dangers. This we must do, and we must not fail, because "there is only one way to fail; it is to abandon the fight before having clenched the win."[44] And, lest we forget, all of us in the academy have "inner Jews" in us. Criticism, probing, questioning, debating, refining, analyzing, discerning, trying to understand in order to heal (*tikkun olam*), every thinker, every intellectual, every academic, every student must in some way have "*some* Jewishness" in them. Being a thinker is being Jewish, being imbued in the Mosaic values of questioning and debating. It is not for nothing that Jews are considered humanity's "first literate people." Finally, we must keep in mind that the enemy staring us down is *not* a fearsome allogenic alien conqueror. Islamism and its antisemitic ancillaries and commissars are conquering, colonialist, domineering, but they are not redoubtable adversaries so long as we do not face them with cultural abdication and capitulation, with our fashionable (woke virtuous) self-loathing and unwillingness to love ourselves and celebrate our cultures and the millennial human civilizations that spawned them.

The Islamist antisemitism that is today seducing, infecting, and consuming our schools, our intellectual communities, our consensus (often consenting) media, our social spaces, and our university quads—erstwhile citadels of knowledge and critical thinking and intellectual ebullience—this new antisemitism of Islamism is not the spawn of a civilization that is an intellectually, morally, or culturally superior system than our own. By all accounts, it is none of the above. It may in fact be inferior. Alas, it flourishes in fertile grounds, in university lecture halls where discernment after thoughtful reflection is given short shrift in favor of jingles and soundbites and memes; where virtuous pedagogy is expected to teach that *all* civilizations and cultures are created equal and are equally valuable; that all value systems and belief systems are worthy of valorization and adulation; that, say, Communism and Capitalism are equally good or equally bad; that Coca-Cola and champagne are both delectable libations. This

---

43 Onfray, "Les abeilles de Spengler," 7.
44 "Il n'y a qu'une façon d'échouer; c'est d'abandonner avant d'avoir réussi." Commonly attributed to Georges Clémenceau.

sort of nihilism is in fact what causes such toxic ideas to triumph. It is our own "intellectual vacuity" and cultural abdication and capitulation and resignation that cause such toxic ideas to triumph...

And so, the problem is us: universities, intellectual elites, educators advocating for inclusiveness (including abhorrent Islamist models, the halalization of our social norms and our sartorial, intellectual, and culinary habits, while at the same time "policing" our everyday language, *vandalizing* our everyday languages, criminalizing the "misgendering" of someone, or refraining from whishing someone a Merry Christmas lest they be offended...). *This* is the real problem. The problem is a civilization willingly folding, forbidding itself from saying who and what it is; a civilization willingly apostatizing itself, abominating its history, criminalizing its traditional values for ostensibly being normatively immutably eternally and irreparably colonialist, white, heterosexual, cisgender, patriarchal, and structurally racist...

This is where the rehabilitation and normalization of antisemitism on university campuses and in the public squares comes from. This is where the shallow disingenuous mantra "Arabs, Muslims, Palestinians are Semites, and can't be antisemites" comes from.

CHAPTER 4

What Hamas Really Wants: The Ideology of the Islamic Resistance Movement

Cole Bunzel

If the horrific events of October 7, 2023, ought to have made anything clear, it is that Hamas never ceased to bear violent, annihilationist intentions toward Israel, contrary to what many over the years had claimed or suggested. On that morning, approximately 4,000 Hamas militants, together with some 2,000 other Gazans, broke through the Gaza-Israel border and rampaged across Israeli villages and *kibbutzim*, killing some 1,200 innocent people, the majority of them civilians, and kidnapping some 250 others. While Hamas would later try to distance itself from some of the worst atrocities against civilians, claiming that "the Palestinian fighters were keen to avoid harming civilians," even as it acknowledged that "[m]aybe some faults happened,"[1] evidence abounds that the intention was to commit a massacre. On the body of one dead Hamas fighter in Kibbutz Be'eri, for instance, was found a notebook with orders reading, "Kill as many people and take as many hostages as possible."[2] Indeed, the pictures and videos posted to social media by Hamas that day bespoke exceptional cruelty and bloodlust motivated by profound hatred. In addition to the photos and videos of slaughtered Israelis and foreigners, there was the infamous phone call between one Hamas militant and his parents back in Gaza, in which he boasted to them about his murderous

---

1 "Our Narrative . . . Operation Al-Aqsa Flood," Hamas Media Office, January 21, 2024, 7–8.
2 Shira Rubin and Joby Warrick, "Hamas Envisioned Deeper Attacks, Aiming to Provoke an Israeli War," *Washington Post*, November 13, 2023, https://www.washingtonpost.com/national-security/2023/11/12/hamas-planning-terror-gaza-israel/.

deeds. "Dad, I am speaking to you from a Jew's phone," he can be heard telling his father in the captured recording. "I killed her and her husband, I killed ten with my own hands. . . . I am in Meflasim, father. I killed ten. Ten! Ten with my own bare hands. Their blood is on my hands. . . . Mother, your son is a hero."[3]

The verbal messages sent by the Hamas leadership that day lent clarity to the aims and ambitions of the October 7 attack, which Hamas called Operation Al Aqsa Flood. In an audio statement announcing the operation, Hamas military leader Mohammed Deif began by listing off a host of grievances against Israel, from the injustice of the Jewish state's establishment to more Israeli policies toward the West Bank and Gaza, but he made clear that forcing change in Israeli policy was not the purpose of the assault. "Today, yes, today," he thundered, "our people resume their revolution, rectify their path and return to the plan of liberation and the establishment of the state through blood and martyrdom. . . . Today is the day of the great revolution that will end the last occupation and the last racist apartheid regime in the world." Deif then called on Palestinians in the West Bank and in Israel to rise up and join in the great revolution, and he further appealed to the so-called Resistance Axis that includes Iran, Syria, Lebanese Hezbollah, the Shiite militias in Iraq, and the Houthis in Yemen: "To the brothers in the Islamic resistance in Lebanon, Iran, Yemen, Iraq, and Syria," he said, "the day has come when your resistance joins the people of Palestine."[4]

Indeed, according to well-sourced reports, the October 7 attack was intended not as a one-off but as a catalyst for a larger regional confrontation culminating in the destruction of Israel and the full "liberation" of Palestine. Planning for the attack went back years and was confined to a small circle of Hamas leaders in Gaza around Yahya Sinwar, Hamas's leader in the strip from 2017 till his death in October 2024.[5] After a short confrontation with Israel in May 2021, Sinwar sought to give the impression that he wanted calm and quiet as he focused on Hamas's governance project in Gaza. But this was a deception.

---

3   "Listen: 'Your Son Killed 10 Jews,' Hamas Terrorist Tells Gazan Parents," *Jerusalem Post*, October 24, 2023, https://www.jpost.com/middle-east/article-769989.

4   Mohammed Deif [Muhammad al-Dayf], "Khitab 'Tufan al-Aqsa,'" Institute for Palestine Studies, October 7, 2023, https://www.palestine-studies.org/ar/node/1654998. Translation from "We Announce the Start of the al-Aqsa Flood," Oasis Foundation, December 14, 2023, https://www.oasiscenter.eu/en/we-announce-the-start-of-the-al-aqsa-flood.

5   According to one report, the five leaders who planned the attack were Yahya Sinwar, his brother Muhammad Sinwar, Mohammed Deif, Rouhi Mushtaha, and Ayman Nofal. See "'al-Tufan' . . . badaʾa bi-sabʿin min 'nukhbat al-nukhba' wa-khamsat masʾulin khattatu lahu," *Asharq Al-Awsat*, January 9, 2024, https://aawsat.news/bqn48.

In the meantime, Sinwar courted Hezbollah and Iran, urging them to join the fray once Hamas began its attack.[6] Yet the response of the Resistance Axis fell far short of his expectations. According to one report, Sinwar had misread "ambiguous pledges of support" from Iran and Hezbollah "as firm commitments to open secondary fronts."[7] Other reporting similarly indicates that the Hamas leadership in Gaza expected far more from the Resistance Axis than proved forthcoming.[8] Given the secrecy surrounding the plot, many of its details, including its timing, were withheld from these partners. Nor was most of the Hamas leadership made aware in advance. Of Hamas's overseas leadership, only Ismail Haniyeh, the head of Hamas's political office, had been briefed.[9] Most were given notice only hours before, and some only learned about it from the news.

Yet, while Hamas's leaders may not all have known about the operation in advance, and some even appear to have faulted Sinwar for launching such a brazen and grisly attack that was sure to invite massive Israeli retaliation,[10] there was no sign of disagreement or dissension in public. Even as some denied that atrocities against women and children had taken place, all praised the attack as an act of righteous and divinely sanctioned violence, the ultimate goal of which was to destroy Israel. As Haniyeh, in Qatar, stated in an address broadcast on Al Jazeera on October 7, "Our objective is clear: we want to liberate our land, our holy sites, our al-Aqsa, our prisoners. This is the goal that is worthy of this battle, worthy of this heroism, worthy of this courage." Addressing Israel, he continued, "We have only one thing to say to you: Get out of our land. Get out of our sight. Get out of our Jerusalem and our al-Aqsa. We don't want to see you on this land.

---

6 Ronen Bergman, Adam Rasgon, and Patrick Kingsley, "Secret Documents Show Hamas Tried to Persuade Iran to Join Its Oct. 7 Attack," *New York Times*, October 12, 2024, https://www.nytimes.com/2024/10/12/world/middleeast/hamas-israel-war.html.

7 Ehud Yaari and Matthew Levitt, "Growing Internal Tensions between Hamas Leaders," The Washington Institute for Near East Policy, December 21, 2023, https://www.washingtoninstitute.org/policy-analysis/growing-internal-tensions-between-hamas-leaders.

8 Georges Malbrunot, "Comment le Hamas a organisé dans le plus grand secret son attaque contre Israël," *Le Figaro*, December 26, 2023, https://www.lefigaro.fr/international/comment-le-hamas-a-organise-dans-le-plus-grand-secret-son-attaque-contre-israel-20231226; Yoni Ben Menachem, "Sinwar's Apparent Betrayal of Iran, Hezbollah and Even Hamas," Jewish News Syndicate, March 12, 2024, https://www.jns.org/sinwars-apparent-betrayal-of-iran-hezbollah-and-even-hamas/.

9 Bergman, Rasgon, and Kingsley, "Secret Documents."

10 Yaari and Levitt, "Growing Internal Tensions between Hamas Leaders."

This land is ours; Jerusalem is ours, everything is ours. You are intruders on this pure and blessed land. There is no place for you."[11]

Later that month, Khaled Meshaal, Haniyeh's predecessor as Hamas's political leader, similarly remarked that "October 7 paved a large highway toward the elimination of Israel."[12] Perhaps most notorious were the comments of Ghazi Hamad, a Hamas politburo member based in Lebanon, who affirmed in a late October interview that Hamas's intention was to repeat the violence of October 7 attack until Israel was finally annihilated. "Israel is a country that has no place on our land," he stated.

> We must remove that country, because it constitutes a security, military, and political catastrophe to the Arab and Islamic nation, and must be finished. . . . We must teach Israel a lesson, and we will do this again and again. The Al-Aqsa Flood is just the first time, and there will be a second, a third, a fourth, because we have the determination, the resolve, and the capabilities to fight.[13]

Another senior Hamas official, the Lebanon-based Ali Baraka, boasted in an interview on October 8 about how Hamas had deceived Israel: "We made them think that Hamas was busy with governing Gaza, and that it wanted to focus on the 2.5 million Palestinians [in Gaza], and has abandoned the resistance altogether. All the while, under the table, Hamas was preparing for this big attack."[14]

Israel had indeed been deceived. The thinking among most Israeli politicians and intelligence officials was that while Hamas might initiate rocket attacks of limited scope every year or so, it did not seek a larger confrontation that could

---

11 "Haniyya: afqadna Isra'il tawazunaha wa-hadafuna tahrir ardina wa-asrana," Al Jazeera, October 7, 2023, https://www.middleeastmonitor.com/20231009-haniyeh-outlines-context-and-objectives-of-hamas-operation-al-aqsa-flood/. Translation, with some modifications, from "Haniyah Outlines Context and Objectives of Hamas Operation Al-Aqsa Flood," *Middle East Monitor*, October 9, 2023, https://www.middleeastmonitor.com/20231009-haniyeh-outlines-context-and-objectives-of-hamas-operation-al-aqsa-flood/.

12 "Hamas Leader Abroad Khaled Mashal on Turkish TV: October 7 Paved the Highway towards Removing Israel," MEMRI TV, October 31, 2023, https://www.memri.org/tv/hamas-leader-abroad-khaled-mashal-october-seventh-elimination-israel-opportunity-for-china-russia. Translation slightly modified.

13 "Hamas Official Ghazi Hamad: We Will Repeat the October 7 Attack, Time and Again, Until Israel Is Annihilated," MEMRI, November 1, 2023, https://www.memri.org/reports/hamas-official-ghazi-hamad-we-will-repeat-october-7-attack-time-and-again-until-israel.

14 "Senior Hamas Official Ali Baraka: We Have Been Secretly Planning the Invasion for Two Years," MEMRI, October 11, 2023, https://www.memri.org/reports/senior-hamas-official-ali-baraka-we-have-been-secretly-planning-invasion-two-years-russia.

invite large-scale Israeli retaliation. As Israel's national security adviser Tzachi Hanegbi stated in a radio interview just days before October 7, "Since the round of fighting in May two years ago, there is a decision by Hamas leadership to display unprecedented restraint and forbearance. For over two years there hasn't been a single rocket fired under Hamas initiative from Gaza. Hamas is very, very restrained and understands the consequences of further defiance."[15] The guiding belief was that Hamas was driven as much by self-preservation as by militant ideology. Beginning in 2018, Gaza began receiving millions of dollars in monthly financial assistance from Qatar, money intended to alleviate the humanitarian situation in Gaza but that also helped to prop up Hamas's government.[16] For Hamas to start a major war would be to put all that at risk.

Another group to have been deceived was the academic and analytical community. Many elements of this group believed not only that Hamas was deterred but indeed that it was evolving into a more moderate and pragmatic actor, one that Israel and the international community could profitably engage. Such thinking went back years, beginning with Hamas's decision to compete in the Palestinian legislative elections in 2006 and its seizure of full control of Gaza the following year. For some analysts, the responsibilities of governance would inevitably have a moderating effect on Hamas. The epitome of this line of thinking came in a *Foreign Affairs* article in 2009 titled "Hamas 2.0," which argued that "Hamas' decision to join the Palestinian government in 2006, and its subsequent takeover of Gaza, have led to a significant ideological softening. . . . In a surprisingly short time, Hamas has largely abandoned religious rhetoric and calls for the violent liberation of Palestine, in favor of the increasingly secular and pragmatic task of state building." This was a "fundamental shift within Hamas" that gave the lie to "the movement's supposedly inflexible ideology."[17] In the same vein, the Harvard scholar Sara Roy, in a 2011 book about Hamas's social services sector, observed that "Hamas has a history of nonviolent accommodation and political adaptation, ideological reflexivity and transformation,

---

15 Yaniv Kubovich and Jonathin Lis, "Why Israel's Defenses Crumbled in Face of Hamas's Assault," *Haaretz*, October 8, 2023, https://www.haaretz.com/israel-news/2023-10-08/ty-article/.premium/six-significant-failures-that-lead-to-one-point-collapse-vs-hamas/0000018b-0f15-dfff-a7eb-afdd0bb80000.

16 Mark Mazzetti and Ronen Bergman, "'Buying Quiet': Inside the Israeli Plan that Propped Up Hamas," *New York Times*, December 10, 2023, https://www.nytimes.com/2023/12/10/world/middleeast/israel-qatar-money-prop-up-hamas.html.

17 Michael Bröning, "Hamas 2.0," *Foreign Affairs*, August 5, 2009, https://www.foreignaffairs.com/articles/middle-east/2009-08-05/hamas-20.

and political pragmatism that the West should welcome."[18] She similarly made light of Hamas's religiosity, stating that "Hamas's fundamental impulse is political and nationalist, not religious, which has accounted for its pragmatism and flexibility."[19]

Such views do not hold up well in light of October 7.[20] In the last analysis, given the choice between governance and resistance, Hamas chose resistance, and in a manner so brutal and heinous as to make the choice not just clear but irrevocable. Hamas, as it turned out, had been neither deterred nor transformed.

The timing of October 7 was of course determined by more than one factor. It was timed to coincide with the Jewish holiday of Simchat Torah, to take advantage of the tumultuous situation in Israel over a controversial judicial reform, and to disrupt efforts at achieving normalization of between Israel and Saudi Arabia.[21] Yet the fundamental motivation behind the attack was no doubt ideological. What Hamas showed was that it remained committed to a religiopolitical ideology that holds Israel's existence to be an affront to God. The purpose of this chapter will be to reexamine Hamas's ideology in light of the events of October 7 that caught so many off guard. Drawing on its own statements and documents stretching back decades, the chapter highlights the persistence of this central theme in Hamas's ideology, namely its deep-rooted and unbending rejection of Israel's right to exist on land that rightfully belongs to the Muslim Palestinians alone. Even as some Hamas leaders appeared willing to engage in tactical accommodation with Israel, rejectionism remained a fundamental feature of the Hamas ideology shared by all.

The Hamas Charter

Known by the acronym Hamas, the Islamic Resistance Movement (Harakat al-muqawama al-Islamiyya) was founded in late 1987 as an outgrowth of the Palestinian branch of the Muslim Brotherhood. Founded in Egypt in 1928, the Muslim Brotherhood is a Sunni Islamist movement that was formed with a view to combatting secularizing and Westernizing influences in Egypt and the

---

18 Sara Roy, *Hamas and Civil Society in Gaza: Engaging the Islamist Social Sector* (Princeton, NJ: Princeton University Press, 2011), 48–49.
19 Ibid., 165.
20 For more on the pre-October 7 misreading of Hamas by a broad range of experts, see Armin Rosen, "How Hamas Fooled the Experts," *Tablet*, October 12, 2023, https://www.tabletmag.com/sections/israel-middle-east/articles/how-hamas-fooled-the-experts.
21 Bergman, Rasgon, and Kingsley, "Secret Documents."

broader Muslim world. The mainstay of the Brotherhood's philosophy, as the group developed into a broad-based social and political movement in Egypt in the 1930s and 1940s, was that Islam constitutes an "all-encompassing system" (*nizam shamil*) comprehending everything from social and moral issues to law and governance.[22] While issues of national liberation and anti-imperialism featured in the Brotherhood's discourse, particularly as concerned the British presence in Egypt, the focal point of the movement was the Islamization of society and politics.

In the 1930s, the Brotherhood began sending envoys to nearby countries to spread its vision. The first Palestinian branch of the Muslim Brotherhood was founded in 1945 in Jerusalem, and by November 1947 the Brothers had set up some two dozen branches across British-Mandate Palestine.[23] Yet, despite its rapid rise, the Palestinian Muslim Brotherhood was a marginal political actor in the Palestinian arena for decades, the militant scene being dominated by secularist and leftist groups. The focus of its attention was in the educational and social arenas.[24] While not disavowing violence in principle, the Palestinian Brothers argued that in the present circumstances it was necessary to prioritize the Islamization of society—that is, the inculcation of proper Islamic beliefs, values, and practices—before the struggle for liberation against Israel could be effectively engaged. In adopting this path, the Brothers ceded the ground for armed struggle to the non-Islamist groups that coalesced, in the mid-1960s, around the Palestine Liberation Organization (PLO), led by the Fatah party of Yasser Arafat. Yet, by the late 1970s, the Brotherhood found itself gaining in influence as an Islamist tide swept the region, and by the mid-1980s, the group's approach to militancy began to shift.

Upon the outbreak of the First Intifada in December 1987, the Political Bureau of the Muslim Brotherhood in Gaza, headed by Sheikh Ahmed Yassin, released the first communiqué in the name of the Islamic Resistance Movement. Addressed to "Our steadfast Muslim masses," the communiqué praised the Intifada not only as "a resounding rejection of the occupation [i.e., Israel]" but also as an event that would "awaken the consciences of those among us who are gasping after a sick peace, after empty international conferences, after treasonous

---

22 Hasan al-Banna, *Majmu 'at rasa 'il al-imam Hasan al-Banna* (Alexandria, Egypt: Dar al-Da'wa, 1998), 372.
23 Abd al-Fattah Muhammad El-Awaisi, *The Muslim Brothers and the Palestine Question, 1928–1947* (London: I. B. Tauris, 1998), 152, 155.
24 On the history of the Palestinian Muslim Brotherhood up to the formation of Hamas, see Khaled Hroub, *Hamas: Political Thought and Practice* (Washington, D.C.: Institute for Palestine Studies, 2000), 11–41.

partial settlements like Camp David."²⁵ The Intifada, it was hoped, would reignite the spirit of Palestinian rejectionism with respect to Israel. "In the preceding decade," the communiqué noted, "the Palestinian position had softened considerably. There were signs from the Palestinian camp signaling the possibility of accepting compromises that were contrary to the provisions of the Palestinian National Charter [i.e., the charter of the PLO]."²⁶ Hamas was thus born out of a rejection of any compromise with Israel. As the communiqué explained, "Hamas is a popular jihadi movement (*haraka jihadiyya sha'biyya*) that seeks to liberate Palestine in its entirety from the Mediterranean Sea to the River Jordan," aiming for "the establishment in it of an independent Islamic state."²⁷

The most important early document produced by Hamas was of course its charter (*mithaq*), which was issued on August 18, 1988.²⁸ Despite some later attempts to downplay its significance, the charter, as its principal author ʿAbd al-Fattah Dukhan would later recount, was the product of hours of deliberations among the founding leaders of Hamas. "We had the honor," recalled Dukhan in a 2011 interview,

> to discuss the Hamas charter in the home of al-Hajj Muhammad al-Najjar, may God have mercy on him, in Khan Yunis. Agreement was reached on all its articles and clauses in that meeting, which lasted long hours and which was composed of a group of the founders including Sheikh Yassin and others. We then sent the charter to our brothers in the West Bank for their observations and modifications, and the result was that the brothers in the [West] Bank agreed with all its clauses.²⁹

---

25 See translation, ibid., 265–266.
26 Ibid., 293.
27 Ibid., 295. Translation slightly modified.
28 The version of the Arabic text I have consulted is found in ʿAbdallah ʿAzzam, *Hamas: al-judhur al-tarikhiyya wa-l-mithaq* (Jordan: Maktab Khidamat al-Mujahidin, 1990), 119–153. Unless otherwise stated, translations of this text are my own. For English translations of the entire charter, see Hroub, *Hamas*, 267–291; and "Hamas Covenant 1988," Avalon Project, https://avalon.law.yale.edu/20th_century/hamas.asp. For an excellent earlier analysis of the charter's main points, see Meir Litvak, "The Islamization of the Palestinian-Israeli Conflict: The Case of Hamas," *Middle Eastern Studies* 34 (1998): 148–163.
29 "Al-Qiyadi Dukhan yakshifu baʿd tafasil taʾsis Hamas," al-Markaz al-Filastini li-l-Iʿlam, November 14, 2011, https://palinfo.com/news/2011/11/14/34561/. For Dukhan's role as the charter's principal author, see Azzam Tamimi, *Hamas: Unwritten Chapters* (London: Hurst & Company, 2007), 164.

The charter, then, was a reflection of the consensus views of the Hamas leadership as the movement took form in the late 1980s, and it had the full endorsement of Sheikh Yassin, who had emerged as the group's spiritual leader. Consisting of five chapters and thirty-six articles, the charter's purpose, as is stated in the introduction, was "to clarify [Hamas's] form, reveal its identity, explain its position, clarify its aspiration, discuss its hopes, and call for aiding it, supporting it, and joining its ranks."[30]

The charter made clear that Hamas was an Islamist movement affiliated with the Muslim Brotherhood. Early on it states that Hamas is "a wing among the wings of the Muslim Brotherhood in Palestine," going on to praise the Brotherhood as a "global organization" distinguished by its all-encompassing approach to Islam.[31] Echoing this theme, the charter repeatedly states that Hamas takes Islam as a "a way of life" (*manhaj hayat*), meaning that for the group religion applies to all aspects of life, from family and social matters to politics and war.[32] Yet, above all, Hamas is defined as a group committed to waging jihad for "the purpose of liberating Palestine."[33] Hamas "strives to raise the banner of God over every inch of Palestine ... no matter how long it takes," and therein "to establish the Islamic state."[34] This was not to say that the followers of the other Abrahamic faiths cannot live there, but that only "in the shadow of Islam" can they live together there in peace and security.[35] Islam must remain the dominant political force in the country, as God has ordained. Exactly how the envisioned state would be structured and run is not discussed, and the charter suggests that Hamas has no interest in assuming political power. Hamas, it states, disavows any interest in "personal fame or material position or social status."[36] Its principal purpose is to wage jihad, the centrality of which is stressed in the group's slogan: "God is its objective, the Messenger is its model, the Quran is its constitution, and jihad in God's path and death in God's path are its highest aspirations."[37] Indeed, jihad is presented as the only legitimate means of reestablishing Muslim sovereignty in Palestine. As the charter states, "there is no solution to the Palestinian issue

---

30 Azzam, *Hamas*, 118.
31 Ibid., 119 (art. 2).
32 Ibid., 120 (art. 5), 121 (art. 6), 144 (art. 27), 153 (conclusion).
33 Ibid., 118 (introduction).
34 Ibid., 121 (art. 6), 123 (art. 7), 125 (art. 9).
35 Ibid., 121 (art. 6).
36 Ibid., 153 (art. 36).
37 Ibid., 123 (art. 8).

except through jihad ... initiatives and proposals and international conferences are a waste of time."[38]

In emphasizing the path of jihad as the only proper course, the charter seeks to inscribe Hamas within the long history of Muslim warriors who fought to reclaim Palestine from invading forces, beginning with the struggle of Saladin against the Crusaders.[39] In the decades-long struggle against Zionism, Hamas is described as "a link in the chain of jihad confronting the Zionist assault" going back to the efforts of 'Izz al-Din al-Qassam in the 1930s.[40] The jihad against the Zionists in Palestine is portrayed as defensive jihad and thus an individual duty (*fard 'ayn*) binding on all able-bodied Muslims. In traditional Islamic law, jihad can take the form of offensive or missionary jihad (*jihad al-talab*) or it can be defensive. In the former case, the duty to fight falls on the community at large, meaning that so long as a sufficient number fulfills it, the rest are dispensed from it. In the case of defense jihad, the duty is binding on the individual. In the case of a defensive jihad, typically involving a situation in which a Muslim territory has been invaded by a non-Muslim enemy, the duty falls on all individuals to partake in the fight to recover it.[41] In the charter, Hamas is keen to emphasize the defensive nature of the struggle: "When the enemy invades Muslim territory, then jihad against him and resisting him become an individual duty binding on every male and female Muslim."[42] Shortly thereafter the point is reiterated: "When the enemies seize a part of Muslim territory, its liberation is an individual duty binding on every Muslim, and so the banner of jihad must be raised to oppose the seizure of Palestine by the Jews."[43]

It may also be noted in this connection that in the classical Muslim division of the world into two spheres, the abode of Islam (*dar al-Islam*) and the abode of unbelief (*dar al-kufr*) or the abode of war (*dar al-harb*), a country that has become part of the abode of Islam ought never to revert to the abode of unbelief.[44] Yet,

---

38   Ibid., 129 (art. 13).
39   Ibid., 151–152 (art. 34).
40   Ibid., 122 (art. 7).
41   See Michael Cook, *Ancient Religions, Modern Politics: The Islamic Case in Comparative Perspective* (Princeton, NJ: Princeton University Press, 2014), 222.
42   'Azzam, *Hamas*, 128 (art. 12).
43   Ibid., 131 (art. 15).
44   Majid Khadduri, *War and Peace in the Law of Islam* (Baltimore, MD: Johns Hopkins University Press, 1955), 52–53. Some Muslim jurists did establish criteria by which a Muslim land could revert to being part of the *dar al-kufr* in the event that it was reconquered by non-Muslims. See Khaled Abou El Fadl, "Islamic Law and Muslim Minorities: The Juristic Discourse on Muslim Minorities from the Second/Eighth to the Eleventh/Seventeenth Centuries," *Islamic Law and Society* 1 (1994): 141–187, at 161–162.

for Hamas, Palestine was not just any territory belonging to the abode of Islam. It had been specially designated by God as "an Islamic *waqf* land," meaning that it belonged exclusively to the Muslims in perpetuity. The term *waqf* means "an endowment." As the charter states, "The Islamic Resistance Movement believes that the land of Palestine is an Islamic *waqf* land [endowed] for the benefit of Muslims throughout the generations and until the Day of Resurrection. It is forbidden to abandon it or part of it or to renounce it or part of it."[45] Here it must be stated that the description of Palestine as an Islamic *waqf* land—indeed of any territory as such—was a Hamas innovation.[46] In the charter, the basis for this assertion is a tradition according to which ʿUmar ibn al-Khattab, the second caliph in Sunni Islam, decided, in correspondence with his commanders, that the recently conquered lands of Iraq and Greater Syria (al-Sham) would not be divvied up and distributed as booty between the soldiers and the caliph as per existing custom. Instead, he declared, according to the charter, "the land should remain in the hands of its holders to benefit from it and from its wealth; but the abstract ownership (*raqaba*) of the land ought to be endowed as a *waqf* for all generations of Muslims until the Day of Resurrection, while the [original] owners would have usufruct rights (*manfaʿa*) only."[47]

The reason for using the phrase "Islamic *waqf* land" was likely that the term *waqf* connoted the idea of property, in this case land, endowed in perpetuity, and that the term appears in the verbal form *aqifuhu* ("I shall endow it") in one of the traditions ascribed to the Caliph ʿUmar. In Islamic law, a *waqf* is a charitable trust or endowment created by an individual who designates a piece of privately-owned property for a charitable purpose. The beneficiaries enjoy the right to use and benefit from it in the sense of being entitled to usufruct (*manfaʿa*), but they are not entitled to its abstract ownership (*raqaba*).[48] The tradition ascribed to ʿUmar, however, pertained to how the territories conquered by the early Muslim state were to be treated and classified. What ʿUmar established was that lands conquered by the Muslims were to be *fayʾ*, meaning property seized by the Muslim community that could remain in the hands of its owners "provided that they pay a special tax signifying that the abstract ownership belongs

---

45 ʿAzzam, *Hamas*, 127 (art. 11). Translation from Yitzhak Reiter, "'All of Palestine if Holy Muslim *Waqf* Land': A Myth and Its Roots," in *Law, Custom, and Statute in the Muslim World: Studies in Honor of Aharon Layis*, ed. Ron Shaham (Leiden: Brill, 2007), 173–197, at 175.
46 Reiter, "'All of Palestine if Holy Muslim *Waqf* Land,'" 181.
47 ʿAzzam, *Hamas*, 128 (art. 11). Translation from Reiter, "'All of Palestine if Holy Muslim *Waqf* Land,'" 175–176.
48 Reiter, "'All of Palestine if Holy Muslim *Waqf* Land,'" 181–187.

to the State Treasury for the benefit of the Muslim community."[49] The money collected from this tax would be spent in the interest of the Muslims. In one version of the tradition, ʿUmar states with respect to the conquered territories, "I shall endow it as *fayʾ* (*ahbisuhu fayʾan*) to be enjoyed by them [the soldiers] and by the Muslims"; in another he states, "I shall endow it (*aqifuhu*) for the Muslims."[50] The institutions of *fayʾ* and *waqf* have in common the separation of usufruct from abstract ownership, but otherwise they are not related.[51] The practical meaning of ʿUmar's reform was of a fiscal nature: the lands conquered by the Muslims would become subject to taxation as opposed to being divvied up among the soldiers and the caliph. Hamas gave the tradition a new meaning, claiming that ʿUmar decided that all lands conquered by the Muslims in the seventh century, including especially Palestine, were unalienable Muslim property till the end of time.[52]

Apart from its classification as "Islamic *waqf* land," the charter also stresses the special significance of Palestine to Islam, describing the al-Aqsa mosque in Jerusalem as "the third holy place after the two holy places [i.e., Mecca and Medina]" and the site of the Prophet's night journey (*masra*) mentioned in the Quran. Both the *waqf* designation and this sanctified status gave further urgency to the defensive jihad for the liberation of Palestine.[53]

Beyond militancy, the charter lays great emphasis on education, arguing that that education in Palestine and across the Arab world needs to be reformed so as to combat "the ideological assault" (*al-fikr al-ghazwi*) that the Muslims have been subjected to from missionaries, Orientalists, and the imperialist West. The proposed educational reforms ought to emphasize that "the issue of Palestine … is a religious issue," a fact that had been lost on the current generation.[54] One group that had succumbed to this "ideological assault" was the PLO, which the charter claimed had adopted "the idea of the secular state." While praising the PLO for its efforts to liberate Palestine, the charter maintained that the PLO's secularism was a fatal flaw and an unbridgeable barrier separating it from Hamas. "Secular thought is entirely opposed to religious thought," it stated. "We cannot replace

---

49 Ibid., 182.
50 Muwaffaq al-Din Ibn Qudama, *al-Mughni sharh mukhtasar al-Khiraqi*, 15 vols., ed. ʿAbdallah al-Turki and ʿAbd al-Fattah Muhammad al-Ḥilw (Riyadh: Dar Hajr, 1986), 3:187; ʿAli Ibn ʿAsakir, *Tarikh madinat Dimashq*, 80 vols., ed. ʿUmar al-ʿAmri (Beirut: Dar al-Fikr, 1995), 2:195–96; cf. Reiter, "'All of Palestine is Holy Muslim *Waqf* Land,'" 184–185.
51 Reiter, "'All of Palestine if Holy Muslim *Waqf* Land,'" 181–189.
52 ʿAzzam, *Hamas*, 128 (art. 11).
53 Ibid., 130 (art. 14).
54 Ibid., 131–132 (art. 15).

the current and future Islamic nature of Palestine and adopt secular thought." However, if the PLO were to reform itself and adopt Islam "as a way of life," Hamas would eagerly join forces with it: "we would be your soldiers and the fuel of your fire that burns the enemies."[55]

Another noteworthy feature of the charter is its embrace of antisemitic tropes that paint the Jews as a conniving and conspiratorial people bent on global domination, tropes of course inspired by European antisemitism. The charter accuses the Jews of being behind the French Revolution, the Communist Revolution, the First World War, the Second World War, and more besides. Furthermore, the Jews created the League of Nations and then United Nations "in order to rule the world," and "they have taken control of the global media." They have further established "secret organizations" such as the Freemasons, the Rotary Clubs, and the Lions Clubs in order to advance their Zionist agenda.[56] This Zionist agenda, according to the charter, has "no limits." After seizing Palestine, the Jews intend "to expand from the Nile to the Euphrates," and from there to expand further. "Their plotting is found," it claims, "in the Protocols of the Elders of Zion," referring to the fabricated antisemitic tract from early twentieth-century Russia.[57] The Hamas leaders' belief in these antisemitic conspiracy theories from Europe added an extra dimension to the Hamas ideology beyond Islamic doctrines.

It was not long before the ideology on display in Hamas's charter was enacted in physical violence. Following the outbreak of the First Intifada, Hamas's first major violent act was the kidnapping and murder of two Israeli soldiers in April 1989, an event that prompted a massive Israeli crackdown on the group including mass arrests and deportations. Sheikh Yassin was arrested and sentenced to life in prison (though he would be released in 1997 as part of an arrangement following the botched assassination of another Hamas leader, Khaled Meshaal, in Jordan).[58] Two years later, in 1991, came the consolidation of Hamas's military wing under the name of the ʿIzz al-Din al-Qassam Brigades, in honor of the antizionist Syrian militant active in the 1930s.[59] The first successful suicide bombing, a car bombing, came in April 1994, killing eight and wounding forty in the northern Israeli town of Afula. Many more such attacks followed in the

---

55 Ibid., 143–144 (art. 17).
56 Ibid., 138–139 (art. 22).
57 Ibid., 149 (art. 32).
58 Beverly Milton-Edwards, *Islamic Politics in Palestine* (London: I. B. Tauris, 1996), 152–153; Tareq Baconi, *Hamas Contained: The Rise and Pacification of Palestinian Resistance* (Stanford, CA: Stanford University Press, 2018), 25–26.
59 Baconi, *Hamas Contained*, 27.

coming years, and with the outbreak of the Second Intifada in September 2000 the pace of attacks picked up dramatically. The period between September 2000 and March 2004 saw fifty-two suicide bombings carried out by Hamas, resulting in 288 dead and over 1,000 injured.[60]

The *Hudna* and the "Phased Solution," Part I

In September 1993, the Oslo Accords were signed between Israel and the PLO, leading to the creation of the Palestinian Authority the next year as an interim self-governing entity in the West Bank and Gaza in anticipation of a permanent peace settlement. In the process, PLO Chairman Arafat recognized Israel's right to exist and revised the PLO charter accordingly. As was to be expected, Hamas vehemently denounced the accords as a betrayal of Islam, an act of "submission to the Zionist enemy." Calling the accords "the agreement of shame and humiliation," Hamas pledged to continue "our jihad against the enemy . . . until victory and liberation," even as Hamas called for unity and vowed to avoid a Palestinian civil war.[61]

It was in this context that Hamas proposed an alternative approach to possible negotiations with Israel, one based on the Islamic legal concept of an armistice (*hudna*). In traditional Islamic law, while a state of permanent war exists between the abode of Islam and the abode of unbelief, a temporary cessation of hostilities is possible under the rubric of a *hudna* should this be deemed beneficial to the Muslims. The foundational precedent for such a ceasefire was the Prophet Muhammad's treaty with the people of Mecca known as the Treaty of al-Hudaybiyya (*sulh al-Hudaybiyya*). Agreed to in the year 628, the treaty followed several years of fighting between the Muslims of Medina and the pagan Quraysh of Mecca, the most recent being a long siege of Medina the year before. The treaty stipulated that "warfare shall be laid aside by the people for ten years, during which the people shall be safe and refrain from [attacking] each other."[62]

---

60 Matthew Levitt, *Hamas: Politics, Charity, and Terrorism in the Service of Jihad* (New Haven, CT: Yale University Press, 2006), 12.
61 "Fa-l-taʿlu rayat al-jihad . . . wa-l-tasqut rayat al-dhill wa-l-ʿar," *Filastin al-Muslima* 11 (November 1993): 5. See further, on Hamas's response to Oslo, Meir Hatina, "Hamas and the Oslo Accords: Religious Dogma in a Changing Political Reality," *Mediterranean Politics* 4 (1999): 37–55; Wendy Kristianasen, "Challenge and Counterchallenge: Hamas's Response to Oslo," *Journal of Palestine Studies* 28 (1999): 19–36.
62 Ayman S. Ibrahim, *Muḥammad's Military Expeditions: A Critical Reading in Original Muslim Sources* (Oxford: Oxford University Press, 2024), 166.

In practice, the treaty lasted less than two years. The Prophet deemed it null and void after an ally of the Quraysh attacked an ally of the Muslims. The abrogation of the treaty was soon followed by the Muslim conquest of Mecca in 630. On the basis of al-Hudaybiyya, most classical Muslim jurists determined that a *hudna* between the Muslims and their enemies could not exceed a period of ten years. Others deemed a longer or shorter *hudna* permissible if the Muslim ruler judged this to be in the interest of the Muslims. Regardless of its length, virtually all jurists agreed that a *hudna* must be temporary, as a permanent *hudna* would imply the invalidation of the duty of jihad.[63]

In the aftermath of the Oslo Accords, Hamas began floating the idea of a timebound *hudna* as an Islamic alternative to the kind of negotiated settlement agreed to by the PLO.[64] The first proposal of this kind came in an interview with Sheikh Yasin from prison in October 1993, subsequently published in the Arab press. Asked what he would do if asked to make an agreement with Israel, Yasin responded: "It might be possible to sign a *hudna* agreement for ten or twenty years, provided that Israel unconditionally withdraw from the [West] Bank, the [Gaza] Strip, and East Jerusalem to the 1967 borders and grant the Palestinian people complete freedom in determining their fate and future."[65] After this interview, the proposal of a *hudna* with Israel became a regular theme in Hamas's discourse.

In discussing the issue, Hamas's leaders emphasized that a *hudna* would not imply recognition of Israel, and that recognition would never be considered. The very point of a *hudna* was to preserve the Palestinian claim to the land on which Israel had been established, so that the jihad to recover the land could be resumed at a future date. The *hudna* concept constituted part of what Hamas sometimes described as "the phased solution" (*al-hall al-marhali*) to the liberation of Palestine, meaning that it represented one phase in the long struggle to destroy the Jewish state. As ʿAbd al-ʿAziz al-Rantisi, another of Hamas's founders, stated in an interview shortly after Yasin's, "With regard to the *hudna* as a phased solution, we do not oppose this, for it preserves the right of the Palestinians to demand the return of their land, and the *hudna* in this circumstance means not

---

63 Majid Khadduri, "Hudna," in *Encyclopaedia of Islam*, new ed., 13 vols., ed. H. A. R. Gibb et al. (Leiden: Brill, 1960–2004), 3:546–547; Rudolph Peters, *Jihad: A History in Documents*, 3rd ed. (Princeton, NJ: Marcus Wiener Publishers, 2016), 38–40; ʿAbdallah Qadiri al-Ahdal, "Hukm ʿaqd al-hudna maʿ al-ʿaduww li-l-hajja," Sayd al-fawāʾid, http://saaid.org/Doat/ahdal/74.htm.

64 On this subject, see Hroub, *Hamas*, 81–84; Khalid Safi, "Mawqif al-Shaykh Ahmad Yasin min al-hudna maʿ al-kiyan al-ṣahyuni," in *Aʿmal muʾtamar al-imam al-shahid Ahmad Yasin* (Gaza: Islamic University in Gaza, 2005), 1177–1214.

65 Jamal Khashuqji, "al-Shaykh Ahmad Yasin zaʾim 'Hamas' li-atbaʿihi: tawqiʿ hudna maʿ Israʾil mumkin," *al-Hayat*, November 1, 1993, https://www.sauress.com/alhayat/31871405.

recognizing Israel. Shaykh Ahmad Yasin drew its limit at a period of ten years, which accords with the Treaty of al-Hudaybiyya and does not contradict the Sharia."[66] As is clear from this comment, even though Yasin had actually mentioned a period of ten or twenty years, the precedent of the Treaty of al-Hudaybiyya formed the basis of the Hamas *hudna* and "phased solution."

Regardless of its length, Hamas was consistent in stressing the timebound nature of a *hudna*, as Palestine was a *waqf* land that could not under any circumstances be conceded to non-Muslims. In the same interview quoted above, Yassin described Palestine as a *waqf* land at several points, explaining how this fact influenced his conception of a phased solution. Asked whether the Oslo Accords could figure into a phased solution, Yasin responded by saying, "I believe in the phased solution, but there is nothing in this agreement [i.e., the Oslo Accords] that achieves the ultimate objectives of the Palestine people. Furthermore, I should like to tell you that Palestine is an Islamic *waqf* land that no leader or generation has the right to concede, for it belongs to the Muslim generations."[67] The phased solution was thus a kind of graduated jihad unfolding in stages; a lull in the fighting, in the form of a *hudna*, could be countenanced, but the ultimate goal of reconquering all of Palestine would forever remain.

Two years later, in an interview with the Hamas-affiliated *Filastin al-Muslima* magazine, Yasin offered a more detailed synopsis of his thinking on the *hudna* question. Here he contrasted the notion of making peace with Israel with agreeing to a *hudna*. "If peace is meant in the sense of a *hudna* and cessation of hostilities for a limited period," he stated, "then that peace is something that Islam permits for the imam of the Muslims to enter into. This happens when he perceives strength in the enemy and weakness in the Muslims, and deems additional time is necessary to prepare and build [for war]." Here again, Yasin made clear that a *hudna* must needs be of limited duration and calculated to benefit the Muslims, and that its purpose was to pave the way for the resumption of hostilities on more favorable terms. Once again, he emphasized the point that Palestine was a *waqf* territory that could not be relinquished by any Muslim leader or generation. Yasin noted, regarding the length of any proposed *hudna*, that "many jurists judged that it must not exceed ten years in accordance with the action of the Prophet in the Treaty of al-Hudaybiyya," though he did not indicate whether he accepted this view.[68] In another interview, from 1995, Yasin

---

66 Quoted in Safi, "Mawqif al-Shaykh Ahmad Yasin," 1189.
67 Khashuqji, "al-Shaykh Ahmad Yasin."
68 "Al-Shaykh al-mujahid Ahmad Yasin yatahaddathu li-'Filastin al-Muslima,'" *Filastin al-Muslima* 13 (March 1995): 24–26, at 24.

suggested fifteen years as a valid duration, insisting that the important point was that the *hudna* not last forever.[69] Beginning in 1997, Yasin even brought up the possibility of renewing the *hudna* should circumstances favor that, in which case it might last longer than the original term.[70] But he contrasted this approach with the idea of "comprehensive and enduring peace," which Hamas would never countenance.[71] Given that Hamas's leadership had conceived of a *hudna* as nothing more than a military tactic for regrouping and rearming, Israel did not engage with Hamas's offers any time during this period.

The introduction of the *hudna* concept into Hamas's discourse marked the beginning of what might be referred to as Hamas's tendency to doublespeak—that is, its utilization of different registers at different times and for different audiences, sometimes appearing more radical and sometimes more practical or moderate. Another feature of the Hamas doublespeak during this period was a newfound effort to distinguish between Jews and Zionists on certain occasions, particularly in public pronouncements.[72] In a 1998 interview, Yasin famously stated, "we do not oppose the Jews because they are Jews; we oppose the Zionist state that arose on our land and on what is rightly ours."[73] He even claimed in the same interview that "we desire peace," referring to the *hudna* proposal.[74] Yet despite such utterances, anti-Semitic themes and annihilationist rhetoric remained a pronounced feature of Hamas's discourse.[75]

---

69 Hroub, *Hamas*, 83.
70 Ibid., 84.
71 Quote in Safi, "Mawqif al-Shaykh Ahmad Yasin," 1195.
72 Hroub, *Hamas*, 50–51; Floor Jansen, *Hamas and Its Positions Towards Israel: Understanding the Islamic Resistance Organization through the Concept of Framing*, Netherlands Institute of International Relations, January 2009, 44, https://www.clingendael.org/publication/hamas-and-its-positions-towards-israel; Imad Alsoos, "From Jihad to Resistance: The Evolution of Hamas's Discourse in the Framework of Mobilization," *Middle Eastern Studies* 57 (2021): 833–856, at 838. Hroub vastly overstates the case in claiming that "[s]uch language vanished from the movement's literature and political discourse." In reality, Hamas never dissociated itself from its charter and continued to cultivate a culture of hatred for Jews qua Jews. See, for instance, "Hamas' Indoctrination of Children to Jihad, Martyrdom, Hatred of Jews," MEMRI, November 3, 2023, https://www.memri.org/reports/hamas-indoctrination-children-jihad-martyrdom-hatred-jews.
73 Quoted in Ahmad Mansur, *al-Shaykh Ahmad Yasin shahid ʿala ʿasr al-intifada* (Cairo: al-Dar al-ʿArabiyya li-l-ʿUlum, 2004), 305.
74 Ibid.
75 See, e.g., "A Senior Hamas Figure Delivers a Speech Replete with Anti-Semitic Motifs—Yet Another Expression of Hamas's Long-standing Tradition of Anti-Semitism," Meir Amit Intelligence and Terrorism Information Center, December 27, 2018, https://www.terrorism-info.org.il/en/senior-hamas-figure-delivers-speech-replete-anti-semitic-motifs-yet-another-expression-hamass-long-standing-tradition-anti-semitism/.

The *Hudna* and the "Phased Solution," Part II

In the mid-2000s, following the assassinations of Yassin and al-Rantisi in 2004 and Israel's disengagement from Gaza in 2005, Hamas would shift even further in the direction of ostensible moderation as it entered the political arena for the first time. In previous years, Hamas had rejected the idea of participating in national elections sponsored by the Palestinian Authority on the grounds that to do so would be to confer legitimacy on the Oslo Accords that had created it. But in early 2005, Hamas changed tack, declaring its intention to run in the Palestinian legislative elections expected to be held later that year, though postponed to January 2006. To justify its decision, Hamas claimed that the Oslo Accords had effectively failed with the outbreak of the Second Intifada and the non-realization of a Palestinian state, and so participation in Palestinian Authority elections no longer conferred legitimacy on an agreement that recognized the state of Israel.[76]

The electoral platform announced by Hamas's "Change and Reform" list did not shy away from the priority of "resistance," noting that its participation came "in the framework of its comprehensive program for the liberation of Palestine and the return of the Palestinian people to their land and country." It further stated that "resistance in all its form is a natural right of the Palestinian people to end the occupation and establish the Palestinian state," and further claimed, pursuant to the idea of Palestine as a *waqf* land, that "historic Palestine is a part of the Arab and Islamic lands and is a right belonging to the Palestinian people that does not diminish with the progress of time and that no military or so-called legal measure will change." Despite such rhetoric, most of the platform was devoted not to the notion of resistance but to the social and economic policies Hamas was proposing, including as regards education and housing.[77] The Palestinian Authority had become notorious for corruption and inefficiency, and Hamas was running primarily as a principled Islamic alterative. But Hamas's rejectionism was also a key part of its electoral platform.

Following Hamas's surprising election victory, in which it won a majority of the seats in the Palestinian Council, the so-called Middle East Quartet (the United States, Russia, the European Union, and the United Nations) issued a statement

---

76 Baconi, *Hamas Contained*, 83.
77 "Al-Barnamaj al-intikhabi, katlat al-taghyir wa-l-islah," https://web.archive.org/web/20160113104721/ http://islah.ps/new/index.php?page=viewThread&id=128. Cf. Khaled Hroub, "A 'New Hamas' through Its News Documents," *Journal of Palestine Studies* 35 (2006): 6–27, at 10. I do not agree with Hroub's observation of "the virtual absence of military resistance from the platform."

calling on the "future Palestinian government" to commit to "nonviolence, recognition of Israel, and acceptance of previous agreements and obligations" pursuant to the peace process. The statement further warned that "future assistance to any new government would be reviewed by donors against that government's commitment" to those principles.[78] Israel, meanwhile, declared that it would not deal with a Palestinian government that included Hamas.[79] In response to such threats, Hamas's leaders undertook a media blitz in the Western press decrying such policies as punishing the winner of a free and fair election but also standing firm on their principles. In the *Los Angeles Times*, Khaled Meshaal, then head of Hamas's political bureau, stated that the Palestinian people "chose Hamas because of its pledge never to give up the legitimate rights of the Palestinian people and its promise to embark on a program of reform." The people had voted for resistance, and therefore resistance must continue. "[N]othing in the world will deter us from pursuing our goal of liberation and return," he declared. "We shall never recognize the legitimacy of a Zionist state created on our soil in order to atone for somebody else's sins or solve somebody else's problem." Meshaal then raised the issue of a *hudna*, saying, "if you are willing to accept the principle of a long-term truce, we are prepared to negotiate the terms. Hamas is extending a hand of peace to those who are truly interested in a peace based on justice."[80] But Meshaal's "peace based on justice" was clearly one that did not include Israel. A few weeks later, Ismail Haniyeh, the newly installed Palestinian prime minister, similarly referred to the possibility of "a long-term *hudna*" in an interview with *The Washington Post*, citing Yasin's previous proposal. Here he mentioned the idea of "a peace in stages," which was the same as the "phased solution" mulled by Hamas's leader in the 1990s.[81] In March, Hamas issued two political programs for its future government emphasizing the same and other

---

78 "Quartet Statement Following Hamas Victory in Palestinian Legislative Elections," January 30, 2006, https://www.usip.org/sites/default/files/file/resources/collections/peace_agreements/quartet_statement.pdf.
79 "Israel Rules Out Working with Hamas Gov't," *Asharq Al-Awsat*, January 29, 2006, https://eng-archive.aawsat.com/theaawsat/news-middle-east/israel-rules-out-working-with-hamas-govt.
80 Khaled Meshaal, "'We Shall Never Recognize . . . a Zionist State on Our Soil," *Los Angeles Times*, February 1, 2006, https://www.latimes.com/archives/la-xpm-2006-feb-01-oe-meshal1-story.html.
81 "'We Do Not Wish to Throw Them into the Sea,'" *Washington Post*, February 25, 2006, https://www.washingtonpost.com/archive/opinions/2006/02/26/we-do-not-wish-to-throw-them-into-the-sea/56c26504-1608-4d18-b118-ba89ed4ffb66/.

themes; the first of these noted the prospect of a *hudna*, while both alluded to the idea of the phased solution.⁸²

Somewhat later in the year, in September, Ahmed Yousef, a political adviser to the Hamas prime minister, announced that the Hamas-led government had delivered to Israel a proposal for a ten-year *hudna*. Israel rejected this, calling on Hamas to agree to the conditions set out by the Quartet instead, including recognizing Israel and disavowing violence.⁸³ Two months later, Yousef published an op-ed in the *New York Times* elaborating on his view of a *hudna* and presenting Hamas as though it were committed to peace.⁸⁴ "We Palestinians are prepared," he wrote, "to enter into a hudna to bring about an immediate end to the occupation and to initiate a period of peaceful coexistence during which both sides would refrain from any form of military aggression or provocation." The *hudna* would mean "a decade of coexistence and negotiations" in which to resolve "the important issues like the right of return and the release of prisoners. If the negotiations fail to achieve a durable settlement, the next generation of Palestinians and Israelis will have to decide whether or not to renew the hudna and the search for a negotiated peace." To reassure skeptics, Yousef added, "This offer of hudna is no ruse, as some assert, to strengthen our military machine, to buy time to organize better or to consolidate our hold on the Palestinian Authority." Yousef's proposal may not have been a ruse in the sense of deliberate deception, but it was a ruse in the sense of being too good to be true, in hinting at an amicable resolution whereby the two sides work out their differences and arrive at an outcome agreeable to all. At no point did either Yousef or Haniyeh indicate a willingness to tolerate the existence of a Jewish state, and there is no reason to believe that Hamas would have deviated from its unflinching rejectionism. Indeed, two years earlier, Yousef had written an essay in Arabic on the *hudna* concept in which he stressed the importance of being able "to resume our uprising and our resistance until the disappearance of the occupation [i.e., Israel] and the attainment of our national rights." A *hudna* with Israel, he wrote,

---

82 Ahmad Fayyad, "Muhaddadat al-barnamaj al-siyasi li-hukumat Hamas al-qadima," Al Jazeera, March 12, 2006, https://aja.me/dap5s; "al-Barnamaj al-siyasi li-hukumat Hamas," March 19, 2024, https://www.ikhwanonline.com/article/18832.
83 "Hamas tatrahu al-hudna badilan li-l-iʿtiraf wa-Israʾil tarfidu," Al Jazeera, September 22, 2006, https://aja.me/3kap4.
84 Ahmed Yousef, "Pause for Peace," *New York Times*, November 1, 2006, https://www.nytimes.com/2006/11/01/opinion/01yousef.html.

would never mean "recognizing the enemy and its occupation of our land or conceding any of our national rights."[85]

Following the swearing in of the Hamas-dominated parliament in February 2006, Israel instituted a partial blockade of Gaza that stalled the flow of goods, money, and people, a measure intended to force Hamas to satisfy the Quartet's conditions regarding the peace process.[86] The closest Hamas ever came to doing so was in the Mecca Agreement of February 2006, which paved the way for a Palestinian national unity government between Hamas and Fatah. According to the agreement's fourth article, the Hamas prime minister agreed "to respect the Arab and international legitimacy resolutions and agreements signed by the PLO," which of course included the Oslo Accords.[87] Yet while this pledge to "respect" the Oslo Accords may have appeared a breakthrough, elsewhere Hamas's leaders made sure to disabuse anyone of that notion. As Mousa Abu Marzouk, the Hamas political bureau's vice president at the time, later stated, "The difference is great between respect (*ihtiram*) and recognition (*i'tiraf*); I respect does not mean that I implement. This is what happened in the case of the Mecca Agreement; we respect old agreements, but this does not mean we recognize them."[88] Hamas's commitment to respecting past agreements such as the Oslo Accords thus did not mean very much.

The year and a half following Hamas's shocking electoral victory was a period of profound tension between Hamas and the dominant Fatah faction of the Palestinian Authority, headed by President Mahmoud Abbas. Following the collapse of the short-lived unity government and clashes between Hamas and Fatah security forces, Hamas seized control of Gaza in a violent coup on June 15, 2007. Hamas's view was that it was acting to thwart a US-backed Fatah coup against its government. In the *New York Times*, Ahmed Yousef sought to portray Hamas's move as an effort "to provide political stability and establish law and order" following a period of "civil unrest ... precipitated by the American and Israeli policy of arming elements of the Fatah opposition who want to attack Hamas and force

---

85 Ahmad Yusuf, "Mafhum al-hudna fi al-Islam wa-atharuha 'ala al-mawdu' al-Filastini," December 2004, https://web.archive.org/web/20061004173308/ http://www.passia.org/meetings/2004/Hassan-Yousef-2004.doc.
86 Steven Erlanger, "Hamas Leader Faults Israeli Sanction Plan," *New York Times*, February 18, 2006, https://www.nytimes.com/2006/02/18/world/middleeast/hamas-leader-faults-israeli-sanction-plan.html.
87 Robert Satloff, "The Mecca Accord (Part I): The Victory of Unity over Progress," The Washington Institute for Near East Policy, February 12, 2007, https://www.washingtoninstitute.org/policy-analysis/mecca-accord-part-i-victory-unity-over-progress.
88 Quoted in Leila Seurat, *The Foreign Policy of Hamas: Ideology, Decision Making and Political Supremacy* (London: I. B. Tauris, 2022), 49–50 (with minor adjustment to transliteration).

us from office." He went on to decry efforts to portray Hamas as "an extreme and dangerous force," noting that Hamas "has consistently offered a 10-year ceasefire with the Israelis to try to create an atmosphere of calm in which we resolve our differences."[89]

For the first time in its history, Hamas found itself the sole governing authority in charge of one of the Palestinian territories, ruling over Gaza's population of approximately two million people. Governance presented Hamas with a dilemma as far as its violent resistance to Israel was concerned, as continuing to stage attacks (mostly in the form of rockets in this period) would put Gaza's welfare in jeopardy, while refraining from doing so would mean compromising on the group's principles. Hamas sought to have it both ways. As Meshaal put it in a speech in February 2006, "The world will see how Hamas can encompass resistance and politics, resistance and government. Government is not our goal; it is a tool. . . . Democracy is our internal choice to reform our house, whereas resistance is our choice in facing the enemy. There is no conflict between the two."[90] Hamas thus pretended that governance and resistance were in no way contradictory. The reality, however, was that Hamas's commitment to fighting and ultimately destroying Israel made governance increasingly untenable, given the ongoing Israeli—and Egyptian—blockade of Gaza. From Israel's perspective, if Hamas remained committed to its destruction, then it had no choice but to prevent the group from enriching itself and expanding its military capabilities. Hence the necessity of the blockade, which expanded significantly upon Hamas's seizure of power in June 2007.

Over the next seventeen years, Hamas and Israel would engage in a series of small-scale confrontations during which Hamas would fire barrages of rockets toward Israel and the latter would respond with airstrikes against Hamas targets. These confrontations included the Israeli military operations known as Cast Lead (December 2008–January 2009), Pillar of Defense (November 2012), Protective Edge (July–August 2014), and Guardian of the Walls (May 2021). Throughout this period, even as it amassed an arsenal of rockets and built up its military infrastructure, including by building an extensive system of underground tunnels, Hamas sought to curry international sympathy by portraying itself as the victim of Israeli aggression. In doing so, it periodically raised the prospect of a *hudna* with Israel, sometimes gaining favorable coverage in the West, including in a "special report" published by the United States Institute for

---

89 Ahmed Yousef, "What Hamas Wants," *New York Times*, June 20, 2007, https://www.nytimes.com/2006/11/01/opinion/01yousef.html.
90 Baconi, *Hamas Contained*, 104–105.

Peace in June 2009.[91] The report stated with great confidence that "Hamas has, in practice, moved well beyond its charter," noting that it "has sent repeated signals that it may be ready to begin a process of coexisting to Israel."[92] Among the evidence cited was a recent *New York Times* interview with Meshaal, who stated, "We are with a state on the 1967 borders, based on a long-term truce. This includes East Jerusalem, the dismantling of settlements and the right of return of the Palestinian refugees." Asked how long was "long-term," he responded by saying "ten years."[93] Hamas again floated the offer of a *hudna* in 2015 only to be rebuffed once more by Israel, which viewed Hamas's disarmament as a precondition for any long-term truce that would include the lifting of the blockade.[94]

The 2015 offer was followed two years later, in May 2017, by Hamas's promulgation of a new political manifesto titled "A Document of General Principles and Policies."[95] The brainchild of Meshaal, the document was intended to showcase Hamas's alleged moderation since the issuing of its charter some thirty years earlier. As Meshaal stated in an interview shortly after the new document's unveiling, "This document reflects our position for now, which means that we are not a rigid ideological organization. This document also shows that we are a dynamic and adaptive organization and that we are eager to change if it is in the best interests of our people."[96] Yet a careful reading of the document reveals more continuity than change. While avoiding the unmistakably antisemitic rhetoric of the 1988 charter, the new document clearly maintained Hamas's rejection of Israel's

---

91 See Paul Scham and Osama Abu-Irshaid, "Hamas: Ideological Rigidity and Political Flexibility," United States Institute of Peace, January 1, 2009, https://www.usip.org/publications/2009/06/hamas-ideological-rigidity-and-political-flexibility. For a more measured study of the *hudna* concept in this period, see Dag Tuastad, "Hamas's Concept of a Long-term Ceasefire: A Viable Alternative to Full Peace?," Peace Research Institute Oslo, November 2010, https://www.prio.org/publications/7356.
92 Scham and Abu-Irshaid, "Hamas," 2.
93 Ibid., 19–20.
94 Shlomi Eldar, "Israel Should Be Wary of Hamas' Truce Proposal," *Al-Monitor*, March 11, 2015, https://www.al-monitor.com/originals/2015/03/israel-hamas-hudna-truce-gaza-humanitarian-crisis-abbas.html; Shlomi Eldar, "What's behind Hamas's Offer of Cease-fire to Israel?," *Al-Monitor*, May 8, 2018, https://www.al-monitor.com/originals/2018/05/israel-egypt-gaza-palestine-hamas-long-term-truce-hudna.html.
95 "A Document of General Principles & Policies" (English version), May 2017, https://web.archive.org/web/20170623063620/https://hamas.ps/en/post/678/A-Document-of-General-Principles-and-Policies. For a valuable analysis of the document, see Jean-Francois Legrain, "Hamas According to Hamas: A Reading of Its Document of General Principles," in *Routledge Handbook of Political Islam*, ed. Shahram Akbarzadeh, 2nd ed. (London: Routledge, 2020), 79–90.
96 Ali Younes, "Meshaal: 'We Want to Restore Our National Rights,'" Al Jazeera, May 2, 2017, https://www.aljazeera.com/features/2017/5/2/meshaal-we-want-to-restore-our-national-rights.

right to exist, stating that Palestine "is a blessed sacred land that has a special place in the heart of every Arab and every Muslim," and therefore "there shall be no recognition of the legitimacy of the Zionist entity."[97] The destruction of Israel was the only long-term solution Hamas could countenance: "Hamas rejects any alternative to the full and complete liberation of Palestine, from the river to the sea."[98] The part of the document that received the most attention in the Western press was a single sentence seemingly endorsing the idea of a two-state solution. As the *Guardian* reported, "Hamas has unveiled a new political program softening its stance on Israel by accepting the idea of a Palestinian state in territories occupied by Israel in the six-day war of 1967."[99] This was not, however, what the sentence in question actually said. The sentence, which immediately followed a line about Hamas's rejection of "any alternative to the full and complete liberation of Palestine," was as follows: "However, without compromising its rejection of the Zionist entity and without relinquishing any Palestinian rights, Hamas considers the establishment of a fully sovereign and independent Palestinian state, with Jerusalem as its capital along the lines of the 4th of June 1967, with the return of the refugees and the displaced to their homes from which they were expelled, to be a formula of national consensus."[100] While appearing to some as marking a breakthrough, the sentence actually said nothing new. It was merely a rephrasing of the familiar "phased solution" concept going back to the 1990s, whereby Hamas would accept full sovereignty on the West Bank and Gaza as the first phase of a longer struggle for liberation. The concept does not mean true coexistence in two states but presupposes the resumption of jihad in pursuit of the only tolerable outcome: Palestinian victory and Israel's demise.

Yahya Sinwar and the Promise of the Latter Days

In retrospect, the far more critical development to have happened in 2017 was the election that February of Yahya Sinwar as overall leader of Hamas in Gaza, succeeding Ismail Haniyeh, who would go on to replace Meshaal as head of Hamas's political bureau. A long-time prisoner, Sinwar was freed in 2011 as part of a hostage deal for Israeli soldier Gilad Shalit, having spent the preceding

---

97 "A Document of General Principles & Policies," 2, 6.
98 Ibid., 6.
99 Patrick Wintour, "Hamas Presents New Charter Accepting a Palestine Based on 1967 Borders," *Guardian*, May 1, 2017, https://www.theguardian.com/world/2017/may/01/hamas-new-charter-palestine-israel-1967-borders.
100 "A Document of General Principles & Policies," 6.

twenty-two years in Israeli jail for the confessed murder of four Palestinians he suspected of collaborating with Israel.[101] Prior to this, he had co-founded and led Hamas's internal security apparatus tasked with identifying and punishing suspected collaborators. In this role he developed a reputation for exceptional cruelty, mercilessly torturing and executing accused traitors. But Sinwar was no mere brute. In prison he devoted himself to the study of Israeli society and politics, consuming Israeli newspapers and television and acquiring fluency in Hebrew. He also rose to become the leader of the Hamas prisoners in Israeli jails, a position of quite some significance within the Hamas structure.

In 2017, the election of Sinwar was perceived as a victory for Hamas's military wing and its less pragmatic, more hardline approach to pursuing Hamas's vision.[102] In fall of that year, Sinwar seemed to confirm those perceptions when he stated, in a closed meeting with Gazan youth, "Over is the time Hamas spent discussing recognizing Israel. Now Hamas will discuss when we will wipe out Israel."[103] Presumably, Sinwar was referring to the more conciliatory approach adopted by Haniyeh and his team, even though they were never suggesting recognition of Israel. Despite his tough talk, over time Sinwar managed to convince a good number of well-informed Israelis that he was a leader Israel could work with, that in fact he was a pragmatist looking to solidify Hamas's rule in Gaza and enable the territory's economic development. In a 2018 interview with the Israeli newspaper *Yedioth Aharonoth*, Sinwar even came across as ready to lay down arms, at least for the time being. "I don't want any more wars," he said. "What I want is an end to the siege. My first commitment is to act in the interest of my people; to protect them and to defend their right for freedom and independence."[104] Months earlier, Israel had approved a deal with Qatar for the Gulf state to transfer millions of dollars per month to Gaza for the purpose of alleviating the humanitarian situation there, payments that continued until 2023. Meantime, Israel gradually increased the number of work permits granted to Gazans working in Israel or the West bank to some 18,000 on the eve

---

101 For Sinwar's biography, see David Remnick, "The Life of Yahya Sinwar, the Leader of Hamas in Gaza," *New Yorker*, August 3, 2024, https://www.newyorker.com/magazine/2024/08/12/yahya-sinwar-profile-hamas-gaza-war-israel.
102 See, for instance, Shlomi Eldar, "How Hamas' New Gaza Leader Came to Power," *Al-Monitor*, February 14, 2017, https://www.al-monitor.com/originals/2017/02/gaza-palestinians-hamas-israel-mohammed-al-deif-yahya-sinwar.html.
103 Dov Lieber, "Hamas Chief: We Won't Discuss Recognizing Israel, Only Wiping It Out," *Times of Israel*, October 19, 2017, https://www.timesofisrael.com/hamas-chief-we-wont-discuss-recognizing-israel-only-wiping-it-out/.
104 Francesca Bori, "Hamas Leader Sinwar: 'I Don't Want Any More Wars,'" Ynet, October 4, 2018, https://www.ynetnews.com/articles/0,7340,L-5363595,00.html.

of October 7.¹⁰⁵ These Israeli policies were no doubt informed by the view of Sinwar as a pragmatic actor capable of compromise, not someone hellbent on pursuing Israel's destruction at all costs.

That perception, of course, turned out to be false. Many were those Sinwar managed to deceive. As a former Israeli military intelligence officer later remarked, "We didn't understand him at all, in an insane way. Zero."¹⁰⁶ "I was naïve," reflected Shlomi Eldar, a veteran journalist and author of books on Hamas, about his failure to grasp the direction Sinwar was taking the group.¹⁰⁷ Even as astute an observer of Palestinian militancy as Ehud Yaari saw Sinwar as belonging to the group of Hamas leaders "who believe that Hamas can no longer escape the reality of their responsibility for the civilian population in Gaza," as opposed to "the military chiefs like Mohammed Deif and Marwan Issa, who believe that Hamas is not about serving the people but is about Jihad."¹⁰⁸ The reality, as he later acknowledged, was that Sinwar's "true priority was spearheading an assault on Israel that he hoped would galvanize Muslims around the region to join the fight."¹⁰⁹ Indeed, Sinwar deliberately set out to convince Israeli leaders that he was a pragmatist who wanted calm, particularly following the brief May 2021 war. According to the captured minutes of Hamas's planning meetings for the October 7 attack, the intention was to "hide our intentions" and "camouflage the big idea (our big project)" by giving the impression that "Gaza wants life and economic growth."¹¹⁰

There were signs, however, that Sinwar had other objectives in mind. One of the most telling was a conference he sponsored on September 30, 2021, at the Commodore Hotel in Gaza City. Titled "The Promise of the Latter Days Conference: Palestine after Liberation," the meeting was held for the purpose of drawing up plans and making preparations for the administration of Palestine following its full and complete liberation, an event assessed by the participants as lying in the very near future. The phrase "the promise of the latter days"

---

105 Nidal Al-Mughrabi, "Israel Sends Thousands of Cross-border Palestinian Workers Back to Gaza," Reuters, November 3, 2023, https://www.reuters.com/world/middle-east/thousands-gazan-workers-sent-back-israel-occupied-west-bank-witnesses-2023-11-03/.
106 Neri Zilber, "'Dead Man Walking': How Yahya Sinwar Deceived Israel for Decades," Financial Times, November 5, 2023, https://www.ft.com/content/de78c7a0-f8f0-403e-b0db-eb86d6e76919.
107 Roundtable discussion with Shlomi Eldar, Stanford University, October 18, 2024.
108 Ehud Yaari, "Gazan Futures: Prospects of a Long-term Armistice of Hudna with Hamas," Fathom, June 2021, https://fathomjournal.org/gazan-futures-ehud-yaari-on-the-prospects-of-a-long-term-armistice-or-hudna-with-hamas/.
109 Yaari and Levitt, "Growing Internal Tensions between Hamas Leaders."
110 Bergman, Rasgon, and Kingsley, "Secret Documents."

(*waʿd al-akhira*) is a reference to a Quranic verse in which God says, addressing the children of Israel who are being delivered from Pharaoh, "and when the promise of the latter days comes to pass, We will bring you gathered together."[111] While traditionally the phrase was interpreted in an eschatological vein (in the sense of "the promise of the hereafter"), in contemporary Islamist circles the verse is commonly understood as referring to God's promise to destroy the Jewish state following the ingathering of the Jews in their ancient land.[112] It was in this sense that Sinwar used the phrase in a 2018 speech, saying that "every new event reaffirms that we are drawing ever nearer to of the promise of the latter days whereby this occupation will be swept away."[113] Fittingly, the 2021 conference was organized by a group called "The Promise of the Latter Days Committee," formed in 2014, which describes itself as "a Palestinian national committee that believes in the inevitability of Palestine's liberation and is convinced of liberation's nearness, and that is composed of a group of Palestinian national establishments and persons."[114]

The conference's proceedings took up such issues as which currency would be used in the immediate aftermath of liberation (not the shekel), how the country would be administered before presidential and parliamentary elections could be held, how the inflow of Palestinian refugees would be managed, and how the international community should be engaged, among other things. The sense that Palestine's full liberation was just around the corner permeated the proceedings. In a speech at the conference, the committee's chairman, Hamas official Kanaan Obaid, stated, "We have a registry of the numbers of Israeli apartments and institutions, educational institutions and schools, gas stations, power stations, and sewage systems, and we have no choice but to get ready to manage them.... We believe that the liberation [will come] within a few years."[115] All these mat-

---

111 Qur'an 17:104.
112 For traditional interpretations, see Uri Rubin, *Between Jerusalem and Mecca: Sanctity and Redemption in the Qurʾān and the Islamic Tradition* (Berlin: Walter de Gruyter, 2023), 45–46; for an example of the modern Islamist interpretation, see "Surat al-Israʾ ... wa-nubuʾ at zawal al-dawla al-sahyuniyya," Akhbar al-Khalij, October 13, 2023, https://akhbar-alkhaleej.com/news/article/1344800.
113 "Al-Sinwar yaʿridu silahan ghanimathu al-Qassam min al-quwwa al-Israʾiliyya," ʿArabi 21, November 16, 2018, https://arabi21.com/story/1137959. Sinwar related this message on behalf of the commander of the al-Qassam Brigades, Mohammed Deif.
114 "Muʾtamar waʿd al-akhira bi-Ghazza al-yawm li-stishraf waqiʿ Filastin baʿd al-tahrir," Filastin Online, September 30, 2021, https://felesteen.news/post/94849.
115 "Hamas-Sponsored 'Promise of the Hereafter' Conference for the Phase Following the Liberation of Palestine and Israel's 'Disappearance,'" MEMRI, October 4, 2021, https://www.memri.org/reports/hamas-sponsored-promise-hereafter-conference-phase-following-liberation-palestine-and.

ters and more were later addressed in a set of recommendations issued by The Promise of the Latter Days Committee shortly after the conference.[116] Among these was a recommendation regarding the proper treatment of the country's Jews, or rather "the settler Jews on the land of Palestine." Here the committee counselled a policy of "distinction" between "the belligerent Jew, who must be fought [and killed]; the fleeing Jew, who may be left alone or pursued to be tried for his crimes; and the non-belligerent Jew who submits, and who may either be absorbed or compelled to leave after a certain time." There were some Jews, however, who would be compelled to stay. According to another recommendation of the committee, those Jews possessing certain valuable skills, such as in the areas of medicine, engineering, and technology, ought to be prevented from leaving, so as not to flee with all the skills and knowledge "that they gained while living on our land."

The triumphalist spirit of the conference was perhaps best captured in a speech written by Sinwar and delivered in absentia via a member of Hamas's political office present at the conference. In the remarks, Sinwar stated,

> We have no concern and no business save liberation, and we rely on God's promise to us of victory.... We are working and striving to recover what is rightly ours in our land. Victory is nigh, and our sponsorship of this conference flows from our perception of the victory's nearness.... [Our] military preparation, planning, and training, in both present and past, above ground and in its depths, in the darkness of the sea and in the sky above, spring from our belief in the nearness of liberation. This means that there is a need to prepare for what comes next, given that its future occurrence is an undeniable reality.[117]

In hindsight, these were the words that conveyed Sinwar's true thinking and intentions in the years leading up to October 7. The Israeli political leadership and Israeli intelligence did not take them seriously. As one former Fatah official close to the Hamas leadership told an Israeli journalist after October 7, "They [Israeli intelligence] didn't take heed of the data. They knew about the

---

116 "Tawsiyat muʾtamar waʿd al-akhira: Filastin baʿd al-tahrir," al-Markaz al-Filastini li-l-Iʿlam, September 30, 2021, https://palinfo.com/news/2021/09/30/60902/.

117 "Waʿd al-akhira ... al-Sinwar: tahrir Filastin huwa markaz al-ruʾya al-istratijiyya li-Hamas," Filastin Online, September 30, 2021, https://felesteen.news/post/94855; Rajab al-Madhun, "'Filastin baʿd al-tahrir': Ghazza tatallamasu al-mustaqbal," al-Akhbar, October 1, 2021, https://al-akhbar.com/Palestine/319010.

conference at the Commodore Hotel, which was even reported in the Israeli media. But they didn't attach any importance to it. It sounded so crazy, they thought it was nothing."[118] Indeed, on the very morning of October 7, 2023, a top-secret Israeli intelligence memorandum made the following assessment: "It is estimated that Hamas is not interested in escalation and entering into a confrontation at the present time."[119]

Conclusion

One of the unavoidable conclusions to be drawn from the foregoing is that Yahya Sinwar played a crucial, indeed a decisive, role in steering Hamas toward the attack of October 7. Sinwar was convinced that the final victory over Israel was drawing near, believing that a massive, surprise assault on Israel would spark the larger confrontation he envisioned, one involving all the elements of the Iranian-led Resistance Axis. Thus would the "promise of the latter days" be fulfilled. Sinwar, of course, was proved wrong. On October 16, 2024, more than a year into Israel's military operation against Hamas in Gaza, he was finally killed, shot in the head by an Israeli soldier during a firefight in southern Gaza. Hamas's battalions were largely destroyed, and Gaza's civilians paid a heavy price for Sinwar's blunder. What remains in store for Gaza is uncertain, but the days of Hamas rule are presumably numbered. Sinwar's grand vision for the reconquest of Israel seems ever more remote.

And yet while Sinwar was indispensable in putting the October 7 attack in motion, it would be a stretch to say that Hamas under Sinwar had become a fundamentally different organization, that "Sinwar's personality changed Hamas, totally," as the Israeli journalist Shlomi Eldar has argued.[120] This is because Sinwar did not come out of nowhere. Hamas, it is true, has long been divided between its more conciliatory political wing and its more hardline military wing, the one willing to accept tactical accommodation with Israel and the other deeply

---

118 Shlomi Eldar, "Hamas Actually Believed It Would Conquer Israel," *Haaretz*, April 5, 2024, https://www.haaretz.com/israel-news/2024-04-05/ty-article-magazine/.highlight/hamas-actually-believed-it-would-conquer-israel-and-divided-it-into-cantons/0000018e-ab4a-dc42-a3de-abfad6fe0000.
119 Bergman, Rasgon, and Kingsley, "Secret Documents."
120 Chanan Tigay, "This Israeli Journalist Reported on Hamas for Decades. But Oct. 7 Took Him by Surprise," *Jewish News of Northern California*, October 25, 2024, https://jweekly.com/2024/10/25/this-israeli-journalist-reported-on-hamas-for-decades-but-oct-7-took-him-by-surprise/.

reluctant to forgo military confrontation. Leaders such as Ismail Haniyeh and Khaled Meshaal belong to the former camp, Mohammed Deif and Marwan Issa to the latter. Sinwar, as it turned out, also belonged to the latter group. Yet even the representatives of the political wing, as was shown earlier, fervently celebrated October 7 as a glorious achievement. In private some of them acknowledged that Sinwar's gambit was misguided, but their misgivings related to Sinwar's strategic approach and not to his larger ideological vision. As one pair of well-informed analysts wrote in the months following October, Hamas's "external leaders have conveyed to foreign diplomats that Sinwar should have settled for a far more limited terrorist operation to capture hostages and pave the way for prisoner exchanges."[121] What these external leaders, representatives of the political wing, did not say—and never would or could—is that Hamas should renounce terrorism completely and come to a political agreement with Israel that resolves the conflict on amicable terms. The only compromise they have ever been willing to countenance is a time-limited *hudna* framed as part of a "phased solution" culminating, inevitably, in Israel's destruction. At times this idea could be phrased in seemingly more palatable terms, but the underlying principle was always the same. To the extent, then, that the strategy of October 7 was premised on the uncompromising, annihilationist vision shared by all Hamas leaders, they all bear responsibility for the attack.

Militant organizations can of course evolve. Ideology need not be set in stone. But the development that one observes in Hamas's ideology over the years relates more to rhetoric than to substance. It remains to be seen whether Hamas, or whatever is left of it, will ever be capable of serious change. Until then, Hamas is an actor with no constructive role to play in the future of the Israeli Palestinian conflict.

---

121 Yaari and Levitt, "Growing Internal Tensions between Hamas Leaders."

PART 2

THE GLOBAL DELUSIONS

CHAPTER 5

Does Terrorism Succeed? New Lessons from Hamas, the Global Intifada, and Antisemitism in America

Max Abrahms

Introduction

The Hamas massacre on October 7, 2023, killed over 1,100 people, the majority of whom were Israeli civilians.[1] As President Joe Biden and numerous reports noted at the time, this attack was not only the most lethal in Israeli history but the deadliest for Jews since the Holocaust.[2] Operation Al Aqsa Flood, as Hamas refers to it, ranks as the second most lethal terrorist attack in the history of modern terrorism, behind only the September 11, 2001 Al Qaeda attack in the United States.[3] Operation Al Aqsa Flood was highly unusual in terms of not only the lethality, but also with regard to its political effects.

Over the last couple of decades, a large body of empirical research within political science has examined the question of whether terrorism is politically

---

1 "Israel's Dead: The Names of Those Killed in Hamas Attacks, Massacres and the Israel-Hamas War," *Haaretz*, July 25, 2024.
2 "Hamas Attack 'deadliest day for Jews since the Holocaust,' Says Biden, as Israeli Jets Pound Gaza," *Guardian*, October 12, 2023, https://www.theguardian.com/world/2023/oct/12/israel-hamas-war-biden-jews-holocaust-palestine-iran-warning; "Hamas's Attack Was the Bloodiest in Israel's History," *Economist*, October 12, 2023, https://www.economist.com/briefing/2023/10/12/hamass-attack-was-the-bloodiest-in-israels-history.
3 An attack by Hutu extremists on April 13, 1994 killed 1,180 people according to the Global Terrorism Database.

effective behavior for the perpetrators. The answer is generally "no." It is true that theoretical work on terrorism often asserts that it is strategic behavior for nonstate actors to attack the population to achieve their political goals.[4] So common is this viewpoint that I refer to it as the Strategic Model of Terrorism.[5] But empirical studies on terrorism have rather consistently found that this tactic seldom pays. Specifically, numerous studies have shown that terrorists rarely achieve their stated political demands;[6] terrorist attacks on civilians actually lower the odds of government concessions even after controlling for many tactical confounds;[7] terrorist violence tends to backfire on the perpetrators politically and organizationally;[8] terrorism typically fails to amplify the grievances of

---

4   See, for example, Andrew H. Kydd and Barbara F. Walter, "The Strategies of Terrorism," *International Security* 31, no. 1 (2006): 49–80; David A. Lake, "Rational Extremism: Understanding Terrorism in the Twenty-First Century," *Dialogue IO* 1, no. 1 (2002): 15–28; H. E. Lapan and T. Sandler, "Terrorism and Signaling," *European Journal of Political Economy* 9, no. 3 (1993): 383–397; Robert A. Pape, "The Strategic Logic of Suicide Terrorism," *American Political Science Review* 97, no. 3 (2003): 343–361.
5   Max Abrahms, "What Terrorists Really Want: Terrorist Motives and Counterterrorism Strategy," *International Security* 32, no. 4 (2008): 78–105.
6   Max Abrahms, "Why Terrorism Does Not Work," *International Security* 31, no. 2 (2006): 42–78; Martha Crenshaw, "Theories of Terrorism: Instrumental and Organizational Approaches," *The Journal of Strategic Studies* 10, no. 4 (1987): 13–31; Seth G. Jones and Martin C. Libicki, *How Terrorist Groups End: Lessons for Countering al Qa'ida* (Santa Monica, CA: RAND Corporation, 2008), https://www.rand.org/pubs/monographs/MG741-1.html; Bonnie Cordes et al., *Trends in International Terrorism: 1982 and 1983* (Santa Monica, CA: RAND Corporation, 1984); Richard English, *Does Terrorism Work?: A History* (Oxford: Oxford University Press, 2016); Walter Laqueur, "The Futility of Terrorism," *Harper's* 252, no. 1510 (1976): 99–105; Thomas C. Schelling, "What Purposes Can 'International Terrorism' Serve?," *Violence, Terrorism, and Justice* 18 (1991): 32.
7   Khusrav Gaibulloev and Todd Sandler, "Hostage Taking: Determinants of Terrorist Logistical and Negotiation Success," *Journal of Peace Research* 46, no. 6 (2009): 739–756, https://doi.org/10.1177/0022343309342076; Anna Getmansky and Tolga Sinmazdemir, "Settling on Violence: Expansion of Israeli Outposts in the West Bank in Response to Terrorism," *Studies in Conflict & Terrorism* 41, no. 3 (2018): 241–259, https://doi.org/10.1080/1057610X.2017.1283196; Max Abrahms and Matthew S. Gottfried, "Does Terrorism Pay? An Empirical Analysis," *Terrorism and Political Violence* 28, no. 1 (2016): 72–89, https://doi.org/10.1080/09546553.2013.879379; Max Abrahms, "The Political Effectiveness of Terrorism Revisited," *Comparative Political Studies* 45, no. 3 (2012): 366–393, https://doi.org/10.1177/0010414011433104.
8   Audrey Kurth Cronin, *How Terrorism Ends: Understanding the Decline and Demise of Terrorist Campaigns* (Princeton, NJ: Princeton University Press, 2009), https://press.princeton.edu/books/hardcover/9780691139487/how-terrorism-ends; Max Abrahms, *Rules for Rebels: The Science of Victory in Militant History* (New York: Oxford University Press, 2018), https://global.oup.com/academic/product/rules-for-rebels-9780198811558; Max Abrahms, "Al Qaeda's Scorecard: A Progress Report on Al Qaeda's Objectives," *Studies in Conflict & Terrorism* 29, no. 5 (2006): 509–529, https://doi.org/10.1080/10576100600701990; Virginia Page Fortna, "Do Terrorists Win? Rebels' Use of Terrorism and Civil War Outcomes," *International*

the perpetrators;⁹ and the terrorist violence tends to empower hardliners in the target country most opposed to politically accommodating the perpetrators.¹⁰

Of course, the question of whether terrorism pays depends on what we are measuring. Understandably, political scientists have tended to focus on the effects of the terrorist violence to the target country. From this vantage point, the October 7 attack was an enormous failure. It provoked the Israel Defense Forces to mount a devastating military assault against the Hamas terrorist organization based in Gaza; substantially weakened its ability to generate pre-attack levels of terrorist violence; killed and harmed many thousands of Palestinians in the course of the counterterrorism response; and strengthened Zionist sentiment among Israelis

---

Organization 69, no. 3 (2015): 519–556, https://doi.org/10.1017/S0020818315000089; Max Abrahms, "Is Terrorism an Effective Tactic?: Evolution in the Conventional Wisdom," in *The Routledge Companion to Terrorism Studies*, ed. Max Abrams (London: Routledge, 2025), 265–270; Virginia Held, "Terrorism, Rights, and Political Goals," in *Violence, Terrorism, and Justice*, ed. R. G. Frey and Christopher W. Morris (Cambridge: Cambridge University Press, 1991), 59–85.

9   Alex P. Schmid and Janny de Graaf, *Violence as Communication: Insurgent Terrorism and the Western News Media* (London: Sage Publications, 1982), https://unesdoc.unesco.org/ark:/48223/pf0000049900; Charles Tilly, *The Politics of Collective Violence* (Cambridge: Cambridge University Press, 2003); Max Abrahms, "Al Qaeda's Miscommunication War: The Terrorism Paradox," *Terrorism and Political Violence* 17, no. 4 (2005): 529–549, https://doi.org/10.1080/095465591009421; Max Abrahms, "The Credibility Paradox: Violence as a Double-Edged Sword in International Politics," *International Studies Quarterly* 57, no. 4 (2013): 660–671, https://doi.org/10.1111/isqu.12026; Max Abrahms, "Why Terrorists Are Misunderstood," *The Evolution Institute's This View of Life* (2020), https://www.prosocial.world/posts/why-terrorists-are-misunderstood.

10 Claude Berrebi and Esteban F. Klor, "Are Voters Sensitive to Terrorism? Direct Evidence from the Israeli Electorate," *American Political Science Review* 102, no. 3 (2008): 279–301, https://doi.org/10.1017/S0003055408080246; Claude Berrebi and Esteban F. Klor, "On Terrorism and Electoral Outcomes: Theory and Evidence from the Israeli-Palestinian Conflict," *Journal of Conflict Resolution* 50, no. 6 (2006): 899–925, https://doi.org/10.1177/0022002706293678; George A. Bonanno and John T. Jost, "Conservative Shift among High-Exposure Survivors of the September 11th Terrorist Attacks," *Basic and Applied Social Psychology* 28, no. 4 (2006): 311–323, https://doi.org/10.1207/s15324834basp2804_4; Christophe Chowanietz, "Rallying around the Flag or Railing against the Government? Political Parties' Reactions to Terrorist Acts," *Party Politics* 17, no. 5 (2011): 673–698, https://doi.org/10.1177/1354068810372582; Agustin Echebarria-Echabe and Emilia Fernández-Guede, "Effects of Terrorism on Attitudes and Ideological Orientation," *European Journal of Social Psychology* 36, no. 2 (2006): 259–265, https://doi.org/10.1002/ejsp.294; Anna Getmansky and Thomas Zeitzoff, "Terrorism and Voting: The Effect of Rocket Threat on Voting in Israeli Elections," *American Political Science Review* 108, no. 3 (2014): 588–604, https://doi.org/10.1017/S0003055414000288; Eric D. Gould and Esteban F. Klor, "Does Terrorism Work?," *The Quarterly Journal of Economics* 125, no. 4 (2010): 1459–1510, https://doi.org/10.1162/qjec.2010.125.4.1459.

and the Jewish Diaspora.[11] Rather than creating a Palestinian state, Operation Al Aqsa Flood has taken that possibility off the table for the foreseeable future.

This chapter contends, however, that the October 7 terrorist attack was successful in a way previously neglected in the political science literature. Although a massive failure dyadically in terms of eliciting from Israel a punishing response to Hamas and its aspirations of Palestinian statehood, the terrorist perpetrators sparked an unprecedented pro-Hamas "global intifada" directed against the Jewish Diaspora in the United States and other Western countries. In this way, Hamas succeeded in not only broadening its organizational appeal geographically but also in undercutting and threatening the security of international Jewry—understudied outcomes the Foreign Terrorist Organization appears to value.[12]

This chapter consists of two main sections. The first section details the effects of the October 7 terrorist attack on the Jewish Diaspora, with a particular focus in the United States. This section highlights how Operation Al Aqsa Flood increased support for Hamas in the United States and extended its "terror" campaign into the Jewish Diaspora. The second section explores several hypotheses for why Hamas support in the United States increased after the October 7, 2023, massacre. The short answer is antisemitism. Operation Al Aqsa Flood and the controversial Israeli military response in Gaza supplied a geopolitical pretext for antisemites in the West to realize their previously hidden agenda of hate.

Post-Attack Hamas Support in the United States

For obvious reasons, terrorist support is notoriously difficult to measure scientifically.[13] Despite the inherent measurement challenges, evidence abounds that Operation Al Aqsa Flood visibly increased support for Hamas

---

11 "Oct. 7 Attack Made Israel Stronger," *Wall Street Journal*, January 31, 2024, https://www.wsj.com/articles/oct-7-attack-made-israel-stronger-hamas-palestinians-jewish-state-herzl-4b628804.

12 Charles B. Strozier, "The Apocalyptic Aims of Hamas," *Psychoanalysis, Self and Context* 19, no. 1 (2024): 3–6, https://doi.org/10.1080/24720038.2023.2292052; Devorah Margolin and Matthew Levitt, "The Road to October 7: Hamas's Long Game, Clarified," *CTC Sentinel* 16, no. 10 (2023): 1–10, https://ctc.westpoint.edu/the-road-to-october-7-hamas-long-game-clarified/; Jeffrey Herf, "The Ideology of Mass Murder," in *Responses to 7 October: Antisemitic Discourse*, ed. Rosa Freedman and David Hirsh (London: Routledge, 2024), 24–29.

13 Alex P. Schmid and Albert J. Jongman, *Political Terrorism: A New Guide to Actors, Authors, Concepts, Data Bases, Theories, and Literature* (New Brunswick, NJ: Transaction Books, 1988); Victor Asal and R. Karl Rethemeyer, "The Nature of the Beast: Organizational Structures and the Lethality of Terrorist Attacks," *The Journal of Politics* 70, no. 2 (2008): 437–449, https://doi.org/10.1017/S0022381608080419.

in the United States. The intifada in the United States that erupted after the massacre stirred anti-Israel protests across the country, with at least eighteen states featuring terrorist flags or signs bearing the logo of Hamas as well Hezbollah and the Popular Front for the Liberation of Palestine.[14] The Anti-Defamation League (ADL) noted: "Protesters have regularly indicated their endorsement of groups that the U.S. recognizes as Designated Foreign Terrorist Organizations (FTOs) . . . including Hamas, Hezbollah, and the Popular Front for the Liberation of Palestine (PFLP) by cheering on their actions in speeches and chants or displaying those groups' logos on flags and other paraphernalia."[15] It is important to emphasize two points about these displays for Hamas, which were unprecedented in number. The first is that public support for Hamas was apparently not limited to its social welfare services to Palestinians. The protesters were explicit that they support Hamas for its terrorist violence in particular. The protesters frequently held signs of the most well-known terrorist leaders such as Abu Obaida, spokesperson for the ʿIzz al-Din al-Qassam Brigades, Hamas's militant wing. The second point is that Hamas support was not limited to rogue individuals acting in defiance of the broader protests. As the Anti-Defamation League has demonstrated in its reports on the intifada in America: "These expressions [of support for Hamas] are not limited to a few individuals on the sidelines of rallies. Rather, in numerous cities and towns across the country, references to these terrorist groups and their violent actions have been met by raucous cheers from protest attendees and their symbols have been proudly displayed at the protests and in footage posted by organizers after the fact."[16]

For example, Nerdeen Kiswani, a leader of the anti-Israel group Within Our Lifetime (WOL), wore a button bearing the image of Abu Obaida at an April 1, 2024, protest outside of a synagogue in Teaneck, New Jersey. Protesters in Manhattan likewise chanted the previous day, "Abu Obaida, ya habib [love], adrab adrab [strike, strike] Tel Aviv."[17] In a July protest in Washington, D.C., against Israeli Prime Minister Netanyahu's visit to Congress, the anti-Israel activists wore Hamas headbands and waved Hamas flags.[18] Outside of Netanyahu's

---

14 "Anti-Israel Protesters Glorify Terror Groups, Violence," Anti-Defamation League (ADL), January 2024, https://www.adl.org/resources/blog/anti-israel-protesters-glorify-terror-groups-violence.
15 Ibid.
16 Ibid.
17 Ibid.
18 Trey Yingst (@TreyYingst), "On the left is a photo of Hamas spokesman Abu Obaida taken during our 2019 interview in Khan Younis. On the right is a photo that my colleague," X (formerly Twitter), July 24, 2024, https://x.com/treyyingst/status/1816221738243391587.

hotel, a protester yelled "Allahu Akbar, Hamas." The activists made clear that their objection was not limited to the Israeli prime minister. The protester screamed at Jews on the streets of Washington, D.C.: "Jewish motherfuckers. We're gonna kill all of you. We're gonna burn you."[19] To terrorize American Jews, anti-Israel activists also graffitied "Hamas is coming" on the national monument.[20] On Capitol Hill, the pro-Hamas activists dressed as terrorists and held a sign that read, "Allah is gathering all the Zionists for the Final Solution."[21] Reporters have documented in Chicago numerous other occasions when groups of anti-Israel activists dressed up as Hamas terrorists and paid allegiance to its military wing and spokesperson.[22] Protesters unabashedly displayed their support for Hamas. For the one-year anniversary of the October 2023 terrorist massacre, other protesters in Chicago shouted: "All Chicago is Hamas! The entire country is with Hamas!"[23] At other rallies in Chicago, anti-Israel activists have walked around with Hamas flags, screaming "I am Hamas, I support them one million percent."[24] Such displays of Hamas support since its 2023 terrorist massacre have been evident in other major cities as well. At anti-Israel rallies in Los Angeles, for example, activists shouted "I am Hamas" as they made death threats to American Jews at a kosher restaurant.[25] Some of these cases of political extremism have escalated to action. In Squirrel Hill, Pennsylvania, for example, a Chabad House was vandalized by a self-described "Hamas operative" wearing a Hamas headband.[26] To make clear their support for Hamas and its Operation Al Aqsa Flood massacre against Jews, anti-Israel groups often use the word "flood" to publicize the intifada events in the United States. Palestine Action, the

---

19 Nioh Berg (@NiohBerg), X (formerly Twitter), February 8, 2025, https://x.com/NiohBerg/status/1816092039659880892.
20 Isaac de Castro (@isaacdecastrog), X (formerly Twitter), February 9, 2025, https://x.com/isaacdecastrog/status/1816306219784761364.
21 Christina Hoff Sommers (@CHSommers), "Just seen on Capitol Hill," X (formerly Twitter), July 24, 2024, https://x.com/CHSommers/status/1816185123597082687.
22 Kassy Dillon (@KassyAkiva), X (formerly Twitter), February 8, 2025, https://x.com/KassyAkiva/status/1826437183227498897; Eyal Yakoby (@EYakoby), X (formerly Twitter), February 8, 2025, https://x.com/EYakoby/status/1826366679137616104.
23 Eyal Yakoby (@EYakoby), X (formerly Twitter), November 5, 2024, https://x.com/EYakoby/status/1845572001332613609.
24 Eyal Yakoby (@EYakoby), X (formerly Twitter), February 7, 2025, https://x.com/EYakoby/status/1825750233147486552; Eyal Yakoby (@EYakoby), X (formerly Twitter), February 7, 2025, https://x.com/EYakoby/status/1825749439585067042.
25 "ADL Records Dramatic Increase in U.S. Antisemitic Incidents Following Oct. 7," Anti-Defamation League (ADL), February 7, 2024, https://www.adl.org/resources/press-release/adl-records-dramatic-increase-us-antisemitic-incidents-following-oct-7.
26 Eyal Yakoby (@EYakoby), X (formerly Twitter), December 1, 2024, https://x.com/EYakoby/status/1851739573224607941.

US-based faction of a global antizionist collective, advertises anti-Israel protests with calls to "flood the gates."[27] Within Our Lifetime issued numerous "call[s] to flood NYC for Palestine," while other groups, such as CODEPINK, used the same "flood" reference to describe protests in other American cities.[28]

American universities around the country have featured some of most virulent and overt Hamas support. As one study concluded, "The current anti-Israel protest movement on and off the college campuses is driven by over 150 pro-terrorism groups, with the vast majority supporting Hamas and/or the October 7 terrorist attacks. The actual number of pro-terrorism groups involved in protests is certainly higher.... The backbone of the protest movement can reasonably be characterized as Hamas."[29] For example, Students for Justice in Palestine openly celebrate the Hamas military wing and its 2023 terrorist rampage.[30] At the UCLA "encampment," the activists wrote in chalk, "Oh Qassam [referencing the ʿIzz al-Din al-Qassam Brigades, Hamas's military wing], oh beloved we want to burn Tel Aviv" and "Oh Abu Obaida we will show you that the Arab people are all with you." At a protest at Columbia University in New York—also in April 2024—protesters chanted, "Al-Qassam you make us proud" and displayed signs bearing the names and images of convicted terrorists.[31] At Stanford University, an encampment was staffed by a student with a Hamas headband.[32] Students at the University of Michigan donned terrorist outfits.[33] Similar pro-Hamas encampments popped up at scores of other universities around the country,

---

27 "Time to Escalate: Anti-Israel Activists Intensify Protests with Violent Direct Actions," Anti-Defamation League (ADL), February 7, 2024, https://www.adl.org/resources/blog/time-escalate-anti-israel-activists-intensify-protests-violent-direct-actions.

28 "Pro-Palestinian Protesters Stage Walkout on Low Steps on Oct. 7," *Columbia Spectator*, October 7, 2024, https://www.columbiaspectator.com/news/2024/10/07/pro-palestinian-protesters-stage-walkout-on-low-steps-on-oct-7/; "Palestine," CODEPINK, https://www.codepink.org/palestine.

29 Ryan Mauro, *Marching toward Violence: The Domestic Anti-Israeli Protest Movement* (Washington, D.C.: Capital Research Center, 2024), 6, https://capitalresearch.org/article/marching-toward-violence-the-domestic-anti-israeli-protest-movement/.

30 Eyal Yakoby (@EYakoby), X (formerly Twitter), August 22, 2024, https://x.com/EYakoby/status/1826743926763782240.

31 "Anti-Israel Protesters Glorify Terror Groups, Violence," Anti-Defamation League (ADL), January 2024, https://www.adl.org/resources/blog/anti-israel-protesters-glorify-terror-groups-violence.

32 "Stanford Forwards Encampment Photo to FBI," *Stanford Daily*, April 30, 2024, https://stanforddaily.com/2024/04/30/stanford-forwards-encampment-photo-to-fbi/.

33 Max Abrahms (@MaxAbrahms), X (formerly Twitter), February 12, 2025, https://x.com/maxabrahms/status/1828911340561354817.

including at seven of the eight Ivy League colleges.[34] Notably, only a handful of the protest groups have condemned Hamas and the October 7 massacre.[35]

Surveys of American public opinion reveal pro-Hamas sympathy, particularly on the political left. An Associated Press survey carried out for the one-year anniversary of Operation Al Aqsa Flood found that Democratic respondents were evenly divided over whether the subsequent war in Gaza is the fault of Israel or Hamas. By contrast, only a quarter of Republican respondents agreed that the Israeli government bears responsibility.[36] A February 2024 Pew survey also found considerable Hamas support sympathy among Americans, especially on the political left. Among all Americans, only 60% of respondents registered a "very unfavorable" view of Hamas. And among Democrats, the Israeli government and Hamas are held in the same esteem. Compared to Republicans, Democrats were over three times as likely to agree that "Hamas's reasons for fighting Israel are at least somewhat valid." Among Democrats ages eighteen to twenty-nine, 44% say Hamas's reasons for fighting are valid. Within this demographic cohort, a greater percentage say that Hamas has valid reasons for fighting than say the same about Israel (44% vs. 35%). Notably, less than 50% of Muslim Americans agreed with the statement that the October 7 attack was "unacceptable." Within this group of Americans, 37% register a favorable view of Hamas.[37]

Hamas is an antisemitic organization.[38] The Jewish targets of the October 7 attack were disproportionately peaceniks at *kibbutzim* and the Nova concert.[39]

---

34 "Campus Antisemitism Surges amid Encampments and Related Protests at Columbia and Other Universities," Anti-Defamation League (ADL), May 3, 2024, https://www.adl.org/resources/blog/campus-antisemitism-surges-amid-encampments-and-related-protests-columbia-and-other.
35 Mauro, *Marching toward Violence*, 26.
36 "Poll: Democrats, Republicans Split on Israel's Responsibility for War's Escalation," *Times of Israel*, October 30, 2024, https://www.timesofisrael.com/poll-democrats-republicans-split-on-israels-responsibility-for-wars-escalation/.
37 Pew Research Center, *Americans' Views of the Israel-Hamas War and U.S. Involvement*, March 21, 2024, https://www.pewresearch.org/wp-content/uploads/sites/20/2024/03/PRC_2024.3.21_Israel-Hamas_REPORT.pdf.
38 "Israel-Hamas War," *Jerusalem Post*, July 2024, https://www.jpost.com/israel-hamas-war/article-822367; *The Essential Guide to October 7*, Jewish People Policy Institute (JPPI), July 2024, https://jppi.org.il/wp-content/uploads/2024/07/The-Essential-Guide-To-October-7-digital.pdf; "Remarks by President Biden on the Terrorist Attacks in Israel," White House, October 10, 2023, https://www.whitehouse.gov/briefing-room/speeches-remarks/2023/10/10/remarks-by-president-biden-on-the-terrorist-attacks-in-israel-2/; Pew Research Center, *Americans' Views of the Israel-Hamas War and U.S. Involvement*, March 21, 2024, https://www.pewresearch.org/wp-content/uploads/sites/20/2024/03/PRC_2024.3.21_Israel-Hamas_REPORT.pdf.
39 "The Folly of the Campus Encampments," *Jerusalem Post*, May 7, 2024, https://www.jpost.com/opinion/article-815885; "Israeli Peace Activist Murdered by Hamas Is Memorialized

On that bloody day, Hamas bragged about killing "Jews," not right-wing supporters of the Benjamin Netanyahu government or even Zionists.[40] And Hamas has ambitions to kill Jews worldwide, not just inside of Israel.[41] Understandably, then, the surge in overt Hamas support in the United States after the October 7 attack from the global intifada struck fear in American Jewry. One survey conducted a month after the terrorist massacre found that the percentage of Jewish students who said they feel comfortable with others on campus knowing they are Jewish dropped by nearly half.[42] The ADL reported:

> A plurality of Jewish students do not feel physically safe on campus. Prior to 10/7, two-thirds (66.6%) of Jewish students said they felt "very" or "extremely" physically safe on campus, compared to less than half (45.5%) post-10/7. Feelings of emotional safety among Jewish students changed even more dramatically—two-thirds (65.8%) of Jewish students said they felt "very" or "extremely" emotionally safe before 10/7, which fell to a third (32.5%) after 10/7."[43]

In sum, support in America for Hamas terrorists has been undeniable since Operation Al Aqsa Flood. It has been documented in many anti-Israel protests throughout the country, particularly at universities, as well as in multiple reports on anti-Israel groups. National surveys of the American public also find surprisingly high levels of popular support for the Foreign Terrorist Organization, especially among citizens on the political left. Predictably, the data also indicate a concomitant rise within American Jewry of feeling unsafe. This aforementioned analysis suggests that the extant academic literature on the effectiveness of terrorism should be broadened to include the effects of terrorism on Diaspora

---

    in Gaza Evacuee Camp," *Times of Israel*, August 2024, https://www.timesofisrael.com/israeli-peace-activist-murdered-by-hamas-is-memorialized-in-gaza-evacuee-camp/.
40 Israel Defense Forces (@IDF), X (formerly Twitter), October 22, 2023, https://x.com/IDF/status/1716874448694096095.
41 "Germany Charges Four for Setting Up Hamas Weapons Depots across Europe," *Times of Israel*, February 9, 2024, https://www.timesofisrael.com/germany-charges-four-for-setting-up-hamas-weapons-depots-across-europe/; "Germany Charges Four over Hamas Weapons Depots in Europe," *Barron's*, February 9, 2024, https://www.barrons.com/news/germany-charges-four-over-hamas-weapons-depots-in-europe-a5146af8.
42 "Campus Antisemitism: A Study of Campus Climate during and after the Hamas Terrorist Attacks," Anti-Defamation League (ADL), February 2024, https://www.adl.org/resources/report/campus-antisemitism-study-campus-climate-and-after-hamas-terrorist-attacks.
43 Ibid.

communities in foreign countries. The next section examines why Hamas support became markedly more prominent in the United States after the October 7, 2023, terrorist massacre.

Why Did Operation Al Aqsa Flood Increase Hamas Support in the West?

My basic contention is that the October 7, 2023, Hamas terrorist massacre and inevitable, forceful Israeli counterterrorism response to it in the Gaza Strip created a pretext for antisemites in the West to realize their previously hidden biases and hatred against Jews due to diminished reputational costs for bigotry. Bigots have acted rationally, seizing on the international opprobrium of Israel to actualize their latent Jew-hatred at a time when the audience costs are at a nadir. Cloaked in the rhetoric of antizionism, antisemitism found unprecedented popularity especially on the American left, manifesting in numerous ways including Hamas support.

The empirical basis for this explanation did not begin in October 2023. Studies have long established that Middle East conflict related to Israel predicts rising antisemitism in the West.[44] Brian Levin, founding director of the Center for the Study of Hate and Extremism at California State University, San Bernardino, notes: "When violent conflicts occur in the Middle East, there are those in the U.S. that exploit these horrifying events to inflame antisemitism."[45] Holly Huffnagle, who directs the American Jewish Committee's efforts to combat antisemitism in the United States, has likewise observed: "We often see an increase in antisemitic acts whenever there is a conflict in the Middle East."[46] In sum, there is an empirical basis to this proposed causal mechanism that precedes the October 7, 2023, massacre in which conflicts involving Israel galvanize mistreatment of Jews.

It is important to underscore that the global intifada movement that Hamas incited has been directed against Jews in the Diaspora rather than Israel.

---

44 Stephen Collinson, "Analysis: Antisemitism Thrives in an Unstable World," CNN, October 31, 2023, https://www.cnn.com/2023/10/31/politics/antisemitism-unstable-world-analysis/index.html.

45 "How the Gaza Crisis Has Fueled Antisemitism in the U.S.," NBC News, November 9, 2023, https://www.nbcnews.com/news/us-news/gaza-crisis-antisemitism-us-hamas-israel-palestine-rcna123163.

46 "How the Gaza Crisis Has Fueled Antisemitism in the U.S.," NBC News, November 9, 2023, https://www.nbcnews.com/news/us-news/gaza-crisis-antisemitism-us-hamas-israel-palestine-rcna123163.

Although in the name of Palestine, the global intifada has threatened the Jewish Diaspora—not Israel. In fact, the global intifada has actually strengthened Zionist support among Jewish and non-Jewish Americans according to numerous indicators such as survey data, observations in the media, sales of Israeli flags and other Judaica, as well as the number of Jews making *aliya* (moving to Israel).[47] The global intifada helped to elect the most pro-Israel presidential administration in American history. Donald Trump campaigned in 2024 on combating the global intifada movement, crushing Hamas, safeguarding Israel, and then went on to appoint to high-level positions likeminded supporters such as Mike Huckabee, Steve Witkoff, and Marco Rubio.[48]

If my causal mechanism is correct, then we would expect to find rising antisemitism in America after October 7, 2023, beyond the noticeable increase in Hamas support. Across multiple data sources and methodologies, the period after Operation Al Aqsa Flood saw a tremendous rise in antisemitism in the United States. One group found a 388% increase in reported incidents of harassment, vandalism, and assault against American Jews.[49] The average monthly rate of antisemitic incidents witnessed by Jewish students soared twenty-two-fold from the previous academic school year. The monthly rate of observing antisemitic vandalism for Jewish students rose by roughly twenty-one times, while the rate of experiencing antisemitic incidents increased 16.25 times.[50] According to FBI Director Christopher Wray, antisemitism in America after October 7, 2023, reached "historic levels." Although making up less than 3% of the American population, 60% of religious-based hate crimes were directed against Jews.[51] In many cases, there was no visible connection of the antisemitism to Hamas, such as

---

47 "AJC Survey Shows American Jews are Deeply and Increasingly Connected to Israel," American Jewish Committee (AJC), June 10, 2024, https://www.ajc.org/news/ajc-survey-shows-american-jews-are-deeply-and-increasingly-connected-to-israel; "Thousands of North Americans Making Aliyah After Oct. 7," Jewish News Syndicate (JNS), July 14, 2024, https://www.jns.org/thousands-of-north-americans-making-aliyah-after-oct-7/; Stewart Ain, "Since Oct. 7, Stars of David and Israeli Flags Have Been Flying Off the Shelves," *The Forward*, March 17, 2024, https://forward.com/news/592232/judaica-sales-oct-7-israel-star-david/.
48 "Trump Promises to Kick 'Foreign Jihad Sympathizers' Out of America," *Campus Reform*, November 6, 2024, https://www.campusreform.org/article/trump-promises-kick-foreign-jihad-sympathizers-america-flashback/26736; "Your Complete Guide to Trump's Jewish Advisers and Pro-Israel Cabinet," *The Forward*, November 13, 2024, https://forward.com/news/674101/trump-cabinet-israel-rubio-huckabee-jewish/.
49 "ADL Records Dramatic Increase."
50 Ibid.
51 Stephen Collinson, "Analysis: Antisemitism Thrives in an Unstable World," CNN, October 31, 2023, https://www.cnn.com/2023/10/31/politics/antisemitism-unstable-world-analysis/index.html.

when a Beverly Hills home of a Holocaust survivor was daubed with antisemitic graffiti reading "F— Jews."[52] Such antisemitic incidents could be perpetrated by antisemites from the political left or right. Indeed, even antisemites who align with Hamas sometimes hail from the far right. For example, the American white supremacist leader Nick Fuentes, who hosts a popular antisemitic podcast, said after Operation Al Aqsa Flood that he favors Hamas "over all these tricky Zionist Jews."[53] In sum, empirical evidence abounds that Hamas support after its October 7 manifested in America by tapping into antisemitism which had previously been more muted presumably due to the audience costs of displaying bigotry.

Other explanations for the rise in Hamas support in the United States have a weaker empirical basis. They will be discussed below.

1. Rising Hamas Support in America was an Expression of Solidarity with Palestinians in Response to the Israeli Military Campaign in Gaza

This explanation lacks empirical support because the global intifada in America preceded the Israeli invasion of Gaza on October 27, 2023. Within a week of Hamas's October 7, 2023, terrorist massacre, approximately 150 rallies sprung up across the United States featuring pro-Hamas rhetoric.[54] For example, a woman at an anti-Israel rally in Portland, Maine shouted, "All of us [are] Hamas!"[55] According to one count by the ADL, there were 312 reported US antisemitic incidents from October 7 to October 23, including harassment, vandalism, and assault—many of which celebrated Hamas.[56] By October 9, just two days after Operation Al Aqsa Flood, anti-Jewish threats on the Telegram platform surged

---

52   Ibid.
53   Ryan Mauro, *Marching toward Violence: The Domestic Anti-Israeli Protest Movement* (Washington, D.C.: Capital Research Center, 2024), 5, https://capitalresearch.org/article/marching-toward-violence-the-domestic-anti-israeli-protest-movement/.
54   "Support for Hamas Terror at Anti-Israel Rallies Across the U.S.," Anti-Defamation League (ADL), November 2023, https://www.adl.org/resources/article/support-hamas-terror-anti-israel-rallies-across-us.
55   Ibid.
56   "U.S. Antisemitic Incidents Up About 400% since Israel-Hamas War Began, Report Says," Reuters, October 25, 2023, https://www.reuters.com/world/us/us-antisemitic-incidents-up-about-400-since-israel-hamas-war-began-report-says-2023-10-25/.

by 488%.⁵⁷ By October 25, the messaging platform Telegram saw a 1,000% increase in the daily average of "violent messages mentioning Jews and Israel in white supremacist and extremist channels."⁵⁸ Offline, more serious antisemitic incidents became routine. In Salt Lake City, Utah, a synagogue was forced to evacuate after receiving a bomb threat.⁵⁹ Across America, Jews were assaulted before the Israeli invasion.⁶⁰ In one such assault, a man punched a twenty-nine year-old woman in the face in New York City's Grand Central Terminal. The victim of the hate crime told NYPD officers that, when she asked the man why he assaulted her, he replied, "You are Jewish," before fleeing.⁶¹ The day after the largest terrorist attack on Jews in history, a protester attending a pro-Hamas rally in New York City was seen brandishing a swastika, leading Mayor Eric Adams to condemn the antisemitic protest.⁶² Within a week of Operation Al Aqsa Flood, there were already a dozen pro-Hamas protests in several US cities, including New York, Washington, Philadelphia, San Francisco, and Chicago. These rallies showed support for Hamas terrorism rather than social welfare work.⁶³ Before the Israeli invasion of Gaza, US Senator Jacky Rosen (D-NV) joined Senators Marsha Blackburn (R-TN), James Lankford (R-OK), and Chris Van Hollen (D-MD) in introducing a bipartisan resolution denouncing antisemitism at institutions of higher education due to the "spike in antisemitic incidents on college campuses across the nation."⁶⁴ University administrators themselves acknowledged the spike in antisemitism and celebration of Hamas immediately after the October 7 terrorist attack.⁶⁵

---

57 "Antisemitism Surges around World as Israel, Hamas Clash," *Voice of America* (VOA), October 15, 2023, https://www.voanews.com/a/antisemitism-surges-around-world-as-israel-hamas-clash/7306956.html.
58 "Antisemitic Incidents Spike following Hamas Attack on Israel, Anti-Defamation League Reports," *CBS News*, October 25, 2023, https://www.cbsnews.com/news/antisemitic-incidents-spike-following-hamas-attack-israel-anti-defamation-league/.
59 "Antisemitism Surges around World."
60 "ADL Records Dramatic Increase."
61 "Antisemitic Incidents Spike."
62 "Antisemitism Surges around World."
63 Ibid.
64 "Rosen Helps Introduce Bipartisan Resolution Condemning Antisemitism on College Campuses," Office of Senator Jacky Rosen, October 25, 2023, https://www.rosen.senate.gov/2023/10/25/rosen-helps-introduce-bipartisan-resolution-condemning-antisemitism-on-college-campuses/.
65 "Standing in Solidarity," Office of the President, Columbia University, October 2023, https://president.columbia.edu/news/standing-solidarity; "Tensions over Israel-Hamas War Roil College Campuses," *Washington Post*, October 18, 2023, https://www.washingtonpost.com/education/2023/10/18/university-israel-hamas-college-tensions/.

2. Rising Hamas Support in America Was Motivated to Reverse US Support of Israel

The empirical flaw with this claim is that visible signs of Hamas support and other forms of antisemitism increased markedly across Western countries immediately after Operation Al Aqsa Flood. Even before the Israeli invasion of Gaza, London police recorded a 1,353% increase in antisemitic crimes.[66] The British organization Community Security Trust reported an immediate 300% surge in antisemitic incidents throughout the United Kingdom, such as vandalizing kosher restaurants with Palestine slogans.[67] Before the Israeli invasion of Gaza, French Interior Minister Gérald Darmanin reported on social media that France saw a massive spike in antisemitic incidents, 588, resulting in 336 arrests.[68] Minister Darmanin also told French radio that his country suffered 100 antisemitic acts in the days after October 7, most involving graffiti displaying "swastikas, 'death to Jews,' calls to intifadas."[69] Home to Europe's most numerous Jewish population, France saw thousands defy a government prohibition against pro-Hamas rallies, with police using water cannons and tear gas to disperse them. Paris police chief Laurent Nuñez said he was concerned rallies would be "the scene of behaviors, slogans and acts of a principally anti-Jewish nature, inciting racial hate and making excuses for the (Hamas) terrorist attacks."[70] The European Union reported a 400% increase in antisemitic incidents since October 2023.[71] Politico noted "jubilant pro-Hamas rallies" in various European countries, with an "avalanche of social media posts rejoicing in the carnage of the attack on southern Israel."[72] Before the Israeli invasion of Gaza, Germany security monitors reported a 240% increase in antisemitic incidents.[73] The groundswell of Hamas of pro-Hamas support and antisemitism was not limited

---

66 Dov Waxman, "Antisemitism Has Moved from the Right to the Left in the US—and Falls Back on Long-Standing Stereotypes," The Conversation, November 2, 2023, https://theconversation.com/antisemitism-has-moved-from-the-right-to-the-left-in-the-us-and-falls-back-on-long-standing-stereotypes-215760.
67 "Antisemitism Surges around World."
68 "Antisemitic Incidents Spike."
69 Howard Mortman, "Europe Is Still Teeming with Antisemitism," Politico Europe, November 6, 2023, https://www.politico.eu/article/europe-is-still-teeming-with-antisemitism/.
70 Ibid.
71 *Experiences and Perceptions of Antisemitism—Third Survey on Discrimination and Hate Crime against Jews in the EU*, European Union Agency for Fundamental Rights (FRA), 2024, https://fra.europa.eu/en/publication/2024/experiences-and-perceptions-antisemitism-third-survey#publication-tab-1.
72 Mortman, "Europe Is Still Teeming with Antisemitism."
73 "ADL Records Dramatic Increase."

to Europe, extending to Australia and Russia, where pro-Hamas Muslim mobs went on Jew hunts at an airport in Dagestan.[74]

3. The Rise of Hamas Support in America Is an Artifact of Measurement Error

A common charge against Jews is that reports of antisemitism are unreliable because data often come from Jewish or Jewish-aligned organizations. But US law enforcement agencies such as the FBI shared the assessment that Operation Al Aqsa Flood galvanized a dangerous uptick in threats against American Jewry.[75] For this reason, law enforcement immediately after the October 7 terrorist massacre began supplying enhanced security to Jewish schools and synagogues in America.[76] Foreign intel services in the West likewise warned that pro-Hamas support and other forms of antisemitism were soaring in their countries as well after the October 7 terrorist massacre.[77] In addition to assessments of governments, the trend was found by non-Jewish organizations using a variety of methodologies.[78] Significantly, the rise in antisemitism was registered not only by Jews in American society. Surveys show that non-Jews in America also personally witnessed heightened antisemitism after October 7, 2023.[79] And, in an interesting survey, non-Jewish students erroneously assumed to be Jewish reported extraordinarily high levels of antisemitism directed against them after the October 7 Hamas terrorist rampage. Of this group, 29.5% reported being the targets of antisemitic remarks. Slightly less than one in five (18.8%) non-Jewish

---

74 Stephen Collinson, "Analysis: Antisemitism Thrives in an Unstable World," CNN, October 31, 2023, https://www.cnn.com/2023/10/31/politics/antisemitism-unstable-world-analysis/index.html.
75 Ibid.
76 Waxman, "Antisemitism Has Moved from the Right to the Left in the US."
77 Mortman, "Europe Is Still Teeming with Antisemitism."
78 See, for example, *Experiences and Perceptions of Antisemitism*.
79 "New AJC Report: 46% of American Jews Altered Behavior Out of Fear of Antisemitism," American Jewish Committee (AJC), February 2024, https://www.ajc.org/news/new-ajc-report-46-of-american-jews-altered-behavior-out-of-fear-of-antisemitism; "Increasing Numbers of Americans Say Antisemitism Is a Serious Problem," YouGov, February 2024, https://today.yougov.com/politics/articles/48112-increasing-numbers-of-americans-say-antisemitism-is-a-serious-problem; "Large Majorities of Americans Say Antisemitism Is a Serious Problem, AJC Survey Finds," NPR, February 13, 2024, https://www.npr.org/2024/02/13/1230928104/large-majorities-americans-antisemitism-serious-problem-ajc; "Campus Antisemitism: A Study of Campus Climate."

students reported having personally experienced an antisemitic incident.[80] In fact, we know that antisemitism is highly underreported given its prevalence since October 7, 2023. Surveys show that most victims of antisemitism (55%) do not report it for fear of more discrimination against them.[81]

Conclusion

Over the last couple decades, a major research question in terrorism studies has focused on whether the tactic works. In general, the answer appears to be no. But this research program has concentrated on the effect of the perpetrators on the target country in terms of its willingness and likelihood of granting political concessions.[82] In many ways, Operation Al Aqsa Flood was a colossal failure. Consistent with the academic literature, Hamas's terrorism rampage on October 7, 2023, elicited a powerful Israeli military response that substantially degraded the Foreign Terrorist Organization, negatively affected Gazans, and impended Palestinian national aspirations. But Operation Al Aqsa Flood and the resultant global intifada in the West demonstrate that terrorism can be effective in another way—by promoting discrimination and violence against minorities in other countries that the terrorist group hates. The October 7 terrorist attack and result Israeli response spurred unprecedented support in America for Hamas and antisemitism more generally particularly on the political left by

---

80 "Campus Antisemitism: A Study of Campus Climate."
81 Ibid.
82 Max Abrahms, ed., *The Routledge Companion to Terrorism Studies: New Perspectives and Topics* (London: Routledge, 2024); Max Abrahms, "Denying to Win: How Image-Savvy Militant Leaders Respond When Operatives Harm Civilians," *Journal of Strategic Studies* 43, no. 1 (2020): 47–73, https://doi.org/10.1080/01402390.2018.1511742; Max Abrahms, "The Strategic Model of Terrorism Revisited," in *The Oxford Handbook of Terrorism* (Oxford: Oxford University Press, 2019), 445–457; Max Abrahms, *Rules for Rebels: The Science of Victory in Militant History* (Oxford: Oxford University Press, 2018); Abrahms and Gottfried, "Does Terrorism Pay? An Empirical Analysis"; Max Abrahms and Philip B. K. Potter, "Explaining Terrorism: Leadership Deficits and Militant Group Tactics," *International Organization* 69, no. 2 (2015): 311–342, https://doi.org/10.1017/S0020818314000416; Abrahms, "The Credibility Paradox"; Abrahms, "The Political Effectiveness of Terrorism Revisited"; Abrahms, "What Terrorists Really Want"; Abrahms, "Al Qaeda's Scorecard"; Abrahms, "Why Terrorism Does Not Work"; Max Abrahms, Matthew Ward, and Ryan Kennedy, "Explaining Civilian Attacks: Terrorist Networks, Principal-Agent Problems and Target Selection," *Perspectives on Terrorism* 12, no. 1 (2018): 23–45, https://www.jstor.org/stable/26487513; Max Abrahms and Karolina Lula, "Why Terrorists Overestimate the Odds of Victory," *Perspectives on Terrorism* 6, no. 4/5 (2012): 46–62, https://www.jstor.org/stable/26296883.

reducing the audience costs of engaging in bigotry and extremism. The conflict between Israel and Hamas seemingly tapped into latest antisemitism in America and the West more generally, manifesting in previously invisible Hamas support. Alternate explanations have weaker empirical support. Alternate explanations rest on a weaker empirical basis. The hypotheses that Hamas support in America rose out of solidarity with Palestinians in response to the Israeli military campaign or reverse US support for Israel or that the apparent rise in Hamas support is an artifact of measurement errors do not withstand scrutiny. Future research should further explore how terrorism can work beyond the dyadic relationship of perpetrators and target country.

CHAPTER 6

Deterrence after October 7[1]

Ben Fishman

The events since October 7 constitute a modern-day test case of deterrence against terrorist groups and state actors. The language of deterrence and corresponding actions in the different cases of Israel and the United States against Hamas, Hezbollah, and Iran show how the United States and Israel have adopted different approaches to the region's conflicts. Further, the post-October Middle Eastern wars have had implications for deterrence in major conflicts in Europe and Asia.

Following a brief review of the events following Hamas's brutal attack on Israel, this chapter will consider how deterrence fits into Israel's historic national security "concept," how the post-Cold War theories of deterrence relate to the present conflict, and how the United States and Israel have applied deterrence after October 7, before examining lessons for other global conflicts. It concludes with speculation about how deterrence will apply in the second Trump administration.

Hamas Attacks, Israel Responds, and the Cycle of Escalation

Over the last year, Israel has fought lengthy and ongoing wars against Hamas and Hezbollah, non-state terrorist groups sponsored by Iran. Because the events of October 7 and their psychological and political implications have been documented in other chapters, I will provide only a brief overview of what happened that day, focusing on how those atrocities opened Israel to its longest and most

---

1   The author thanks Elizabeth Surman for superb research assistance and Michael Eisenstadt for guiding my thinking about deterrence.

complicated war and on what military measures are deemed necessary to restore safety and normalcy to the country.

Following October 7, Israel launched a major offensive into Gaza, Operation Swords of Iron, to rescue hostages and destroy Hamas, according to Prime Minister Netanyahu's maximalist goal. The more realistic goal favored by Israel's defense establishment was to destroy Hamas's military capabilities, in part because Hamas represents an ideology and political movement and is not just a terrorist group. Israel mobilized reserves and launched a major ground and air invasion targeting Hamas's leadership, weapons, and tunnel network. Rescuing hostages proved a more complicated effort. Out of a total of 250 who were taken, only eight have been rescued as of this writing.[2] More than 100 were released as part of trade during a brief November ceasefire. Among the hostages are twelve American citizens, four of whom are thought to be in Gaza and alive.

Hezbollah did not join Hamas in an invasion of Israel on October 7 as Hamas leader Yahya Sinwar allegedly hoped (perhaps warned off by a strong message from President Biden discussed below). However, it did fire enough munitions that led to the departure of more than 68,000 citizens from the North.[3]

When Israel invaded Gaza with ground forces to expose tunnels and destroy Hamas's military capabilities, it also engaged in an extensive bombing campaign that destroyed much of the territory's infrastructure. The human toll in Gaza as a result of Hamas's attack has been beyond devastating. Gaza's Health Ministry reported that, as of December 1, over 44,000 Gazans have died since October 7.[4] That number may be disputed, but the magnitude of human loss is indisputably tragic.[5] The World Bank's Preliminary Damage Assessment estimated that Gaza would cost $18.5 billion to rebuild just as of January 2024, which only accounts for infrastructure, not the ongoing and future humanitarian crisis.[6] Whether this response is considered a "just war" or "genocide" is the subject of other essays in

---

2   Matthew Mpoke Bigg, Ephrat Livni, and Aryn Baker, "Dozens of Hostages Remain in Gaza: What We Know," *New York Times*, September 3, 2024, https://www.nytimes.com/article/hostages-in-gaza-hamas.html.
3   "325 Days of War: Data Compilation of the Northern and Southern Communities," Taub Center, August 26, 2024, https://www.taubcenter.org.il/en/the-north-and-south/.
4   "Reported Impact Snapshot: Gaza Strip," UN OCHA, December 10, 2024, https://www.ochaopt.org/content/reported-impact-snapshot-gaza-strip-10-december-2024.
5   Gabriel Epstein, "Here's the Real Problem with the U.N.'s Revised Gaza Death Toll," *Washington Post*, May 24, 2024, https://www.washingtonpost.com/opinions/2024/05/24/united-nations-gaza-death-toll-adustment/.
6   "Joint World Bank, UN Report Assesses Damage to Gaza's Infrastructure," April 2, 2024, World Bank Group, https://www.worldbank.org/en/news/press-release/2024/04/02/joint-world-bank-un-report-assesses-damage-to-gaza-s-infrastructure.

volume. Regardless, trauma in Israel exists, both real physical and psychological, especially since 97 hostages (out of 240 taken on October 7) whose conditions are unknown remain in captivity more than one year into their captivity.[7] The families of those hostages have been demanding a ceasefire and hostage trade backed by mass protests, but the government's policy has not changed.

Beginning in April 2024, the war escalated when Iran attacked with drones and missiles nominally in response to Israel's targeted killing of three senior Iran Quds Force commanders in Lebanon. Most of those missiles and long-range drones were defeated before they reached Israel by a combination of Israeli fighter jets and the Iron Dome defense system as well as American sea and air-based interceptions. Arab military forces reportedly participated in the operation and opened their air space.[8] Because of the relatively limited damage, Israel's response was relatively limited as well.

On the northern front, Hezbollah and Palestinian militants initiated a cross border attack on October 8 that began a cycle of attacks and reprisals for several months.[9] In September, Israel escalated its campaign, called Operation Northern Arrows, to take on Hezbollah as it did Hamas. On September 18, it previewed a comprehensive attack with an operation that blew up hundreds of Hezbollah pagers. Damaging the communications system prefaced an air campaign that successfully led to the killing of Hezbollah's leader Hassan Nasrallah and several of the organization's other top officials. Israel subsequently launched a ground invasion into southern Lebanon. As of the beginning of November, Israel struck Beirut and other locations to degrade Hezbollah's military infrastructure, and Hezbollah has hit the areas around Haifa thirty-seven times and Tel Aviv fourteen times.[10]

---

7   Peter Saidel, Summer Said, and Anat Peled, "Hamas Took More Than 200 Hostages from Israel. Here's What We Know," *Wall Street Journal*, September 1, 2024, https://www.wsj.com/world/middle-east/hamas-hostages-israel-gaza-41432124; Michael Singh, "Denial or Punishment? The U.S.-Israel Debate about How Best to Deter Iran," The Washington Institute for Near East Policy, February 6, 2024, https://www.washingtoninstitute.org/policy-analysis/denial-or-punishment-us-israel-debate-about-how-best-deter-iran.

8   Stuart Winer, "Report: Gulf States, Including Saudi Arabia, Provided Intelligence on Iran Attack," *Times of Israel*, April 15, 2024, https://www.timesofisrael.com/report-gulf-states-including-saudi-arabia-provided-intelligence-on-iran-attack/.

9   "Hezbollah, Hamas Claim Attacks on Israel from Lebanon," Reuters, October 10, 2023, https://www.reuters.com/world/middle-east/salvo-rockets-fired-south-lebanon-towards-israel-security-sources-2023-10-10/.

10 Hanin Ghaddar et al., "Mapping Clashes along the Israel-Lebanon Border," The Washington Institute for Near East Policy, June 4, 2024. https://www.washingtoninstitute.org/policy-analysis/mapping-clashes-along-israel-lebanon-border; Daniel Byman, Seth G. Jones, and

In response to the deaths of Nasrallah and Hamas leader Ismael Haniya in early August, Iran launched a far more sophisticated attack, firing 200 ballistic missiles at Israel. Although there were no direct casualties, some of the missiles penetrated Israel's air defense systems and struck near strategic sites like the Mossad Headquarters and the Nevatim air base.[11]

After nearly a month consulting with the United States on the scope of its retaliatory strike—no targeting of Iran's nuclear or oil installations and minimizing civilian casualties—Israel launched a multi-stage air and missile offensive targeting Iran's air defenses and ballistic missile infrastructure. As of this writing, Iran is considering further escalation despite the first deployment of the US THAAD ballistic missile defense system to Israel.[12]

Deterrence and Israel's National Security "Concept"

The Gaza War challenged the key tenets of Israel's national security policy or "concept" set initially by Israel's founding father David Ben Gurion. He stipulated that the Jewish state must have a superior army that could ensure victory and defend the county; that superiority would deter hostile countries from attacking Israel; an exceptional intelligence corps would detect emerging threats; and wars should be short since Israel could not sustain extended wars given its limited ability to retain the mobilization of reserves.[13]

Over seventy-five years, these precepts have mostly remained constant. When they have failed, Israel has suffered its greatest defeats: October 1973, the long war in Lebanon, the Second Intifada, the 2006 war with Hezbollah, and now the Gaza War. Military superiority has never been the issue. Rather, intelligence failures, poor decision-making, and extended deployments have all led to strategic

---

Alexander Palmer, "Escalating to War between Israel, Hezbollah, and Iran," CSIS, October 4, 2024, https://www.csis.org/analysis/escalating-war-between-israel-hezbollah-and-iran.
11   David Gritten, Matt Murphy, and Patrick Jackson, "What We Know about Iran's Latest Missile Attack on Israel," BBC, October 3, 2024, https://www.bbc.com/news/articles/c70w1j0l4880.
12   "Background Press Call on Israel's Targeted Strikes against Military Targets in Iran," White House, October 26, 2024, https://www.whitehouse.gov/briefing-room/press-briefings/2024/10/25/background-press-call-on-israels-targeted-strikes-against-military-targets-in-iran/.
13   Gur Laish, "The Long War Phenomenon: Is a New Security Concept Required After October 7?" BESA Center Perspectives Paper No. 2,295, August 19, 2024, https://besacenter.org/the-long-war-phenomenon-is-a-new-security-concept-required-after-october-7/.

defeats as documented in post-war commissions.[14] In the Gaza War, Israel experienced a strategic surprise due to a failure in both tactical intelligence (by not communicating the warning of a possible attack throughout the military system) and strategically by miscalculating that the wall around Gaza and complex surveillance system would prevent a complex attack by Hamas.[15] Israel also grossly overestimated the extent to which Hamas under Sinwar was satisfied with the status quo effectively running Gaza with funding from the Qataris and others, which the Israeli leadership supported. It turned out Sinwar had different aspirations.

Over the last decade, Israel pursued a different strategy to counter Iran and its regional proxies. Israel has followed "gray zone" operations developed by former IDF Chief of Staff Gadi Eisenkot (unacknowledged operations, such as assassinations, cyber-attacks, bombings, etc.), which aimed to prevent all-out war on several fronts. Israel called this The Campaign Between the Wars—known by its Hebrew acronym, MAMBAM. Eisenkot described the aims of MAMBAM to "deter the enemy and keep war at bay; weaken enemies and other malign forces in the region; reduce the enemy's force build processes; help create optimal conditions for IDF to win the next war; help generate legitimacy for Israel to use force while simultaneously damaging the enemy's legitimacy."[16] But with the Hamas operation followed by an all-out IDF response, the "gray zone" became a hot zone with Hamas, and then with Hezbollah. Even if the IDF considered the Palestinian arena apart from other regional threats, ignoring Hamas and Sinwar's strategy made Israel vulnerable to an October 7-like attack. According to one former senior Israel defense official, MAMBAM "failed completely."[17]

Regardless of these failures, Israel has maintained a "qualitative military edge" (QME) over its neighbors even as more advanced technology has proliferated. A 2008 US law required the United States to ensure that any US sales or transfers to other regional actors had to be evaluated in terms of QME.[18]

---

14 Scott Abramson, "How Israelis Probe Their Failings," *Mosaic*, July 1, 2024. https://mosaic-magazine.com/essay/israel-zionism/2024/07/how-israelis-probe-their-failings/.

15 Amnon Sofrin, "The Intelligence Failure of October 7—Roots and Lessons," Jerusalem Strategic Tribune, November 26, 2023, https://jstribune.com/sofrim-the-intelligence-failure-of-october-7-roots-and-lessons/; Michel Wyss, "The October 7 Attack: An Assessment of the Intelligence Failings," *CTC Sentinel*, https://ctc.westpoint.edu/the-october-7-attack-an-assessment-of-the-intelligence-failings/.

16 Gadi Eisenkot and Gabi Simoni, "Guidelines for Israel's National Security Strategy," The Washington Institute for Near East Policy, Policy Focus 160, 2019.

17 Interview with Zohar Palti, November 5, 2024, Washington, D.C.

18 US Congress. *Public Law 110-429—United States-Israel Energy Cooperation Act*, §201, October 15, 2008. https://www.govinfo.gov/content/pkg/PLAW-110publ429/pdf/PLAW-110publ429.pdf.

The October 7 attack and its aftermath has also demonstrated how Israel's dependence on the United States to retain its military superiority is an evolution away from its ethos of self-reliance. In case of extended wars, Israel has relied on extensive resupply from the United States, starting in 1973. Currently, the United States provides Israel with $3.8 billion of annual military assistance provided most recently by a ten-year MOU signed in 2018.[19] Since the Gaza War, the United States has added $12.6 billion in support, including ammunition, bombs, and restocking Iran Dome interceptors.[20] These funds demonstrate additional evidence of Israel's reliance in case of extended wars. Another result of the extended mobilization has been the negative impact on Israel's economy. As of late September, estimated costs for the war were approximately $67 billion, not counting the October salvos with Iran and Hezbollah. In October, Moody's lowered Israel's credit rating by two grades in the second reduction of this year.[21]

Israel also suffered diplomatically as a result of the October wars. In the region, it has put enormous political pressure on its peace treaty partners, Egypt and Jordan, increased the stress on its relationship with the UAE, and put off indefinitely normalization with Saudi Arabia. Indeed, Crown Prince Mohammed bin Salman described Israel's behavior in Gaza as genocide.[22] Beforehand, he only sought some progress between Israel and the Palestinians to pursue normalization in addition to a series of bilateral agreements with the United States.

Mechanisms and Language of Deterrence

The post-October-7 wars have illuminated the different mechanisms of deterrence by denial and deterrence by punishment. Denial means "to deter an action by making it infeasible or unlikely to succeed." In contrast, deterrence by punishment "threatens severe penalties, such as nuclear escalation or severe economic

---

19 "Ten-Year Memorandum of Understanding Between the United States and Israel," U.S. Embassy in Israel, October 1, 2018, https://il.usembassy.gov/ten-year-memorandum-of-understanding-between-the-united-states-and-israel/.

20 Jim Zanotti and Jeremy Sharp, "Israel and Hamas Conflict in Brief: Overview, U.S. Policy, and Options for Congress," Congressional Research Service, October 4, 2024, https://crsreports.congress.gov/product/pdf/R/R47828.

21 Sharon Wrobel, "Moody's Lowers Israel's Credit Rating for 2nd Time This Year, amid Hezbollah Escalation," *Times of Israel*, September 28, 2024, https://www.timesofisrael.com/moodys-slashes-israels-credit-rating-amid-hezbollah-escalation-war-costs-to-economy/.

22 Jennifer Gnana, "MBS Condemns Israel's 'Genocide' in Gaza as Saudi Frustrations Mount," *Al Monitor*, November 11, 2024, https://www.al-monitor.com/originals/2024/11/mbs-condemns-israels-genocide-gaza-saudi-frustrations-mount.

sanctions, if an attack occurs. The focus of deterrence by punishment is not the direct defense of the contested commitment but rather threats of wider punishment that would raise the cost of an attack."[23] There are several other theoretical types of deterrence that address the scope and timelines, but they are less relevant to the post-October 7 world.

How Israel and the United States Describe Deterrence Illustrates Their Key Differences

Since October 7, Israel has adopted an almost exclusively punitive approach to Iran and its proxies. It prosecuted a vicious ground and air war to destroy Hamas operators, its leaders, and military infrastructure. It did so regardless of the hostages taken by Hamas and domestic pressure for a ceasefire. Then Israel launched Operation Northern Arrows to eliminate Hezbollah's top leader and degrade its military capabilities, specifically Iranian-provided long-range rockets.

Table 1 demonstrates how senior Israeli officials articulated an offensive strategy at each phase of the conflict. If Israel had positioned itself defensively with walls and the Iron Dome before the war, it switched immediately to punish its adversaries after October 7. The words "destroy," "wipe out," and "exact a price" exemplify senior Israeli officials' rhetoric—and actions—after October 7. Prime Minister Netanyahu explicitly articulated this punitive strategy during his September speech to the UN General Assembly: "If you strike us, *we will strike you*" (emphasis mine).[24]

Another variation of the punitive strategy that Israel has attempted to adopt, or at least use to justify, its actions to the United States, is to "escalate to de-escalate[?]."[25] This nuclear deterrence concept from the Cold War posits that once a conflict escalates, one side will be incentivized to de-escalate (e.g., folding in poker). To justify its complex attacks against Hezbollah, Israel reportedly told US security officials that this was their strategy until a ceasefire could endure. While US-led negotiators pursue negotiations to restore calm on the Lebanese

---

23 Michael J. Mazarr, "Understanding Deterrence," RAND Corporation, 2018, https://www.rand.org/content/dam/rand/pubs/perspectives/PE200/PE295/RAND_PE295.pdf.
24 "In UN Remarks, Netanyahu Says Israel Will Keep 'Degrading Hezbollah' until Objectives Are Met," PBS, September 27, 2024, https://www.pbs.org/newshour/politics/watch-live-israeli-prime-minister-benjamin-netanyahu-delivers-remarks-at-2024-un-general-assembly.
25 Barak Ravid, "U.S. Fears War in Lebanon but Hopes Israeli Attacks Push Hezbollah to a Deal," Axios, September 21, 2024, https://www.axios.com/2024/09/21/us-israel-lebanon-hezbollah-war-pressure-diplomatic-deal.

border, Israel has deployed 50,000 troops in Lebanon, frequently bombing Hezbollah targets, and Hezbollah continues to launch rockets against Israel.[26] Even though Israel has a number of impressive tactical achievements, punitive deterrence alone has come up short as a strategy.

On some occasions, punitive deterrence is most effective when an attack is planned carefully and executed precisely. Israel launched a complex and effective retaliatory attack targeting Iran's air defense systems and its ballistic missile and drone infrastructure. The attack reportedly was coordinated with but assisted by the United States.

Table 1. Israel's Deterrence by Punishment

Date	Context	Speaker	Quote (emphases added)	Source
10/07/23	October 7	Prime Minister Netanyahu	"The IDF will immediately use all its strength to *destroy Hamas's capabilities*. We will destroy them and we will *forcefully avenge this dark day* that they have forced on the State of Israel and its citizens. . . . All of the places which Hamas is deployed, hiding and operating in, that wicked city, *we will turn them into rubble*."	Israel's Ministry of Foreign Affairs
10/12/23	October 7	Defense Minister Gallant	"*We will wipe out this thing called Hamas.* Hamas—the Islamic State of Gaza—will be wiped from the face of the earth. *It will not continue to exist.* There will be no situation in which Israeli children are murdered and we all go about our business."	Times of Israel
04/14/24	Iran's first attack on Israel	Minister Gantz. Member of War Cabinet	"In the face of the Iranian threat, we will build a regional coalition, and *we will exact a price from Iran* in the way and at the time that is right for us."	JNS

(*Continued*)

---

26 "Israeli Media: 50,000 Troops Fail to Capture a Single Village in Lebanon," *Middle East Monitor*, November 3, 2024, https://www.middleeastmonitor.com/20241103-israeli-media-50000-troops-fail-to-capture-a-single-village-in-lebanon/.

Table 1. (*Continued*)

Date	Context	Speaker	Quote (emphases added)	Source
07/21/24	Israel's attack on Yemen	Prime Minister Netanyahu	"From the beginning of the war, I made it clear that *Israel will act against all attackers*, which is why we struck Houthi targets in Yemen yesterday in response to the deadly drone attack near the U.S. Consulate in Tel Aviv. The targeted port is used for smuggling weapons from Iran to the Houthis, who have attacked Israel and other nations. The international community must support Israel's actions to *defend against this Iranian terror axis* and *ensure the aggressors pay a heavy price.*"	X
09/18/24	Pager attacks	IDF Chief Halevi	"The rule is that every time we work on a certain stage, the next two stages are already ready to advance. At each stage, *the price for Hezbollah must be high.*"	Reuters
9/27/24	Speech to UN	Prime Minister Netanyahu	"If you strike us, *we will strike you*.... For too long, the world has appeased Iran. That *appeasement must end*.... *Israel has every right to remove this threat* and return our citizens to their home safely. And that's exactly what we're doing."	PBS
10/1/24	Iran's attack on Israel	Netanyahu	"Iran made a big mistake tonight—and *it will pay for it*. The regime in Iran does not understand *our determination to defend ourselves and our determination to retaliate* against our enemies."	CNN
10/18/24	Sinwar's assassination	Defense Minister Gallant	"Sinwar died while beaten, persecuted and on the run—he didn't die as a commander, but as someone who only cared for himself. This is a clear message to all of our enemies—*the IDF will reach anyone who attempts to harm the citizens of Israel or our security forces*, and we will bring you to justice."	CBS
10/19/24	Strike on Netanyahu's home	Prime Minister Netanyahu	"Nothing *will deter us*. The agents of Iran who tried to assassinate me and my wife today made a bitter mistake."	Times of Israel

Date	Context	Speaker	Quote (emphases added)	Source
10/25/24	Israel's strike on Iran	IDF Spokesperson Hagari	"If the regime in Iran were to make the mistake of beginning a new round of escalation, *we will be obligated to respond*. Our message is clear: all those who threaten the State of Israel and seek to drag the region into wider escalation *will pay a heavy price*. We demonstrated today that *we have both the capability and the resolve to act decisively*. And we are prepared *on offense and defense to defend the State of Israel* and the people of Israel."	X
10/31/2	Anticipating Iran's possible response	Prime Minister Netanyahu	"The supreme objective that I have set for the IDF and the security services is to *prevent Iran from attaining nuclear weapons*.... I have not taken, we have not taken, and *we will not take, our eyes off this objective*."	Fox News

The United States: Deterrence by Denial

Immediately after October 7, President Biden stressed his support for Israel, its right to defend itself, and his outrage against Hamas's attacks that killed and took more than 200 hostages, including Americans. More importantly, he offered the weight of the United States military behind Israel. He warned "any country, organization, anyone thinking of taking advantage of the situation, I have one word: Don't. Don't."[27] This emphasis on defending Israel and enhancing US capabilities to symbolically and materially contribute to Israel's self-defense were a constant theme of US statements—deterrence by denial—as Table 2 demonstrates.

For example, according to reports, Hamas leader Yahya Sinwar wanted Hezbollah to join Hamas's attack.[28] Declassified intelligence may eventually

---

27 "Remarks by President Biden on the Terrorist Attacks in Israel," White House, October 10, 2023, https://www.whitehouse.gov/briefing-room/speeches-remarks/2023/10/10/remarks-by-president-biden-on-the-terrorist-attacks-in-israel-2/.

28 Ronen Bergman, Adam Rasgon, and Patrick Kingsley, "Secret Documents Show Hamas Tried to Persuade Iran to Join Its Oct. 7 Attack," *New York Times*, October 12, 2024, https://www.nytimes.com/2024/10/12/world/middleeast/hamas-israel-war.html.

reveal Nasrallah's—and Iran's—assessment of October 7. But Biden's deployment of the USS Gerald Ford Carrier Strike Group to the eastern Mediterranean likely affected their reluctance to join October 7.[29] Neither Hezbollah nor Iran tested the United States for several months following October 7.

Throughout the following year, the United States stressed that it would support Israel's defense in a conflict and deployed more and increasingly sophisticated assets to the region. But, while the United States played a significant role helping Israel defend itself from the April[30] and October[31] Iranian missile attacks, it left the retaliatory strikes to Israel—even if it negotiated the extent of the strikes to avoid Iran's energy sources and nuclear sites and minimize civilian casualties. Further, the Biden administration sent the Terminal High Altitude Area Defense (THAAD) to Israel to further deter Iran's response to Israel's attack. Significantly, this was the first time US combat soldiers (THAAD operators) deployed to Israel. Yet, for over a year, the United States has stepped up its deterrence by denial to defend Israel, but the United States itself has not participated in attacking Iran, Hezbollah, or Hamas, not even attempts to rescue American hostages in Gaza.

The exceptions were US retaliation against attacks by Shi'a militias in Iraq and against the Houthis, who effectively closed commercial shipping in the Red Sea. According to CENTCOM counts, the United States conducted seventy-one operations against the Houthis in September and October, including both defensive actions and preemptive strikes against UAVs, UASs, anti-ship ballistic missiles, as well as the B-2 mission described below. This is in addition to at least 102 US-UK strikes on Houthi capabilities as of April 24, 2024.[32] The few times Houthi drones and rockets reached Israeli territory (out of more

---

29 Idrees Ali and Phil Stewart, "U.S. Publicly Announces Submarine Move to Middle East amid Israel-Iran Tensions," Reuters, August 11, 2024, https://www.reuters.com/world/middle-east/us-publicly-announces-submarine-move-middle-east-amid-israel-iran-tensions-2024-08-12/.
30 "Statement from President Joe Biden on Iran's Attacks against the State of Israel," White House, April 14, 2024, https://www.whitehouse.gov/briefing-room/statements-releases/2024/04/13/statement-from-president-joe-biden-on-irans-attacks-against-the-state-of-israel/.
31 "Background Press Call on Israel's Targeted Strikes Against Military Targets in Iran," White House, October 26, 2024, https://www.whitehouse.gov/briefing-room/press-briefings/2024/10/25/background-press-call-on-israels-targeted-strikes-against-military-targets-in-iran/.
32 Michael Knights, "Assessing the Houthi War Effort since October 2023," *CTC Sentinel*, April 2024, https://ctc.westpoint.edu/assessing-the-houthi-war-effort-since-october-2023/.

than 200 missiles and 170 drones launched at Israel in the last year,[33] Israel bombed Yemen in response on July 20, September 29, and December 26.[34] Israel's most recent attack hit Sanna's airport among other targets and killed six.[35]

One puzzle for future analysis is to what extent the US defense umbrella after October 7 enabled Israel to take such a punitive approach against Iran and its proxies. In other words, will the combination of punitive deterrence from Israel and deterrence by denial be a sufficient deterrent against Iran and its proxies' malign activities, or worse, compel Iran to race to a nuclear weapon?

At some point, the United States will have to demonstrate its own seriousness to prevent Iran from developing a nuclear weapon, especially if it doesn't want Israel to attempt a raid on its own. To date, the closest the United States has come to a significant offensive measure and warning to Iran is when it struck underground Houthi targets with a long-ranged B-2 bomber. The Pentagon explained that the purpose of the strike was to "Target facilities that our adversaries seek to keep out of reach, no matter how deeply buried underground, hardened, or fortified."[36] However, if that message was intended to intimidate Iran, Iran may have interpreted the threat in the exact opposite manner: if the United States is using its most sophisticated weapon and still can't make a serious dent in the Houthis' capability to close traffic to the Red Sea, the United States. will remain a paper tiger. Indeed, a Houthi spokesman said, "we will confront [the bombing] with escalation, and America will pay a heavy price."[37]

---

33 Emanuel Fabian, "Houthi Drone Crashes in South as Terror Group Said to Brace for Major Israeli Attack," *Times of Israel*, December 25, 2024, https://www.timesofisrael.com/houthi-drone-crashes-in-south-as-terror-group-said-to-brace-for-major-israeli-attack/.

34 "Israel Strikes Houthi Targets in Yemen, Killing at Least Four People," Reuters, September 29, 2024, https://www.reuters.com/world/middle-east/israel-launches-strikes-yemeni-houthi-targets-2024-09-29/; Ameneh Mehvar, Sherwan Hindreen Ali, et al., "Middle East Overview September 2024," ACLED, October 4, 2024, https://acleddata.com/2024/10/04/middle-east-september-2024-special-issue-middle-east-crisis/#keytrends5.

35 "Israel Strikes Houthi Targets in Yemen, Killing Six," Reuters, December 27, 2024, https://www.reuters.com/world/middle-east/israel-strikes-yemens-sanaa-airport-ports-power-stations-2024-12-26/.

36 Todd Lopez, "U.S. Strikes Underground Targets in Yemen," U.S. Department of Defense, October 17, 2024, https://www.defense.gov/News/News-Stories/Article/article/3938958/us-strikes-underground-targets-in-yemen/.

37 Tom O'Connor, "Houthis Vow 'America Will Pay a Heavy Price' for Bombing Yemen Amid Crisis," *Newsweek*, October 4, 2024, https://www.newsweek.com/houthis-vow-america-will-pay-heavy-price-bombing-yemen-amid-crisis-19648.

Table 2. US Deterrence by Denial

Date	Context	Speaker	Quote (emphases added)	Source
10/08/23	Deployment of the Ford carrier strike group to the eastern Mediterranean	A senior defense official	"These posture increases were intended to serve as an unequivocal demonstration in deed and not only in words of U.S. support for Israel's defense and serve as a deterrent signal to Iran, Lebanese Hezbollah, and any other proxy across the region who might be considering exploiting the current situation to escalate the conflict. Those adversaries should think twice."	USNI News
10/10/23	October 7	President Biden	"The United States has also enhanced our military force posture in the region *to strengthen our deterrence*... Let me say again—to any country, any organization, anyone thinking of taking advantage of this situation, I have one word: *Don't. Don't.*"	White House
04/13/24	Iran's attack on Israel	President Biden	"I condemn these attacks in the strongest possible terms. At my direction, to support the defense of Israel, the U.S. military moved aircraft and ballistic missile defense destroyers to the region over the course of the past week." "Thanks to these deployments and the extraordinary skill of our servicemembers, we helped Israel take down nearly all of the incoming drones and missiles."	White House
08/11/24	Deployment of submarine to the region	Pentagon Statement	"Secretary Austin reiterated the United States' commitment to take every possible step to defend Israel and noted the strengthening of U.S. military force posture and capabilities throughout the Middle East in light of escalating regional tensions."	Reuters

Date	Context	Speaker	Quote (emphases added)	Source
09/28/24	Nasrallah's assassination	President Biden	"The United States fully supports Israel's right to defend itself against Hezbollah, Hamas, the Houthis, and any other Iranian-supported terrorist groups. Just yesterday, I directed my Secretary of Defense to *further enhance the defense posture of U.S. military forces in the Middle East region to deter aggression* and reduce the risk of a broader regional war."	White House
10/01/24	Iran's attack on Israel	Secretary of Defense Austin	"We condemn this outrageous act of aggression by Iran, and *we call on Iran to halt any further attacks,* including from its proxy terrorist groups.... Our forces remain postured to protect U.S. troops and partners in the Middle East, and the Department maintains significant capability to defend our people, *provide further support for Israel's self-defense, and deter further escalation.*"	Defense Department
10/02/24	U.S. B-2 bomber strike on Yemen	Secretary of Defense Austin	"This was a unique demonstration of the United States' ability to target facilities that our adversaries seek to keep out of reach, *no matter how deeply buried underground, hardened, or fortified.*... The United States will not hesitate to take action to defend American lives and assets; *to deter attacks against civilians and our regional partners;* and to protect freedom of navigation and increase the safety and security in these waterways for U.S., coalition, and merchant vessels. We will continue to make clear to the Houthis that *there will be consequences* for their illegal and reckless attacks."	Defense Department

(Continued)

Table 2. (*Continued*)

Date	Context	Speaker	Quote (emphases added)	Source
10/17/24	Sinwar's assassination	Secretary of Defense Austin	"The killing today of Yahya Sinwar, the leader of the terrorist group Hamas, by Israeli forces is a *major achievement in counterterrorism*... The United States fully supports Israel's right to defend itself against Hamas and other terrorist groups. At President Biden's direction, our forces in the Middle East stand *ready to defend Israel, deter aggression, and reduce the risk of all-out war* in the region."	Defense Department
10/21/24	Anticipating Israel's strike on Iran	Secretary of Defense Austin	"We're going to do—continue to do—everything we can… to dial down the tensions and hopefully *get both parties to begin to de-escalate*."	*Times of Israel*
10/25/24	THAAD deployment and Israel's response to Iran	President Biden (readout of call with Prime Minister Netanyahu)	"Should Iran choose to respond, *we are fully prepared to once again defend against any attack*. We recently *deployed a THAAD battery*, which is a ballistic missile defense system, to Israel. And we have worked to *strengthen Israel's air defense systems* in the run-up to tonight's response."	White House

Despite the concrete and rhetorical defense assistance the United States has provided since October 7, Israel has never really responded seriously to American requests to allow more humanitarian assistance into Gaza or to prosecute the war while limiting civilian casualties. The only time the issue came to a head occurred when Secretary of State Blinken and Secretary of Defense Austin sent a letter to two of their counterparts on October 13 warning Israel that, if Israel did not improve humanitarian conditions in Gaza within thirty days, the administration would review its military assistance to Israel.[38] Israel demonstrated enough progress so that the administration could justify that Israel had met the standard of a humanitarian response. But the political firestorm produced by the leaked letter deepened the mistrust of supporters of President Biden and Prime Minister Netanyahu, particularly in the days running up to the US election. For

---

38   Barak Ravid (@BarakRavid), "Secretary of State Blinken & Secretary of Defense Austin sent a letter on Monday to Israel . . . ," X (formerly Twitter), October 15, 2024, https://x.com/BarakRavid/status/1846182689222664471.

such a strong bilateral security relationship exemplified by US support to Israel after October 7, tension will remain over the issue of Palestinian rights and a Palestinian state. Even the dealmaker President Trump may wade into the issue as part of a regional peace agreement.

Broader Global Implications

Other partners and allies are most likely looking at the US reaction to Israel's wars against Hezbollah, Hamas, and Iran with great interest. The manner in which the United States deployed significant assets in defense of Israel yet adopted a deterrence by denial strategy will be examined closely by Ukraine and NATO as well as America's Indo-Pacific allies. Has the United States' commitment to Israel's defense made our allies more or less confident in their own security? If the United States has practiced deterrence by denial in the Middle East, can they be confident that such deterrence will be sufficient to address their own security needs against the great powers China and Russia?

Europe

When Russia invaded Ukraine, the Biden administration immediately condemned Russia's violation of Ukraine's territorial integrity and worked to rally NATO allies behind Ukraine. Biden used a dramatic train ride from Poland to Kyiv to demonstrate his commitment to defending the country against Russian aggression. Traveling just before the war's first anniversary, Biden proclaimed, "One year later, Kyiv stands. And Ukraine stands. Democracy stands. The Americans stand with you, and the world stands with you."[39] The US benefits strategically the longer Russia is fighting a long war, draining its resources, personnel and exploiting their technology.

Although America's strategic rationale for defending Ukraine is clear, the United States has made every decision to increase support for Ukraine based on a judgment of how Russia will respond. For example, when the United States decided to provide High Mobility Artillery Rocket Systems (HIMARS) in June 2022, it modified the system's range so the system could not strike as deeply into

---

39 Evan Vucci et al., "Biden Declares 'Kyiv Stands' in Surprise Visit to Ukraine," Associated Press, February 20, 2023, https://apnews.com/article/russia-ukraine-zelenskyy-biden-f00af220669457d5ba07127c7e57a27b.

Russia.[40] In May 2023, the president authorized the defense department to train eighteen F-16 pilots with other European allies providing the fighter jets. And in November, the Biden administration authorized the supply of anti-personnel landmines and longer-range missiles. As of late September, the United States has provided Ukraine with nearly $60 billion in a combination of direct assistance or drawdown authority—a process by which the United States can deliver its own equipment to partners.[41]

Despite billions of dollars in support for Ukraine to defend itself, the strategic goal of deterring Russia from achieving territorial gains or global aspirations remains elusive. Russian internal discord has not materialized and the June 2023 revolt from Wagner chief Yevgeny Prigozhin was quickly put down. Most recently, North Korea has deployed thousands of troops to aid Russia. There is no end in sight for the war if the United States continues to arm and fund Ukraine without changing the war's dynamics. More dangerously, Russia could truly escalate the war by deploying tactical nuclear weapons as Putin has threatened.[42]

The US response to the wars in Ukraine and Israel featured certain similarities: in both cases it provided significant resources and arms, but it has been unwilling to engage directly with the initiators of the conflicts (Russia and Iran). For Israel, the United States deployed the most significant military assets available immediately following October 7. While the United States played a serious role defending Israel from the April and September Iranian missile attacks, it has yet to fire a shot at Iran or its proxies save for a few strikes against Iraqi militias aligned with Iran who were attacking US forces in western Syria. Where the United States has engaged against the Houthis, it has failed to defeat the Yemeni group and reopen the Red Sea—a key function of the US Navy.

If the United States is reluctant to engage Iran and its proxies with force—deterrence by punishment—the likely lesson Ukraine will take from the Middle

---

40 Michael R. Gordon and Gordon Lubold, "U.S. Altered HIMARS Rocket Launchers to Keep Ukraine from Firing Missiles into Russia," *Wall Street Journal*, December 5, 2022, https://www.wsj.com/articles/u-s-altered-himars-rocket-launchers-to-keep-ukraine-from-firing-missiles-into-russia-11670214338.

41 "Fact Sheet on U.S. Security Assistance to Ukraine," September 26, 2024, U.S. Department of Defense, https://media.defense.gov/2024/Sep/26/2003554492/-1/-1/1/20240926-UKRAINE-FACT-SHEET-PDA-66-AND-USAI-T21.PDF.

42 Laurence Arnold and Ramsey Al-Rikabi, "Will Putin Use Nuclear Weapons? What Russia's Doctrine Change Means," Bloomberg, November 19, 2024, https://www.bloomberg.com/news/articles/2024-11-19/will-putin-use-nuclear-weapons-what-russia-s-doctrine-change-means?sref=FVpgSLg0.

East since October 7 is that the United States will not participate offensively to protect Ukraine. The United States will fund and supply Ukraine with arms, but nothing more.

Asia

In 2022, the Biden administration released a strategy document on expanding its presence and strengthening its alliances in the Indo-Pacific. The strategy encompasses multiple initiatives, including economic, trade, and climate cooperation.[43] In terms of regional security, the document focuses on two developments: (1) the formalization of trilateral cooperation between the United States, Japan, and South Korea—where Japanese-Korean tensions limited cooperation in the past, and (2) the formalization of an Australian-US-UK partnership (AUKUS) to better coordinate security in the region. The United States also initiated a more sustained dialogue with India, holding five 2+2 dialogues between the respective secretaries of state and defense.[44]

At the same time, Chinese and North Korean provocations have also increased. In response to China's October 18 military exercises in the Taiwan Strait, a Pentagon spokesperson said, "This military pressure operation is irresponsible, disproportionate, and destabilizing. Deterrence remains strong in the Indo-Pacific, and the Department remains confident in its current force posture and operations in the region."[45]

On October 30, North Korea tested a new ballistic missile capable of hitting the U.S. mainland. They have also sent troops to aid Russa's campaign against Ukraine. US and allied deterrence or "extended deterrence" has clearly not affected these provocative behaviors.

In response to the ballistic missile test, the United States, South Korea, and Japan issued a joint statement: "The United States reiterates that its commitments

---

43 "The United States' Enduring Commitment to the Indo-Pacific: Marking Two Years since the Release of the Administration's Indo-Pacific Strategy," U.S. Department of State, February 9, 2024, https://www.state.gov/wp-content/uploads/2024/02/Indo-Pacific-Strategy-Second-Anniversary-Fact-Sheet.pdf.
44 "Joint Statement on the Fifth Annual India-U.S. 2+2 Ministerial Dialogue," U.S. Department of Defense, November 10, 2023, https://www.defense.gov/News/Releases/Release/Article/3586228/joint-statement-on-the-fifth-annual-india-us-22-ministerial-dialogue/.
45 "Statement from Pentagon Press Secretary Maj. Gen. Pat Ryder on PRC Military Drills near Taiwan," U.S. Department of Defense, October 14, 2024, https://www.defense.gov/News/Releases/Release/Article/3934707/statement-from-pentagon-press-secretary-maj-gen-pat-ryder-on-prc-military-drill/.

to the defense of the ROK and Japan are ironclad and backed by the full range of capabilities, including nuclear. In addition, the three countries will continue to strengthen our trilateral security cooperation to deter and respond to the DPRK's advancing nuclear and ballistic missile threats more effectively."[46] Additionally, the United States led a trilateral aerial exercise with fighter craft escorting a long-range stealth bomber. The test of this action will be whether there are further ballistic missile tests and if so, when.

China has positioned itself to launch an offensive against Taiwan, seize the South China Sea Islands, or, more dangerously, join the DPRK in destabilizing the Korean Peninsula. At the same time, the DPRK continues to develop its nuclear arsenal and test ballistic missiles that could be used for retaliatory purposes.

The lessons for our Asian partners from the US response to Israel's post-October wars are twofold: President Biden rushed to embrace Israel's right to defend itself and provided Israel additional means to do so; but regardless of symbolism, our partners look for examples of how the United States would actually participate in the defense of treaty allies Japan, Korea, and the Philippines, and to support Taiwan, which the United States is not obligated to defend. One important difference between the US posture in the Middle East and the Indo-Pacific is the credible commitment of around 100,000 US troops and dozens of assets in the region. The deaths of American soldiers have traditionally been a *casus belli*. China or the DPRK would have to consider that factor as part of any potential offensive actions.

Looking Forward

It is too early to predict how the second Trump administration will treat the Israel-Iran conflict and its regional offshoots. However, judging from early statements about Israel and Iran as well as the track record of the first Trump administration, it is more than likely that Trump will continue practicing deterrence by denial in the region if not selective disengagement.

During his transition, Trump and officials in his first administration have suggested he wants Israel to conclude the war in Gaza.[47] The Trump administration

---

46 "Joint Statement on the Republic of Korea-U.S.-Japan Trilateral Vice Foreign Ministerial Meeting," U.S. Department of State, October 16, 2024, https://www.state.gov/joint-statement-on-the-republic-of-korea-u-s-japan-trilateral-vice-foreign-ministerial-meeting-2/#:~:text=The%20Deputy%20Secretary%20reiterated%20that,and%20the%20Japan%2DUS%20Alliance.

47 Jacob Magid, "Trump Told Netanyahu He Wants Gaza War over by Time He Enters Office," *Times of Israel*, October 30, 2024. https://www.timesofisrael.com/trump-told-netanyahu-he-wants-gaza-war-over-by-time-he-enters-office-sources/.

is expected to return to "maximum pressure" (sanctions) against Tehran—intimating they will decrease kinetic behavior to Iran's malign behavior and focus more on strengthening the sanctions regime. Yet at the same time, one senior official on the transition team said, "If nobody believes you have a credible threat of military force, then you're going to lose deterrence."[48] How the next administration will establish such a credible threat without using force against Iran or elsewhere remains unanswered.

During his first administration, Trump favored deterrence by denial with the exception of the killing of IRGC Quds Force commander Qassem Suleimani, who was responsible for the deaths of hundreds of Americans in Iraq. But Suleimani was also a target of opportunity because Israel and the United States had highly specific intelligence on his location. Ultimately, Trump could face a decision if maximum pressure fails and Iran makes a concerted effort to change from nuclear enrichment to weaponization. October 7 also demonstrates how even the best intelligence with high levels of certainty is never perfect.

When it comes to Europe, Trump is likely to remain skeptical about NATO and maintain his cozy relationship with Putin. (Trump speaks with him regularly, whereas Biden has shunned the Russian president.) Trump is likely to favor a negotiated settlement with Russia to end the Ukraine War, as opposed to NATO and Biden's firm support for Ukraine. In combination with Trump's negative view of the NATO alliance and the Article V commitment, overall deterrence against Russia may decrease.

Trump's policy on China is more difficult to predict. On the one hand, the president-elect and many of his appointees are so-called China Hawks who view China primarily as a threat. Trump's intended tariffs against China are part of that strategy. But it's unclear whether the new administration will view the alliance structures built in the last four years as beneficial or treat them with little regard, similar to NATO. If Trump presents himself as a dealmaker, as he did in his high-profile meeting with President Xi and Kim Jong-Un during his first term, our Asian partners will lose their sense of security. One lesson US allies—NATO, Ukraine, our Asian partners, and even Israel—should take from October 7 is that they will likely require at least some form of deterrence by denial from the United States as key parts of their own national security strategies, especially against China and Russia.

---

48 Robbie Gramer and Eric Bazail-Emil, "A Sneak Peek on Trump's Iran Policy," Politico, November 8, 2024. https://www.politico.com/newsletters/national-security-daily/2024/11/08/a-sneak-peak-on-trumps-iran-policy-00183727.

CHAPTER 7

US-Israel Relations in the Wake of October 7

Jonathan Rynhold

Introduction

This chapter examines US-Israel relations in the year following the murderous Hamas attack on Israel on October 7, 2023. It focuses on three main questions. First, what have been the main factors driving US-Israel relations during the war? Second, what has been the impact of the war on the special relationship? Third, what are the implications of these for the relationship going forward?

The special relationship between Israel and the United States is grounded on four foundations. There are shared strategic interests, shared values and Israel's resonance in American political culture, and the influence of pro-Israel lobby in domestic American politics.[1] Since the 1970s, the strategic relationship has become increasingly institutionalized, thereby constituting a fourth foundation.

The chapter begins by describing President Biden's approach to Israel. It then analyzes the relations between the US administration and the Israeli government in the year following October 7, 2023, before turning to the role of Congress. Finally, the impact of the war on American public opinion, including Jewish opinion, is analyzed.

The chapter argues that the main factor driving US-Israel relations was President Biden's and Prime Minister Netanyahu's perceptions of their country's strategic interests. On the most basic level regarding the identity of common enemies, these interests overlapped. The exceptional level of cooperation

---

1   Jonathan Rynhold, "The Special Relationship between the United States and Israel," in *The Routledge Handbook on Contemporary Israel*, ed. Guy Ben-Porat et al. (London: Routledge, 2022): 183–196.

that this engendered was safeguarded from domestic critics by President Biden's strong personal sympathy for Israel, which was itself deeply intertwined with his overarching approach to US foreign policy. This sympathy was typical of the traditional support for Israel among the American public. However, during the war it became clear that this outlook was no longer shared by large swathes of the younger generation. This presents the major challenge to the special relationship in the future.

The Biden Administration's Approach to Israel

If an issue is important to the president, then they will be the most important player in determining foreign policy.[2] This was particularly the case for Biden who was renowned for trusting his gut more than the views of aides and experts.[3] Biden was a classic representative of the post-Second World War pro-Israel liberal internationalist. Synthesizing ideology, values, and strategic interests, this approach asserted that US security was best achieved by "making the world safe for democracy." America needed to lead, to protect its democratic allies in the "free world" by containing the Soviet Union, while promoting liberal norms of Human Rights, humanitarianism, self-determination, and democracy.[4]

For leading advocates of this strategy such as Democratic Presidents Johnson, Clinton, and Biden, Israel was an emotive part of the narrative that underlay their commitment to this strategy. The story of America's failure to stand up to Nazism the concomitant failure to prevent the Second World War and the Holocaust were seen as evidence as to moral and strategic bankruptcy of isolationism.[5]

President Biden declared many times, "I'm a Zionist."[6] Indeed, Biden often recalled how his father spoke to him as a young child about the Holocaust and the moral obligation to protect of the newly created State of Israel. Biden took this to heart, taking each of his children and grandchildren to visit the Dachau

---

2   William Quandt, *Peace Process* (Washington, D.C.: Brookings/University of California Press, 2005).
3   Yasmeen Abutaleb, "On Foreign Policy, Biden's Gut Is His Guide," *Washington Post*, April 3, 2023; Bob Woodward, *War* (New York: Simon & Schuster, 2024), 190.
4   Joseph R. Biden Jr., "Why America Must Lead Again: Rescuing U.S. Foreign Policy After Trump," *Foreign Affairs* 99, no. 2 (March/April 2020): 64–75, https://www.foreignaffairs.com/articles/united-states/2020-01-23/why-america-must-lead-again.
5   Franklin Foer, "Biden Will Be Guided by His Zionism," *Atlantic*, October 10, 2023, https://www.theatlantic.com/ideas/archive/2023/10/israel-hamas-war-biden/675592/.
6   Ibid.

concentration camp.[7] When asked by an interviewer why he felt so strongly about the October 7 massacre, Biden replied, "Israel is going after a group of people who have engaged in barbarism that is as consequential as the Holocaust. The Jews have been subjected to abuse, prejudice, and attempts to wipe them out for over 1000 years.... It violates every... principle my father taught me."[8]

Israel also has a special place in the hearts of liberal internationalists of Biden's generation, because of its pioneering achievements and especially its democratic character. There were less than thirty democracies in the world in 1948, and only two countries that received their independence after the Second World War—Israel and India—have remained democratic throughout, and India was neutral in Cold War. All of this made the fate of Israel of special concern.[9] Biden often told the story of his conversation with Prime Minister Golda Meir in Israel as a freshman senator just before the Yom Kippur War, which reinforced his sense of Israel's vulnerability[10] and which he recalled as "one of the most consequential meetings I've ever had in my life."[11]

Biden was also part of a cohort of Democrats who entered Congress deeply affected by the Vietnam War. The War made them more cautious than their predecessors about military intervention.[12] Although he supported the 2003 invasion of Iraq, by 2007 Biden had come to view intervention in Iraq as a mistake. Indeed, he was the most vociferous opponent of increasing American troops levels in Iraq when the Obama administration came into office in January 2009.[13] "America," he argued, "needed to get out of the nation-building business."[14] One of his first acts as president was to complete the withdrawal from Afghanistan.

---

7   Nettanel Slyomovics, "Biden's Secret Weapon vis-à-vis Netanyahu," *Haaretz*, November 3, 2023, https://www.haaretz.com/israel-news/2023-11-03/ty-article-magazine/.highlight/bidens-secret-weapon-vis-à-vis-netanyahu/0000018b-91e7-db7e-af9b-fbe75acf0000.

8   "President Joe Biden: The 2023 60 Minutes Interview Transcript," CBS News, October 15, 2023, https://www.cbsnews.com/news/president-joe-biden-2023-60-minutes-transcript/.

9   Jonathan Rynhold, *The Arab-Israeli Conflict in American Political Culture* (Cambridge: Cambridge University Press, 2015), chapter 1.

10 "Remarks by President Biden on the October 7th Terrorist Attacks and the Resilience of the State of Israel and its People," White House, October 18, 2023, https://www.whitehouse.gov/briefing-room/speeches-remarks/2023/10/18/remarks-by-president-biden-on-the-october-7th-terrorist-attacks-and-the-resilience-of-the-state-of-israel-and-its-people-tel-aviv-israel/.

11 Alexander Ward, *The Internationalists* (London: Penguin, 2024), 83–84.

12 Joe Biden, *Promises to Keep* (New York: Random House, 2007), 48.

13 Ward, *The Internationalists*, 16–17, 31.

14 Ibid., 32.

Still, the "forever wars" in Iraq and Afghanistan did not turn Biden into an isolationist. Instead, Biden sought to *defend*,[15] rather than extend, the "free world." Secretary of State Blinken defined the struggle thus:

> A fierce competition is underway to define a new age in international affairs.... Russia, with the partnership of Iran and North Korea, as well as China—are determined to alter the foundational principles of the international system.... While their... ideologies and interests differ, these revisionist powers all want to entrench autocratic rule at home... and they all seek to erode the foundations of the United States' strength.[16]

The administration recognized that these actors were increasing their level of cooperation significantly.[17] In the Middle East, Russia and Iran sold arms to each other and cooperated and in Syria. China conducted several joint military exercises with Russia and Iran,[18] while trying to slowly undermine the US position in the Gulf though its Belt and Road Initiative.[19]

Rather than expending resources on lost causes like democratizing Iraq and Afghanistan, the Biden administration sought to concentrate on the most important issue areas and geographic areas in this global competition: Europe, Asia, and the Middle East.[20] The administration referred to this as "disciplined" American leadership."[21]

Maintaining a pro-American balance of power in the Middle East remains a vital US interest because of the irreplaceable role of its fossil fuels in ensuring the stability of the free world.[22] The United States has an interest in preventing a

---

15 Robert Singh, "The Biden and Trump Doctrines in Comparative Perspective," in *The Trump and Harris Doctrines*, ed. Stanley Renshon and Peter Suedfeld (Cham, Switzerland: Springer, 2024), 17–40.
16 Antony Blinken, "America's Strategy of Renewal," *Foreign Affairs* 103, no. 5 (2024). See also Jake Sullivan, "The Sources of American Power," *Foreign Affairs* 102, no. 6 (2023): 8–29.
17 Blinken, "America's Strategy of Renewal"; Andrea Kendall-Taylor and Richard Fontaine, "The Axis of Upheaval: How America's Adversaries Are Uniting to Overturn the Global Order," *Foreign Affairs* 103, no. 3: 50–63.
18 "China, Iran and Russia Hold Joint War Games in Gulf of Oman," Al Jazeera, March 12, 2024, https://www.aljazeera.com/news/2024/3/12/china-iran-and-russia-stage-joint-naval-drills-in-gulf-of-oman.
19 Rachel Moreland, "Shifting Sands: U.S. Gulf Policy Recalibrates as China's Regional Ambitions Grow," *Middle East Policy* 31, no. 1 (2024): 149–161.
20 Biden, "Why America Must Lead Again"; Sullivan, "The Sources of American Power."
21 Blinken, "America's Strategy of Renewal"; Sullivan, "The Sources of American Power."
22 Jonathan Rynhold, "The Future of U.S.-Israeli Relations," *Survival* 63, no. 5 (2021): 121–146.

regional conflict that could threaten the flow of energy, especially when Russian oil is already under sanctions. Such a situation would provide Putin with more resources with which to fight the war against Ukraine. In addition, the United States has an interest in preventing a hostile power, like Iran or China, gaining control over the majority of the region's oil. In those circumstances, they would be able to convert the revenue and market dominance into military and political power, with serious consequences for the overall global balance of power.

To achieve its global strategic objectives, the administration prioritized the rejuvenating and extending of alliances,[23] with "fellow democracies as the first port of call."[24] Israel has long been America's strongest and most reliable ally in the Middle East. In the past, Israel's value as a strategic asset was tempered by the strain America's close relations with Israel put on relations with its Arab allies. However, with the signing of the Abraham Accords—added to the preexisting peace agreements with Egypt and Jordan—this constraint has been greatly reduced. None of these countries broke diplomatic relations with Israel in the year following October 7, 2023. Indeed, the leaders of Jordan, the UAE, and Saudi Arabia told Blinken in person that they wanted Israel to defeat Hamas.[25] Moreover, Israel and America's regional allies, including Saudi Arabia, actually cooperated during the war within the framework of CENTCOM, the US regional military command in the Middle East.

US-Israel Relations: October 2023–October 2024

President Biden used his "bully pulpit" to provide Israel with extremely strong rhetorical support, referring to Hamas's attack as "an act of sheer evil"[26] in which the atrocities they committed were "worse that ISIS," the equivalent of "15 9/11s."[27] He also pointed out that more Jewish people had been murdered on

---

23 Blinken, "America's Strategy of Renewal"; Sullivan, "The Sources of American Power"; Steve Clemons, "The Biden doctrine," *Atlantic*, August 22, 2016, https://www.theatlantic.com/international/archive/2016/08/biden-doctrine/496841/; Jessica T. Mathews, "What Was the Biden Doctrine? Leadership Without Hegemony," *Foreign Affairs* 103, no. 5 (September/October 2024): 64–75.
24 Blinken, "America's Strategy of Renewal."
25 Woodward, *War*, 128, 129, 135.
26 Evan Osnos, "Joe Biden's Last Campaign," *New Yorker*, March 4, 2024 www.newyorker.com/magazine/2024/03/11/joe-bidens-last-campaign,
27 "Remarks by President Biden on the October 7th Terrorist Attacks." This was a speech Biden wrote personally. Woodward, *War*, 137.

October 7 that on any day since the end of the Second World War.[28] All of this bolstered the legitimacy for Israel's massive military campaign to defeat Hamas. He returned to these themes a year later following the killing of the architect of the October 7 attack, the head of Hamas in Gaza, Yahya Sinwar, describing it as generating similar feelings to those felt throughout America following the killing of Bin Laden.[29] Aside from rhetoric, Biden also became the first US president to visit Israel in wartime.

The Biden administration viewed the Israel-Hamas War in terms of the wider struggle to defend the "free world" with Hamas and Putin both seeking to "annihilate a neighboring democracy."[30]

The administration could not fail to notice the unprecedented political support Russia and China gave to Hamas. They also recognized the major role of Iran as the primary enabler of October 7[31] and subsequent attacks on Israel (and well over a hundred on US forces) by Hezbollah, the Houthis, and others in Iraq and Syria.[32]

Israel began the war with a ground campaign involving 300,000 soldiers. This included attacks on Hamas's military using civilian shields in, under, or by hospitals, mosques, and schools.[33] The president and secretary of state severely criticized Hamas for using civilian shields.[34] At the same time, the administration

---

28 "Remarks by President Biden on the October 7th Terrorist Attacks."
29 Hannah Sarisohn, "Biden: Sinwar's Death Is a 'good day for Israel, the U.S. and the world,'" *Jerusalem Post*, October 17, 2024, www.jpost.com/breaking-news/article-825063.
30 Osnos, "Joe Biden's Last Campaign."
31 Ronen Bergman et al., "Secret Documents Show Hamas Tried to Persuade Iran to Join Its Oct. 7 Attack," *New York Times*, October 12, 2024, https://www.nytimes.com/2024/10/12/world/middleeast/hamas-israel-war.html; Emanuel Fabian, "IDF Says It Found Proof Hamas Developed Cruise Missile Capabilities, Aided by Iran," *Times of Israel*, January 7, 2024, https://www.timesofisrael.com/idf-says-it-found-proof-hamas-developed-cruise-missile-capabilities-aided-by-iran/; Samia Nakhoul and Parisa Hafezi, "IRGC, Hezbollah Helping Direct Houthi Attacks on Shipping," Reuters, January 20, 2024, https://www.reuters.com/world/middle-east/irgc-hezbollah-helping-direct-houthi-attacks-shipping-iranian-sources-2024-01-20/.
32 Eran Lerman, "Biden's Decision and the American Military Deployment," *Jerusalem Strategic Tribune*, November 5, 2023, https://jstribune.com/lerman-bidens-decision-and-the-american-military-deployment/.
33 Amos Harel, "For Israel, the Raid on Gaza's Al-Shifa Hospital Is a Firm Message to Hamas," *Haaretz*, November 16, 2023, https://www.haaretz.com/israel-news/2023-11-16/ty-article/.premium/for-israel-the-raid-on-gazas-al-shifa-hospital-is-a-firm-message-for-hamas/0000018b-d4eb-d423-affb-f7eb5c7b0000.
34 Gadi Zaig, "Hamas Commits a War Crime When It Places Its Headquarters under a Hospital, Biden Said," *Jerusalem Post*, November 16, 2023, https://www.jpost.com/middle-east/article-123456; Jack Forrest, "Blinken Calls Out Other Countries for Not Demanding Hamas Surrender and 'stop hiding behind civilians,'" CNN, December 21, 2023, https://www.cnn.com/2023/12/21/politics/blinken-hamas-civilians/index.html.

demanded and generally received from Israel evidence to justify these attacks.[35] But the justification for civilian casualties was set at a lower bar than in previous rounds, allowing Israel to adopt more permissive rules of engagement.[36] Overall, American acceptance (if not always support) for Israel continuing the war over such an extended period, was unusual.

Israel's defense establishment was particularly impressed with the speed with which the United States began to supply Israel with arms.[37] Between October 7, 2023, and the end of August 2024, the United States delivered more than 50,000 tons of armaments and military equipment, as well providing about $14 billion in aid, over and above the annual sum of $3.8 billion.[38] The president withstood pressure from within his party and from some figures in the administration[39] to stop supplying Israel with defensive weapons or make military aid conditional. The administration also vetoed several UN Security Council resolutions hostile to Israel.[40]

For the United States, a central objective was to prevent an escalation of the conflict[41] into a full-scale regional war in which US forces would directly fight Iran. Indeed, part of the rationale for the military aid referred to above was to deter Iran and thereby prevent the escalation of the war.[42] There were two addi-

---

35 Franklin Foer, "The War That Would Not End," *Atlantic*, September 25, 2024, https://www.theatlantic.com/international/archive/2024/09/israel-gaza-war-biden-netanyahu-peace-negotiations/679581/.

36 Jacob Magid, "Ex-Biden Aide Claims Israel Has More Tolerance for Causing Civilian Casualties Than U.S.," *Times of Israel*, October 9, 2024, https://www.timesofisrael.com/ex-biden-official-claims-israel-has-higher-tolerance-for-civilian-casualties-than-us/.

37 Lerman, "Biden's Decision and the American Military Deployment."

38 Ibid.; Emanuel Fabian, "Israel Says U.S. Shipments of Arms and Equipment during War Exceed 50,000 Tons," *Times of Israel*, August 26, 2024, https://www.timesofisrael.com/israel-says-us-shipments-of-arms-and-equipment-during-war-exceeds-50000-tons/; Oded Yaron and Ben Samuels, "Revealed: The Munitions U.S. Supplied Israel for Gaza War," *Haaretz*, November 16, 2023, https://www.haaretz.com/israel-news/security-aviation/2023-11-16/ty-article/.premium/shells-laser-guided-missiles-and-bunker-busters-the-munitions-the-u-s-supplied-israel/0000018b-d3b9-dffa-adef-f7b990750000.

39 Foer, "The War That Would Not End"; "Emails Show Early U.S. Concerns of Israeli War Crimes," *Jerusalem Post*, October 5, 2024, www.jpost.com/middle-east/article-823219.

40 Farnaz Fassihi et al., "U.S. Vetoes Israel-Hamas Cease-Fire Resolution at U.N. Security Council," *New York Times*, December 8, 2023; Jacob Magid, "U.S. Blocks Security Council Motion Blaming Israel for Deadly Gaza Aid Convoy Incident," *Times of Israel*, March 1, 2024; Jacob Magid, "U.S. Vetoes Security Council Resolution Granting Palestinians Full-Member Status at UN," *Times of Israel*, April 19, 2024, https://www.timesofisrael.com/us-vetoes-security-council-resolution-granting-palestinians-full-member-status-at-un/.

41 Foer, "The War That Would Not End"; Sullivan, "The Sources of American Power."

42 Lulu Garcia-Navarro, "Antony Blinken Insists He and Biden Made the Right Calls: The Interview," *New York Times*, January 4, 2025, https://www.nytimes.com/2025/01/04/us/politics/antony-blinken-interview.html.

tional concerns, first that China and Russia would seek to take advantage of the concentration of America's energy on the Middle East, by taking aggressive action in their own regions. There were real concerns that the United States did not have enough of certain types of arms to supply both Ukraine and Israel sufficiently.[43] Second, such a war, and especially its economic impact in the form of higher oil prices, would damage the Democrats' chances in the 2024 elections.[44]

The United States paid a price for its restraint. According to Congressional testimony in March 2024 by General Michael Kurilla, head of CENTCOM, the administration's restraint in responding to attacks by Iran and its proxies was emboldening them. From October 2023 through mid-February 2024, attacks by Iranian-backed proxies resulted in at least 186 casualties among US troops serving in the Middle East.[45]

In any case, at the very outset Biden acted decisively to deter Iran and its allies from joining the war, both through his stark rhetorical threat—"don't"[46]—and by quickly and publicly moving US military assets to the region, including two aircraft carriers and a nuclear submarine armed with Tomahawk missiles.[47] After Israel assassinated a senior commander in the elite Quds Force of the Islamic Revolutionary Guards Corps (IRGC) in Damascus on April 1, 2024, Iran made it clear that it would attack Israel directly. Subsequently, secret American diplomacy seems to have influenced the Iranians not to attack Israeli population centers.[48] When Iran launched its attack on Israel on April 13—directly from

---

43 Vera Bergengruen, "For Antony Blinken, the War in Gaza Is a Test of U.S. Power," *Time*, January 11, 2024, https://time.com/collection/davos-2024-ideas-of-the-year/6551990/antony-blinken-israel-gaza-us-power/.
44 Jacob Magid, "The U.S. Aims to Wrap Up Gaza War. How Does That Square with Its Goal of Toppling Hamas?," *Times of Israel*, May 14, 2024, www.timesofisrael.com/the-us-aims-to-wrap-up-gaza-war-how-does-that-square-with-its-goal-of-toppling-hamas/.
45 Suzanne Maloney, "Iran's Order of Chaos: How the Islamic Republic Is Remaking the Middle East," *Foreign Affairs* 103, no. 3 (May/June 2024): 97–109, https://www.foreignaffairs.com/iran/irans-order-chaos-suzanne-maloney.
46 "Remarks by President Biden on the October 7th Terrorist Attacks."
47 Amos Harel, "Israel Walks Fine Line between Gaza and Lebanon, Awaiting Hezbollah's Next Move," *Haaretz*, October 13, 2023, https://www.haaretz.com/israel-news/2023-10-13/ty-article/.premium/dogged-by-nightmares-israel-walks-a-thin-line-between-gaza-and-lebanon/0000018b-255b-d680-af9b-27dfe0390000; Avi Scharf, "U.S. Sends Attack Submarine with Tomahawk Missiles to Middle East," *Haaretz*, November 6, 2023, https://www.haaretz.com/israel-news/security-aviation/2023-11-06/ty-article/.premium/u-s-sends-attack-submarine-with-tomahawk-missiles-to-middle-east/0000018b-a605-d9c0-a5fb-ef5d7b330000.
48 Edward Wong, "U.S. and Iranian Officials Held Indirect Talks in Oman on Risks of a Wider War," *New York Times*, May 18, 2024, https://www.nytimes.com/2024/05/18/world/middleeast/us-iran-oman-talks.html.

its own territory for the first time—the administration coordinated an unprecedented international coalition including both NATO and Arab allies including Jordan, Bahrain, the UAE, and Saudi Arabia, which actively helped to defend Israel.[49] And, while Israel assassinated Ismail Haniyeh, the head of Hamas's political wing in Teheran, the United States deterred direct Iranian retaliation by moving two US carrier strike groups and other military assets into the region, and by sending stern warnings to Tehran through a back channel.[50]

There was an extremely high level of consultation between the United States and Israel. This was symbolized by Blinken participating in an Israeli cabinet meeting, by the US secretary of state for defense and the Israeli defense minister speaking over eighty times during the year, and by the presence of American officials embedded in IDF operation centers.[51] This was designed to serve as a "bear hug" to help restrain Israel. Israel would certainly have much preferred a more robust American response to Iranian involvement in the war, but in general, Israel acquiesced to United States' concerns regarding escalation. Here the United States had extra leverage, as Israel could not easily defend itself alone from a large array of missiles launched from multiple sites across the region. Two notable examples of the administration restraining Israel were the Israeli decision not to escalate the war with Hezbollah in October 2023[52] and its very limited response to the Iranian missile attack in April.[53]

However, when Israel undertook audacious acts with potentially major repercussions—for example, assassinating the head of Hezbollah, Hassan Nasrallah—it did not inform the United States until just beforehand, fearing the United States would try to prevent such acts.[54] While this policy angered

---

49 Dan Lamothe and Alex Horton, "U.S. Details Pentagon's Role in Defending Israel from Iranian Attack," *Washington Post*, April 14, 2024; "How the U.S. Forged a Fragile Middle Eastern Alliance to Repel Iran's Israel Attack," *Wall Street Journal*, https://www.wsj.com/world/middle-east/how-the-u-s-forged-a-fragile-middle-eastern-alliance-to-repel-irans-israel-attack-4a1fbc00; Tzvi Joffre, "U.S. Intercepts Over a Dozen Houthi Drones, Missiles; IDF Intercepts Drone toward Eilat," *Jerusalem Post*, December 26, 2023, https://www.jpost.com/breaking-news/article-779556.
50 Foer, "The War That Would Not End."
51 Ibid.; Nancy Youssef, "U.S. Frustrated by Israel's Reluctance to Share Iran Retaliation Plans," *Wall Street Journal*, October 9, 2024, www.wsj.com/world/middle-east/u-s-frustrated-by-israels-reluctance-to-share-iran-retaliation-plans-f132ebc7.
52 Woodward, *War*, 121–125; Emanuel Fabian, "Gallant tells U.S. Envoy Hochstein There's a 'short window' for a Deal with Hezbollah," *Times of Israel*, January 4, 2024, www.timesofisrael.com/gallant-tells-us-envoy-hochstein-theres-a-short-window-for-a-deal-with-hezbollah/.
53 Ronen Bergman and Patrick Kingsley, "Why Israel Decided to Pare Down Attack on Iran," *New York Times*, April 23, 2024, https://www.nytimes.com/2024/04/23/world/middleeast/israel-iran-attack.html.
54 Youssef, "U.S. Frustrated by Israel's Reluctance to Share Iran Retaliation Plans."

senior administration figures, it provided the United States with deniability, thereby lowering the chances of retaliation against US targets and thus lowering the chances of the United States getting dragged into the conflict directly. The United States made a point of publicly declaring it had no foreknowledge of, or role in, the assassination or the Israel retaliatory strike on Iran in April 2024; and, in an extremely unusual move, it also contacted Iran directly to convey the message.[55]

There were many significant disagreements between the allies: over the provision of humanitarian aid, the extent of civilian casualties, terms for a ceasefire, and Israel's refusal to engage in post-war planning regarding Gaza. In the first few months, American reservations were mainly expressed in private, but, after January 2024, these became increasingly expressed in public.

From the administration perspective, the U.S. had an interest in Israel being seen to comply with humanitarian norms because it would help them sustain domestic and international legitimacy to support their global grand strategy, as well as their support for Israel. As Blinken told Netanyahu on October 12, "From our perspective humanitarian assistance for the Palestinians and civilian protection is a moral imperative. But even if you disagree with that, it's a strategic imperative."[56] Or, as the president declared upon arriving in Israel on October 18, "What sets us apart from the terrorists is we believe in the fundamental dignity of every human life. ... If you give that up, then the terrorists win. And we can never let them win."[57]

On several occasions, the United States got Israel to increase humanitarian aid[58] and delay or scale back military operations out of concern for civilian casualties. Initially, Israel announced a total siege of Gaza until Israeli hostages were released. Pressure from the administration helped Netanyahu to overcome opposition in the cabinet, effectively ending the siege before it began.[59] Prompted by Congressional Democrats, the administration also made Israel provide a report that it was complying with international law when using American arms.[60] They used considerable leverage to pressure Israel on these issues, but this did not

---

55 "Blinken: U.S. Not Involved in Iranian Strike, Seeks De-escalation," *Jerusalem Post*, April 19, 2024, www.jpost.com/israel-hamas-war/article-797943; Woodward, War, 158, 161.
56 Woodward, *War*, 127. See also Sullivan, "The Sources of American Power."
57 "Remarks by President Biden on the October 7th Terrorist Attacks."
58 Garcia-Navarro, "Antony Blinken Insists."
59 Woodward, *War*, 126, 131–135.
60 Hannah Sarisohn, "Biden Gives Israel 45 Days to Submit Report on International Law Violations or Lose Military Aid," *Jerusalem Post*, February 10, 2024, www.jpost.com/israel-hamas-war/article-786097.

include heavy pressure to stop the war altogether,[61] in part out of a fear that this would encourage Iran and Hezbollah to escalate the conflict.[62]

As the humanitarian situation deteriorated, the administration became very angry at the government's failure to stop far-right activists who were reducing the amount of aid entering Gaza.[63] Three days after the IDF mistakenly hit a convoy of aid in which seven *World Kitchen* aid workers were killed on April 1, 2024, Biden spoke to Netanyahu on the phone providing him with a detailed list of actions Israel had to take regarding the humanitarian situation in Gaza. "If you don't do that and we don't see results," Biden threatened, "then you've lost me. I'm out."[64] The Israeli government then released a four-page document of actions it would take that was almost verbatim the things that Biden had been telling Netanyahu going back to December.[65] Israel also quickly managed to double the amount of aid trucks going into Gaza to the administration's satisfaction.[66]

For the Israeli government, the most important goal was to destroy Hamas's conventional military forces and end its governance over Gaza. As Netanyahu's closest advisor Ron Dermer put it,

> the existential threat is that if we do not wipe out an organization that did what they did to us on October 7, then that imperils the whole future of the country because all the buzzards circling around Israel are going to look and see they can get away with it. ... It's not enough to just hit it hard. It's not enough to deplete their capacity ... we have to show all of the enemies in the region that if they do this type of attack, they don't survive it.[67]

---

61 Dion Nissenbaum et al., "Israel Agrees to U.S. Request to Delay Invasion of Gaza," *Wall Street Journal*, October 25, 2023, https://www.wsj.com/world/middle-east/israel-battles-on-multiple-fronts-as-conflict-risks-spreading-a5e537ec; Amir Tibon, "Reliance on U.S. Weapons Forces Netanyahu to Accept Biden's War Requests," *Haaretz*, December 5, 2023; Anshel Pfeffer, "In Dramatic Pivot, Israel Says It Intends to 'Flood' Gaza with Humanitarian Aid," *Haaretz*, March 13, 2024, https://www.haaretz.com/israel-news/2024-03-13/ty-article/.premium/israel-changes-its-policy-on-supplies-to-gaza-intends-to-flood-in-aid-idf-says/0000018e-390e-db12-a9ef-fbff14c50000.
62 Woodward, *War*, 151, 182.
63 "U.S. Outraged at Israeli Protesters' Assault on Aid Convoy: 'Utterly unacceptable,'" *Times of Israel*, May 20, 2024, www.timesofisrael.com/us-outraged-at-israeli-protesters-assault-on-aid-convoy-utterly-unacceptable/.
64 Woodward, *War*, 159.
65 Ibid.
66 Lazar Berman and Jacob Magid, "After PM's Call with Biden, Ministers Okay Steps to Swiftly Ramp Up Aid Flow to Gaza," *Times of Israel*, April 4, 2024, www.timesofisrael.com/after-pms-call-with-biden-ministers-okay-steps-to-swiftly-ramp-up-aid-flow-to-gaza/.
67 Woodward, *War*, 116.

In contrast, the administration spoke of "degrading"[68] Hamas's capabilities to the point where they could not repeat an October 7-style attack. Based on the US experience in Afghanistan and Iraq,[69] the US military were skeptical that Israel could totally defeat Hamas. They argued for a less intensive form of warfare based on raids and targeted strikes, one which would cause fewer civilian casualties. On several occasions, what Americans thought to be impossible, such as evacuating about a million civilians from Rafah in short order, turned out to be possible, though sometimes only after initial American operational concerns were addressed.

The administration did pressure Israel to alter the scale and character of its military operations. Things came to a head when Biden expressed firm opposition to Israel conducting a large-scale military offensive in Rafah, terming it a "red line."[70] The president publicly declared that he would not supply the weapons Israel would need to conduct a massive offensive campaign in Rafah.[71] The United States then delayed the supply of thousands of bombs and refused to supply the 2,000 pound bombs altogether.[72] Subsequently, Israel conducted smaller operations in Rafah.[73] Although these were more aggressive than the administration liked, they considered them well-reasoned with provisions to protect civilian life. [74]

Another source of tension in the relationship was the negotiations for a ceasefire. The president took a strong personal interest in the hostages, some of whom were also US citizens. In November 2023, with intensive US, Egyptian, and Qatari mediation, fifty hostages were released during a brief ceasefire. Efforts then turned to obtaining a second ceasefire and hostage deal.

The administration assigned the bulk of the blame to Sinwar for the failure to achieve a deal. Even when Israel put forward what the administration thought were very generous terms in early April that were acceptable to Hamas leaders in Doha,

---

68 "The Biden Administration Doesn't Think Israel Can Fully Win in Gaza," Politico, May 14, 2024, www.politico.com/news/2024/05/14/biden-israel-gaza-00157949.
69 Foer, "The War That Would Not End"; Woodward, *War*, 135–137.
70 Kevin Liptak, MJ Lee, and Kayla Tausche, "Inside Biden's Decision to Go Public with His Ultimatum to Israel," CNN, May 10, 2024, www.edition.cnn.com/2024/05/09/politics/inside-bidens-public-ultimatum/index.html.
71 Jacob Magid, "In Bluntest Threat Yet, Biden Says Israel Will Have to Choose between Rafah Op, U.S. Arms," *Times of Israel*, May 9, 2024, www.timesofisrael.com/in-bluntest-threat-yet-biden-says-israel-will-have-to-choose-between-rafah-op-us-arms/.
72 John Hudson, "U.S. Pauses Shipment of Thousands of Bombs to Israel amid Rafah Rift," *Washington Post*, May 7, 2024.
73 Michael Gordon and Vivian Salama, "U.S. Pushes to Shape Israel's Rafah Operation, Not Stop It," *Wall Street Journal*, March 27, 2024, www.wsj.com/world/middle-east/behind-closed-doors-the-u-s-pushes-to-shape-not-stop-the-rafah-operation-302403e6.
74 Foer, "The War That Would Not End;" Garcia-Navarro, "Antony Blinken Insists."

Sinwar rejected the deal.⁷⁵ Just before leaving office, in an interview in the *New York Times,* Blinken put the blame for the lack of a ceasefire squarely on Hamas:

> The two biggest impediments to getting [a ceasefire] over the finish line . . . both go to what drives Hamas. One has been whenever there has been public daylight between the United States and Israel and the perception that pressure was growing on Israel. . . . Hamas has pulled back from agreeing to a cease-fire and the release of hostages. . . . The other thing that got Hamas to pull back was their belief, their hope that there would be a wider conflict, that Hezbollah would attack Israel. . . . One of the things that I found a little astounding throughout is. . . . Why there hasn't been a unanimous chorus around the world for Hamas to put down its weapons, to give up the hostages, to surrender. . . . Where is the world, saying, Yeah, do that! End this! Stop the suffering of people that you brought on!⁷⁶

Nonetheless, Blinken also stated that "There have been times when actions that Israel has taken . . . made it [a hostage deal] more difficult.⁷⁷" Ultimately, freeing the hostages was a higher priority for the administration that for the Israeli government, which set the total defeat of Hamas as a higher priority. As Netanyahu told Vice President Harris on July 25, 2024,

> If Hamas remains in power in Gaza, it's a victory to Hamas. It's a defeat to Israel. We want a deal that will release the hostages and we are willing to pay with a ceasefire for a period of time to achieve this. Your administration is saying we want a ceasefire, implicitly an end to the war, that along the way releases the hostages. That is not acceptable . . .⁷⁸

The administration became angry with Netanyahu because they felt that he was acting duplicitously by formally agreeing to a position and then acting in such a way as to undermine the chances of success.⁷⁹ On May 31, the president publicly

---

75 Woodward, *War*, 160.
76 Garcia-Navarro," Antony Blinken Insists."
77 Ibid.
78 Woodward, *War*, 202.
79 Foer, "The War That Would Not End"; Woodward, *War*, 181.

announced a ceasefire initiative which he claimed was Israeli in origin, though it turned out Israel was not fully in agreement with the (incomplete) plan as interpreted by the United States.[80]

Well before the war, the administration prioritized facilitating the normalization of relations between Israel and Saudi Arabia, which in turn was a condition for pushing through a formal defense treaty between the United States and Saudi Arabia. By doing this, Biden would prevent the Saudis from slipping out of the American orbit—they had been developing friendlier relations with China. To advance this objective, they sought to leverage a permanent ceasefire. Normalization would require Israel to recommit to an "over the horizon process that includes a vision for a demilitarized Palestinian state."[81] As the Biden administration saw it, Hamas could not be defeated by military force alone, because, as Blinken told Israel's war cabinet, "Hamas is an idea, and you cannot destroy an idea." Only a political pathway to a Palestinian state could do that, he argued. In the first instance that meant handing over Gaza to a "revitalized," reformed Palestinian Authority.[82] In response, Dermer staked out the Israeli position: "It's one thing to have a bad idea, it's another thing to have a bad idea in control of territory! Our goal is to remove the territorial control that Hamas has over Gaza. We have to dismantle this army."[83]

Meanwhile, Netanyahu sought to avoid presenting a plan for "the day after" in Gaza as his right-wing coalition were intensely opposed to the creation of such a Palestinian state. For Netanyahu to accept this would almost certainly mean the collapse of his government. The administration became so frustrated with the far-right members of the Israeli coalition on this and humanitarian issues that they publicly called on Netanyahu to form a different coalition. Furthermore, Netanyahu's constantly backtracked on understandings reached privately with the administration on these issues lead to a serious deterioration in the relations between President Biden and the Israeli prime minister, which were not great to begin with.[84]

---

80 Lazar Berman, "Netanyahu: We Will Destroy Hamas, Biden's Version of Hostage Deal 'incomplete,'" *Times of Israel*, Jume 3, 2024, www.timesofisrael.com/netanyahu-we-will-destroy-hamas-bidens-version-of-hostage-deal-incomplete.
81 Woodward, *War*, 129, 146–147; Garcia-Navarro, "Antony Blinken Insists."
82 Ben Samuels and Amir Tibon, "U.S. Sees Palestinian Authority as Possible Solution in Gaza, Yet Israel Is Working to Weaken It," *Haaretz*, November 1, 2023, https://www.haaretz.com/us-news/2023-11-01/ty-article/.premium/u-s-sees-palestinian-authority-as-possible-solution-in-gaza-as-israel-works-to-weaken-it/0000018b-8b8a-db7e-af9b-ebcb50e30000.
83 Woodward, *War*, 139.
84 Dion Nissenbaum and Vivian Salama, "Biden-Netanyahu Relationship at Boiling Point as Rafah Invasion Looms," *Wall Street Journal*, February 15, 2024, www.wsj.com/world/middle-east/

US Domestic Politics and Congress

During the war, the scale of anti-Israel activity—including student encampments, demonstrations, and protests—far surpassed anything seen before. While the "uncommitted" group of thirty delegates at the Democratic Party convention threatened not to vote Democrat in the presidential election, unless the administration significantly shifted its policy in anti-Israel direction.[85] On the other hand, "never Trump" Republicans, whose vote the Democrats were targeting, were very pro-Israel.[86] In parallel, a December 2023 poll found that Democrats were almost evenly divided over whether the United States supporting Israel too much, too little, or the right amount.[87] Those opposed to Israel sounded louder because the far left (and far right) tend to be more active than moderates.[88] Ultimately, these divisions meant there was little to be gained be taking a firmer stance in either direction, a conclusion reinforced when assessing the potential role of Jewish and Arab/Muslim communities in the elections. For, while the Arab vote was important in the swing state of Michigan, American Jews were important in the swing state of Pennsylvania, which had more electoral college votes than Michigan.[89] Most swing-state Democratic candidates did not support Bernie Sanders's bid to block aid to Israel.[90]

---

biden-netanyahu-relationship-at-boiling-point-as-rafah-invasion-looms-b893bec5.
85 Nate Cohn, "Trump Leads in 5 Key States, as Young and Nonwhite Voters Express Discontent with Biden," *New York Times*, May 13, 2024.
86 Nicholas Grossman, "How Much Will Gaza Affect Joe Biden's Re-election Chances?," *The Bulwark*, May 10, 2024, https://www.thebulwark.com/p/israel-gaza-hamas-biden-reelection-polls; Mark Penn, "The Simple Math That Could Swing the Election to Biden," *New York Times*, May 12, 2024.
87 Megan Brenan, "Americans Divided Over U.S. Involvement in Middle East," *Gallup*, January 5, 2024, https://news.gallup.com/poll/548084/americans-divided-involvement-middle-east.aspx.
88 "Beyond Red vs. Blue: The Political Typology," Pew Research Center, November 9, 2021, https://www.pewresearch.org/politics/2021/11/09/beyond-red-vs-blue-the-political-typology-2/.
89 "New Poll Finds Arab American Voters Evenly Divided in the 2024 Presidential Election," Arab American Institute, October 2, 2024, https://www.aaiusa.org/library/press-release-new-poll-arab-american-voters-evenly-divided-in-race-for-white-house-f989m; Marc Levy, "Some Jewish Voters in Swing States Reconsider Their Devotion to Democrats," Associated Press, October 21, 2024, https://apnews.com/article/jewish-voters-pennsylvania-2024-elections-trump-harris-09297d8c0843ae2b1698c9d2dfb80fd9.
90 Marc Rod, "Most Swing-state Democrats Disavow Sanders' Bid to Block Aid to Israel," *Jewish Insider*, September 30, 2024, www.jewishinsider.com/2024/09/senate-democrats-swing-states-bernie-sanders-aid-israel/.

Nonetheless, the impending US elections led Israel to limit its second strike against Iran on October 25, 2024, to military targets. The administration feared an Israeli attack on the Iranian nuclear program would lead to a regional war, and that an attack on Iran's oil industry would, at a minimum, cause a spike in oil prices[91]— though, even here, part of the reason Israel relented was that the United States imposed harsh new sanctions on Iran's oil industry leading to a dramatic cut in revenue.[92] Either way, aside from this, electoral considerations had little substantive influence over US-Israel relations during the war. Yet, the administration had to invest considerable time and energy into managing the domestic politics of the war. With President Biden publicly identifying himself as a Zionist, the administration tried to balance things to deflect opposition among Democrats to its continued support for Israel's military campaign, by having Vice President Kamala Harris make public statements that were critical of Israeli policy, especially regarding the humanitarian situation and the high number of casualties,[93] by increasing oversight over how Israel used American arms, and by delaying and withholding a few arms transfers and by applying limited, but symbolically significant and precedent setting sanctions, against far-right Israeli figures and institutions.[94]

Meanwhile, Congressional activity related to the war reflected the broader divide between Republicans and Democrats over Israel, as well as the divide within the Democratic Party. This was most apparent when Netanyahu addressed a joint session of Congress, with about seventy Democrats boycotting the event, including Vice President Harris.[95] Congressional initiatives designed to pressure Israel were the province of the left of the Democratic Party.[96] They sought to condition the transfer of military aid and offensive weapons to

---

91 Shira Rubin and Ellen Nakashima, "Netanyahu Tells U.S. that Israel Will Strike Iranian Military, Not Nuclear or Oil, Targets," *Washington Post*, October 14, 2024, www.washingtonpost.com/world/2024/10/14/israel-iran-strike-nuclear-oil-military/.

92 Danny Zaken, "How the U.S. Persuaded Israel to Hold Back on Iranian Oil Targets," *Israel Hayom*, October 22, 2024, www.israelhayom.com/2024/10/22/how-washington-persuaded-israel-to-hold-back-on-iranian-oil-targets/.

93 Woodward, *War*, 139, 201.

94 Ben Samuels, "Biden's Executive Order on Violent Israeli Settlers Is a Game-changer," *Haaretz*, February 2, 2024, https://www.haaretz.com/us-news/2024-02-02/ty-article/.premium/bidens-executive-order-on-violent-israeli-settlers-is-a-game-changer/0000018d-699e-dd6e-a98d-fdbe10460000.

95 Jacob Magid, "Some 70 Democrats Boycotted Netanyahu Speech, Tlaib Protests during Address," *Times of Israel*, July 24, 2024, https://www.timesofisrael.com/liveblog_entry/some-70-democrats-boycotted-netanyahu-speech-tlaib-protests-during-address/.

96 Ben Samuels, "Leahy Law: What You Need to Know about the Law Roiling U.S.-Israel Ties," *Haaretz*, April 27, 2024, https://www.haaretz.com/israel-news/2024-04-27/ty-article/.premium/explained-the-u-s-law-that-may-lead-to-santions-on-west-bank-idf-battalion/0000018f-1c19-d502-a5bf-fcff5dfe0000.

Israel. But they were actually weakened when AIPAC helped defeat anti-Israel lawmakers Jamaal Bowman and Cori Bush in the Democratic Party primaries.[97] Nonetheless, in an unprecedented situation, the left were sometimes joined by pro-Israel Democrats.[98] On April 4, three days after seven aid workers died when the IDF unintentionally hit a World Central Kitchen convoy delivering aid in Gaza, the former House speaker Nancy Pelosi signed on a letter "to withhold this and any future offensive arms transfers until a full investigation into the airstrike is completed,"[99] while Senate Majority leader Chuck Schumer publicly called for Netanyahu to be replaced.[100]

For all that, ironically, it was the Republicans that held up the aid $17 billion military aid package for Israel—in part because Trump did not want to give the president "a win," but in part because many Republicans opposed giving the aid to Ukraine, which was part of the package. This was a symptom of the growth of isolationist opinion within the GOP.[101] Historically, isolationists have been hostile to the idea of a close US-Israel relationship.[102] The high-profile Fox News commentator Tucker Carlson adopted this stance during the war.[103]

American Public Opinion

Traditionally, every major demographic group surveyed by the main pollsters sympathized with Israel over the Palestinians. Although Republicans were

---

97 Matthew Kassel, "AIPAC Emerges as Moderate Force in Political Primaries," *Jewish Insider*, August 29, 2024, https://jewishinsider.com/2024/08/aipac-political-primaries-pro-israel-group-mainstream-lawmakers/.
98 Marc Rod, "After Netanyahu's Rejection of Two-State Solution, Five New Senate Democrats Support Conditioning Israel Aid," *Jewish Insider*, January 19, 2024, https://jewishinsider.com/2024/01/after-netanyahus-rejection-of-two-state-solution-five-new-senate-democrats-support-conditioning-israel-aid/.
99 "Pelosi Joins Call by 37 Democrats for Biden to Halt Transfer of U.S. Weapons to Israel," *Times of Israel*, April 6, 2024, www.timesofisrael.com/pelosi-joins-call-by-37-democrats-for-biden-to-halt-transfer-of-us-weapons-to-israel/.
100 Barak Ravid, "Schumer's Anti-Netanyahu Speech Stuns Israel," Axios, March 14, 2024, https://www.axios.com/2024/03/14/schumer-israel-netanyahu-speech-reaction.
101 Kevin Freking, "Aid Package for Israel Fails in the House," Associated Press, February 7, 2024, https://apnews.com/article/congress-israel-hamas-military-aid-speaker-johnson-a0f135bcee-45afcbe2a90453c4aa894a.
102 Rynhold, *The Arab-Israeli Conflict*, chapters 2–3.
103 Ben Samuels, "Tucker Carlson Questions U.S. Support for Israel War—Could the GOP Follow?," *Haaretz*, October 11, 2023, https://www.haaretz.com/us-news/2023-10-11/ty-article/.premium/tucker-carlson-questions-u-s-support-for-israel-war-could-the-gop-follow/0000018b-19c2-dcc0-a3df-9de2ad700000.

generally far more supportive of Israel during the war, still three-quarters of Democrats consistently supported Israel[104] and a large majority agreed that protecting Israel should be an important goal of US foreign policy (59% to 20%).[105] However, these figures masked a deep divide between the parties.

Between 2002 and 2017 there was a massive rise in Republicans support for Israel. This correlated closely with the increase in the number of Republicans who agreed that "Islam encourages violence more than other religions," which grew from about a third in 2002 to about 70% in 2017. In comparison, only about a quarter of Democrats agreed with this statement in both 2002 and 2017. Democrats also became increasingly dovish in this period. Taken together, these trends made Democrats less and less supportive of Israel's use of military force against its extremist Islamist enemies.[106]

Moreover, since 2015, there was a sharp decline in Democrats' sympathy for Israel. From the 1990s until 2014, on average, Democrats favored Israel over the Palestinians by a margin of at least 2:1. However by 2020, Gallup polls showed that about half favored Israel and half the Palestinians. Left-wing "progressive" and "liberal" Democrats tended to favor the Palestinians more, while "moderates" tended to favor Israel.[107]

This negative trend among Democrats was due to the interaction between three long-term cultural processes in America and three triggers emanating from Israel and the Middle East. First, in the twenty-first century, Democrats have become increasingly liberal, secular, and dovish, whereas since 2015 Israel has been led by the most conservative, religious, and hawkish government in its history. Second, levels of negative affective partisanship between Democrats and Republicans have grown to unprecedented proportions. In 2015, Prime Minister Netanyahu opposed the JCPOA nuclear deal with Iran by working closely with the Republican-led Congress against the Obama administration. This came to be perceived by Democrats as Israel taking sides with the Republicans in American domestic politics. This perception was greatly reinforced by the close relationship between Trump and Netanyahu 2017–2020.[108] But the most significant

---

104 "Monthly Polls: December 2023–October 2024," Harvard CAPS/Harris Poll, https://harvardharrispoll.com.
105 Laura Silver et al., "Majority in U.S. Say Israel's Reasons for Fighting Hamas Are Valid," *Pew Research Center*, March 24, 2024, https://www.pewresearch.org/2024/03/21/majority-in-u-s-say-israel-has-valid-reasons-for-fighting-fewer-say-the-same-about-hamas/.
106 Rynhold, *The Arab-Israeli Conflict*, chapters 2–3.
107 Jonathan Rynhold, "Democrats' Attitudes toward the Israeli-Palestinian Conflict," *Middle East Policy* 27, no. 4 (2020): 48–61, https://doi.org/10.1111/mepo.12526.
108 Rynhold, "Democrats' Attitudes toward the Israeli-Palestinian Conflict."

opinion trend has been generational in character. Until the middle of the second decade of the twenty-first century, generational differences in attitudes to Israel were not especially large. In contrast, in this war, the younger generation was far more negative toward Israel than older cohorts.

One reason Americans have been supportive of Israel is that they viewed the U.S. and Israel as sharing democratic values and other positive traits. As young Democrats have become more negative about America, so they have become more negative toward Israel. In 2011, only 8% of Democrats thought that other countries were better than the United States, but by 2023 that number jumped to 36%, reaching 50% among Democrats aged eighteen to twenty-nine.[109] The generational divide was also salient regarding political ideology. According to a 2021 survey, 18% of eighteen- to twenty-nine-year-olds who identified as Democrats belonged to the farthest left element of the Party known as "Progressives," compared to half that percentage for those over fifty.[110] The younger generation are also far more attracted to the Black Lives Matter movement and critical race theory than older generations.[111] In 2012, 28% of Democrats agreed that "racial discrimination is the main reason why black people can't get ahead," with almost no difference between age cohorts. By 2017, 64% of Democrats agreed with that statement, with the largest increase by far occurring among Millennials.[112] In a December 2023 Harvard/Harris survey, about 80% of eighteen- to twenty-four-year-olds supported "an ideology that white people are oppressors and non-white people . . . have been oppressed and as a result should be favored today," compared to about a quarter of those over forty-five.[113]

In the summer of 2014, there were massive protests following the shooting of a black teenager by a white police officer in Ferguson, Missouri, which coincided with a war between Israel and Hamas. This confluence of events began to trigger a link between attitudes towards race relations in the United States and attitudes to the Israeli Palestinian conflict. Pro-Palestinian and left-wing groups wrongly framed the Israeli Palestinian conflict as the equivalent of racial conflict

---

109 Hannah Hartig, "U.S. Is One of the World's Greatest Countries, Say Majority of Americans," Pew Research Center, August 29, 2023, https://www.pewresearch.org/short-reads/2023/08/29/majority-of-americans-say-us-is-one-of-the-greatest-countries-in-the-world/.
110 "Beyond Red vs. Blue: The Political Typology."
111 Jenn Hatfie, "8 Facts about Black Lives Matter," Pew Research Center, July 12, 2023, https://www.pewresearch.org/short-reads/2023/07/12/8-facts-about-black-lives-matter/.
112 "The Generation Gap in American Politics," Pew Research Center, March 1, 2018, https://www.pewresearch.org/politics/2018/03/01/the-generation-gap-in-american-pol. itics/
113 "Monthly Polls: December 2023," Harvard CAPS/Harris Poll, https://harvardharrispoll.com.

in America. The impact of this trend was evident in the attitudes of the younger generation during the Israel-Hamas War that started in 2023.

In a Harvard/Harris poll from December 2023, half of eighteen- to twenty-four-year-olds supported Hamas, compared to around 10% for those over forty-five.[114] Over two-thirds of the youngest cohort agreed that "Jews as a class are oppressors and be treated as oppressors," compared to less than a sixth of those over forty-five. 60% of eighteen- to twenty-four-year-olds also agreed that "Hamas killing 1200 Israeli civilians and the kidnapping of another 250 civilians could be justified by the grievances of the Palestinians," more than triple the percentage for those over forty-five. Finally, over half of eighteen- to twenty-four-year-olds agreed that "Israel should be ended and given to Hamas and the Palestinians," while only a third supported a two-state solution. In contrast, about two-thirds of those over forty-five supported a two-state solution, with about 10% supporting the dissolution of the State of Israel.

American Jews

Antizionist groups like Jewish Voices for Peace[115] that support BDS against Israel received greater media coverage after October 7, leaving the impression that American Jews, especially the younger generation, were becoming less supportive of Israel. Indeed, there was anecdotal evidence that an element of the younger generation of non-Orthodox American Jews,[116] including those in rabbinical school, are becoming increasingly antizionist.[117] Certainly, opinion

---

114 "Monthly Polls: December 2023; March, May, and September 2024," Harvard CAPS/Harris Poll, https://harvardharrispoll.com.
115 Alongside messages praising Nasrallah, the University of Michigan's Jewish Voices for Peace shared a post stating, "'Death to Israel' is a moral imperative." Rachel Fink, "Anti-Zionist U.S. Student Groups Mourn Nasrallah's Death, Vow to Continue His 'Fire of Resistance,'" *Haaretz*, September 29, 2024, https://www.haaretz.com/us-news/2024-09-29/ty-article/.premium/anti-zionist-u-s-student-groups-mourn-nasrallah-vow-to-continue-his-fire-of-resistance/00000192-3dc2-dee0-a9bf-3ff20adf0000.
116 Haley Cohen, "Poll: Overwhelming Majority of American Jews Support Israel's Fight against Hamas," *Jewish Insider*, December 21, 2023, https://jewishinsider.com/2023/12/poll-overwhelming-majority-of-american-jews-support-israels-fight-against-hamas/.
117 Gabby Deutch, "At Conservative and Reform Rabbinical Schools, a Debate over Red Lines on Anti-Zionism," *Jewish Insider*, February 13, 2024, https://jewishinsider.com/2024/02/jewish-rabbinical-schools-conservative-reform-synagogues-israel-anti-zionism/; anecdotal evidence from personal conversations with senior figures in Non-Orthodox educational institutions.

regarding Netanyahu and his government was at best divided,[118] but, overall, American Jews remain very supportive of Israel, its war aims, and the way it prosecuted the war. In a May 2024 survey, 85% described US support for Israel as "important," while emotional attachment to Israel increased by about 10% from the year before across all types of religious and non-religious categories and across all age cohorts. There was also evidence of greater involvement in Pro-Israel activities,[119] including a March for Israel held in November, which drew nearly 300,000 participants. Between October 7, 2023, and July 2024, American Jews donated nearly a billion dollars through their local Jewish federations, and hundreds of millions more through other channels.[120]

Conclusion

This chapter argues that the main factor driving US-Israel relations during the war was the two leaders, President Biden and Prime Minister Netanyahu's, perception of their country's strategic interests. On the local level regarding Gaza, it was mainly Israeli priorities that dominated, while on the regional level, American priorities dominated. For the president, his grand strategy combined comfortably with his deep emotional commitment to Israel when it came to supporting the *defense* of Israel. The personal resonance of Israel's plight also fired Biden's willingness to stand up to those in his administration and party who wanted him to reduce support for Israel. However, outside of these parameters, his sympathy for the country did not translate into administration support for Israeli government policy. Indeed, there were several significant conflicts over policy. Nonetheless, the underlying American commitment to Israeli security was never in doubt. The special relationship proved resilient. This resilience was reinforced by the institutionalization of the strategic relationship, which meant that US and Israeli defense officials worked together intensively throughout, in particular through CENTCOM. The administration expended a lot of energy dealing with the domestic politics of the war, and the fact that

---

118 Becka Alper, "Israel-Hamas War—U.S. Jews' Experiences and Views," Pew Research Center, April 2, 2024, https://www.pewresearch.org/short-reads/2024/04/02/how-us-jews-are-experiencing-the-israel-hamas-war/.
119 Gregory Zuckerman, "Jolted by Oct. 7 Attacks, More U.S. Jews Feel Drawn to Their Faith," *Wall Street Journal*, October 15, 2024, www.wsj.com/us-news/jolted-by-oct-7-attacks-more-u-s-jews-feel-drawn-to-their-faith-219951f4.
120 Theodore Sasson and Chuck Freilich, "What Israeli Leaders Should Know About American Jews," INSS Insight, no. 1882, July 21, 2024. www.inss.org.il/publication/american-jews/.

Netanyahu's political survival depended on his far-right coalition partners was a significant source of rancor. But, at the end of the day, domestic politics played a secondary role.

Looking to the future, CENTCOM represents the type of cooperation that is likely to be supported not only by internationalists but also by isolationist leaning Republicans, such as the Vice President J. D. Vance, because it increases the role of local allies in regional security, thereby allowing the United States to play a lesser role.[121] Nonetheless, while the evangelical base of the Republican party remains firmly pro-Israel, the growth of isolationist tendency within the party could have negative consequences for the willingness of a future administration to provide the level aid and direct US military support to Israel that were evident during this war.

Finally, the war highlighted the way in which the cultural, value-based, foundations of the relationship are weakening. Under America's oldest president the special relationship remained robust, but changing attitudes among the younger generation present a serious challenge going forward. And yet, for a significant proportion of the younger generation, negative attitudes toward Israel were held alongside contradictory attitudes that indicated sympathy towards Israel. Thus, in the same Harvard/Harris Poll, while over half of eighteen- to twenty-four-year-olds agreed than Israel should be ended and given to Hamas and the Palestinians, nearly 70% agreed that Israel has a right to exist as the homeland of the Jewish people. Furthermore, 80% of eighteen- to twenty-four-year-olds agreed that "Israel has a right to defend itself against terror attacks by launching air strikes on targets on heavily populated Palestinian areas with warnings to those citizens," the exact same percentage as for forty-five- to fifty-four-year-olds.

Going forward, this suggests two conclusions. First, there is a sizable group of young Democrats on the left of the party that have cohered into an anti-Israel cohort that will be around for some time, much in the same way that such groups exist on the far left of British and European left-wing parties. Second, a significant part of the younger generation lacks a consistent coherent outlook and will therefore be open to solidifying their outlook in either direction.

---

121 Emily Jacobs, "Vance Puts Pro-Israel Spin on America First Worldview in Quincy Institute Speech," *Jewish Insider*, May 23, 2024, www.jewishinsider.com/2024/05/vance-puts-pro-israel-spin-on-isolationist-worldview-in-quincy-institute-speech/.

CHAPTER 8

See No Evil, Hear No Evil, Speak No Evil: The Erasure of Hamas in UN Human Rights Narratives, and the Implications after October 7[1]

Anne Herzberg

> "The story I found myself part of proposed, in effect, that the ills of Western civilization—racism, militarism, colonialism, nationalism—were embodied by Israel. . . . By selectively emphasizing some facts and not others, by erasing historical and regional context, and by reversing cause and effect, the story portrayed Israel as a country whose motivations could only be malevolent . . ."
> —Matti Friedman[2]

Introduction

On October 7, 2023, the Jewish holiday of Simchat Torah, thousands of combatants from Hamas, Palestinian Islamic Jihad (PIJ), and the Popular Front for the

---

1 Legal advisor and UN representative of the Institute for NGO Research. The author wishes to thank Joshua Kern, Naftali Balanson, and Ariella Esterson for their comments and editorial assistance.
2 Matti Friedman, "When We Started to Lie," The Free Press, September 10, 2024, https://www.thefp.com/p/friedman-when-we-started-to-lie.

Liberation of Palestine (PFLP) crossed over the border from Gaza into Southern Israel, launching an armed attack on dozens of cities, villages, *kibbutzim*, and *moshavim* (farming communities).[3] These combatants systematically murdered, burned alive, dismembered, tortured, and raped thousands of civilians;[4] 360 young people were murdered and subjected to mass sexual violence at the Nova music festival;[5] 240 people (ranging in age from nine months to eighty-six years) from twenty-five different nationalities were taken hostage, 100 of whom remain captive in Gaza one year later as of this writing.[6] The massacre of 1,200 in only a few hours was coupled with thousands of indiscriminate rocket attacks fired by Palestinian armed groups on Israeli population centers including Tel Aviv, Jerusalem, and Be'er Sheva.[7] In the days that followed, Iranian-backed proxies Hezbollah and the Houthis launched attacks on Israel's northern cities and the southern city of Eilat, respectively, shooting ballistic missiles, anti-tank guided missiles (ATGMs), mortars, and explosive drones from Lebanon,

---

3   "1,500 Deaths, 253 Hostages, 6 Months: Marking Half a Year since October 7," *Jerusalem Post*, April 7, 2024, https://www.jpost.com/israel-hamas-war/article-795696.
4   Mapping the Massacre, https://oct7map.com/; "October 7: How Hamas Attacked Israel Minute by Minute," *Haaretz*, April 18, 2024, https://www.haaretz.com/israel-news/2024-04-18/ty-article-static/.premium/what-happened-on-oct-7/0000018e-c1b7-dc93-adce-eff753020000; Geoffrey Gettleman et al., "Screams without Words: How Hamas Weaponized Sexual Violence on October 7," *New York Times*, December 28, 2023, https://www.nytimes.com/2023/12/28/world/middleeast/oct-7-attacks-hamas-israel-sexual-violence.html.
5   Mustafa Abu Ganeyeh and Leonardo Benassatto, "'I was reborn' on Oct. 7 Says Survivor of Hamas Attack on Israeli Festival," Reuters, October 31, 2023, https://www.reuters.com/world/middle-east/i-was-reborn-oct-7-says-survivor-hamas-attack-israeli-festival-2023-10-31/.
6   Peter Saidel et al., "Hamas Took More Than 200 Hostages from Israel: Here's What We Know," *Wall Street Journal*, September 1, 2024, https://www.wsj.com/world/middle-east/hamas-hostages-israel-gaza-41432124; Hostages and Missing Families Forum, https://stories.bringthemhomenow.net/about-them.
7   Bill Hutchinson, "Israel-Hamas War: Timeline and Key Developments," ABC News, November 22, 2023, https://abcnews.go.com/International/timeline-surprise-rocket-attack-hamas-israel/story?id=103816006.

Yemen, Syria, and Iraq.[8] The resulting attacks led to the internal displacement of nearly 200,000 Israelis.[9]

During Hamas's takeover and control of Gaza, which followed Israel's Disengagement in 2005, and up until October 7, it systematically utilized the civilian infrastructure (hospitals, schools, mosques, homes, UN facilities) to shield and conceal weapons as well as command and control centers.[10] Hamas constructed a tunnel network throughout Gaza more extensive than the New York City subway system to smuggle weapons, protect its fighters, maneuver operationally, and kidnap and hold Israeli hostages.[11] This military fortification was financed and operationally supported by Iran.[12] These activities placed the population of Gaza at risk and exacerbated civilian casualties. At the same time, Hamas gained significant strength in the West Bank, poised to assume power.[13] Hamas exploited the humanitarian aid system, placing the burden of social services on the international community, while also diverting billions of dollars,

---

8   "Israel, Hezbollah Exchange Artillery, Rocket Fire," Reuters, October 8, 2023, https://www.reuters.com/world/middle-east/israel-strikes-lebanon-after-hezbollah-hits-shebaa-farms-2023-10-08/; Dana Polak, "Hezbollah: Analysis of Attacks against Israel," Alma Research and Education Center, July 2, 2024, https://israel-alma.org/2024/07/02/hezbollah-intensity-and-range-analysis-of-attacks-against-israel-october-8-2023-to-july-1-2024/; Maha El-Dahan, "Who Are Yemen's Houthis and Why Did They Attack Israel," Reuters, November 1, 2023, https://www.reuters.com/world/middle-east/who-are-yemens-houthis-why-did-they-attack-israel-2023-11-01/.

9   "About 200000 Israelis Internally Displaced amid Ongoing Gaza War, Tensions in North," Times of Israel, October 22, 2023, https://www.timesofisrael.com/about-200000-israelis-internally-displaced-amid-ongoing-gaza-war-tensions-in-north/.

10 "Hamas's Use of Human Shields in Gaza," NATA Strategic Communications Centre, June 2019, https://stratcomcoe.org/cuploads/pfiles/hamas_human_shields.pdf; William Booth, "While Israel Held Its Fire, the Militant Group Hamas Did Not," Washington Post, July 15, 2014, https://www.washingtonpost.com/world/middle_east/while-israel-held-its-fire-the-militant-group-hamas-did-not/2014/07/15/116fd3d7-3c0f-4413-94a9-2ab16af1445d_story.html.

11 Marco Hernandez and Josh Holder, "The Tunnels of Gaza," New York Times, November 10, 2023, https://www.nytimes.com/interactive/2023/11/10/world/europe/hamas-gaza-tunnels.html; "Moving in the Dark: Hamas Documents Reveal Tunnel Battle Strategy," New York Times, September 3, 2024, https://www.nytimes.com/2024/09/02/world/europe/hamas-tunnels-war-documents.html; "How Hamas is Fighting in Gaza," New York Times, July 13, 2024, https://www.nytimes.com/2024/07/13/world/middleeast/hamas-gaza-israel-fighting.html.

12 "Hamas's Military Build-Up in the Gaza Strip," Meir Amit Intelligence and Terrorism Information Center, April 8, 2007, 5, www.terrorism-info.org.il//Data/pdf/PDF1/hamas_080408_501786899.pdf.

13 Nasser Khdour, "Surging Violence: Hamas Attempts to Reshape the West Bank's Political Landscape," Washington Institute, April 5, 2023, https://www.washingtoninstitute.org/policy-analysis/surging-violence-hamas-attempts-reshape-west-banks-political-landscape.

food aid, and material to support its military campaign and personally enrich its leadership.[14] Many Hamas leaders were harbored in Qatar and Turkey.[15]

In the aftermath of October 7, however, these aspects of the conflict were largely missing from UN reporting. UN Secretary General Antonio Guterres, for instance, in remarks made on October 24 to the Security Council, framed the Hamas atrocities as a story of agentless Palestinian victims resisting Israeli oppression: "[T]he attacks by Hamas did not happen in a vacuum. . . . The Palestinian people have been subjected to 56 years of suffocating occupation."[16] His remarks echoed those made by UN Human Rights Council Special Rapporteur for the Palestinians Francesca Albanese, who on October 9 told Qatari media outlet Al Jazeera, "What's happening needs to be put in context, a context of decades of oppression imposed on the Palestinians. . . ."[17]

The role of Hamas, and the nature of the atrocities of October 7, and their aftermath is similarly sanitized on the UN's "Question of Palestine" "history of the conflict" webpage:

> In October of 2023, another escalation between Gaza and Israel began. In July 2024 the International Court of Justice found that Israel's presence in the OPT is unlawful and it should bring it to an end as rapidly as possible, cease settlement activities, evacuate settlers, and make reparations. In September 2024 the General Assembly demanded that Israel end its occupation in 12 months.[18]

---

14 Ella Levy-Weinrb, "Meet the Hamas Billionaires," *Globes*, July 24, 2014, https://en.globes.co.il/en/article-the-phenomenal-wealth-of-hamas-leaders-1000957953; Matthew Levitt, "Ban Hamas in Europe," Washington Institute, September 4, 2003, https://www.washingtoninstitute.org/policy-analysis/ban-hamas-europe.
15 "In Turkey, Qatar Defense Chief Says No Plans to Expel Hamas," *Al-Monitor*, June 2024, https://www.al-monitor.com/originals/2024/06/turkey-qatar-defense-chief-says-no-plans-expel-hamas; "Hamas's Benefactors: A Network of Terror," Joint Hearing, Before The Subcommittee On The Middle East and North Africa, House of Representatives, 113th Congress, Second Session, September 9, 2014, https://www.govinfo.gov/content/pkg/CHRG-113hhrg89738/html/CHRG-113hhrg89738.htm.
16 "Secretary-General's remarks to the Security Council—on the Middle East," October 24, 2023, https://www.un.org/sg/en/content/sg/speeches/2023-10-24/secretary-generals-remarks-the-security-council-the-middle-east%C2%A0.
17 Al Jazeera English (@AJEnglish), X (formerly Twitter), October 9, 2023, https://twitter.com/AJEnglish/status/1711399357277254142.
18 "Timeline of Events," UNISPAL, https://www.un.org/unispal/history/.

Hamas's actions are euphemized as an "escalation," with responsibility assigned solely to Israel because of its "unlawful" presence, "settlement activities," and "occupation."

This discourse serves to enable justification and minimization of the single largest massacre of the Jewish people since the Holocaust. Although it serves a political interest, it does not advance understanding of the truth. That it emanates from UN officials and agencies is not surprising. This discourse reflects longstanding patterns concerning narrative creation in the Israeli Palestinian conflict, where UN reporting has been reduced to activism as a result of its selective and partial presentation of the facts.

The human rights frameworks of the United Nations are a primary space where the crafting of these narratives takes place, and it is carried out in two ways. First, hyperbolic and disproportionate focus is placed on alleged egregious abuses by Israel. Second, the historical context of Israel's founding and its ongoing security challenges, which negate the selected narratives, are erased. This year's International Court of Justice Advisory Opinion on Israel's "policies and practices in the occupied Palestinian territory," for example, reductively describes attacks on Israel by Arab States in 1948, 1967, and 1973, as "war broke out."[19] As to current drivers of conflict, Iran's role is erased.[20]

Nowhere is this dynamic more apparent than with regards to the portrayal of Hamas in UN reporting. Since the mid-1990s, Hamas has been one of the most significant actors in the conflict.[21] Its campaign of suicide bombings beginning in the Oslo period was a major obstacle in reaching final status talks;[22] the violence of the Second Intifada led to the construction of the security barrier and Israel's 2005 Disengagement;[23] Hamas's 2007 takeover of Gaza[24] and subsequent indiscriminate attacks on Israel are responsible for multiple violent confrontations and wars, and paved the way for the October 7 atrocities.

---

19 International Court of Justice Advisory Opinion on the Legal Consequences Arising from the Policies and Practices of Israel in the Occupied Palestinian Territory, Including East Jerusalem, July 19, 2024, paras. 53, 57, and 60.
20 Ibid.
21 Kali Robinson, "What is Hamas," *Council on Foreign Relations*, August 19, 2024, https://www.cfr.org/backgrounder/what-hamas.
22 Meir Hatina, "Hamas and the Oslo Accords: Religious Dogma in a Changing Political Reality," *Mediterranean Politics* 4, no. 1 (1999): 37–53, https://doi.org/10.1080/13629399908414698.
23 Shmuel Even, "'The decision that changed history': Ten Years since the Disengagement from the Gaza Strip," *Strategic Assessment* 18, no. 2 (2015): 73.
24 Bruce Riedel, "Battle for Gaza: Hamas Jumped, Provoked and Pushed," Brookings, August 16, 2007, https://www.brookings.edu/articles/battle-for-gaza-hamas-jumped-provoked-and-pushed/.

One would expect, therefore, that an analysis of the Hamas organization and its conduct would feature prominently in UN human rights reporting on the conflict. Yet, the word "Hamas" appeared only once in the 2024 ICJ advisory opinion,[25] and the group is rarely mentioned in other UN documentation.

This paper will examine how Hamas is defined and discussed in two UN human rights investigatory mechanisms, focusing on reports of the Special Committee to Investigate Israeli Practices and the work of the UN Special Rapporteur "on the situation of human rights in the Palestinian territories occupied since 1967." The paper will first offer a brief overview of UN bodies specifically established to address the Arab Israeli conflict and a summary of Hamas's history and role. It will discuss how narrative and framing operates in the conflict. It will then explore how the Special Committee and the Special Rapporteur mandate have reported on Hamas and how their discourse (or lack thereof) has impacted the construct of narratives and their framing in the conflict. The paper will conclude with the consequences of these narratives for the Arab Israeli conflict, particularly in light of October 7.

UN Arab-Israeli Conflict-Related Mechanisms

The UN played a fundamental role in the establishment of the State of Israel. and the General Assembly has stated that it is "[m]indful of the special responsibility of the United Nations to achieve a just solution to the question of Palestine."[26] The UN Organization's political, judicial, and reporting bodies have also centrally figured in shaping the narratives of how Israel and the Arab Israeli conflict is viewed. The UN Special Committee on Palestine (UNSCOP) was established in May 1947 to formulate a solution to the "Question of Palestine."[27] The Committee's work led to the drafting of the Partition Plan, which recommended to the UN General Assembly (UNGA) that the territory of mandatory Palestine be divided into two states—one Jewish and one Arab.[28] The November 29,

---

25 The sole mention is in a sentence where the court announces it will not examine Israel's responses to October 7: "the request of the General Assembly do not include conduct by Israel in the Gaza Strip in response to the attack carried out against it by Hamas and other armed groups on 7 October 2023." Advisory Opinion, para 81.
26 UNGA Resolution A/RES/43/177 (1988).
27 "Report on the First Committee," Special Committee on Palestine, UN Doc. A/307, May 13, 1947.
28 Steven E. Zipperstein, *Zionism, Palestinian Nationalism and the Law: 1939–1948* (New York: Routledge, 2022).

1947, UNGA vote in favor of the Partition Plan (rejected by Arab states) paved the way for Israel to declare its independence on May 14, 1948.[29] Immediately afterwards, five Arab armies aided by local Arab militias launched war on the nascent Jewish state.[30] UN narratives regarding Israel often embraced the Arab perspective over the Israeli perspective from this point on.[31]

For example, armistice agreements were concluded in the first half of 1949 between the warring parties.[32] In December 1949, the UNGA passed resolution 302(IV), establishing the UN Relief and Works Agency (UNRWA) to address refugees from the war, including approximately 700,000 Arab refugees.[33] This agency was kept outside of the normative refugee framework established in 1950, administered by the UN High Commission for Refugees (UNHCR).[34] The refusal to incorporate UNRWA into the UNHCR framework was in large part due to Arab state opposition to the resettlement of Arab refugees.[35]

During the 1950s and 1960s, the alliance between the Soviet Union and Arab States solidified, and, coupled with new states created in the wake of decolonization, they formed a powerful bloc of nearly two-thirds of the UN membership that could be harnessed for the creation of anti-Israel resolutions and mechanisms.[36]

---

29 UNGA Resolution A/RES/181 (1947).
30 "The Arab-Israeli War of 1948," Office of the Historian, U.S. Department of State, https://history.state.gov/milestones/1945-1952/arab-israeli-war.
31 Robert P. Barnidge Jr., *Self-Determination, Statehood, and the Law of Negotiation: The Case of Palestine* (Oxford: Hart Publishing, 2016); Zipperstein, *Zionism, Palestinian Nationalism*.
32 *The Middle East 1916–2001: A Documentary Record*, Yale Law School Avalon Project, https://avalon.law.yale.edu/subject_menus/mideast.asp.
33 UN Doc. A/Res/302(IV) (1949). In 1948, UNGA Resolution A/RES/194 set up the Palestine Conciliation Commission, the body originally tasked with rehabilitating, resettling, and compensating refugees from the war. The Arab states, however, refused to participate in the framework, leading to its disbanding shortly thereafter. Kobi Michael and Michal Hatuel-Radoshitzky, "Seventy Years to UNRWA—Time for Structural and Functional Reforms," Institute for National Security Studies, September 2020, 16–17, https://www.inss.org.il/wp-content/uploads/2020/09/Memo204_e.pdf.
34 Adi Schwartz and Einat Wilf, *The War of Return: How Western Indulgence of the Palestinian Dream Has Obstructed the Path to Peace* (New York: All Points Books, 2020); Arlene Kushner, "The UN's Palestinian Refugee Problem," *Azure* 22 (2005); Gina Benevento, "UNRWA, Thomas L. Thompson, and Others," *Azure* 24 (2006).
35 Michael and Hatuel-Radoshitzky, *Seventy Years to UNRWA*, 17.
36 See Anne Herzberg, "Apartheid Discourse in the Israeli-Palestinian Conflict: Implications for a Negotiated Peace in the Aftermath of October 7" (paper presented at conference at Goethe University Frankfurt, May 4, 2024, publication forthcoming in conference proceedings); Joshua Kern and Anne Herzberg, "False Knowledge as Power: Deconstructing Definitions of Apartheid that Delegitimise the Jewish State," NGO Monitor, December 2021, https://ngo-monitor.org/pdf/NGOMonitor_ApartheidReport_2021.pdf.

In UN debates, Arab countries adopted positions equating Zionism to settler-colonialism and imperialism, while the Soviets accused Zionism of being on par with the crimes of Naziism and apartheid.[37] The first attempt to codify these positions in a UN legal instrument occurred during the drafting of the Convention on the Elimination of Racial Discrimination (CERD), where the Soviets proposed an amendment characterizing Zionism as a prohibited form of discrimination.[38] While the amendment was rejected, it laid the groundwork for future mechanisms aimed at cementing a one-sided historical narrative of the conflict and denigrating Jewish self-determination.

The establishment of the PLO in 1964 and the Arab defeats and assumption of Israeli control over the territories of the West Bank, Gaza Strip, Golan Heights, and Sinai Peninsula in 1967 and its maintenance in 1973 intensified the rhetoric and precipitated a host of mechanisms singling out Israel within the UN system.[39] In 1968, in Resolution 2443 (XXIII), the General Assembly created the Special Committee to Investigate Israeli Practices Affecting the Human Rights of the Palestinian People and Other Arabs of the Occupied Territories. As noted in the Committee's name, and which would set a precedent for UN mechanisms to come, the mandate of this committee was solely focused on Israel, portrayed Israel as the sole party bearing responsibility for human rights law obligations, and established a narrative of "occupation" to frame the conflict. Although Egypt had controlled Gaza in 1949–1967, and Jordan the West Bank, this legal appellation was not previously applied.

In 1975, the UN General Assembly adopted Resolution 3379 recharacterizing Zionism, the self-determination movement of the Jewish people, as racist, illegal, and illegitimate.[40] The resolution was coupled with the creation of a special mechanism—the Committee on the Exercise of the Inalienable Rights of the Palestinian People (CEIRPP), a second unique framework in the UN system dedicated to Palestinians.[41] The Committee hosts events and issues publications promoting the idea that Israel's founding was a *Nakba* ("catastrophe")

---

37 Herzberg, "Apartheid Discourse"; Zipperstein, *Zionism, Palestinian Nationalism*, 183.
38 James Loeffler, *Rooted Cosmopolitans: Jews and Human Rights in the Twentieth Century* (New Haven, CT: Yale University Press, 2018), 246, 253; Ofra Friesel, "Race versus Religion in the Making of the International Convention against Racial Discrimination, 1965," *Law and History Review* 32, no. 2 (2014): 351; Draft International Convention on the Elimination of All Forms of Racial Discrimination: Report of the Third Committee, United Nations General Assembly, A/6181, December 18, 1965.
39 Herzberg, "Apartheid Discourse."
40 Ibid.
41 UN Committee on the Exercise of the Inalienable Rights of the Palestinian People (CEIRPP) https://www.un.org/unispal/committee/.

and that offer tendentious portrayals of the history of the Arab-Israeli conflict.[42] Its work is facilitated by the Division for Palestinian Rights (formed in 1977), which serves as the bureaucratic arm of the CEIRPP, and a corresponding and unique information agency, UNISPAL (established in 1991), which issues and disseminates reports and NGO materials promoting the Palestinian narrative.[43] In addition to UNISPAL, the DPR maintains a separate "Question of Palestine" UN website and Ask UNPal chat function.[44]

In 1993, following the Vienna World Conference on Human Rights,[45] the UN established the Office of the High Commissioner for Human Rights (OHCHR) to serve as the bureaucracy for the Commission on Human Rights and expanded the capability of the UN to produce reports and execute action items in resolutions issued by the Commission.[46] This period also saw the creation of a mandate for a Special Rapporteur "on the situation of human rights in the Palestinian territories occupied since 1967."[47] This second investigatory mechanism was also foundationally partisan. It is the only Special Rapporteur mandate that does not require annual renewal, and, like the Special Committee, the first investigatory mechanism, the mandate is uniquely focused on reporting on alleged violations by Israel.[48]

In 2005, the Commission on Human Rights was disbanded due in large part to its disproportionate focus on Israel. According to former UN Secretary General Kofi Annan, the "Commission's ability to perform its tasks" had been "overtaken" and "undermined by the politicization of its sessions and the selectivity of its work." The "body's declining credibility had cast a shadow on the

---

42 Juliana Geran Pilon, "The United Nations' Campaign Against Israel," Heritage Foundation, June 1983, 5; Julius Stone, *Israel and Palestine: Assault on the Law of Nations* (Baltimore, MD: Johns Hopkins University Press, 1981), 6. The Anti-Defamation League has documented that CEIRPP "is an anachronistic forum for bias against Israel and the most disturbing manifestation of institutional prejudice against the Jewish State within the U.N.," "35 Years of Demonizing Israel," July 2009, 3, https://www.adl.org/sites/default/files/documents/israel-international/uninternational-organizations/c/CEIRPP-FINAL-REPORT-2009.pdf.
43 "About the Division of Palestinian Rights," CEIRPP, https://www.un.org/unispal/about-division-palestinian-rights/.
44 CEIRPP, https://www.un.org/unispal/.
45 "World Conference on Human Rights, Vienna, 1993," Office of the High Commissioner for Human Rights (OHCHR), https://www.ohchr.org/en/about-us/history/vienna-declaration.
46 "About UN Human Rights," OHCHR, https://www.ohchr.org/en/about-us.
47 "Special Rapporteur on the situation of human rights in the Palestinian territories occupied since 1967," OHCHR, https://www.ohchr.org/en/special-procedures/sr-palestine.
48 Ibid.

reputation of the United Nations system as a whole."⁴⁹ It was replaced with the Human Rights Council (UNHRC), which began operations in 2006.⁵⁰

The UNHRC, however, has proven just as problematic as the Commission. Item 7 of the Council's standing agenda is dedicated to discussing alleged human rights violations in "Palestine"—the only item dedicated to a single country focused debate.⁵¹ In addition to the Item 7 general debate, each year also includes an "interactive dialogue" with the Special Rapporteur.⁵² UN Secretary General Ban Ki-Moon commented that he was "disappointed at the Council's decision to single out only one specific regional item, given the range and scope of allegations of human rights violations throughout the world."⁵³ Debates on Israel have also been expanded to be included during every agenda Item 2 debate.⁵⁴ Nine out of thirty-six special sessions of the Council have focused on Israel, with the next most frequent being Syria (5).⁵⁵ The UNHRC has also instituted forty investigative bodies to address issues of human rights concern.⁵⁶ 25% (ten investigations) were mandated to report on abuses allegedly committed by Israel. The country with the second most investigations (Burundi) numbered three.⁵⁷

---

49 "Secretary-General Elaborates on Reform of Human Rights Structures in Address to Commission on Human Rights," OHCHR, April 7, 2005, https://www.ohchr.org/en/press-releases/2009/10/secretary-general-elaborates-reform-human-rights-structures-address.
50 "About UN Human Rights," OHCHR, https://www.ohchr.org/en/about-us.
51 Tovah Lazaroff, "Western Nations Boycott UNHRC's Agenda Item 7 Debate on Israeli 'human rights abuses,'" *Jerusalem Post*, June 27, 2016, https://www.jpost.com/israel-news/politics-and-diplomacy/western-nations-boycott-unhrcs-agenda-item-7-debate-in-which-countries-discuss-israel-457907.
52 "Human Rights Council Holds Interactive Dialogue with the Special Rapporteur on Occupied Palestinian Territories," July 16, 2020, https://www.un.org/unispal/document/human-rights-council-holds-interactive-dialogue-with-the-special-rapporteur-on-occupied-palestinian-territories-press-release-excerpts/.
53 Jamey Keaten, "World in Chaos, Israel Gets Singular Focus at UN Rights Body," Associated Press, June 13, 2016. The EU and the United States boycott the Item 7 debate because of the inherent bias. Human Rights Council holds general debate on the Human Rights Situation in Palestine and other occupied Arab Territories, UNHRC, March 24, 2014.
54 In 2019, the Council added an "accountability report" related to the conflict to be debated under Item 2 at every March session. In 2021, it added a standing Item 2 interactive dialogue debate with the permanent "Commission of Inquiry on the Occupied Palestinian Territory, including East Jerusalem, and Israel" to the June sessions. In July 2023, the Council moved an annual discussion of an OHCHR database of companies supposedly complicit in Israel's "settlement enterprise" from Item 7 to Item 2 of September sessions.
55 "Special Sessions," UNHRC, https://www.ohchr.org/en/hr-bodies/hrc/special-sessions.
56 "International Commissions of Inquiry, Commissions on Human Rights, Fact-Finding missions and other Investigations," UNHRC, https://www.ohchr.org/en/hr-bodies/hrc/co-is.
57 "Human Rights Council-mandated Investigative Bodies," UNHRC, https://www.ohchr.org/en/hr-bodies/hrc/list-hrc-mandat.

All of these Israel-dedicated mandates were one-sided.[58] Each year, between five and ten reports, and at least three resolutions, are produced on Israel.[59] More resolutions have been passed on Israel than on all other countries combined.[60]

Summing up this UN record at his retirement in 2016, Ban Ki-Moon remarked,

> I have argued that we cannot have a bias against Israel at the UN. . . . Decades of political maneuvering have created a disproportionate number of resolutions, reports and committees against Israel. In many cases, instead of helping the Palestinian issue, this reality has foiled the ability of the UN to fulfill its role effectively.[61]

Nevertheless, despite the ongoing criticism, these flawed mechanisms continue to proliferate.

History of Hamas and Conflict with Israel

Before analyzing the narrative framing and UN reporting, it is important to provide background on Hamas. Much of this information routinely goes unmentioned in UN reporting. Hamas, officially Harakat al-Muqawama al-Islamiya ("Islamic Resistance Movement") was originally founded as a Muslim Brotherhood social and religious offshoot in the 1960s and 1970s.[62] Its form as a terrorist organization, promoting itself as an alternative and rival to the Palestine Liberation Organization, crystallized in the 1980s.[63]

---

58 Anne Herzberg, "NGO Monitor Submission to the UN Biennial Report of the Secretary General," NGO Monitor, January 22, 2021, https://ngo-monitor.org/submissions/ngo-monitor-submission-to-the-un-biennial-report-of-the-secretary-general/; Anne Herzberg, "NGO Monitor Submission to the United Nations Human Rights Council Commission of Inquiry on the 2018 Protests in the "Occupied Palestinian Territory," NGO Monitor, November 15, 2018, https://ngo-monitor.org/wp-content/uploads/2018/11/2018-Gaza-COI-Submission-FINAL.pdf.
59 "Documents and Resolutions," UNHRC, https://www.ohchr.org/en/hr-bodies/hrc/documents.
60 "Resolutions Database," UN Watch, https://unwatch.org/database/resolution-database/.
61 Keaten, "World in Chaos."
62 Devorah Margolin, "Hamas at 35," Washington Institute, December 21, 2022, https://www.washingtoninstitute.org/policy-analysis/hamas-35.
63 Ibid.

In 1988, the group published its Charter,[64] comprising quotes from Islamic religious teachings, antisemitic conspiracy theories, and its declaration to wage war until Israel is eliminated.[65] It presents the conflict as a religious war between Muslims and Jews[66] and is genocidal in outlook.[67] It rejects any form of political compromise or "so-called peaceful solutions."[68] A cornerstone of Hamas ideology is that of "revolution from below," exploiting government and social institutions, most notably educational institutions, to build support and indoctrinate the people beginning from a young age.[69]

During the Oslo process and the adoption of the Oslo agreements (1993–1995), Hamas began a campaign of suicide bus bombings throughout Israel, causing hundreds of casualties.[70] Hamas played an integral part in the terror war known as the "Second Intifada," launched in 2000 by Yasser Arafat following his rejection of the Camp David agreement.[71] Hamas also took inspiration from Israel's unilateral withdrawal from Lebanon in 2000, which it viewed as a victory for Hezbollah.[72] Hamas carried out 40% of the suicide bombings during the Second Intifada, killing hundreds and injuring thousands of Israelis.[73] By the mid-2000s, Hamas was designated as a terrorist organization by the United States, Australia, Canada, the EU, and Japan.[74]

March 2002 saw a month of extreme violence, including fourteen suicide attacks, culminating with the Hamas bombing of the Passover seder at the Park Hotel in Netanya.[75] In April 2002, Israel began Operation Defensive Shield to

---

64 The Covenant of the Islamic Resistance Movement, August 18, 1988 (Hamas Charter), https://avalon.law.yale.edu/20th_century/hamas.asp.
65 Ibid.
66 Ibid., Preamble.
67 Ibid., art. 7, "The Day of Judgement will not come about until Moslems fight the Jews (killing the Jews)."
68 Ibid., art. 13; see also arts. 11, 32.
69 Margolin, "Hamas at 35," 5; Hamas Charter, arts., 15, 18.
70 Yoram Schweitzer, "The Rise and Fall of Suicide Bombings in the Second Intifada," *Strategic Assessment* 13, no. 3 (October 2010): 39–48, https://www.inss.org.il/wp-content/uploads/2022/12/fe-3014381841.pdf.
71 Schweitzer, "The Rise and Fall of Suicide Bombings."
72 "Hamas's Military Build-Up in the Gaza Strip," Meir Amit Intelligence and Terrorism Information Center, April 8, 2007, 5, www.terrorism-info.org.il//Data/pdf/PDF1/hamas_080408_501786899.pdf.
73 Ibid.
74 Margolin, "Hamas at 35." New Zealand followed in 2010 and, in 2021, the thirty-five-nation Organization of American States and the United Kingdom (post-Brexit) designated. Ibid.
75 Matti Friedman, "Ten years after Passover Blast, Survivors Return to Park Hotel," *Times of Israel*, March 27, 2012, https://www.timesofisrael.com/ten-years-after-passover-bombing-survivors-return-to-netanyas-park-hotel/.

dismantle terrorist infrastructure in the West Bank.[76] Israel carried out targeted assassinations of Hamas leaders in Gaza and undertook efforts to prevent weapons smuggling from Egypt.[77] In 2003, Israel began construction of a security barrier in the West Bank, leading to a significant reduction in suicide bombings.[78]

In August 2005, Israel carried out the Disengagement, unilaterally removing all Israeli settlements and IDF forces from Gaza, as well as four West Bank communities.[79] Hamas immediately acted to destabilize the territory by confronting the EUBAM protection force along the border;[80] looting greenhouses left behind by Israel;[81] accelerating the construction of tunnels;[82] and increasing rocket and mortar fire on Israeli communities bordering Gaza.[83]

In January 2006, Hamas won the Palestinian Legislative Council elections, placing it in charge of the Palestinian Authority (PA), and cementing the group's political power in Gaza.[84] On June 25, 2006, Hamas carried out an incursion into Israeli territory via a tunnel, killing two soldiers and kidnapping soldier Gilad Shalit.[85] Two weeks later, Hezbollah attacked an IDF patrol using rocket fire and an attack on communication and control posts as a diversion to its incursion (the same tactics were used October 7), killing eight soldiers and

---

76 "Passover Eve Massacre at Park Hotel in Netanya," Meir Amit Intelligence and Terrorism Information Center, May 2004, https://www.terrorism-info.org.il/Data/pdf/PDF1/JUNE_6_2_1700435765.pdf.
77 "Israel Has a Long History of Targeted Killings. Here's a Look at Some of Them," Associated Press, July 31, 2024, https://apnews.com/article/israel-hamas-haniyeh-hezbollah-assassination-71f26e21f4b5e1ad7887197bf2beb446.
78 Emanuel Fabian, "After terror attacks, Israel reinforces part of West Bank barrier with 9-meter wall," *Times of Israel*, June 22, 2022, https://www.timesofisrael.com/in-wake-of-terror-attacks-israel-reinforces-stretch-of-northern-west-bank-barrier/; Schweitzer, "Rise and Fall," at 45–46.
79 Even, "The Decision that Changed History."
80 Josef Federman, "Once Representing Hope, an EU Mission in Gaza Is Symbol of Sputtering Western Vision," *Times of Israel*, July 7, 2023, https://www.timesofisrael.com/once-representing-hope-an-eu-mission-in-gaza-is-symbol-of-sputtering-western-vision/.
81 "Looters Strip Gaza's Greenhouses," Associated Press, September 14, 2005, https://www.nbcnews.com/id/wbna9331863; Jeffrey Goldberg, "What, Exactly, Is Hamas Trying to Prove?," *Atlantic*, July 13, 2014, https://www.theatlantic.com/international/archive/2014/07/what-exactly-is-hamas-trying-to-prove/374342/.
82 Jonathan Schanzer, "Tunnel Vision," Washington Institute, August 14, 2003, https://www.washingtoninstitute.org/policy-analysis/tunnel-vision.
83 "Rocket and Mortar Attacks against Israel by Date," Jewish Virtual Library, https://www.jewishvirtuallibrary.org/palestinian-rocket-and-mortar-attacks-against-israel.
84 Simon Jeffrey, "Hamas Celebrates Election Victory," *Guardian*, January 26, 2006, https://www.theguardian.com/world/2006/jan/26/israel1.
85 Amos Harel, "How Were Palestinian Militants Able to Abduct Gilad Shalit?," *Haaretz*, October 18, 2011, https://www.haaretz.com/2011-10-18/ty-article/how-were-palestinian-militants-able-to-abduct-gilad-shalit/0000017f-db1f-df0f-a17f-df5f27890000.

kidnapping the bodies of two.[86] It is clear that both Iranian proxy organizations, if not overtly coordinating, were operating with similar strategies and tactics.[87]

In March 2007, Hamas and Fatah formed a unity government, but the cooperation was short-lived.[88] In June 2007, Hamas carried out a coup, killing and exiling Fatah members, taking full control of Gaza, increasing its tunnel fortifications,[89] and intensifying its military attacks on Israel.[90] Israel placed restrictions on the territory to prevent weapons smuggling and diversion of dual-use items.[91] Hamas frequently attacked the crossings into Israel, leading to closures.[92] Egypt often shut down its border with Gaza.[93]

These attacks led to large scale military confrontations with Israel in December 2008–January 2009, November 2012, July–August 2014, and May 2021.[94] These conflicts were marked by ever increasing numbers, range, and sophistication of Hamas rockets fired at Israeli population centers.[95] By May 2021, Hamas was able to subject Tel Aviv and Israel's main airport to sustained attacks.[96] The com-

---

86 Uzi Rubin, "The Rocket Campaign against Israel during the 2006 Lebanon War," Begin-Sadat Center for Strategic Studies Mideast Security and Policy Studies No. 71 (June 2007), https://besacenter.org/wp-content/uploads/2007/06/MSPS71.pdf.
87 "Hamas's Military Build-up," Meir Amit Intelligence and Terrorism Information Center, 4.
88 David Rose, "The Gaza Bombshell," *Vanity Fair*, March 3, 2008, https://www.vanityfair.com/news/2008/04/gaza200804; Steven Erlanger, "Hamas Seizes Broad Control in Gaza Strip," *New York Times*, June 14, 2007, https://www.nytimes.com/2007/06/14/world/middleeast/14mideast.html; "Hamas Coup in Gaza," *IISS Strategic Comments* 13 (June 2007), https://www.tandfonline.com/doi/epdf/10.1080/13567880701539929?needAccess=true.
89 The first tunnels were discovered in 2001. Schanzer, "Tunnel Vision."
90 By February 2008, rockets were able to reach Northern Ashkelon and tunnel entrances were exposed in Israeli border communities. "Hamas's Military Build-up," 3.
91 Adam Ragson, "Hamas: Israel Agreed to Lift Gaza Import Restrictions on Many 'Dual-Use' Goods," *Times of Israel*, April 18, 2019, https://www.timesofisrael.com/hamas-israel-agreed-to-lift-gaza-import-restrictions-on-many-dual-use-goods/.
92 Herzberg, "2018 COI Submission," 39.
93 Kristen Chick, "Israel, Gaza Tensions: Why Egypt Helps Maintain the Blockade," *Christian Science Monitor*, April 2, 2010, https://www.csmonitor.com/World/Middle-East/2010/0402/Israel-Gaza-tensions-Why-Egypt-helps-maintain-the-blockade.
94 "Timeline: Key Events in the Israel-Arab and Israeli-Palestinian Conflict," American Jewish Committee, https://www.ajc.org/IsraelConflictTimeline.
95 Lenny Ben-David, "Hamas's Advanced Weaponry: Rockets, Artillery, Drones, Cyber," Jerusalem Center for Public Affairs, August 1, 2021, https://jcpa.org/article/hamas-advanced-weaponry-rockets-artillery-drones-cyber/.
96 "Gaza Conflict 2021 Assessment," JINSA, October 2021, https://jinsa.org/wp-content/uploads/2021/10/Gaza-Assessment.v8-1.pdf.

ing online in 2011 of Israel's Iron Dome defense system created the perception that these conflicts could be managed despite their increasing severity.[97]

Hamas's fighting tactics became the subject of detailed study by security analysts,[98] who found that its "operational concept rests in large part on the unlawful tactic of deliberately embedding its military operations and assets deep within the urban civilian infrastructure of Gaza."[99] As early as 2003, researchers raised concerns regarding Hamas tunnels and that they could be used to "transport captured Israeli soldiers" and to engage in "complicated attacks against Israeli military targets."[100] Experts also remarked on how Hamas exploited international legal standards and disinformation campaigns as a means to create international pressure on Israel.[101]

Three other notable events would prove prescient for October 7. In 2011, Israel agreed to trade more than 1,000 Palestinian prisoners for IDF soldier Gilad Shalit, who had been held incommunicado in Gaza since 2006.[102] Yahya Sinwar, who would go on to be the architect of October 7, was one of those released.[103] In June 2014, Hamas operatives kidnapped three Israeli boys hitchhiking from a popular West Bank junction.[104] This event was a precursor to the 2014 conflict in Gaza, but also marked Hamas's efforts to seize civilian hostages as part of its military strategy.[105]

Thirdly, and perhaps most significantly, in 2018, Hamas organized a series of violent activities along the border fence separating Gaza and Israel entitled "the

---

97 Azriel Bermant, "A False Sense of Security, Effective Shield or Morale Booster? Israel's Missile Defence," *Fathom*, November 2023, https://fathomjournal.org/a-false-sense-of-security-effective-shield-or-morale-booster-israels-missile-defence/.
98 "Hamas's Military Build-up," 5.
99 Ibid., 30; "An Interim Assessment of the Gaza Conflict 10–21 May 2021," High Level Military Group, July 2021, 16, http://www.high-level-military-group.org/pdf/hlmg-interim-assessment-gaza-conflict-may-2021.pdf.
100 Schanzer, "Tunnel Vision."
101 "Gaza Conflict Assessment," 7.
102 Yoram Schweitzer, "A Mixed Blessing: Hamas, Israel, and the Recent Prisoner Exchange," *Strategic Assessment* 14, no. 4 (January 2012): 23–32, https://www.inss.org.il/wp-content/uploads/2022/12/fe-233001974.pdf.
103 Lahav Harkov, "'No one appealed against Oct. 7 mastermind Sinwar's 2011 prison release,'" *Jewish Insider*, May 21, 2024, https://jewishinsider.com/2024/05/emi-palmor-gilad-shalit-hostage-release-negotiations/.
104 David Horovitz and Mitch Ginsburg, "What Happened on the Night of the Kidnapping," *Times of Israel*, June 30, 2014, https://www.timesofisrael.com/what-happened-on-the-night-of-the-kidnapping/.
105 Anna Schechter, "Hamas 'abduction manual' Shows that Hostage-Taking Was a Central Aim of Attack," NBC News, October 24, 2023, https://www.nbcnews.com/news/investigations/hamas-abduction-manual-shows-hostage-taking-was-central-aim-attack-rcna121794.

Great Return March." Styled by Hamas as spontaneous "marches" calling for a "mass return of 'Palestinian refugees' to the 'homes of their ancestors' within the State of Israel,"[106] these actions, lasting through 2019, involved hostile provocations, including destruction of the fence, the testing of IDF border defenses, and incursions into Israeli territory.[107] In one notable instance, operatives crossed and attempted to take over an IDF post, seize weapons, and abduct an IDF soldier.[108] In hindsight, the "March" appears to have served as preparations for the October 7 invasion and massacre. As explained by a Hamas member, the "March's" purpose was to, "enter our occupied lands, and ignite a revolution against the Zionist enemy . . . what was taken by force will be regained by force alone."[109] The slogan for the 2018 Gaza summer camps was "I am returning to my homeland." In September 2023, just weeks before the Hamas assault, similar activity occurred at the border.[110]

Throughout this period, Hamas took control of the UNRWA union.[111] It built its command and control centers and tunnels under UNRWA and humanitarian aid facilities, such as the Al Shifa hospital.[112] The humanitarian aid community played an important role in Hamas's ability to cement control over the territory and reinforce its military fortifications. First, the presence of dozens of humanitarian actors, including at least thirteen UN agencies and seventy-five aid organizations, relieved Hamas of the duty to provide social services for its people, freeing up money, time, and other resources to focus on its political and military agenda. The aid industry also provided an influx of billions of dollars and goods into the territory which Hamas was able to divert for its military purposes.[113]

---

106 Avinoam Sharon, "Recent Developments in Israeli Law," Versa, May 30, 2018, http://versa.cardozo.yu.edu/viewpoints/recent-developments-israeli-law-0.
107 "News of Terrorism and the Israeli-Palestinian Conflict (October 24–October 29, 2018)," Meir Amit Intelligence and Terrorism Information Center, https://www.terrorism-info.org.il/app/uploads/2018/10/E_262_18.pdf.
108 Ibid.
109 "Fence Cutters Unit in Gaza Proclaims Victory," MEMRI, April 27, 2018, https://www.memri.org/tv/fence-cutters-unit-gaza-proclaims-victory-or-martyrom.
110 "Possible Renewal of the Return Marches," Meir Amit Intelligence and Terrorism Information Center, September 10, 2023, https://www.terrorism-info.org.il/en/possible-renewal-of-the-return-marches/.
111 Khaled Abu Toameh, "Hamas Wins Teachers Union Elections for UN Schools in Gaza," *Jerusalem Post*, March 29, 2009, https://www.jpost.com/middle-east/hamas-wins-teachers-union-elections-for-un-schools-in-gaza.
112 "Finnish TV: Rockets from Gaza Hospital," *Times of Israel*, August 2, 2014, https://www.timesofisrael.com/finnish-tv-rockets-fired-from-gaza-hospital/.
113 Rory Jones, Ian Talley, and Benoit Faucon, "How the West—and Israel Itself—Inadvertently Funded Hamas," *Wall Street Journal*, October 19, 2023, https://www.wsj.com/world/middle-east/hamas-gaza-humanitarian-aid-diverted-cf356c48.

Third, aid activities provided a cover for much of Hamas's military activity such as at UNRWA schools and hospitals.[114] UN agencies and humanitarian groups also vociferously lobbied against any restrictions placed on the territory.[115]

Importantly, Hamas control of UNRWA teachers, and the territory more broadly, allowed it to dictate the educational curriculum and information dissemination, not only to indoctrinate the people of Gaza but also to control and frame narratives being exported from the territory by NGOs and UN agencies.[116]

UN Framing of Narratives in the Conflict

The creation and framing of narratives in conflict situations are a means to control messaging and shape public opinion which can then be leveraged for political decision-making.[117] Framing is also used to direct focus in conflict and to divide parties into opposing forces.[118] As Thankatchan and Thomas note, "identity-based or interest-based conflicts are framed in adversarial or win-lose terms rather than seeking a win-win solution."[119]

The UN, and, in particular, the dedicated Palestinian-focused and human rights mechanisms, have played a leading role in framing the narratives in the Arab Israeli conflict. This is due to the UN organization's role as the primary multilateral institution for debating international relations, conducting diplomacy, and establishing international norms, but also because of its part in Israel's establishment. The co-opting of the body that endorsed the creation of a Jewish state to engage in campaigns and messaging that undermines that history, serves as a powerful rhetorical tactic and political weapon.[120]

---

114 Anne Herzberg, "Hamas Exploitation of Hospitals for Hostage Taking: The Legal Imperative to Investigate Aiding and Abetting of War Crimes," *Fathom*, February 2024.
115 "Principles Under Pressure," Norwegian Refugee Council, 2018, www.nrc.no/globalassets/pdf/reports/principles-under-pressure/nrc-principles_under_pressure-report-2018-screen.pdf.
116 Margolin, "Hamas at 35."
117 Keerthana Thankachan and P. E. Thomas, "Media Framing and Its Effects on Conflict: A Thematic Approach to Framing as a Means of Control," *International Journal of Advanced Academic Studies* 3, no. 4 (2021): 6–13, https://www.allstudyjournal.com/article/626/3-3-50-472.pdf.
118 Ibid., 7, citing J. Rothman, *Resolving Identity-Based Conflict in Nations, Organizations, and Communities* (San Francisco, CA: Jossey-Bass, 1997), 21.
119 Ibid.
120 Barnidge, *Self-Determination, Statehood*. In 2013, Palestinian Authority officials convened a conference at Bir Zeit University with UN Rapporteurs, academics, and NGO representatives. The theme of the conference was how to reframe narratives in the conflict. Several

Hamas also emphasizes the importance of narrative creation in its Charter. It remarks that "Jihad is not confined to the carrying of arms and the confrontation of the enemy" but also "the convening of solidarity conferences, the issuing of explanatory bulletins, favorable articles and booklets, enlightening the masses regarding the Palestinian issue...."[121]

In UN narratives, legal framing is dominant.[122] This framing presents Israel as the perpetrator of violation of international law, and the Palestinians as victims of "occupation," "colonialism," "genocide," "apartheid," and an "indigenous" people who were forcibly displaced from "their" land with a "right of return." These themes echo that of the Hamas Charter which speaks about Israel acting "in a way similar to Nazism and which ... relies on the methods of collective punishment."[123]

Another important framing of the conflict is how violence is employed, the extent to which it is used, who carries it out, and why. Thus, in the Arab Israeli conflict, we see common themes of Israelis as violent and cruel oppressors who "indiscriminately" and "disproportionately" target innocent civilians, imposing a "siege" on the "open air prison" of Gaza, while Palestinians are agentless victims; armed groups like Hamas are presented as "freedom fighters," and "human rights defenders, exercising their "right of resistance." Again, these messages harken back to the Hamas Charter decrying the "Jews" who, "in their Nazi treatment ... made no exception for women or children."[124]

---

participants examined strategies to shift the framing away from Palestinian terrorism to one focused on settlements as the "cause of violence." Others advocated shifting from an "occupation" paradigm to one of "Colonialism, apartheid and ethnic cleansing" because "they resonate negatively worldwide and can serve to mobilize public opinion and political support." Proceedings of an International Law Conference Organized by the Bir Zeit Institute of Law, "Law and Politics: Options and Strategies of International Law for the Palestinian People," *Palestine Yearbook of International Law* 17 (2014): 141, 159. Much of this framing also stems from the close relationship between UN bodies and Palestinian-aligned NGOs. Due to both ideological factors and resource constraints, these actors provide a significant bulk of the material relied upon in UN reporting. UN agencies often do not have the resources to conduct independent fact-finding or verification.

121 Hamas Charter, art. 29.
122 I originally identified this framing as "lawfare." Anne Herzberg, *NGO Lawfare: Exploitation of Courts in the Arab-Israeli Conflict*, NGO Monitor, 2008. Zipperstein calls this phenomenon "transformational legal framing." Zipperstein, *Zionism, Palestinian Nationalism*, 17–18. See also Gerald Steinberg and Anne Herzberg, "The Role of International Legal and Justice Discourse in Promoting the New Antisemitism," in *Anti-Zionism and Antisemitism: The Dynamics of Delegitimization*, ed. Alvin H. Rosenfeld (Bloomington, IN: Indiana University Press, 2019), 142–168.
123 Hamas Charter, art. 20.
124 Ibid.

Often, however, it is the information that is concealed in these narratives that is central role in shaping the framing. For instance, in descriptions of fighting between the Israeli military and Palestinian armed groups, the presence of Palestinian fighters is erased or they are described as "civilians." Their military tactics are ignored, or excused, or denied. The antisemitic and jihadi ideology driving the organization and their political objectives is not factored into the UN reporting.

Despite its full political control of Gaza, Hamas's is euphemized as the "de facto authorities" or the "Ministry of Health."[125] Its driving ideology and governance approaches are rarely discussed. The treatment of its own people is a rarely expressed issue of concern. Religion is downplayed. Corruption, exploitation of development aid, and the role played by international institutions is generally not mentioned.

Violence committed against Israelis is not described in significant detail if mentioned at all. If an accounting of Israeli casualties is provided, great care is taken to clearly delineate civilian from combatant figures ensuring the number is as low as possible, while on the Palestinian side, Palestinian civilian and combatant casualties are conflated to maximize the figures—and the accompanying public outrage.[126]

This framing also places emphasis on third state "accountability" and "responsibility" for supporting Israel, with attention placed on activities by the United States, the United Kingdom, or Germany. In contrast, the role of third-party states, such as Iran, Qatar, Syria, or North Korea, complicit in Palestinian violence, are not mentioned. An analysis of Egypt's control of part of Gaza's border and its policies towards Gaza and the Palestinians is generally absent or attributed to Israel.

In addition to driving public discourse and policy, these UN narratives also serve as control mechanisms.[127] As explained by Benford, once narratives are

---

125 See, e.g., "Quarterly Update on Humanitarian Access: Gaza De Facto Authorities Impede Access of NGO Staff," UN OCHA, https://www.ochaopt.org/content/quarterly-update-humanitarian-access-gaza-de-facto-authorities-impede-access-ngo-staff; "Gaza Initial Rapid Assessment, 27 August 2014," UN OCHA, August 27, 2014, https://reliefweb.int/report/occupied-palestinian-territory/gaza-initial-rapid-assessment-27-august-2014.
126 The following statement is indicative: "Between 7 October 2023 and 30 September 2024, at least 41,615 Palestinians were killed and 96,359 were injured, according to MoH [Ministry of Health] in Gaza." "Humanitarian Situation Update #224 | Gaza Strip," UN OCHA, September 30, 2024, https://www.ochaopt.org/content/humanitarian-situation-update-224-gaza-strip.
127 Robert D. Benford, "Controlling Narratives and Narratives as Control within Social Movements," in *Stories of Change: Narratives and Social Movements*, ed. Joseph E. Davis (Albany, NY: SUNY Press, 2002), 53.

established, those responsible for creating them seek to sustain and enforce them in order to prevent the construction and dissemination of alternative or competing narratives.[128] UN mechanisms responsible for crafting the conflict's narratives, also serve as their enforcers. Therefore, those who seek to reframe the dominant narratives by calling attention to these missing elements or seek to expand the discussion are accused of engaging in "smear campaigns" or branded as "Israeli-state agents."[129] This phenomenon appears to be one reason why after October 7, and as the extent to which Hamas was embedded in UN bodies and infrastructure was exposed through IDF military operations in Gaza, UN statements, and particularly those made by UNRWA officials, have become increasingly extreme.[130]

The next section will look at how two Palestinian-focused UN human rights investigatory mechanisms have contributed to narrative framing and enforcement relating to Hamas.

Reports of the Special Committee and the Special Rapporteur

As mentioned, the Special Committee to Investigate Israeli Practices and the Special Rapporteur for the Palestinians were established in 1968 and 1993 respectively to investigate human rights violations by Israel, and report on an annual basis. Voting bloc dynamics dominated by states hostile to Israel created these mechanisms, imparting them with biased mandates. These one-sided mandates reinforced a narrative that Israel was solely to blame for the conflict and would ensure that the reports produced and the activities conducted under these mandates would further entrench the desired narratives and framing. Consequently, these bodies issue copious statements and engage in advocacy that present Israel as solely responsible for the conflict; demonize the government and the IDF as being motivated by bad faith; present Palestinians as

---

128 Ibid.
129 "The Spread of Misinformation and Disinformation Continues to be Used as a Weapon in #Gaza," UNRWA, September 1, 2024, https://www.unrwa.org/newsroom/official-statements/spread-misinformation-disinformation-continues-be-used-weapon-war-gaza; "Palestinian Rights Committee Bureau Calls for Solidarity, Support to Sustain UNRWA amidst Smear Campaign, Funding Suspensions, Humanitarian Crisis in Gaza," CEIRPP, February 28, 2024, https://reliefweb.int/report/occupied-palestinian-territory/palestinian-rights-committee-bureau-calls-solidarity-support-sustain-unrwa-amidst-smear-campaign-funding-suspensions-humanitarian-crisis-gaza.
130 Ibid.

agentless victims of oppression; minimize Israel's security concerns and the extent and impact of Palestinian terrorism on Israeli civilians; and sanitize or erase the aims and activities of Hamas and other terror organizations, as well as their state sponsors such as Iran and Qatar.

Those in the position of Special Rapporteur have particularly viewed their job as one of narrative shapers and enforcers. John Dugard (Rapporteur in 2001–2008) saw himself as the "political arm" of the UN,[131] engaging in "gladiatorial combat" and "openly confronting" the United States and Israel.[132] Richard Falk (2008–2014) believes the conflict consists of a "legitimacy war" for Palestinians, involving "a worldwide struggle to gain control over the debate about legal entitlements and moral proprieties" and the "crucial role" the UN must play in this effort.[133] Michael Lynk (2016–2022), for his part, saw it as his job to "challenge shibboleths" and "tired thinking."[134]

These Rapporteurs resist a "war on terror paradigm" for the conflict and have worked to obstruct this perspective. Francesca Albanese (2022–present) writes, "the way the situation in the oPt is framed is crucial. Not a conflict: a prolonged occupation that has exhausted any lawful raison d'etre, and morphed into institutionalized apartheid, punctuated by violent instances of war."[135] In his penultimate report to the UNHRC in 2007, Dugard posited and lobbied for a reframing of the conflict from one of violations of international humanitarian law, to one of "colonialism" and "apartheid."[136] Falk, like his colleagues, emphasizes the importance of language framing the conflict from one of "occupation" to "colonial ambitions" and "annexation."[137]

The following provides examples of the Special Committee and Rapporteur reporting and narrative dissemination regarding Hamas at critical inflection points in the conflict between 2002 and October 7, 2023.

During the height of the Second Intifada, the Special Committee's 2002 report makes no mention of Hamas, suicide bombings, or terrorism on Israelis.

---

131 Richard Falk, John Dugard, and Michael Lynk, *Protecting Human Rights in Occupied Palestine: Working Through the United Nations* (Atlanta, GA: Clarity Press, 2022), 317. In addition to commentary, this work compiles selected excerpts from their UN reports. These selections demonstrate what themes these advocates deemed significant, but also what aspects they chose not to highlight.
132 Ibid., 316.
133 Ibid., 206.
134 Ibid., 340.
135 Francesca Albanese (@FranceskAlbs), X (formerly Twitter), April 16, 2022, https://twitter.com/FranceskAlbs/status/1515290650077503493.
136 Falk et al., *Protecting Human Rights*, 20.
137 Ibid., 207.

Rather it accuses Israel of "indiscriminate" and "intense bombardment" on Palestinian towns.[138] It details the numbers of Palestinian deaths and injuries but says nothing about Israeli casualties.[139]

Dugard's 2002 report does not deny the existence of Palestinian terrorism as the Special Committee does in its report, but rather blames its existence on "the military occupation" and the bad motives of Israel ("enforcement of the occupation"):

> That terrorism is a scourge that threatens Israelis and Palestinians alike cannot and should not be denied ... At the same time, it is important not to ignore the main explanation for the acts of terror committed by Palestinians against Israelis—opposition to the military occupation. Or the main explanation for the acts of terror committed by the Israel Defense Forces against Palestinians—enforcement of the occupation.[140]

In contrast to naming the IDF (which he equates with terrorists), Palestinian actors, notably Hamas, are unnamed, and their civilian targets and Islamist and eliminationist motives are obscured.[141]

The theme of bad faith reappears in the 2006 Special Committee report. The Committee acknowledges rocket attacks on Israeli cities and that Israel has a "legitimate desire ... to provide security," but then undercuts that legitimacy by claiming that it "cannot be used as an excuse to justify its mistreatment of the Palestinian people."[142] Moreover, the Committee declares, "It is not possible to equate the responsibilities of Palestinians and Israelis" because of Israel's "excessive use of force and the wide range of collective punishments and humiliations imposed on Palestinians as retaliatory measures." Ignoring the clearly defined objectives of Hamas, the Committee imputes good motives to Palestinians,

---

138 Report of the Special Committee, UN Doc. A/57/207, September 16, 2002, para. 30.
139 Ibid., para 29.
140 "Statement by John Dugard," UNHRC, March 26, 2002, https://www.ohchr.org/en/statements/2009/10/default-title-331.
141 The ascribing of bad faith motives to the IDF is a typical theme in UN and NGO reporting. For instance, in a 2003 HRW regarding the Rafah crossing between Egypt and Gaza, HRW called Israeli concerns of tunnels and weapons smuggling "alarmist" and "consistently exaggerated" in order to "justify the demolition of homes." "Razing Rafah," Human Rights Watch, October 17, 2004, https://www.hrw.org/report/2004/10/17/razing-rafah/mass-home-demolitions-gaza-strip.
142 Report of the Special Committee, UN Doc. A/61/500/Add.1, June 8, 2007, para. 46.

whom they claim have the "aspiration" to "live in conditions of a just and durable peace as a neighbour to Israel."¹⁴³

The sanitizing of Hamas's political objectives and ideology similarly appears in Rapporteur Falk's 2008 report. He positively reports on an incident where tens of thousands of Gazans breached the border with Egypt flooding into the territory as an "exodus and spectacle" and sending a "message" to the Israelis. He calls Hamas a "partner" with Israel and that a June 2008 ceasefire could be viewed as "implicit recognition by Hamas of the State of Israel."

In 2009, Falk focuses on Israel's conduct during Operation Cast Lead, claiming it engaged in a "massive assault on a densely populated urbanized setting" subjecting the " entire civilian population to an inhumane form of warfare."¹⁴⁴ Absent from his report was any mention of Hamas tactics embedding within civilian infrastructure and launching hundreds of indiscriminate rockets on "densely populated urban settings" in Israel or subjecting Israeli society to an "inhumane form of warfare." He places sole blame on Israel for breaking a supposed July 2008 "ceasefire" with Hamas. Falk laments as a "dilemma" the "insistence that Palestinians renounce all forms of armed resistance" quoting dissident Israeli columnist Gideon Levy, upset that "life in Israel is just peachy" and that Israelis are not "paying any price" for the "injustice of occupation."¹⁴⁵

A May 2012 report reflects Falk's distress at the world media for reporting on the threat of Hamas rocket fire on Israeli civilians, which he minimizes "as rarely resulting in Israeli casualties" in contrast to the "far more... perilous existence" for Gazans. He adds that, "unlike the Israelis," the Palestinians have no "Iron Dome." Yet, he makes no mention of Hamas's practice of firing rockets from civilian infrastructure, its diversion of humanitarian aid to the detriment of Palestinians, and its building of tunnels to protect its leadership but the failure to provide civil defense for the general population.¹⁴⁶ Indeed, he praises this practice, claiming casualties to "militants were greatly reduced by avoiding targeted facilities and taking shelter, and damage to rocket launchers was reduced by greater mobility and use of underground launching sites."¹⁴⁷ An ongoing theme in his reports is that Hamas, euphemized as the "'de facto' authorities in Gaza,

---

143 Ibid.
144 Falk, *Protecting Human Rights*, 150.
145 Ibid.,167.
146 Ibid., 184.
147 Ibid., 197.

do not themselves engage in retaliation against Israel but rather seek to maintain an effective ceasefire."[148]

Many Special Committee and Rapporteur reports comment on the "blockade," "siege," or other characterizations of restrictions on imports to Gaza. Few to none, however, connected these restrictions to the threat of diversion of building materials by Hamas for tunnels and rockets, nor did they mention how damage could be attributed to Hamas embedding within and under civilian infrastructure. These policies were also characterized as being motivated by bad faith in order to inflict "collective punishment" on Gaza's civilians.[149] The 2011 Special Committee report, for example,[150] states: "Homes, schools and other infrastructure that were destroyed by Israeli attacks in December 2008 and January 2009 could not be rebuilt due to restrictions on the import of building material."[151]

Another promoted narrative is that the tunnel network in Gaza was used primarily for the smuggling of civilian goods necessitated by Israeli strictures. For instance, "The economy declined significantly and is sustained by illegal imports through tunnels."[152] Little was noted about the military purpose of the tunnels and what the implications would be for the civilian population, or about the thousands, many of them children, employed to build them in dire conditions.[153] Falk, in his 2012 report, also downplays the nature and purpose of Hamas's tunnels while again ascribing nefarious motives to Israel that restrictions in Gaza

---

148 Ibid., 185. See also the 2012 report discussing "the hostilities between Israel, the de facto authorities in the Gaza Strip and Palestinian armed groups in Gaza." "Popular discontent could result in another round of violence," Special Committee, UNHRC, June 27, 2013, https://www.ohchr.org/en/press-releases/2013/06/occupied-territories-popular-discontent-could-result-another-round-violence; Report of the Special Committee, UN Doc. A /68/379, September 11, 2013, https://documents.un.org/doc/undoc/gen/n13/471/02/pdf/n1347102.pdf; Richard Falk, "Gaza Fuel Crisis: UN Expert Calls for Urgent Action to Avert a Humanitarian Catastrophe," UNHRC, November 26, 2013, https://www.ohchr.org/en/press-releases/2013/11/gaza-fuel-crisis-un-expert-calls-urgent-action-avert-humanitarian.
149 Statement of Richard Falk, UNHRC, February 20, 2012, https://www.ohchr.org/en/statements/2012/02/statement-united-nations-special-rapporteur-situation-human-rights-palestinian; General Assembly Provisional Agenda, UN Doc. A/69/150 (2014).
150 Statement of the Special Committee, UNHRC, July 28, 2011, https://www.ohchr.org/en/press-releases/2011/07/systematic-human-rights-violations-continue-occupied-territories-says-un.
151 The September 11, 2013, Special Committee Report includes similar narratives.
152 Statement of Richard Falk, February 20, 2012; Richard Falk, "Collective Punishment in Gaza Must End: Israel's Blockade Enters Its 7th Year," UNHRC, June 14, 2013, https://www.ohchr.org/en/press-releases/2013/06/collective-punishment-gaza-must-end-israels-blockade-enters-its-7th-year-un.
153 "2009/10 Human Development Report: Occupied Palestinian Territory," UNDP, January 2010, hdr.undp.org/system/files/documents/nhdrpalestineen2009-10.pdf.

"signals of the Government of Israel's unlawful efforts to separate the Gaza Strip from Palestine, by forcing Gazans to rely via the tunnels on Egypt to fulfill their basic needs."[154]

Michael Lynk's 2020 report emphasized the "collective punishment" of Palestinians by Israel, calling it an "inflamed scar that runs across the entire 53-year-old Israeli occupation of Palestinian territory." He characterized Israel counter-terror measures as the methods of "belligerent armies, colonial authorities, and Occupying Powers." He notes that, for twenty-five years, UN institutions have "deplored" Israeli "collective punishment."[155] Israel's closure is blamed for turning Gaza into an "impoverished ghetto with a decimated economy and collapsing social service system." His 2022 report accuses Israel of "an indefinite warehousing of an unwanted population of 2 million Palestinians." Hamas—its authoritarian rule, its diversion of aid, its attacks on the humanitarian crossings, its turning of Gaza into a military fortification to launch attacks on Israel as part of its eliminationist agenda—is not ascribed any blame. In fact, Lynk considers rocket fire into Israel as merely a "probably war crime" that occurs apparently only "in times of intense combat in Gaza."[156] He further believes that Hamas, "as ghastly as some of its actions have been," should be incorporated "within a meaningful conflict-resolution strategy."[157]

In 2021, the Special Committee reported on the fourth major round of fighting between Israel and Hamas and echoed earlier reports. The Committee focused on the "substantial damage to civilian infrastructure in Gaza," caused by "Israeli forces' indiscriminate attacks on public and private properties (including businesses, industrial and commercial entities, schools, mosques, banks, farmlands and media outlets) as well as damage to infrastructure, including power, telecommunication, health and water...."[158] Hamas was not held responsible for any of this damage, there was no mention of Hamas exploitation of

---

154 Statement of Richard Falk, February 20, 2012; "UNDP Human Development Report," 94: "Tunnels have become a highly lucrative business... but are dangerous and even lethal to those who work in them. As one older resident of Gaza put it, 'one of the worst forms of insecurity... is their work building and running tunnels. I call this 'suicide in the name of work.' It affects about 25,000 people.'"
155 Falk, *Protecting Human Rights*, 268.
156 Ibid., 358.
157 Ibid., 356–357.
158 Deemed Israeli "aggression" (para 12), Report of the Special Committee, UN Doc. A/76/360, September 29, 2021.

civilian infrastructure to conceal weapons and launch rocket attacks, nor did the Committee discuss that much of damage to power, water, telecommunications, and so on were due to short-falling Hamas rockets or theft of pipes and other material by the terrorist organization.

Albanese takes the analysis to an even more extreme position in her first report as Rapporteur, claiming that Israel's policies towards Gaza "is at the core of the settler-colonial goal to ensure the demographic supremacy and prevent Palestinian self-determination."[159] She blames Israel for "preventing Palestinians from voting and interfering with Palestinian politics" because an "independent formation of a Palestinian [e.g., Hamas-dominated] leadership and political will that could challenge Israeli colonial interests."[160] Moreover, she considers the "violent suppression of popular resistance" to be "collective punishment," but that the "law of self-determination" legitimizes a Palestinian "right to resist."[161] She notes that acts to prevent "resistance" amount to "persecution."[162]

The 2018 reporting grossly downplayed the nature of the 2018 marches, including minimizing the violence employed and the political objectives. The Special Committee, for instance, notes that the purpose of the marches was to call for the Palestinian "right to return to lands from which they were displaced during and after 1948." Yet, it fails to appreciate the violent political objective behind that sentiment. It describes the events as "largely peaceful," in contrast to the serious nature of the violence. While it calls "the commission of violent acts by some" "unacceptable," it "condemns the excessive and disproportionate use of force by Israeli security forces," claiming without evidence that these acts "did not pose a threat to life or serious injury," despite the mass efforts to overrun the fence and attempts to attack soldiers and neighboring civilian communities.[163] The organizing role of Hamas and statements of violent intent by its leaders was absent.[164]

---

159 Francesca Albanese, *Report of the Special Rapporteur on the Situation of Human Rights in the Palestinian Territories Occupied since 1967*, UN Doc. A/77/356, September 21, 2022, para. 46.
160 Ibid., para. 59.
161 Ibid., paras. 6, 30.
162 Ibid., para. 62.
163 "Examination of the List of Fatalities in the 'Return Marches' Reveals that Most of Them are Operatives of Terrorist Organizations, About Half of Whom Affiliated with Hamas," Meir Amit Intelligence and Terrorism Information Center, January 21, 2019, https://www.terrorism-info.org.il/en/examination-list-fatalities-return-marches-reveals-operatives-terrorist-organizations-half-affiliated-hamas/.
164 Special Committee Report, UN Doc. A/73/499, November 9, 2018.

Issued just days prior to October 7, 2023, the Special Committee report remarked on the renewal of violent activity along the Gaza/Israel border fence. The Committee again erased the role of Hamas in organizing the events, instead claiming it was "an idea conceived by a Palestinian poet and envisaged as a non-violent march at the separation fence."[165] The Committee repeated claims by "senior Hamas officials" that the protests were because "the humanitarian situation in Gaza had worsened again in 2023, and the renewed protests were intended to raise international awareness of the humanitarian situation." It lamented that during the 2018 violence, "Israeli forces reinforced their positions at the fence with additional troops, including more than 100 sharpshooters" and repeated claims that the demonstrations were civilian in nature, had clearly stated political aims and, despite some acts of significant violence, did not constitute combat or a military campaign."[166]

UNRWA was also a significant focus in the 2023 Special Committee report criticizing that the agency had been "chronically underfunded for a decade."[167] It argued that US "funding to UNRWA equates to 7 to 9 per cent of the foreign military assistance provided by the United States to Israel each year" and is "supplemented by an additional $1 billion to replenish the Israeli 'Iron Dome' system." Setting aside its lack of knowledge regarding US strategic interests or the inner workings of the US-Israel relationship, the Committee ignored the longstanding and documented criticisms regarding UNRWA's role in prolonging the conflict, exposing children to incitement to violence and antisemitic messaging, Hamas's control of the teachers' union, and exploitation of its facilities for Hamas military installations.

Implications and Conclusions

The examples discussed above demonstrate how narrow, politically driven framing and narrative dissemination and enforcement, constructed in a similarly confined ecosystem, can serve to obstruct policy making and serve as a vector to inflame conflict. For nearly twenty years, the way in which UN bodies engaged

---

165 Special Committee Report, UN Doc. A/78/553, October 25, 2023 (dated after October 7, but authored prior to the events).
166 Ibid., paras. 34–35.
167 Ibid., para. 41.

with Hamas and were involved in Hamas's management of Gaza once it seized full control of the territory, coupled with one-sided UN mechanisms serving as the predominate means through which conflict narratives were created, disseminated, and enforced, has proven disastrous for the region.

The nature of Hamas ideology; its military strategy; and its exploitation of humanitarian aid systems to carry out its political objectives were largely indulged by UN humanitarian agencies and then concealed by UN human rights frameworks. Had they approached Gaza and the problem posed by Hamas rule without these politicized and myopic blinders, perhaps the events of October 7 and the catastrophe that has followed could have been avoided.

As noted by UN Secretary General Anthony Guterres on October 24, 2023, "the attacks by Hamas didn't happen in a vacuum." Indeed.

PART 3

THE CAMPUS AND THE LAND OF MAKE-BELIEVE

CHAPTER 9

Higher Education Responds to October 7

KC Johnson

On August 13, 2024, US District Court Judge Mark Scarsi granted an injunction to Jewish students at UCLA. They had sued after the university allowed anti-Israel protesters to set up an encampment, surrounded by a barrier made of plywood, and then physically block Zionist Jewish students from part of the campus. The court found that UCLA effectively made "certain of its programs, activities, and campus areas available to other students when UCLA knew that some Jewish students . . . were excluded." In 2024, Judge Scarsi concluded, "*Jewish students were excluded from portions of the UCLA campus because they refused to denounce their faith* (emphasis in original)."[1] A UCLA spokesperson lamented that the ruling would "improperly hamstring our ability to respond to events on the ground," but the university eventually decided not to appeal.[2]

One student described the encampment as a "weird" development whose participants simultaneously claimed "to be peaceful and anti-war, but also had a critical mass of people who were in support of Hamas" and who "completely ignored the hostages and the horrific attacks of October 7th."[3] The encampment reflected a broader campus environment where, in the aftermath of October 7, almost 25% of UCLA's Jewish students experienced a physical attack or threat

---

1 *Frankel v. Regents of the Univ. of Cal.*, 2024 U.S. Dist. LEXIS 146433, *3 (Central Dist. Cal. August 13, 2024).
2 Amy Dipierro, "Federal Judge Orders UCLA to Ensure Equal Access to Jewish Students following pro-Palestinian Protests," *EdSource*, August 14, 2024, https://edsource.org/2024/federal-judge-orders-ucla-to-ensure-equal-access-to-jewish-students-following-pro-palestinian-protests/717544.
3 *Antisemitism and Anti-Israel Bias at UCLA*, Task Force Report, October 16, 2024, 27, https://antisemitismreport.org/.

and nearly 40% experienced some form of antisemitic discrimination. Jewish undergraduates regularly encountered inappropriate anti-Israel or antisemitic behavior from teaching assistants. Marches featured such slogans as "Intifada," "from the river to the sea, Palestine will be free," and "kill the Jews."[4] Some professors offered extra credit or excused class attendance and assignments to students who joined the encampment.[5]

Even after the injunction, the attitudes that aroused the court's concern remained. The undergraduate student government—curiously, by secret ballot—had voted ten to three to endorse a pro-BDS resolution.[6] And the head of UCLA's Cultural Affairs Commission allegedly told staffers to do "your research when you look at [job] applicants" because "lots of zionists (sic) are applying."[7]

Since October 7, 2023, virtually every elite college or university has witnessed similar campus developments. Three factors stand out regarding the academy's response to October 7, the subject of this chapter.

First, protests flourished primarily at either elite colleges and universities or at public universities in deep-blue states that draw from a population base that has grown sharply critical of Israel.[8] A statistical analysis from *Washington Monthly* confirmed that "pro-Palestinian protests are overwhelmingly an elite college phenomenon," with protests particularly likely at private institutions that had few Pell Grant students and highly selective admissions standards.[9]

For the faculty, meanwhile, anti-Israel activism came disproportionately from professors in the humanities, law, public health, and some social sciences. That virulent anti-Israel rhetoric, often couched in misleading analysis, came from the nation's finest universities questioned the traditional liberal belief that better education is the solution to eradicating antisemitism. As Dara Horn asked about the post-October 7 academy: "If hatred comes from ignorance, why were

---

4   Ibid., 46.
5   Ibid., 62.
6   Aaron Bandler, "UCLA Student Gov't Passes BDS Resolution," *Jewish Journal*, February 22, 2024, https://jewishjournal.com/community/368513/ucla-student-govt-passes-bds-resolution/.
7   Seth Mandel, "The Codification of Anti-Jewish Hiring Policies," *Commentary*, November 29, 2024, https://www.commentary.org/seth-mandel/the-codification-of-anti-jewish-hiring-policies/.
8   Laura Silver, "Younger Americans Stand Out in Their Views of the Israel-Hamas War," Pew Research Center, April 2, 2024, https://www.pewresearch.org/short-reads/2024/04/02/younger-americans-stand-out-in-their-views-of-the-israel-hamas-war/.
9   Robert Kelchen and Mark Novikoff, "Are Gaza Protests Happening Mostly at Elite Colleges?," *Washington Monthly*, May 24, 2024, https://washingtonmonthly.com/2024/05/24/are-gaza-protests-happening-mostly-at-elite-colleges/.

America's best universities full of this very specific ignorance? And why were so many people trying to justify it, explain it away, or even deny it?"[10]

Second, virtually no campus protest denounced Hamas in any way, even for using Palestinians as human shields or for kidnapping or murdering Israeli Arabs. To the contrary: as the 2024–2025 academic year proceeded, outright pro-Hamas commentary started to grow more pronounced.[11] About the only campus impact of Hamas murdering non-Jews came when the Harvard Nepali Students Association withdrew its signature from an anti-Israel letter after news broke that Hamas had killed ten Nepali students on October 7.[12]

The protesters' unwillingness to condemn Hamas, even if only for the terrorist organization's actions toward Arabs, was even more notable given examples of heroism from Israeli Arabs. For instance, on October 7, a Bedouin construction worker and married father of two, Amer abu Sabila, was in Sderot visiting his brothers. After the attack began, he phoned his parents to assure them he was all right, but he then encountered a Jewish Israeli woman whose husband had been murdered. Abu Sabila drove the woman and her two daughters to the Sderot Police Station and what he thought was safety—only to discover that Hamas had taken over the building. Terrorists murdered him and the Jewish mother, though the two daughters survived. This extraordinary combination of courage and tolerance would seem tailor-made for a campus movement that ostensibly protested Islamophobia. Yet, as spring 2024 encampments renamed campus buildings on behalf of Palestinians killed by Israelis, abu Sabila's name went wholly unmentioned.[13]

Third, while antisemitism in the United States had traditionally come from the right, virtually none of the antizionist campus activism came from the right. Instead, it was almost entirely either a left-wing or an Islamist phenomenon. Rabbi David Wolpe, who briefly served on Harvard's antisemitism advisory group, recognized the existence of an "ideology that grips far too many of the

---

10 Dara Horn, "Why the Most Educated People in America Fall for Anti-Semitic Lies," *Atlantic*, February 15, 2024, https://www.theatlantic.com/ideas/archive/2024/02/jewish-anti-semitism-harvard-claudine-gay-zionism/677454/.
11 Laura Meckler and Susan Svrluga, "Pro-Hamas Messages Intensify on College Campuses," *Washington Post*, November 10, 2024, https://www.washingtonpost.com/education/2024/11/10/pro-hamas-messages-college-campuses/.
12 "Statement by the Harvard Undergraduate Nepali Student Organization," October 10, 2023, https://www.instagram.com/p/CyOyCuBOCnS/.
13 Ilana Curiel, "Bedouin Family Mourns Son Murdered by Terrorists Amid Heroic Act," Ynet, October 27, 2023, https://www.ynetnews.com/magazine/article/skrbfzfzt.

students and faculty, the ideology that works only along axes of oppression and places Jews as oppressors and therefore intrinsically evil."[14]

Quite unlike the case with far-right antisemitism, the ideology behind the recent anti-Israel activism came from well within the academic mainstream and was well represented among the faculty ranks. It thus created a difficult problem even for those administrators who wanted to act. As Boston University professor David Decosimo observed, "Years of faculty searches that have been explicitly ideological and partisan, prizing and hiring for the illiberal radicalism on display in the ... Hamas-praise."[15] Even the American Association of University Professors (AAUP), the organization founded in 1915 to defend academic freedom and the rights of campus dissenters from the prevailing orthodoxy on campus, gave way. In Fall 2024, it reversed its longstanding position and deemed BDS resolutions targeting Israel and Israeli academics as consistent with principles of academic freedom.[16]

The campus response to October 7 proceeded through three distinct periods. The first came immediately after the massacre, with student groups and professors either outright supporting Hamas or (much more frequently) penning public letters providing "context" that minimized the significance of Hamas atrocities. Even with the benefit of hindsight, it remains remarkable that the worst killing of Jewish civilians since the Holocaust led to a wave of protests *against* Israel.

The second period began in late 2023, as the House Education and Workforce Committee convened oversight hearings. A variety of university presidents struggled to defend their responses to anti-Israel campus protesters. The spectacle brought national attention to toxic campus environments and ultimately triggered the resignations of the Harvard, Penn, and Columbia presidents.

The third period occurred as the weather warmed in April and May 2024. (Virtually no relationship existed between the pace of the Gaza conflict—most of the key battles, other than Rafah, had passed by this point—and the intensity of the campus protests.) Almost always in violation of their school's regulations, protesters established encampments to express their hostility to Israel. Though they claimed to be engaging in civil disobedience, the protesters and

---

14 David Wolpe (@RabbiWolpe), X (formerly Twitter), December 7, 2023, https://x.com/RabbiWolpe/status/1732847411175796747.

15 David Decosimo (@DavidDecosimo), X (formerly Twitter), Oct. 24, 2023, https://x.com/DavidDecosimo/status/1716848091175743750.

16 Ryan Quinn, "AAUP Faces Criticism for Reversal on Academic Boycotts," Inside Higher Ed, August 16, 2024, https://www.insidehighered.com/news/faculty-issues/academic-freedom/2024/08/16/aaup-faces-criticism-reversal-academic-boycotts.

their allies ferociously opposed any punishment for their actions, which sometimes included criminal misconduct.

***

On the morning of October 7 at Harvard, a student veteran of anti-Israel activism sprung into action. From a profile in the *New Yorker*: "As Harvard's campus awoke to news of the Hamas attack on Israel, a Palestinian American student... rushed to her friend's apartment, still in pajamas, to compose 'an emergency statement' on behalf of Palestinian allies on campus."[17] The resulting statement, signed by thirty-four student groups, held "the Israeli regime entirely responsible" for "all the unfolding violence." The statement claimed that "the massacres in Gaza have already commenced," even as the IDF desperately sought to save Israeli civilians within Israeli territory; the only Gazans killed at this point were those who had invaded Israel. The statement declined to condemn Hamas's mass murder of civilians, its use of sexual violence, or its kidnapping of hundreds of people. Instead, the thirty-four Harvard student groups demanded "a firm stand against colonial retaliation."[18]

Student groups elsewhere released similarly inflammatory missives—at a time, to reiterate, when Hamas operatives remained on Israeli soil and the full horror of the massacre was emerging. The Columbia chapters of Students for Justice in Palestine and Jewish Voice for Peace expressed "**full solidarity** with Palestinian resistance against over 75 years of Israeli settler-colonialism ... [in] an unprecedented historic moment for the Palestinians of Gaza" in which "**Palestinians launched a counter-offensive against their settler-colonial oppressor** (emphasis in original)."[19] At UCLA, the Undergraduate Student Association Council Cultural Affairs Commissioner released an official statement honoring "the Palestinians on the frontlines taking their land and sovereignty back! From the River to The Sea, Palestine Will Be Free."[20] At Yale, student activists stood "in

---

17 Eren Orebey, "The Anguished Fallout from a Pro-Palestinian Letter at Harvard," *New Yorker*, October 30, 2023, https://www.newyorker.com/news/dispatch/the-anguished-fallout-from-a-pro-palestinian-letter-at-harvard.
18 "Joint Statement by Harvard Palestine Solidarity Groups," October 8, 2023, https://s3.documentcloud.org/documents/24025075/joint-statement-by-harvard-palestine-solidarity-groups.pdf.
19 "Columbia Students for Justice in Palestine Statement of Solidarity," October 9, 2023, https://www.palestine-studies.org/en/node/1654384.
20 Alicia Verdugo (@culturalaffairs), "The Cultural Affairs Commission of UCLA Stands in Solidarity with Palestinians in Their Struggle for Liberation from Israel," Instagram, October 9, 2023, https://www.instagram.com/p/CyMSRCuSlAR/?img_index=2.

solidarity with Palestinian resistance against violent settler colonial oppression" and held "the Zionist regime accountable" for any loss of civilian lives.[21]

Five days after the massacre, the national branch of Students for Justice in Palestine (SJP) organized a day of resistance, and SJP rallies occurred at universities around the country. The SJP messaging toolkit stressed that "settlers are not 'civilians' in the sense of international law, because they are military assets used to ensure continued control over stolen Palestinian land." A promotional poster featured a drawing of a paraglider, recalling the paragliders Hamas used in the attack.[22]

These protests avoided criticizing Hamas or mentioning the fate of hostages being held in Gaza, and instead advanced strongly anti-Israel positions, such as a Palestine from the river to the sea or a renewed intifada.[23] During a second round of direct action, on October 25, Cooper Union protesters chanting "Free Palestine" banged on a library door and a transparent library window behind which sheltered some Jewish students.[24] A University of Washington speaker proclaimed, "We don't want Israel to exist. We don't want these Zionist counter protesters to exist."[25] A Penn student celebrated the "powerful images that came from the glorious October 7th. . . . I felt so empowered and happy."[26]

Students faced criminal charges at both the University of Massachusetts (for occupying a campus building) and Harvard (for assaulting a Jewish student documenting a public anti-Israel protest).[27] At Columbia, a student group

---

21 Yalies4Palestine (@yalies4palestine), Instagram, October 9, 2023, https://www.instagram.com/yalies4palestine/p/CyLbSibAU5A/?hl=en&img_index=1.
22 Melissa Koenig, "Student Groups at Calif. University Face Backlash Over Pro-Palestinian Rally Poster Featuring Paraglider," *New York Post*, October 10, 2023; see also Emma Greem, "How a Student Group Is Politicizing a Generation on Palestine," *New Yorker*, December 15, 2023, https://archive.ph/QJfjP.
23 Video of Columbia Protest, posted by Aviva Klompas (@AvivaKlompas), X (formerly Twitter), October 12, 2023, https://x.com/AvivaKlompas/status/1712588263133790366; Video of UCLA Protest, posted by Aviva Klompas (@AvivaKlompas), X (formerly Twitter), October 12, 2023, https://x.com/AvivaKlompas/status/1712613678166466862.
24 Sharon Otterman, "How a 6-Second Video Turned a Campus Protest into a National Firestorm," *New York Times*, December 18, 2023, https://www.nytimes.com/2023/12/18/us/campus-protest-video.html.
25 Video of University of Washington Protest, posted by Jason Rantz (@jasonrantz), X (formerly Twitter), October 23, 2023, https://x.com/jasonrantz/status/1717277404136403303.
26 Video of University of Pennsylvania Protest, posted by This Is Penn (@this.is.penn), Instagram, November 2, 2023, https://www.instagram.com/this.is.penn/reel/CzKkvDqAdpN/.
27 Video of University of Massachusetts Protest, posted by Kassy Akiva (@KassyAkiva), X (formerly Twitter), October 25, 2023, https://x.com/KassyAkiva/status/1717644714432700697; Sally Edwards, "Harvard Grad Students Charged Following Confrontation at October Pro-Palestine Protest," *Harvard Crimson*, May 18, 2024, https://www.thecrimson.com/article/2024/5/18/graduate-students-charged-hbs-palestine-confrontation/.

scheduled a movie night with an accompanying message from its president: "Zionists aren't invited" and "THE HOLOCAUST WASN'T SPECIAL."[28] Students at George Washington University projected messages of "Glory to our martyrs" and "Free Palestine from the river to the sea" onto the walls of the university library.[29] Students at multiple campuses ripped down posters of kidnapped Israelis; a New York University student (who formerly had interned for the ADL) claimed to "have found it increasingly difficult to know my place as a biracial brown woman."[30]

Some of these students' instructors greeted the Hamas massacre with ill concealed glee. Cornell professor Russell Rickford told an anti-Israel rally that the attack "was energizing. And if [Palestinian civilians] weren't exhilarated by this challenge to the monopoly of violence, by this shifting of the balance of power, then they would not be human. I was exhilarated."[31] Columbia professor Joseph Massad celebrated as "awesome" the "Palestinian resistance's takeover of several Israeli settler-colonies near the Gaza boundary."[32] Yale professor Zareena Grewal asserted that "Israel is a murderous, genocidal settler state and Palestinians have every right to resist through armed struggle."[33] Discussing the fate of innocent civilians in the Israeli south, Grewal was dismissive: "Settlers are not civilians. This is not hard."[34] Speaking to "zionist journalists," University of California-Davis professor Jemma Decristo tweeted

---

28 Carl Campanile, "Columbia University Lesbian Group Disinvites 'Zionists' from Movie Night," *New York Post*, October 25, 2023, https://nypost.com/2023/10/25/metro/columbia-university-lesbian-group-disinvites-zionists-from-movie-night/.
29 Andrew Lapin, "'Glory to our martyrs' Projected onto Building at George Washington University," *Times of Israel*, October 26, 2023, https://www.timesofisrael.com/glory-to-our-martyrs-protected-onto-building-at-george-washington-university/.
30 "New York Student Yazmeen Deyhimi Apologises for Tearing Posters of Israeli Hostages," NDTV, October 18, 2023, https://www.ndtv.com/world-news/nyu-student-yazmeen-deyhimi-apologises-after-video-of-her-tearing-posters-of-israeli-hostages-goes-viral-4492851.
31 Sofia Robinson, "Cornell Professor 'Exhilarated' by Hamas's Attack Defends Remark," *Cornell Daily Sun*, October 16, 2023, https://cornellsun.com/2023/10/16/cornell-professor-exhilarated-by-hamass-attack-defends-remark/.
32 Joseph Massad, "Just Another Battle or the Palestinian War of Liberation?," Electronic Intifada, October 8, 2023, https://electronicintifada.net/content/just-another-battle-or-palestinian-war-liberation/38661.
33 Ari Blaff, "'Settlers Are Not Civilians': Yale Professor Defends Hamas Terrorism," *National Review*, October 11, 2023, https://www.nationalreview.com/news/settlers-are-not-civilians-yale-professor-defends-hamas-terrorism/.
34 Ibid.

(with images of a knife, a machete, and three drops of blood), "They can fear their bosses, but they should fear us more."[35]

The professors who made the most extreme post-October 7 statements came from similar scholarly traditions. None came from STEM, economics, or finance. Rickford is a professor of African American history. Massad is a specialist in Arab politics whose first book attributed homophobia in the Middle East to European imperialists. Grewal's research focuses on race, gender, religion, and nationalism among American Muslims. Decristo is a specialist in the interplay between sound, race, gender, and embodiment. Extreme hostility to Israel functioned as an outgrowth of their research interests.

That said, professors such as the quartet above were the exception. A far more common faculty response focused on public, mass-signed letters purporting to provide context to better understand the events of October 7. The context provided, however, was highly selective. The Hamas attack featured the mass, targeted killing of civilians. But none of the faculty letters mentioned comparable events, such as the Srebrenica massacre in the Yugoslav wars, the September 11 attacks, or the Russian murder of civilians in Bucha or Mariupol during the Ukraine war. The letters were similarly devoid of context for Hamas's use of rape as a weapon of war or its taking of hostages.

Each of the faculty letters either came from humanities departments or attracted signatures mostly from professors in the humanities and softer social sciences. A focus on research themes of race, gender, and ethnicity disproportionately appeared among the signatories. Oriented around concepts of "decolonization," the faculty documents presented residents of a state internationally recognized for more than seventy-five years as a rogue entity of "settler colonialists."[36] The letters' primary purpose seemed to be minimizing or even implicitly justifying Hamas atrocities by presenting a tendentious, one-sided summary of Israeli security policies since the creation of the state.

A public letter signed by 120 full-time City University of New York faculty members typified the genre. The document charged that the CUNY administration, which had issued a statement condemning Hamas, sought to "suppress dissent" from "anti-apartheid" protesters, thereby "rejecting all criticism of Israel." The CUNY signatories implied that the Israeli military response

---

35 Jemma Decristo (@jemmaisOKeh), X (formerly Twitter), October 10, 2023, reposted by Jason Bedrick (@JasonBedrick), X (formerly Twitter), October 19, 2023, https://x.com/JasonBedrick/status/1715036789730431299.
36 For background, see Simon Sebag Montefiore, "The Decolonization Narrative Is Dangerous and False," *Atlantic*, October 27, 2023, https://www.theatlantic.com/ideas/archive/2023/10/decolonization-narrative-dangerous-and-false/675799/.

was *more* troubling than anything Hamas did. There was, the signatories proclaimed, "no equivalence between the October 7 military operation by Hamas and the subsequent military attack by the Israeli state, and certainly no equivalence to the systemic and the violence of Israeli settler colonialism. Israeli state violence has defined Palestinian life in Israel, the West Bank, and the Gaza Strip since 1948."[37]

Similar joint letters came from professors at Columbia (defending student groups' effort to "recontextualize the events of October 7, 2023"), Princeton (endorsing the right of return), Cal-Berkeley ("Israel's attack on Gaza constitutes a deliberate and acknowledged act of genocide"), Harvard (university criticizing "from the river to the sea" was "badly misjudged as an act of moral leadership"), and institutions in New England ("potentially genocidal campaign"); along with disciplinary missives came from sociologists (Israel committing "internationally supported genocide"), linguists (need to address October 7 in "context"), and specialists in ethnic studies ("context is crucial" when discussing "Zionist militarism").[38] Multiple academic departments or programs adopted an anti-Israel perspective as official orthodoxy. Northwestern's Asian American Studies Program put the matter the most bluntly, on its official university webpage: "As Ethnic Studies scholars, we are pro-Palestine."[39]

---

37 "CUNY Faculty and Staff Reject the Palestine Exception to Free Speech," October 17, 2023, https://docs.google.com/document/u/3/d/e/2PACX-1vT1FLJtSCq9kn8uTAwNLlr4V9kkoGWxGsS6PPTwuaDNesQHbprxwiAQhWsv4MBsOpe5vyZBaJsAeyx7/pub.
38 See "An Open Letter from Columbia University and Barnard College Faculty in Defense of Robust Debate about the History and Meaning of the War in Israel/Gaza," October 30, 2023, https://docs.google.com/document/d/1cVLg6RTnqd2BTzuouWbfACnFEex7GQeImDZJnMlUReM/preview?tab=t.0; "Berkeley Faculty for Justice in Palestine," *The Daily Californian*, December 20, 2023, https://www.dailycal.org/opinion/letters-to-the-editor/berkeley-faculty-for-justice-in-palestine/article_7a4bf44c-9a23-11ee-8ebd-af32631a60e4.html; " An Open Letter from Faculty for Justice in Palestine," *Daily Princetonian*, November 29, 2023, https://t.co/JmrAo8sNiY; "Harvard Faculty Statement in Support of Academic Freedom," *Medium*, November 14, 2023, https://medium.com/@acfreedomfacstatement/harvard-faculty-response-to-combating-antisemitism-86ca47e87cdf; Maggie Scales, "More Than 1,000 Professors Call for Cease-fire in Gaza in Open Letter to New England Senators," *Boston Globe*, December 6, 2023, https://www.bostonglobe.com/2023/12/06/metro/israel-hamas-cease-fire-professors-open-letter/; "Statement on Bias in UC Statements," University of California Ethnic Studies Faculty Council, October 16, 2023, https://drive.google.com/file/d/1053yck657ENep688zvPTs6njfAGWBvE6/view; "MLA Delegates Pass Motion Defending Pro-Palestine Speech," Inside Higher Ed, January 08, 2024, https://t.co/KJiZ0yLtgu.
39 "Open Letter to NU Leadership on Islamophobia," Asian American Studies Program, October 17, 2023, https://asianamerican.northwestern.edu/about/news/2023/open-letter-to-nu-leadership-on-islamophobia.html.

No college or university president took anywhere near such extreme positions. And some—such as University of Florida President Ben Sasse—unequivocally condemned Hamas for its actions.[40] But many prominent university presidents struggled both to enforce their school's own rules against anti-Israel protesters or to make clear statements criticizing Hamas—a record that attracted the attention of legislators.

To be sure, university leaders traditionally had eschewed taking public positions on controversial political issues—often by citing the Kalven Report, which embraced institutional neutrality on grounds that "the university is the home and sponsor of critics; it is not itself the critic."[41] But, by the time of George Floyd's murder, most elite schools had embraced a different approach, issuing strong moral condemnations (generally consistent with a liberal worldview) on major issues of the day. Standing up for Israel, by contrast, was not seen as a position associated with the campus left, and many university presidents struggled to address October 7 in public remarks. The presidents or deans at Harvard, Penn, Cornell, and the University of Virginia all issued follow-up statements after their alumni or other university communities protested the temporizing nature of their original reaction.

No university leader struggled with the tensions caused by October 7 more than Harvard President Claudine Gay, who issued three statements. The first came on October 9, where she joined seventeen other senior administrators in a both-sides approach, terming themselves "heartbroken" about "the death and destruction unleashed" by Hamas and "the war in Israel and Gaza now under way."[42] Though the original draft "denounce[d] this [Hamas] act of terror," the final statement removed the language at the urging of Gay's chief of staff.[43] The senior administrators also considered—but declined to include—a passage distancing the university from the student groups' statement and a reference to

---

40 Kelly Garrity, "Senator-turned-university-president Disses Fellow Educators for Silence," Politico, October 15, 2023, https://www.politico.com/news/2023/10/15/ben-sasse-university-president-israel-hamas-00121627.

41 "Kalven Committee: Report on the University's Role in Political and Social Action," November 11, 1967, https://provost.uchicago.edu/sites/default/files/documents/reports/KalvenRprt_0.pdf.

42 Claudine Gay et al., "A Statement from Harvard University Leadership," October 9, 2023, https://www.harvard.edu/president/news-gay/2023/war-in-the-middle-east/.

43 *Antisemitism on College Campuses Exposed*, Republican Staff Report, Committee on Education and Workforce, U.S. House of Representatives, October 31, 2024, 35–38.

Hamas's action as "violent."[44] After harsh criticism of the original statement, Gay issued a second statement the following day, "on the war in the Middle East," in which she left "no doubt" that she condemned Hamas's terrorism and distanced herself from the student groups' missive.[45]

Gay's third, and most passionate, statement (which came on video) defended the student groups' ability to articulate their position. Harvard, she remarked, "rejects the harassment or intimidation of individuals based on their beliefs" and "embraces a commitment to free expression."[46] Gay's administration showed reluctance to employ disciplinary processes against student disruptors, even for behavior—as in a pro-Palestinian student march through campus buildings disrupting classes with chants of "let Gaza live"—that would violate the rules of virtually any university in the country.[47]

The politics of campus antisemitism are unusual. Many prominent Democrats—including the Biden administration (which worried about the "extremely disturbing pattern of antisemitic messages being conveyed on college campuses"), Majority Leader Charles Schumer (D-NY), Governor Josh Shapiro (D-PA), and then-Representative Adam Schiff (D-CA)—strongly criticized the campus protesters.[48] And arguably the two strongest supporters of Israel in Congress—Senator John Fetterman (D-PA) and Representative Ritchie Torres (D-NY)—are Democrats. But policy toward Israel divides the caucus, which also includes antisemitic members from the Squad and progressives responsive to a party base that, especially among younger voters, has grown increasingly hostile to Israel in recent years.

So, with campus antisemitism dividing Democrats but uniting Republicans, it's easy to see why (beyond the policy question) the House Education and Workforce Committee convened early December hearings on how higher education responded to October 7. The initial witnesses—the presidents of Harvard (Claudine Gay), Penn (Liz Magill), and MIT (Nancy Kornbluh)—appeared on

---

44 Ibid.
45 Claudine Gay, "War in the Middle East," October 10, 2023, https://www.harvard.edu/president/news-gay/2023/war-in-the-middle-east/.
46 Claudine Gay, "Our Choices," October 12, 2023, https://www.harvard.edu/president/news-gay/2023/our-choices/.
47 Cam Kettles, "Hundreds Disrupt Classes, March through Harvard Law School, Kennedy School in Support of Palestine," *Harvard Crimson*, October 20, 2023.
48 Jacob Magid, "White House Slams 'Grotesque' Displays of Antisemitism on College Campuses," *Times of Israel*, October 26, 2023; https://www.timesofisrael.com/liveblog_entry/white-house-slams-grotesque-antisemitism-on-college-campuses-by-pro-palestinian-groups/.

December 5, 2023. The exchange that received the most attention came toward the end of the hearing. It involved Representative Elise Stefanik (R-NY), the fourth-ranking Republican in the House and by far the most active questioner in the hearing, and the presidents of Penn and Harvard:

> ELISE STEFANIK: Ms. Magill, at Penn, does calling for the genocide of Jews violate Penn's rules or code of conduct, yes or no?
>
> LIZ MAGILL: If the speech turns into conduct, it can be harassment, yes.
>
> ELISE STEFANIK: I am asking specifically. Calling for the genocide of Jews, does that constitute bullying or harassment?
>
> LIZ MAGILL: If it is directed and severe or pervasive, it is harassment.
>
> ELISE STEFANIK: So, the answer is yes?
>
> LIZ MAGILL: It is a context-dependent decision, Congresswoman...
>
> ELISE STEFANIK: And, Dr. Gay, at Harvard, does calling for the genocide of Jews violate Harvard's rules of bullying and harassment, yes or no?
>
> CLAUDINE GAY: It can be. Depending on the context.
>
> ELISE STEFANIK: What's the context?
>
> CLAUDINE GAY: Targeted as an individual, targeted as—at an individual, severe, pervasive.
>
> ELISE STEFANIK: It's targeted at Jewish students, Jewish individuals. Do you understand your testimony is dehumanizing them? Do you understand that dehumanization is part of antisemitism? I will ask you one more time. Does calling for the genocide of Jews violate Harvard's rules of bullying and harassment, yes or no?
>
> CLAUDINE GAY: Antisemitic rhetoric, when it crosses into conduct—
>
> ELISE STEFANIK: And is it antisemitic rhetoric—

CLAUDINE GAY: Antisemitic rhetoric, when it crosses into conduct, that amounts to bullying, harassment, intimidation. That is actionable conduct, and we do take action.

ELISE STEFANIK: So, the answer is yes, that calling for the genocide of Jews violates Harvard code of conduct, correct?

CLAUDINE GAY: Again, it depends on the context.[49]

Legal commentator Sarah Isgur astutely suggested that the presidents answered questions as if they were testifying at a deposition rather than a congressional hearing.[50] Their highly legalistic responses were not factually inaccurate—free speech principles nominally govern all Ivy League universities—but came across as both misleading and tone-deaf. Expanding DEI and Title IX bureaucracies policing speech deemed harmful to racial minorities or women seemed hard to square with the absolutist conception of free speech the presidents offered, and neither Magill nor Gay addressed the hypocrisy. The sighing and condescension exhibited by Magill and Gay (behavior that, Isgur added, clearly had *not* been recommended by the lawyers who prepped them) created an image of indifference to the fate of Jewish students at their schools.[51] Magill even declined to commit to watching the Israeli government's video of Hamas atrocities.

To commentator Andrew Sullivan, the testimony proved that, for Jews on campus, there actually are no "double standards. There is a single standard: It is fine to malign, abuse and denigrate 'oppressors' and forbidden to do so against the 'oppressed.'"[52]

Magill had come to Washington already under fire for indifference to campus antisemitism—the academic year had begun with the Palestine Writes Literature Festival, with invited participants including the antisemitic former Pink Floyd frontman Roger Waters (who eventually backed out) and Marc Lamont Hill, whom CNN had fired for his anti-Israel extremism. Magill cited

---

49 *Hearings, Holding Campus Leaders Accountable and Confronting Antisemitism* [hereafter *Antisemitism Hearings*], Committee on Education and Workforce, U.S. House of Representatives, 118th Congress, 2nd Session, https://www.youtube.com/watch?v=3J0Nu9BN5Qk.
50 Sarah Isgur and David French, "Podcast: Students Call for Genocide, Presidents Smirk," *The Dispatch*, December 7, 2023, https://thedispatch.com/podcast/advisoryopinions/students-call-for-genocide-presidents-smirk/.
51 Ibid.
52 Andrew Sullivan, "The Day the Empress' Clothes Fell Off," *The Weekly Dish*, December 8, 2023, https://andrewsullivan.substack.com/p/the-day-the-empress-clothes-fell.

academic freedom to defend the conference but showed little curiosity as to why anyone associated with Penn would want to hear from such figures.[53] At the hearing, Representative Jim Banks (R-IN) three times asked her what educational value would come from Waters's appearance. Magill thrice evaded the question and instead robotically responded, "Antisemitism has no place at Penn."[54] She offered no insight on why—if antisemitism had no place at Penn—someone like Waters would be an invited speaker.

Amidst intense political and donor backlash to her performance, Magill posted an online video after returning to campus saying she had reversed herself and concluded that calls for genocide against Jews *would* violate the Penn code.[55] But it was too little, too late, and she resigned her post on December 11, 2023.

The Harvard Corporation initially backed Gay, but the controversy over her testimony led to media scrutiny—most notably from *Washington Free Beacon* reporter Aaron Sibarium—into her relatively sparse scholarly record. Repeated revelations of plagiarized passages in her academic work made her position untenable, and Gay resigned on January 2, 2024, though she remained a tenured professor of political science. Before her resignation, Gay planned a "spring reset" proposal to move beyond her disastrous response to October 7 by balancing a task force on antisemitism with one on Islamophobia.[56]

The controversy over the genocide question obscured one other issue from the hearing. Representative Kathy Manning (D-NC) pressed Gay on a Harvard School of Public Health course, "The Settler Colonial Determinants of Health," which used Palestine as a case study and thus held as fact that Jews were not indigenous to the land of Israel. Gay responded that she knew "about the long history in Israel," but declined to explain how such a course could have been approved. When asked by Manning what Harvard was doing to educate against such false claims, given that the university "is actually teaching courses with the underlying premise that Israel is a colonial—a settler colonial state," Gay blandly responded, "We have faculty."[57]

---

53 Elizabeth Magill et al., "Statement on Palestine Writes Festival," September 12, 2023, https://pan-school.sas.upenn.edu/news/statement-palestine-writes-literature-festival.
54 *Antisemitism Hearings*, https://www.youtube.com/watch?v=3J0Nu9BN5Qk.
55 Penn (@Penn), "A Video Message from President Liz Magill," X (formerly Twitter), December 6, 2023, https://x.com/Penn/status/1732549608230862999.
56 Maureen Farrell and Rob Copeland, "How Harvard's Board Broke Up with Claudine Gay," *New York Times*, January 6, 2024.
57 *Holding Campus Leaders Accountable and Confronting Antisemitism*, U.S. House Committee on Education and the Workforce, YouTube, December 5, 2023, https://www.youtube.com/watch?v=3J0Nu9BN5Qk.

Gay's disinterest in exploring why her university's professors might exhibit anti-Israel bias in the classroom was not surprising. Controversy over such matters dated back at least a generation, when a Columbia committee largely cleared Middle Eastern Studies professors of allegations of in-class bias filed by Jewish students. Reports of similar classroom bias resurfaced soon after October 7. A mandatory course in the MA program of Columbia's School of Public Health featured the professor identifying Jewish donors to Columbia as "wealthy white capitalists" who had laundered "dirty money" and "blood money" through the school; a speaker in the class referred to "so-called Israel."[58] And one student writing a thesis on Israeli artists reported to a Columbia task force that each time the student made an in-class presentation, "the thesis seminar leader would say, 'I hate Israel.'"[59]

Stanford, shortly after October 7, featured similar cartoonish conduct in the classroom. An instructor in a required first-year course departed from the syllabus to discuss the Hamas attack, which he deemed justified, since "Israelis are colonizers." Claiming that "he was simulating what Jews were doing to Palestinians, he took (according to a later Stanford investigation "Jewish students' belongings and mov[ed them] to the edge of the room while the student was turned around and looking out the window."[60]

Events such as this came to light as a result of a Stanford investigation that uncovered "other instances of antisemitism or anti-Israeli bias in the classroom, and incidents where teaching assistants abused their positions and class communication networks to proselytize for their personal views on the Israeli-Palestinian conflict or to urge students to attend protest rallies or demonstrations."[61] The university presidents' disastrous performance before the House committee intensified the significance of these internal investigations; at other schools, lawsuits brought ugly facts to light.

Stanford's subcommittee unanimously concluded that "antisemitism exists today on the Stanford campus in ways that are widespread and pernicious." It wasn't hard to see why—the report opened with a January 2024 incident when approximately 200 Jewish students, faculty, staff, and alumni attended a town hall on campus antisemitism with high-ranking administrators. Jewish attendees "were confronted by

---

58 *Report #2: Columbia University Experiences of Antisemitism* [hereafter *Columbia Antisemitism Report*], Columbia University, Task Force on Antisemitism, August 2024, 22.
59 Ibid., 24.
60 *'It's in the Air': Antisemitism and Anti-Israeli Bias at Stanford, and How to Address It* [hereafter *Stanford Antisemitism Report*], Stanford University, Subcommittee on Antisemitism and Anti-Israel Bias, 15.
61 Ibid., 5.

a 'human tunnel' of about 30 protestors lining the staircase leading to the event"; as they left, "protestors pursued and harassed them, following closely on their heels and chanting loudly: 'Zionists, Zionists you can't hide. We charge you with genocide!'" (The protesters had no way of knowing the attendees' attitude toward Zionism, just that they were Jewish.) One Jewish student reported that the protesters shouted at him, "Go back to Brooklyn!" and "We know your names, we know where you work and soon we are going to find out where you live."[62]

The subcommittee's report described how a particular form of post-October 7 antisemitism manifested itself on campus: "The most common way that antisemitism presents itself in student life is not to exclude all Jewish students but to place on Jewish students a unique burden of showing that they reject the State of Israel and any connection to it." Powerful officials, in turn, threw up their hands: a high-level administrator told a graduate student who complained about the campus culture, "At the end of the day, antisemitism is institutional, there is nothing I can do about it."[63]

Columbia's report revealed a similarly flawed campus culture, documenting a striking number of antisemitic online posts and even instances of physical assault against Jewish students. "On campus," one student recalled, "my friends have been spit on, been called like terrible, terrible names, a very close friend of mine was called, a lover of genocide and then a lover of baby killing. This was only a couple of days after October seventh."[64] Despite (or perhaps because of) Columbia's international student body, the committee found that "Israelis were targeted for being Israeli. . . . The hatred toward Israelis has reached alarming levels on campus." One Israeli student overheard two healthcare professionals saying that "they would not treat her because she was Israeli."[65]

As at Stanford, administrators and instructors often seemed indifferent at best and hostile at worst. Jewish students recalled that Columbia's counseling and psychological services implied "that they just need to learn to accept and cope with antisemitic experiences."[66] While the School of Public Health Class Day speaker demanded divestment from Israel and led chants for Free Palestine, "a dean applauded the speech from the podium and thanked the student for 'an inspiring message.'"[67] A student quoted in the report portrayed a campus culture similar to Stanford's: "We're seeing on campus intimidation, active exclusion,

---

62 Ibid., 30.
63 Ibid., 67.
64 *Columbia Antisemitism Report*, 13.
65 Ibid., 29.
66 Ibid., 9.
67 Ibid., 27.

assault, conspiracies of blood libel and media and financial control, historical erasure, and calls for violence ... settl[ing] subconsciously as the norm amongst the majority of the non-Jewish student body."[68]

Similar themes appeared in a report on CUNY requested by Democratic governor Kathy Hochul. Retired judge Jonathan Lippman explored "an alarming number of unacceptable antisemitic incidents targeting members of the CUNY community"—though mostly "carried out by a small, vocal minority of individuals."[69] Lippman concluded that CUNY needed to recognize that at some schools, a pattern of racial, ethnic, and gender diversity in hiring "has not translated into an environment of tolerance and respect"—to such an extent, "unfortunately," he "heard of too many incidents in which faculty fell short."[70] As if to reinforce Lippmann's concerns, the report coincided with an aborted Rosh Hashanah celebration by Jewish students at CUNY's Baruch College. The head of Baruch's Hillel was "told by the administration that the campus can't guarantee the safety of Jewish students because of other agitators who want to hurt, intimidate or harass them."[71] (CUNY reversed itself after strong criticism.)

Harvard's antisemitism task force was slow to issue its final report, but in May 2024, a cache of previously unreported allegations released by the House Education Committee filled in details from Cambridge. In one harrowing incident, a Jewish undergraduate student was chased back to his dorm, with his pursuers screaming at him: he was so traumatized that he stopped eating at the dining hall. In another incident that "everybody in the Jewish community talks about," a sophomore Israeli student attended a class meeting to see a friend of hers make a presentation. After asking where she was from, the professor told her to leave the room "because some people are uncomfortable you're here."[72] Alan Garber, who had succeeded Gay as president, observed that "a lot of the problem we have is about shunning of Israeli students"—a pattern that appeared

---

68 Ibid., 35.
69 *Antisemitism and Discrimination at the City University of New York: Report of the Honorable Jonathan Lippman, Former Chief Judge of New York and Chief Judge of the New York Court of Appeals, to the Honorable Kathy Hochul, Governor of New York* [hereafter *CUNY Antisemitism Report*], September 23, 2024, 1, 9.
70 Ibid., 19, 124.
71 Carl Campanile, "CUNY's Baruch College Put on Blast for Trying to Block Rosh Hashanah Celebration: 'Appalling,'" *New York Post*, September 17, 2024.
72 *Committee Staff Report, Investigative Update: The Antisemitism Advisory Group and Harvard's Response: Clarity and Inaction*, U.S. House of Representatives, Committee on Education and the Workforce, May 15, 2024, 5.

at other elite institutions as well, and one that undermined higher education's commitment to both equality and internationalism.[73]

In addition to universities' own investigations and documents obtained via congressional subpoena, more insight into specifics of the post-October 7 campus environment came out through lawsuits filed by Jewish students against Harvard (two lawsuits), MIT, New York University, the Art Institute of Chicago, Columbia (four lawsuits), the University of Pennsylvania, Carnegie Mellon, Haverford, Rutgers (two lawsuits), Cooper Union, Northwestern, the University of Virginia, the University of California-Berkeley, the University of California-Davis, and UCLA.[74] An unknown additional number of schools also came under investigation by the Department of Education's Office for Civil Rights (OCR) for Title VI violations.

Universities have settled some of these cases, either directly with plaintiffs or through voluntary resolution letters with OCR. Those that have pursued the legal fight sometimes had to resort to revisionist history—Liz Magill's Penn, for instance, fantastically claimed to have "led the fight against antisemitism."[75] Apart from the lawsuit against UCLA, the strongest victory for Jewish students came when a US district judge denied Harvard's motion to dismiss the complaint against it. "As pled," Judge Richard Stearns wrote, "Harvard's reaction was, at best, indecisive, vacillating, and at times internally contradictory." The complaint documented "Harvard's failure to address what [its leaders] repeatedly publicly recognized as an eruption of antisemitism on the Harvard campus. Indeed, in many instances, Harvard did not respond at all." The court would not "reward Harvard for virtuous public declarations that for the most part... proved hollow when it came to taking disciplinary measures against offending students and faculty. In other words, the facts as pled show that Harvard failed its Jewish students."[76]

Judge Stearns also presided over a lawsuit filed by Jewish students against MIT, which documented harassment of Jewish faculty members and pressure on Jewish students to take down Israeli flags. The complaint highlighted MIT's

---

73   Ibid., 12.
74   David Bernstein, "A List (with Links) of Antisemitism Lawsuits Filed against American Universities," *The Volokh Conspiracy*, May 22, 2024, https://reason.com/volokh/2024/05/22/a-list-with-links-of-antisemitism-lawsuits-filed-against-american-universities/.
75   *Yacoby and Davis v. University of Pennsylvania*, Case No. 2:23-cv-04789 (E.D. Pa.), ECF No. 21, 8.
76   *Kestenbaum v. President & Fellows of Harvard Coll.*, 2024 U.S. Dist. LEXIS 139180, *16–17 (D. Mass.), August 6, 2024.

decision to minimize disciplinary charges against anti-Israel students who had blocked access to a campus building, lest foreign students involved in the incident have their student visas withdrawn. Despite this record, Stearns sided with MIT, arguing that the university at least attempted to address on-campus discrimination against Jewish students, which was all that Title VI required. He conceded that MIT's response hadn't been particularly successful but speculated this was because the university failed "to anticipate the bigoted behavior that some demonstrators... would exhibit as events unfolded. The transgressors were, after all, mostly MIT students whom the school (perhaps naively) thought had internalized the values of tolerance and respect for others... that a modern liberal university education seeks to instill."[77] The court's indictment of the MIT student body could have applied to scores of elite universities since October 7.

Some encouraging news did exist in the post-October 7 academy. Since the 1970s, relations between Blacks and Jews sometimes have been tense, and in recent years, the Squad has identified younger legislators of color with vitriolically anti-Israel policies. Even so, virtually no anti-Israel protests occurred at HBCUs. Nor were antisemitic episodes common at religious schools, despite a long record of right-wing antisemitism, often with religious roots, in US history. According to Harvard's Crowd Counting Consortium, virtually no anti-Israel protests occurred at religiously conservative colleges or universities. Schools located in more conservative parts of the country likewise saw minimal anti-Israel activity.[78]

In the 2023 and 2024 football seasons, quarterback Jake Retzlaff was one of only a handful of Jewish students at Brigham Young University, an overwhelmingly Mormon institution. "As campuses across America erupted in protests over the war in Gaza, and as many of those protests curdled into virulent antisemitism," the *Atlantic*'s McKay Coppins wrote, "Retzlaff was struck by how different his classmates seemed from the people in viral video clips hurling epithets at Jewish students.... 'I'd love to ask them about their faith,' Retzlaff [said]. 'What are the odds that they're faithful at all? I'd bet you they're not.'"[79] BYU

---

77   *StandWithUs Ctr. for Legal Just. v. Mass. Inst. of Tech.*, 2024 U.S. Dist. LEXIS 134141, *13 (D. Mass.), July 30, 2024).
78   For protest data, see *Crowd Counting Consortium: A Public Interest and Scholarly Project to Document Protests and Demonstrations in the United States*, Harvard Kennedy School, Ash Center for Democratic Governance and Innovation, https://ash.harvard.edu/programs/crowd-counting-consortium/.
79   McKay Coppins, "The Jewish Quarterback at a Mormon College: Faith and Football at Brigham Young University," *Atlantic*, October 18, 2024, https://www.theatlantic.com/ideas/archive/2024/10/jewish-quarterback-mormon-college-byu/680292/.

is one of the most conservative universities in the country (Trump carried the school's home county by almost forty points), but Retzlaff's experience hardly seems atypical among students who spent the post-October 7 period outside the realm of elite or blue-state public universities.

In April and May, events at the country's most prestigious institutions quickly overwhelmed feel-good stories like Retzlaff's. Beginning on April 17 at Columbia, anti-Israel encampments spread to at least 122 other colleges and universities.[80] Each of these protests at the very least violated campus time/place/manner restrictions; some featured ugly rhetoric; a few crossed the line into outright criminal conduct. In contrast to the fall student activism, most spring protests also had an explicit goal of distancing universities from Israel through adoption of a BDS resolution.

The initial Columbia encampment coincided with then-President Minouche Shafik's turn to testify before the House Education Committee. The next day, Shafik requested that the New York Police Department remove the protesters. Students quickly erected a second encampment, whose leaders included a student who had remarked (during a previous disciplinary process, no less) that "Zionists don't deserve to live. . . . Be grateful that I'm not just going out and murdering Zionists."[81] Amidst faculty backlash against Shafik's use of the NYPD, the president allowed the encampment to remain in place for two weeks. Columbia professors served as marshals to shield the protesters from the media; curiously for a public protest at a university, encampment participants often masked their faces and refused to speak to reporters.[82] In a move that Jewish students, according to a subsequent Columbia report, found "especially troubling," some faculty members even moved their classes to the encampment. English professor Bruce Robbins said that he wanted to show that he "supported the encampment," even though two of his students—whom he suspected were "former members of the Israeli military"—stayed away.[83] After negotiations with the administration broke down, some protesters occupied Columbia's Hamilton

---

80 For the count, see Kelchen and Novikoff, "Are Gaza Protests Happening Mostly at Elite Colleges?"

81 Olivia Land, "Suspended Columbia Student Who Declared 'Zionists don't deserve to live' Sues University," *New York Post*, October 1, 2024, https://nypost.com/2024/10/01/suspended-columbia-student-who-declared-zionists-dont-deserve-to-live-sues-university/.

82 Nora Moses and Hudson Warm, "Students Walk Out of Class to Stand with Gaza," Yale Daily News, January 17, 2024, https://yaledailynews.com/blog/2024/01/17/students-walk-out-of-class-to-stand-with-gaza/.

83 Anemona Hartocollis, "Taking Cues from Students, U.C.L.A. Faculty Members Join the Protests," *New York Times*, May 2, 2024, https://www.nytimes.com/2024/05/02/us/ucla-faculty-protests.html.

Hall, and Shafik again called in the NYPD. More than 100 people were arrested, although the Manhattan District Attorney later dropped all charges against Columbia students.[84]

Surveying the scene, *Atlantic* essayist Michael Powell "could not shake the sense that too many at this elite university, even as they hoped to ease the plight of imperiled civilians, had allowed the intoxicating language of liberation to blind them to an ugliness encoded within that struggle."[85] Shafik offered a more legalistic conclusion: the encampment and related protests had "create[ed] a hostile environment in violation of Title VI, especially around our gates, that is unsafe for everyone."[86]

Although Columbia's encampment attracted the most attention, arrests also occurred at City College, MIT, Emerson College, UMass-Amherst, Dartmouth, UCLA, the University of New Hampshire, the University of Wisconsin, Stanford, and the University of Michigan. In the Michigan case, the office of the state's attorney general, Dana Nessel, filed charges against eleven students for obstruction or trespassing. Squad member Rashida Tlaib (D-Michigan) claimed that her fellow Democrat "decided if the issue was Palestine, she was going to treat it differently, and that alone speaks volumes about possible biases within the agency she runs." Nessel, who is Jewish, responded that Tlaib "should not use my religion to imply I cannot perform my job fairly as Attorney General. It's antisemitic and wrong."[87]

Superficially, universities took two differing approaches to the encampments. Some appeased the protesters. Facing a demand from 195 professors (almost one-eighth of the Brown faculty) to avoid punishment for student protesters whose actions the instructors deemed "in line with our educational mission," Brown President Christina Paxson allowed the protesters to present a divestment resolution before the trustees in exchange for their standing down.[88] (The

---

84 Chelsia Rose Marcius, "Why Bragg Dropped Charges against Most Columbia Student Protesters," *New York Times*, June 23, 2024, https://www.nytimes.com/2024/06/23/nyregion/columbia-protest-charges-bragg.html.
85 Michael Powell, "The Unreality of Columbia's 'Liberated Zone,'" *Atlantic*, April 22, 2024, https://www.theatlantic.com/ideas/archive/2024/04/columbia-university-protests-palestine/678159/?gift=SGP_jVpjFhhw1gdjNwRqmRo-uMox_ruc23MZW870Kcw.
86 Statement from Columbia University President Minouche Shafik, Columbia University, April 29, 2024, https://president.columbia.edu/news/statement-columbia-university-president-minouche-shafik-4-29.
87 Clara Hendricksen, "Michigan Attorney General Nessel Calls U.S. Rep. Tlaib's Accusation of Bias Anti-Semitic," *Detroit Free Press*, September 22, 2024.
88 "Faculty Letter in Support of BrownU Jews for Ceasefire Now," November 21, 2023, https://docs.google.com/document/d/1KcPZJ6eXOPXhXdtyrDCDm1IN8-09Savro45i-JxBJEg/edit?tab=t.0.

trustees ultimately rejected the resolution; Trustee Joseph Edelman resigned to protest the "morally reprehensible" decision to hold the vote "based on weakness toward student activists."[89]) One of the two Northwestern professors who negotiated with encampment leaders privately sought to "get some amazing wins" for them.[90] The University of Minnesota's interim president, Jeff Ettinger, ended protesters' occupation of a campus building by issuing a statement endorsing the Palestinian right of resistance and return. He later noted—in a hearing before the State Senate—that he had not realized what he had signed because the protesters presented their key demand in Arabic. "That was a mistake by our administration," Ettinger explained.[91]

Other universities—such as Michigan, Columbia, or Harvard—seemed to take a harder line, eventually initiating disciplinary actions. But after receiving disciplinary records through subpoena, the House Education Committee found that the vast majority of anti-Israel protesters at Columbia and Harvard were not punished. None was expelled.[92]

On June 14, 2024, Dean Josef Sorett maintained that the Columbia leadership was "steadfast" in its "commitment to combatting the rise in antisemitism that has affected our campus."[93] But it seemed their heart was not really in the fight. The *Washington Free Beacon* had posted screenshots of texts between four senior administrators mocking Jewish campus leaders discussing students' experiences with antisemitism.[94] Columbia removed three but curiously allowed the most powerful of the four, Sorett, a scholar on religion and race, to remain in his

---

89 Joseph Edelman, "Why I Am Resigning as a Brown Trustee," *Wall Street Journal*, September 8, 2024, https://www.wsj.com/articles/why-i-am-resigning-as-a-brown-trustee-gaza-antisemitism-protesters-1479f433.

90 "U.S. House of Representatives: Staff Report on Antisemitism," December 18, 2024, 8, https://www.speaker.gov/wp-content/uploads/2024/12/House-Antisemitism-Report.pdf.

91 Exchange between Sen. Ron Latz and Interim President Joseph Ettinger, June 25, 2024, posted by KC Johnson (@kcjohnson9), X (formerly Twitter), June 27, 2024, https://x.com/kcjohnson9/status/1806412336439456227.

92 *Foxx: Columbia's Refusal to Enforce Rules Against Antisemites is Disgraceful*, U.S. House of Representatives, Committee on Education and the Workforce, August 19, 2024, https://edworkforce.house.gov/news/documentsingle.aspx?DocumentID=411857.

93 Josef Sorett to Board of Visitors, June 14, 2024, posted by Eliana Johnson (@elianayjohnson), X (formerly Twitter), June 14, 2024, https://x.com/elianayjohnson/status/1801694798581023071.

94 Eliana Johnson and Aaron Sibarium, "Columbia Administrators Fire Off Hostile and Dismissive Text Messages, Vomit Emojis during Alumni Reunion Panel on Jewish Life," *Washington Free Beacon*, June 12, 2024, https://freebeacon.com/campus/columbia-administrators-fire-off-hostile-and-dismissive-text-messages-vomit-emojis-during-alumni-reunion-panel-on-jewish-life/.

position.[95] Shafik herself resigned shortly before the fall classes began. And for spring 2025, the university assigned Joseph Massad to teach a course on the origins and effects of Zionism, responding to criticism by claiming that "we seek to provide a learning environment and classrooms that promote intellectual inquiry and analytical thinking along with civility, tolerance and respect."[96]

A few days after the university presidents' disastrous performance in the House hearing, Harvard psychology professor Steven A. Pinker asked the question the university leaders had avoided: "Why are universities so surprisingly congenial to Hamas in the first place?"[97] Former Harvard president and Obama cabinet official Lawrence Summers theorized that "the issues around antisemitism and ... the failure to confront it can't be separated from the broader issues of political diversity ... and identity politics."[98] These issues seem unlikely to be solved soon. As troubling as it might seem, events since October 7 revealed that—at least at elite institutions—the do-nothing Stanford administrator might have correctly understood the chances for addressing the problem: "At the end of the day, antisemitism is institutional, there is nothing I can do about it."[99]

---

95 Sharon Otterman, "3 Columbia University Deans Who Sent Insulting Texts Have Resigned," *New York Times*, August 6, 2024, https://www.nytimes.com/2024/08/08/nyregion/columbia-university-deans-resign-text-messages-antisemitism.html.

96 Jaley Cohen, "Columbia Professor Resigns after University Allows Anti-Israel Academic to Continue Teaching Course on Zionism," *Jewish Insider*, December 17, 2024, https://jewishinsider.com/2024/12/columbia-university-joseph-massad-lawrence-muzzy-rosenblatt-israel/.

97 Benjamin Hunt, "Why October 7 May Mark a Turning Point for Universities," *New York*, December 16, 2023, https://nymag.com/intelligencer/2023/12/why-the-israel-hamas-war-may-be-a-turning-point-in-academia.html.

98 Larry Summers CNN interview with Dana Bash, December 5, 2023, video posted by KC Johnson (@kcjohnson9), X (formerly Twitter), December 6, 2023, https://twitter.com/kcjohnson9/status/1732165162612719628.

99 *Stanford Antisemitism Report*, 67.

CHAPTER 10

The Political Economy of Antisemitism and Israel Hatred in Twenty-First-Century America

Alex Joffe and Asaf Romirowsky

Introduction

The post-October 7 campus protests have spurred closer reexamination of the sources and nature of anti-Israel movements in the United States and elsewhere. While their origins go back to the 1960s, the BDS movement has been a presence in American society since the beginning of the twenty-first century and stands at the core of opposition to Israel's existence.

Groups such as Students for Justice in Palestine (SJP) and Jewish Voice for Peace (JVP) have grown from tiny, campus *groupuscules* into national organizations with thousands of followers. Other groups such as the American Friends Service Committee[1] have extended the reach of the BDS movement into churches and the labor movement. The longstanding relationship of these groups with American Muslim Brotherhood organizations such as the Council on American Islamic Relations (CAIR) was foundational to the explosion of antisemitic hatred seen throughout American society after October 7, particularly to its extension into local and national politics. Israel boycotts are now debated on the floor of the US Congress and have been passed in city councils around the country.

---

1   Alex Joffe and Asaf Romirowsky, "The Progressive Saviour Complex: Quakers, American Jews and Israel," *Fathom*, July 2021, https://fathomjournal.org/fathom-long-read-the-progressive-saviour-complex-quakers-american-jews-and-israel/?highlight=joffe th.

The many BDS groups are closely aligned and overlap with broader anti-American and anti-Western movements, including Antifa, ANSWER, Black Lives Matter, climate change activism, revolutionary socialism, and many others.[2] Indeed, as the antisemitic tsunami emerged after October 7, it has become apparent that many of these organizations and movements are in fact components of a larger phenomenon, an anti-Westernism rooted in the shared animus of the communist and Islamic worlds and their Western extensions, that is to say, the "red-green alliance" or Islamo-leftism.

This phenomenon has been well established in Europe for over two decades and now extends fully to the United States.[3] This chapter will address the political economy of these organizations, a topic that has not received the scholarly attention it deserves or, for that matter, is required for a full assessment of their aims and of the extent of their support in America. The funders include both "red" and "green" components, that is to say, communist and Islamist or political Islamic, but also a variety of left-wing foundations that are embraced and funded by the US government.

The question of how or whether these movements are centrally directed is beyond the scope of this study. Enough evidence exists to demonstrate they work in concert but also that certain elements continually seek to center all attention and efforts on the cause of "Palestine." The concept of "intersectionality," in its expansive rather than original sense, proclaims that "no one is free until everyone is free" and has been used to make "Palestine" a practical and philosophical pivot for all other movements. This has produced occasional friction but little real controversy since shared antisemitism is a unifying factor. Anti-colonialism, anti-nationalism, anti-Enlightenment, climate activism, human rights, and anti rationalism are all unified and even subsumed by antisemitism.

As the language of these movements has converged on "Palestine," close affinities have been revealed with Soviet-style antisemitism, developed in the 1950s and 1960s and disseminated throughout the Soviet bloc and the Arab worlds.[4] All contemporary components are fundamentally antisemitic in that they seek

---

2   Ryan Mauro, *Marching toward Violence: The Domestic Anti-Israeli Protest Movement* (Washington, D.C.: Capital Research Center, 2024), https://capitalresearch.org/app/uploads/Marching-Toward-Violence.pdf.
3   Pierre-André Taguieff, *Rising from the Muck: The New Anti-Semitism in Europe* (Chicago, IL: Ivan R. Dee, 2004).
4   Izabella Tabarovsky, "Zombie Anti-Zionism," *Tablet*, July 30, 2024, https://www.tabletmag.com/sections/arts-letters/articles/zombie-anti-zionism; Izabella Tabarovsky, "The Cult of 'Antizionism,'" *Tablet*, September 30, 2023, https://www.tabletmag.com/sections/arts-letters/articles/cult-of-antizionism-icsz; Izabella Tabarovsky, "Soviet Anti-Zionism and Contemporary Left Antisemitism," *Fathom*, May 2019, https://fathomjournal.org/soviet-anti-zionism-and-contemporary-left-antisemitism/.

to deprive Jews of the right to sovereignty, focus disproportionately on Israel and Jews in a pantheon of villains, which includes the United States, and invariably invoke conspiracy theories and fantasies of cosmic evil. Antisemitism is a primary means to undo the present by creating a counter-history using real and invented elements in order to undermine a shared sense of the past and thus social cohesion in the present, and to seize power for the future.

With the exception of political Islam, which is religiously and culturally conservative but adept at allying with, and manipulating others through, the strategic use of minority and victim status, as well as dissimulation, these movements are almost exclusively on the political, cultural, and religious left. Their ideologies have spread throughout society via educational systems (both K–12 and higher education), "diversity, equity, and inclusion" (DEI) and "environmental, social, governance" (ESG) mechanisms in corporate and governmental settings, the NGO sector, particularly organizations dedicated to "human rights," and the media. Messages are amplified artificially through social media including by foreign state actors. The organizations themselves form interlocking directorates of personnel and ideologies which circulate freely as individuals move, for example, from the NGO to higher education and governmental sectors. And all share the same funders.

Political Economy

A political economy unites all the components of contemporary antisemitism. As suggested, these are largely on the political and cultural left, but may in fact include elements of the far right which are covertly funded as agent provocateurs by foreign actors or domestic communists.

The economy centers on the 1) red-green alliance actors and 2) background entities acting as funders and amplifiers. The nature of the backing is financial but also political, meaning creation of social and other connections for mutual training, support, and message amplification. Certain entities act as funders alone while others act both as funders and organizers.

The political economy of contemporary antisemitism may be parsed in many ways. The approach used here is to examine the extremist funders, the "reds" and "greens," and then the progressive left. Each are ideological but in different ways.

Both the red and the greens are frank and united about their anti-Western revolutionary intent, communist on the one hand and Islamic on the other. Israel should be destroyed and America must follow. There is no practical political program; genocidal intent is implicit with respect to Israel and even Jews, and both act as revolutionary vanguards.

The ideology behind the progressive left and its quasi-official amplifiers in government and NGOs is acquiring and retaining absolute political power. This is accomplished in part by funding anti-Israel and other entities who act as agents provocateurs, inspiring fear and establishing dominance over spaces and discourse, moving the lines of acceptable speech and behavior toward targeting Jews, Israel, and Christians in the name of human rights, resistance, liberation, and so on, and generating public demands for "something to be done" and "safety."

Israel is the latest target after the panics of Black Lives Matter, Russiagate, transgenderism, and COVID have run their courses. This latter issue has been immensely influential since it unified elements of government, some of which fund NGOs, foundations, academia, the wealth high tech class and their media platforms, and empowered the government-connected "disinformation industry." These narrative-making and enforcement mechanisms have been discredited with respect to COVID but remain in place and when it comes to Israel and Jews, are supplemented by foreign powers that have bought influence throughout American society such as Qatar and China.

Three nominally separable movements thus vie for dominance in American society using Israel and Jews as foils. The threats to Israel and Jews emerge from a series of fundamentally contradictory forces; racists posing as anti-racists; defenders of democracy—inside and outside of government—who use covert anti-democratic means to subvert normal politics; defenders of human rights who defend and deny rape and murder; Muslim settler colonialists in the West who attack purported Jewish settler colonialism. Intellectual and social contradictions, however, are no obstacle.

The Reds

Influence operations by foreign communist parties from the Soviet era to the modern Chinese Communist Party have a long history of funding of domestic organizations including peace groups and environmental NGOs in the United States and in Europe.[5] The goals of disrupting Western social cohesion and

---

5 Richard Felix Staar, *Foreign Policies of the Soviet Union* (Stanford, CA: Hoover Institution Press, 1991), 79–88; Darren E. Tromblay, *Political Influence Operations: How Foreign Actors Seek to Shape U.S. Policy Making* (Lanham, MD: Rowman & Littlefield, 2018); *CCP Political Warfare: Federal Agencies Urgently Need a Government-Wide Strategy*, U.S. Department of Defense, House Committee on Oversight and Reform, October 24, 2024.

subverting political processes have been a constant for a century, with, as noted above, the Soviet Union displaying particular animus towards Israel and Jews.

Soon after October 7, reports began to appear regarding several New York area groups, notably The People's Forum and Within Our Lifetime, which have key roles in organizing violent anti-Israel demonstrations. The People's Forum describes itself as "movement incubator for working class and marginalized communities to build unity across historic lines of division at home and abroad" through "popular education, our cultural work and our media laboratory."[6]

The group's anti-Western focus was made clear by a speaker in New York City who stated: "When we finally deal that final blow to destroy Israel. When the state of Israel is finally destroyed and erased from history, that will be the single most important blow we can give to destroying capitalism."[7] This is a recapitulation of the classic antisemitic theme of Jewish control of capitalism.

It quickly became apparent that The People's Forum was being funded by wealthy entrepreneur Neville Roy Singham and his wife Jodie Evans,[8] a co-founder of CODEPINK. The People's Forum provides funding to seemingly grassroots protests, while Codepink is well known for disrupting Congressional hearings and for support of Hamas, North Korea, and other causes. The People's Forum Executive Director Manolo De Los Santos is a probable Cuban intelligence operative.[9] Singham also funds the ANSWER Coalition and the Party for Socialism and Liberation, which are involved in anti-police and climate protests.

Singham is a Singapore-based software businessman with close connections to the Chinese Community Party,[10] and his network of organizations is active supporting Chinese-backed causes in Africa, India, and the United States.[11] Operatives from The People's Forum also work at other institutions including the Kairos Center for Religions, Rights, and Social Justice at Union Theological

---

6   See "About Us," The People's Forum, https://peoplesforum.org/about/.
7   Jason Curtis Anderson (@JCAndersonNYC), X (formerly Twitter), January 17, 2025, https://twitter.com/jcandersonnyc/status/1746908368021725630.
8   Michael Shellenberger, "Meet the American Millionaire Marxists Funding Anti-Israel Rallies," *New York Post*, November 16, 2023, https://nypost.com/2023/11/16/opinion/meet-the-american-millionaire-marxists-funding-anti-israel-rallies/.
9   "May 1: NYPD Liberates Occupied Columbia," *The Daily Scroll*, May 1, 2024, https://the-dailyscroll.substack.com/p/may-1-nypd-liberates-occupied-columbia.
10 Mara Hvistendahl et al., "A Global Web of Chinese Propaganda Leads to a U.S. Tech Mogul," *New York Times*, August 5, 2023, https://www.nytimes.com/2023/08/05/world/europe/neville-roy-singham-china-propaganda.html.
11 "January 18: The NYC-CCP Connection," *The Daily Scroll*, January 18, 2025, https://thedailyscroll.substack.com/p/january-18-the-nyc-ccp-connection.

Seminary, the affiliated divinity school of Columbia.[12] The message of American and Israeli perfidy and the critique of "capitalism" is thus sanitized and amplified by a quasi-academic institution.

The role of The People's Forum helps bring into view relationships between various BDS, pro-Hamas, anti-capitalist, and anti-American groups, including its alliance with the "Democratic Socialists of America" (DSA). The DSA's reported 2024 financial crisis, brought about as many donors abandoned the group precisely because of its Hamas support,[13] still leaves an unknown number of members in elected positions, including as Democrats, and especially unelected positions,[14] such as on school boards.[15]

Another more overt communist backer of anti-Israel and anti-American protests is James "Fergie" Chambers, one of the heirs to the telecommunications and automotive conglomerate Cox Enterprises, and with an inherited net worth of several hundred million dollars.[16] Chambers, who has also lived in Russia and is a convert to Islam, is an avowed communist who states his hatred of the United States clearly: "We need a revolution. . . . I see success as the dissolution of the United States government and an end to the U.S. empire." He has made his approach to Israel no less clear, stating We need to "make people who support Israel actually afraid to go out in public."[17] He also described the Hamas massacre of October 7 as "a moment of hope and inspiration for tens of millions of people."[18]

---

12 Jon Levine, "China-linked Tech Tycoon Neville Singham Has Secret Group of Operatives at Columbia University," *New York Post*, August 31, 2024, https://nypost.com/2024/08/31/us-news/neville-singham-has-secret-group-of-operatives-at-nycs-columbia-university/.
13 Carl Campanile, 'Democratic Socialists Face Seven-Figure 'Crisis' Amid Palestinian Support That May Force Dreaded Layoffs of Staff," *New York Post*, January 21, 2024, https://nypost.com/2024/01/21/news/democratic-socialists-face-seven-figure-crisis-amid-palestinian-support-that-may-force-dreaded-layoffs-of-staff/.
14 Jon Levine, "How DSA Educators Spread Far-Left 'Poison' in America's Schools," *New York Post*, December 19, 2023, https://nypost.com/2023/12/19/news/how-dsa-educators-spread-far-left-poison-in-americas-schools/.
15 Liza Featherstone, "Democratic Socialists Are Running for School Board—and Winning," *Jacobin*, January 2, 2024, https://jacobin.com/2024/01/school-board-elections-dsa-nyc-conservatives-far-right-local-politics.
16 Dan Adler, "Citizen Chambers," *Vanity Fair*, May 2024, https://archive.vanityfair.com/article/2024/5/citizen-chambers.
17 David Peisner, "Fergie Chambers Is Heir to One of America's Richest Families—and Determined to See the U.S. Fall," Rolling Stone, March 24, 2024, https://www.rollingstone.com/culture/culture-features/fergie-chambers-cox-enterprises-heir-overthrow-us-1234983156/.
18 Kiera Butler, "There's a Communist Multi-Millionaire Fomenting Revolution in Atlanta," Mother Jones, March 21, 2024, https://www.motherjones.com/politics/2024/03/theres-a-communist-multi-millionaire-fomenting-revolution-in-atlanta/.

Chambers is notable for helping create and fund "Palestine Action U.S." (now renamed "Unity of Fields"), which is the North American branch of the British based "Palestine Action." Both groups have undertaken direct action vandalizing Israeli owned businesses especially defense manufacturer Elbit Systems,[19] as well as Jewish organizations in Britain connected to Israel.[20] Unity of Fields has also taken credit for vandalizing sites around Columbia University and the homes of Brooklyn Museum trustees in the name of "Palestine."[21]

Chambers has also supported other violent far left causes including protests against a police training facility in Atlanta ("Cop City"), which brought together a variety of far-left groups including the leading BDS group, the American Friends Service Committee, as well as local activists.[22] In the United States, the post-October 7 unification of BDS, Muslim, and communist/antifa groups has been evident from other online sources including shared toolkits, talking points, and organizing advice on anti-Israel and anti-capitalist issues.[23]

The role of anti-capitalist groups, including those focused on climate such as "Just Stop Oil," which claims to "resist those who are responsible for mass death via extreme heating and those committing genocide in Gaza,"[24] have considerable overlap in tactics, including vandalism of public monuments and art. In the US donations to "Just Stop Oil" have come from a variety of left-wing philanthropists and celebrities such as film writer/director Adam Mackay, whose activism includes joining the staunchly anti-Israel Green Party and signing public statements condemning Israel over Gaza.[25]

---

19 "Palestine Action," InfluenceWatch, 2025, https://www.influencewatch.org/organization/palestine-action/.
20 Mathilda Heller, "Palestine Action Carries Out Multi-Location Vandalism to Mark Balfour Declaration Signing," *Jerusalem Post*, November 3, 2024, https://www.jpost.com/diaspora/article-827281.
21 "Palestine Action."
22 "5 Things You Need to Know about 'Cop City,'" American Friends Service Committee, https://afsc.org/news/5-things-you-need-know-about-cop-city; "Network for Strong Communities," InfluenceWatch, https://www.influencewatch.org/non-profit/network-for-strong-communities/; Butler, "There's a Communist Multi-Millionaire."
23 "Jan 26: We Charge Genocide Toolkit—Int'l Day of Action," https://docs.google.com/document/d/10UO-nRpdnBf_fcI5qhw1RQJ2n-12KIM2NBL-c45Mjqk/.
24 "Just Stop Genocide," Just Stop Oil, October 26, 2023, https://juststopoil.org/2023/10/26/just-stop-genocide/.
25 Damien Gayle, "Just Stop Oil's 'Spring Uprising' Protests Funded by US Philanthropists," *Guardian*, April 29, 2022, https://www.theguardian.com/environment/2022/apr/29/just-stop-oils-protests-funded-by-us-philanthropists; Adam McKay, "It Is Time to Abandon the Democratic Party," Variety, November 6, 2024, https://variety.com/2024/film/news/adam-mckay-time-to-abandon-democratic-party-trump-victory-1236202362/.

Internationally, the public face of the unified anti-Israel/anti-capitalism movement is exemplified by climate personality Greta Thunberg, who quickly reoriented her activism and has now appeared at many pro-Hamas rallies, stating already in December 2023, "You cannot be neutral in a genocide."[26] Thunberg's own funding is largely circular, based on prizes received from institutions which are themselves funded by various organizations and institutions.

The unification of the climate message with pro-Palestinian messaging was echoed by the radical group "Extinction Rebellion," which in Britain is largely funded by hedge fund billionaire Chris Hohn, and which has participated in anti-Israel protests along with Muslim groups.[27] Hohn's financial support for climate causes and thus for pro-Palestinian groups properly belongs under the category of progressives but usefully illustrates the far-left oligarchic support for "intersectional" movements which include explicitly communist and Muslim organizations.

Indirect communist support for the pro-Palestinian movement has been received through the Chinese propaganda platform TikTok, which after October 7 began to feed tremendous quantities of anti-Israel messaging to its users. TikTok has been shown to begin feed anti-Israel content nearly immediately to new users.[28] This was consistent with the platform's strategy of reflecting the Chinese Communist Party's political interests by artificially amplifying or suppressing messaging on controversies outside of China.[29] Similar patterns had been noted during earlier periods of US domestic unrest, namely the George Floyd and BLM protests, which were artificially amplified by TikTok.

---

26 Greta Thunberg, Alde Nilsson, Jamie Mater, and Raquel Frescia, "We Won't Stop Speaking Out about Gaza's Suffering—There Is No Climate Justice without Human Rights," *Guardian*, December 5, 2023, https://www.theguardian.com/commentisfree/2023/dec/05/gaza-climate-justice-human-rights-greta-thunberg.
27 Damien Gayle, "Backlash over European Climate Activists' Support for Palestine," *Guardian*, October 23, 2023, https://www.theguardian.com/environment/2023/oct/23/backlash-over-european-climate-activists-support-for-palestine; Rupert Neate, "Billionaire Philanthropist Leads World's Top-Performing Hedge Funds," *Guardian*, January 17, 2022, https://www.theguardian.com/business/2022/jan/17/billionaire-philanthropist-leads-worlds-top-performing-hedge-funds.
28 Jeff Horwitz and Georgia Wells, "What TikTok Is Showing America's Youth About the War in Gaza," *Wall Street Journal*, November 13, 2023, https://www.wsj.com/tech/tiktok-israel-gaza-hamas-war-a5dfa0ee.
29 *A Tik-Tok-ing Timebomb: How TikTok's Global Platform Anomalies Align with the Chinese Communist Party's Geostrategic Objectives*, Network Contagion Research Institute, December 21, 2023, https://networkcontagion.us/wp-content/uploads/A-Tik-Tok-ing-Timebomb_12.21.23.pdf.

Denigrating Israel and the United States in order to improve China's image globally and in the States is explicit.

The concurrent controversy regarding the United States forcing the Chinese owner of the platform to sell its majority stake in order to operate in the States similarly revealed an artificial effort to blame the initiative on Israel or Jews.[30] Given that TikTok and other social media platforms such as Instagram have become the primary vectors for information among Gen X consumers, the negative impact on younger American's views of Israel have been measurable.[31]

The Greens

American Muslim and Arab influence on the American political and cultural scene is older than generally realized. As early as the 1930s and 1940s, newspapers and then organizations such as the Arab National League and Conference of Americans of Arabic-Speaking Origin began expressing opposition to Zionism and the establishment of Israel. During the late 1940s and 1950s, these efforts were enhanced by semi-official American elements connected to the CIA, State Department, and ARAMCO through cut-out groups such as the Institute of Arab American Affairs.

By the 1950s and especially the 1960s onward, a growing network of domestically based Muslim organizations took root, implanted in the United States by Muslim Brotherhood members who came as students to organize the growing number of Muslim immigrants and students. These organizations included the Muslim Student Association, North American Islamic Trust, International Institute of Islamic Thought, Islamic Society of North America, Muslim American Society, and in 1993, the Council on American-Islamic Relations (CAIR). Most are connected in a network with the American Muslim Brotherhood which in 1991 issued its "Explanatory Memorandum on the General Strategic Goal for

---

30 Yair Rosenberg, "The Jews Aren't Taking Away TikTok," *Atlantic*, April 17, 2024, https://www.theatlantic.com/ideas/archive/2024/04/antisemitism-conspiracy-theories-tiktok/678088/.

31 Laura E. Adkins, "Young Americans Are Turning against Israel—and You Can Thank TikTok," *Forward*, December 21, 2023, https://forward.com/opinion/574346/freepalestine-tiktok-israel-china/; Alicia Warren, "China, TikTok Role in Anti-Israel College Protests Is 'an act of war,' Expert Says," Fox Business, May 2, 2024, https://www.foxbusiness.com/politics/chinas-role-anti-israel-college-protests-act-war-expert-says.

the Group in North America," discovered in an FBI raid and which outlined a long-term project for the Islamization of America.[32]

During the era of Pan-Arabism student organizing worldwide was a strategy in which the Muslim Brotherhood as well as Ba'athist and Nasserite organizations participated. One outgrowth in 1959 was the General Union of Palestinian Students, which became an important locus for Palestinian politics, including representatives from Europe.[33] The ascent of former student leader Yassir Arafat to the head of the Fatah movement and then the Palestine Liberation Organization was due in part to mastery of student politics.

A General Union of Palestinian Students chapter was created at San Francisco State University during the 1970s but fell into abeyance until it was revived in 2000 as Students for Justice in Palestine. This is the period when the Muslim Brotherhood began a unification effort of North American Muslim institutions which includes the North American Islamic Trust (which owns the vast majority of US mosques), the Islamic Council of North America, and other entities. The anti-Israel and antisemitic messaging presented in American mosques has been well documented by researchers at the Middle East Media Research Institute, not least of all through videos made by the mosques themselves.[34]

The individual responsible for the recreation of SJP, Hatem Bazian, is a Brotherhood operative who later went on to found Zaytuna College, a Berkeley based seminary. The National Students for Justice in Palestine remains part of the Muslim Brotherhood network but acts as an umbrella organization. A subsequent unification effort that created the US Council of Muslim Organizations from 2011 to 2013, an umbrella organization that some have argued put the American Muslim Brotherhood under effective Turkish control.[35]

Foreign financial support for the other individual key players in the North American BDS movement such as the Palestine Youth Movement, Arab American Action Network, and the Arab American Institute is unclear. Support for these and other groups from progressive funders such as the

---

32 Lorenzo Vidino, "The Muslim Brotherhood's U.S. Network," Hudson Institute, January 25, 2011, https://www.hudson.org/national-security-defense/the-muslim-brotherhood-s-u-s-network.
33 Ido Zelkovitz, *Students and Resistance in Palestine: Books, Guns and Politics* (London: Routledge, 2014), 18–21.
34 "Sermons by Imams in the West," MEMRI, https://www.memri.org/subjects/sermons-by-imams-in-the-west.
35 "USCMO Founding," US Council of Muslim Organizations, https://uscmo.org/uscmo-founding/.

Tides Foundation, Rockefeller Brothers Fund, and other anti-Israel groups is discussed below.

In 2024, one component of the antisemitism network, however, the Vancouver-based Samidoun Palestinian Prisoner Solidarity Network, was shut down by US and Canadian authorities who designated it a sham charity that serves as an international fundraiser for the Popular Front for the Liberation of Palestine."[36] Samidoun has been a key organizer of campus protests around the United States, Canada, and Europe, and founder and leader Khaled Barakat (also designated a PFLP fundraiser) and his wife Charlotte Kates have spoken at many protests.[37]

Understanding the funding behind the huge network of Muslim organizations has been extraordinarily difficult. Judging from the various individuals involved, initial support was apparently received from the Muslim World League, World Association of Muslim Youth, and other Saudi entities. It is also clear that considerable support is now received through private foundations created by American Muslims. As SJPs entered the mainstream in academia as ostensibly student run organizations, local chapters received funding (along with Muslim Student Associations, which are classified by the IRS as religious organizations) from student activity fees collected by universities themselves. Most of these organizations appear to be Sunni in orientation, but the Muslim Students Association Persian-Speaking Group (MSA-PSG) seems to be an organization created by and connected directly to the Islamic Republic of Iran for the purpose of influencing US campuses.[38]

Capturing student governments, which allocated funding, was part of the long-term strategy to dominate campus cultures. This process was greatly accelerated by the huge increases in foreign students accepted onto American campuses in the last ten to twenty years. From the point of view of universities' efforts to become "global" institutions, rather than American ones, coincided with other trends towards globalization, and conveniently filled not only

---

36 "United States and Canada Target Key International Fundraiser for Foreign Terrorist Organization PFLP," U.S. Department of the Treasury, October 15, 2024, https://home.treasury.gov/news/press-releases/jy2646.

37 "The NGO Network Orchestrating Antisemitic Incitement on American Campuses," NGO Monitor, April 25, 2024, https://ngo-monitor.org/reports/ngo-network-orchestrating-antisemitic-incitement-on-american-campuses/.

38 Eitan Fischberger, "Tehran's Trojan Horse: Meet the American Student Nonprofit Pledging Allegiance to the Iranian Regime," Middle East Forum, December 4, 2024, https://www.meforum.org/fwi/fwi-news/tehrans-trojan-horse.

campuses with foreign students, who paid full tuition, but also helped launch a slew of foreign campuses, not least of all in the Arab world.

One area where foreign Arab and Muslim funding has clearly made an impact is on universities themselves. Revelations continue regarding the tens and hundreds of billions of dollars contributed to American universities, from elite institutions like Harvard to obscure ones like the University of North Texas. Qatar, Saudi Arabia, and Turkey are the largest contributors. Estimates range up to $18 billion of support from Organization of the Islamic Conference states between 2014 and 2019. Qatar alone has provided more than a billion dollars each to various American universities including Texas A&M and Cornell.[39] This is in addition to vast Qatari investments in other global economic sectors including real estate, sports, hospitality, energy, and food and beverage.[40]

The impact of this funding is at once difficult to measure directly in social or cultural terms and palpably vast. Given its vast scale and sheer pervasiveness, it is influence-buying at a profound level. The implications for antisemitism are obvious but felt indirectly. Studies have shown a clear correlation between the amounts of money received from foreign sources and the number of antisemitic incidents reported on particular campuses.[41] Tens of billions of dollars in Qatari funding to US universities and think tanks such as the Brookings Institution[42]—which also created an overseas unit in Qatar itself—has undoubtedly helped change the atmosphere of campuses.

Campus cultures have been changed over the past twenty-five years in that the needs of the institution to attract and retain money, to placate donors who may or may not articulate their intentions or demands, have been realized in desensitizing institutions to antisemitism from students and faculty alike. From

---

39 *Cornell University's Ten Billion Dollar Sale: Soft Power, Qatar, The Muslim Brotherhood, and an Antisemitism Crisis on Campus*, Institute for the Study of Global Antisemitism and Policy (ISGAP), March 2024, https://isgap.org/wp-content/uploads/2024/03/Cornell_Ten_Billion_Dollar.pdf; *Hijacking Higher Education, Qatar, The Muslim Brotherhood, and Texas A&M: Buying Nuclear Research and Student Information*, vol. 2, ISGAP, February 2024, https://isgap.org/wp-content/uploads/2024/02/TAMUQ_Report_Volume_Two-1.pdf.

40 *Networks of Hate: Qatari Paymasters, Soft Power, and the Manipulation of Democracy*, ISGAP, December 5, 2023, https://isgap.org/wp-content/uploads/2023/12/Networks-of-Hate_5DEC.pdf.

41 *The Corruption of the American Mind: How Foreign Funding of Higher Education in the United States Predicts the Erosion of Democratic Values and Antisemitic Sentiment on Campus*, ISGAP, January 2024, https://isgap.org/wp-content/uploads/2024/01/The-Corruption-of-the-American-Mind_V2-2.pdf.

42 Eli Lake, "Qatar's War for Young American Minds," The Free Press, October 24, 2023, https://www.thefp.com/p/qatars-war-for-young-american-minds.

the bottom up, the immense growth of foreign students has supercharged campus antisemitism.

This is coupled with top-down changes facilitated by funding sources and generational changes. Qatari funding in particular has been critical to propaganda activities aimed at K–12 teachers who are offered overseas experiences and curricular materials which emphasize Arab and Islamic experiences and delegitimize Israel and Judaism.[43]

University faculties have gradually been filled by a younger cadre of "scholar activists" with Third World inclinations, with intellectual ideologies claiming that only "natives" can teach or understand particular cultures such as the Middle East and Islam, and who are to a large extent either foreign born or first generation children of immigrants, the pedagogical enterprise has been unsubtly reengineered from the top down. Israel, Jews, whiteness, settler colonialism, all have become suspect and then hated categories. The absolute identification of Israel as a "white" "oppressor" "colonizer" gives license to radical violence in the name of combating "settler colonialism" and "decolonization."[44]

Finally, with the pervasive growth of "diversity, equity, and inclusion" (DEI) ideology and bureaucracies—in which Jews have come to be enshrined as the ultimate privileged white supremacist group, and Israel the supreme example of settler colonial society—the institutions are even less inclined to create or maintain pedagogical evenhandedness or social comity. The ideological enforcers of the DEI industry maintain conformity, let faculty politicize classrooms and students harass and intimidate on the quad. They have in a sense enacted a coup against administrations, which have thus far been held hostage to donors who helped set the entire process in motion with billions of dollars in gifts. In economic terms, DEI has become an important mechanism for universities themselves to reengineer faculties and impose ideological enforcement which is

---

43 "The Influence of Qatar on American High Schools: Collusion of Haters and Educators," Americans for Peace and Tolerance, September 16, 2020, https://www.peaceandtolerance.org/2020/09/16/the-influence-of-qatar-on-american-high-schools-collusion-of-haters-and-educators/; Susan Edelman, "Antisemitism in NYC Schools Fueled by Foreign Actors, Activist Says," *New York Post*, October 26, 2024, https://nypost.com/2024/10/26/us-news/anti-israel-foreign-actors-activists-have-infiltrated-nyc-schools-report/; Richard Goldberg, "Crack Down on Anti-Semitic K–12 Curricula," *City Journal*, April 30, 2024, https://www.city-journal.org/article/crack-down-on-anti-semitic-k-12-curricula.

44 Simon Sebag Montefiore, "The Decolonization Narrative Is Dangerous and False," *Atlantic*, October 27, 2023, https://www.theatlantic.com/ideas/archive/2023/10/decolonization-narrative-dangerous-and-false/675799/.

uniformly anti-Israel and antisemitic. In the case of the University of Michigan this amounted to a $250 million enterprise funded by the state.[45]

Direct foreign funding of the American Islamic groups behind pro-Palestinian agitation, though long alleged, has been difficult to document. Evidence from the early twenty-first century, however, shows an elaborate pattern of direct support from institutions such as the Organization of the Islamic Conference, the World Assembly of Muslim Youth, the governments of Saudi Arabia and Kuwait, and individuals such as UAE Sheikh Hamdan bin Rashid Al Maktoum and Saudi Al-Walid bin Talal. In addition, there are loans, contributions, pledges, and mortgages from Arab and Muslim banks, embassies, and governments.[46] The overall pattern indicates that CAIR acted as an unregistered foreign agent on behalf of different governments and organizations to influence US policy and society at large.[47]

It appears likely that similar methods continue to transfer foreign funds into US Islamist organizations. Outside of a few signature cases such as the Holy Land Foundation, US law enforcement has been reluctant to become involved. In November 2024, however, a magistrate overseeing a defamation suit filed by a former CAIR employee ordered the organization to reveal the sources of funding behind its Washington Trust Foundation.[48] This ruling has the potential to reveal the full sources of the American Muslim Brotherhood network, and along with it the funding behind other American Muslim networks—Shi'a, Turkish, and more.

It is clearer that the American Muslim Brotherhood network has itself contributed funds to global jihadist organizations including Hamas. Most notable are connections between Hamas and American Muslims for Palestine,[49] the

---

45 Nicholas Confessore, "The University of Michigan Doubled Down on D.E.I. What Went Wrong?," *New York Times Magazine*, October 16, 2024, https://www.nytimes.com/2024/10/16/magazine/dei-university-michigan.html.
46 Michael Walzer, "Unsettling Ideology," Jewish Review of Books, Fall 2024, https://jewishreviewofbooks.com/political-philosophy/17162/unsettling-ideology/.
47 "CAIR and the Foreign Agents Registration Act," Center for Security Policy's CAIR Observatory, March 17, 2010, https://cairunmasked.org/wp-content/uploads/2010/03/CAIR_and_the_Foreign_Agents_Registration_Act_03-22-10_v1.0.pdf.
48 Victor Nava, "Controversial Muslim Group CAIR Forced to Reveal Sources of Funding After Defamation Case Against Former Employee Backfires," *New York Post*, November 25, 2024, https://nypost.com/2024/11/25/us-news/controversial-muslim-group-cair-forced-to-reveal-sources-of-funding-after-defamation-case-against-former-employee-backfires/.
49 Jonathan Schanzer, *Congressional Testimony: Foundation for Defense of Democracies—House Ways and Means Committee, From Ivory Towers to Dark Corners: Investigating the Nexus Between Antisemitism, Tax-Exempt Universities, and Terror Financing*, House Ways and Means Committee, November 15, 2023, https://gop-waysandmeans.house.gov/wp-content/uploads/2023/11/Schanzer-Testimony.pdf.

sponsor of Students for Justice in Palestine, and successor of the Holy Land Foundation which had been found guilty in an American court for responsibility in the death of David Boim.

Iranian contributions to antisemitic movements in the United States. are even more difficult to track. The role of Iranian American millionaires such as Francis Najafi, who funds anti-Israel organizations (some of which were created during the Obama administration to amplify its messages) such as NIAC, J Street, the Quincy Institute, and Jewish Currents is suggestive of Iran working through a well-placed cutout.[50]

An unconfirmed report indicated that the April 15 disruptions were organized by the Intelligence Organization of the Islamic Revolutionary Guard Corps working through a variety of local groups such as Within Our Lifetime.[51] One of the most important developments in the economic sphere were reports linking the "A15 Action" global blockage of shipping and transportation centers to the Iranian Revolutionary Guard Corp (IRGC).[52] The April 2024 effort was executed by Antifa and Palestinian groups but documents leaked by Iranian anti-regime elements suggest the effort was ordered by the IRGC's intelligence branch. The groups involved overlap with BDS organizations but emphasize direct action over boycotts and have a revolutionary communist orientation.

The US government has not confirmed these connections, but, in testimony to Congress, US Director of National Intelligence Avril Haines noted that Iran continued to "stoke discord and undermine confidence in our democratic institutions" through cyber and influence campaigns.[53] White House spokesman John Kirby confirmed "that Iran has been funding and encouraging some of the protest activity here in the United States" but there is no public sign that the intelligence community or law enforcement is addressing the problem. At the same time, a report indicates that US intelligence agencies have seen signs of

---

50   Alana Goodman, "Meet the Iranian Donor Bankrolling Anti-Israel Jewish Groups," *Washington Free Beacon*, May 20, 2024, https://freebeacon.com/israel/meet-the-iranian-donor-bankrolling-anti-israel-jewish-groups/.

51   Vahid Beheshti (@Vahid_Beheshti), "BREAKING: The leaked top-secret letter of the Islamic Republic's Ministry of Intelligence," X (formerly Twitter), November 5, 2024, https://twitter.com/Vahid_Beheshti/status/1779786659229298775.

52   Dan Diker and Tirza Shorr, "The April 15 Trade Blockade Around the World," Jerusalem Center for Security and Foreign Affairs, April 15, 2024, https://jcpa.org/the-april-15-trade-blockade-around-the-world/.

53   Avril Haines, "Statement from Director of National Intelligence Avril Haines on Recent Iranian Influence Efforts," Office of the Director of National Intelligence, July 9, 2024, https://www.dni.gov/index.php/newsroom/press-releases/press-releases-2024/3842-statement-from-director-of-national-intelligence-avril-haines-on-recent-iranian-influence-efforts.

Iranian and Russian online influence operations designed to prevent the reelection of former President Trump.[54]

Foreign intervention in US politics and culture is not limited to funding. Analyses have shown that in Britain a sophisticated Iranian and Hamas network helped mobilize massive antisemitic street demonstrations which threatened state security and British Jews in the streets.[55] The strong Iranian relationship with South Africa's ruling African National Congress, including financial investments, as well as electoral considerations aimed at South Africa's 900,000 Muslim voters, have been suggested to be motivations for that country's legal assault on Israel in the International Court of Justice.[56]

Qatari support for Islamist groups, and the upswing in officially sanctioned antisemitism within China, suggest strategic plans to disrupt American politics and culture.[57] This is complemented by Muslim Brotherhood influence operations in cyberspace aimed at Israel both internally and internationally.[58]

Progressives

A keystone to American antisemitism is support from foundations and the US government. This shocking realization cuts against the grain regarding

---

54 Dustin Volz, "Iran Is Working to Undercut Trump in Presidential Election, U.S. Spy Agencies Say," *Wall Street Journal*, July 29, 2024, https://www.wsj.com/politics/elections/iran-is-working-to-undercut-trump-in-presidential-election-u-s-spy-agencies-say-7f67fad7.
55 Charles Hymas, "Pro-Palestine Protests in UK 'Stirred Up by Iranian and Hamas Network,'" *Telegraph*, October 19, 2023, https://www.telegraph.co.uk/news/2023/10/19/pro-palestine-protests-uk-iranian-hamas-network/.
56 Samantha Aschieris, "South Africa's Ties to Hamas, Iran Exposed amid Financial Troubles, Genocide Case," Just the News, January 25, 2024, https://justthenews.com/government/diplomacy/south-africas-ties-hamas-iran-exposed-amid-financial-troubles-genocide-case; Carlo Strenger, "Another Main Reason South Africa's Ruling Party Filed a Genocide Petition against Israel," *Haaretz*, January 18, 2024, https://www.haaretz.com/opinion/2024-01-18/ty-article-opinion/.premium/another-main-reason-south-africas-ruling-party-filed-a-genocide-petition-against-israel/0000018d-1cf4-dd75-addd-fef523410000; Jacob Siegel, "Lawfare at The Hague," Quillette, January 17, 2024, https://quillette.com/2024/01/17/lawfare-at-the-hague/.
57 Josh Rogin, "China's Online Antisemitism: A New Tool against the West," *Washington Post*, January 8, 2024, https://www.washingtonpost.com/opinions/2024/01/08/china-antisemitism-online-tool-west-gaza/.
58 Refaella Goichman, "'We're playing with Israelis' minds': Inside Telegram Group Helping Thousands Spread Disinformation," *Haaretz*, January 18, 2024, https://www.haaretz.com/israel-news/security-aviation/2024-01-18/ty-article/.premium/exposed-telegram-group-with-thousands-of-pro-palestinian-users-spreading-disinformation/0000018d-1c5c-d022-ad9d-1e7c69830000.

the alleged liberal basis of the progressive movement and guarantees of equal protection under the law by the government. But the growth of foundations, along with NGOs as the "third sector," has generated a vast non-profit industry purporting constitute "civil society" that operates almost exclusively," under the premises of human rights as a universal secular religion and the governance principles of "transnational progressivism."[59]

The relationships between tax-exempt foundations, NGOs, and the government are complex. Often, they stand in opposition, but foundations have become in some cases so wealthy and influential that they act as competitors to governments, creating initiatives without oversight. Sometimes they are too attractive to governments to ignore as adjuncts. Governments have also found it convenient to promote policies covertly by funding NGOs. In addition, there is a revolving door between activist NGOs, supporting foundations, think tanks, and universities; personnel are shared and there is a pattern of mutual support and ideological validation and reinforcement. There is also a "halo effect" afforded to many of these organizations—with the possible exception of government—by media and other commentators who are often literally part of the same political economy, for example from academic centers for "human rights," amplifies the reach of antisemitic and anti-Israel propaganda.

Foreign support for NGOs as tools to manipulate public opinion and policy is another problem with particular relevance to the political economy of antisemitism. European states and supra-national bodies such as the European Union have long funded "human rights" organizations such as Human Rights Watch and Amnesty International, as well as local Palestinian NGOs which in turn attack Israel as extensions of European policy. States such as Saudi Arabia, Qatar, and Turkey funding "human rights" NGO is another old problem. The problem is not limited to the Middle East and in fact may have greater economic implications elsewhere, such as Chinese non-profits under government control that advocate for "green energy" projects with donations to Western universities and advocacy groups, which in turn push for policies that directly benefit Chinese firms.[60]

---

59 Joan Roelofs, *Foundations and Public Policy* (Albany, NY: SUNY Press, 2003); Michael Ignatieff, *Human Rights as Politics and Idolatry* (Princeton, NJ: Princeton University Press, 2003); John Reader, "The Discourse of Human Rights—A Secular Religion?," *Implicit Religion* 6 (2003): 41–51; John Fonte, "Liberal Democracy vs. Transnational Progressivism: The Ideological War Within the West," *Orbis* 46, no. 3 (Summer 2002): 449–467.

60 Thomas Catenacci, "Ex-CCP Officials Funneled Millions to US Universities, Nonprofits To Promote Green Energy, Tax Forms Show," *Washington Free Beacon*, December 10, 2024, https://freebeacon.com/energy/ex-ccp-officials-steered-millions-to-us-based-green-groups-universities-for-climate-initiatives/.

More broadly, the evidence of foundation funding aligns with data showing that the global movement for Hamas and the Palestinians was constructed over decades with European Union, NGOs, and US foundations.[61] However, the pro-Hamas protests, in their celebratory, "genocide," and ceasefire phases, and organizational connections with other movements such as BLM, the Women's March, and Occupy Wall Street, demonstrate that the deeper intent is not support for "Palestine" and changes in US policy but creating fissures in American society.

Within the United States, foundations such as the Tides Foundation, Rockefeller Brothers Fund, Ford Foundation, Omidyar Foundation, and the Open Societies Foundation all contribute to the funding of BDS as well as to climate, human rights, and other protest movements, in order to obscure sources of funding. Tides in particular acts as the fiscal sponsor of the Arab Resource and Organizing Committee, IfNotNow, Jewish Voice for Peace, Adalah Justice Project, and other anti-Israel protest groups and bail funds active on campuses. Fiscal sponsorship is a method for organizations without tax-exempt status to receive funds from a recognized entity, which in turn shields the identity of contributors from view.

Rockefeller Brothers Fund and Soros network funding supports Jewish Voice for Peace and IfNotNow,[62] while the Tides Foundation and Omidyar Network fund other BDS groups such as the Adalah Justice Project.[63] The role of the Tides Foundation and the Rockefeller Brothers Fund (RBF) in supporting BDS has been especially well documented.[64] Reports indicate that RBF, along with the Ben & Jerry's Foundation and donor-advised funds administered by Charles Schwab, were among those supporting the January 3 protests in New York City that included the Palestinian Youth Movement, the New York branch of the Democratic Socialists of America, Writers against War on Gaza, Jewish Voice for

---

61 Gary Wexler, "The Inside Story of How Palestinians Took Over the World," *Jewish Journal*, November 18, 2023, https://jewishjournal.com/commentary/columnist/365220/the-inside-story-of-how-palestinians-took-over-the-world/.

62 "Rockefeller Brothers Fund," NGO Monitor, https://www.ngo-monitor.org/funder/rockefeller_brothers_fund/; Alana Goodman, "Soros-Backed Groups Storm U.S. Capitol, Accuse Israel of Genocide," *Washington Free Beacon*, October 19, 2023, https://freebeacon.com/democrats/soros-backed-groups-storm-u-s-capitol-accuse-israel-of-genocide/.

63 Joseph Simonson and Andrew Kerr, "This 'Grassroots' Anti-Israel Group Is Actually Part of a Left-Wing Dark Money Behemoth," *Washington Free Beacon*, October 27, 2023, https://freebeacon.com/democrats/this-grassroots-anti-israel-group-is-actually-part-of-a-left-wing-dark-money-behemoth/.

64 River Page, "San Francisco Taxpayers Funded the Bay Bridge Protests," Pirate Wires, January 26, 2025, https://www.piratewires.com/p/aroc-bridge-protests; "Rockefeller Brothers Fund."

Peace, Al-Awda, and Critical Resistance. Numerous smaller foundations such as the Firedoll and Sparkplug Foundations support individual groups such as Jewish Voice for Peace, Palestine Children's Relief Fund, International Jewish Anti-Zionist Network, and Arab American Action Network, while also contributing to larger dark money operations such as the Alliance for Global Justice.[65]

Even more obscure non-profits such as WESPAC have critical roles.[66] The example of WESPAC, the Westchester Peace Action Committee Foundation, illustrates the manner in which many BDS and antisemitic groups are supported. WESPAC acts as the "fiscal sponsor" of National SJP, Samidoun, the Palestinian Youth Movement, Within Our Lifetime, Jewish Voice for Peace, Adalah-NY, and the US Campaign for Palestinian Rights.[67] As such, it is also tied to Hamas-connected American Muslim Brotherhood organizations including American Muslims for Palestine, which directs SJPs, Linda Sarsour's MPower Change, as well as other groups such as Palestine Legal, the lawfare arm of the BDS movement.[68]

The case of the Open Societies Foundation, created by George Soros with the initial aim of changing post-Soviet Central and Eastern Europe, is especially well documented. The role of the foundation, as well as those belonging to family members, in creating J Street and other organizations which aimed to change American Jewish and the broader American public's attitudes towards Israel, Iran, and Middle East policy from the Obama administration onward must be judged successful. Villainizing AIPAC in particular and positing J Street as an alternative has been critical to the project of splitting the American Jewish community from within.

Foundations and government grants are also linked to "dark money" outfits that function as extensions of the Democratic Party. An example of this is Arabella Advisors, run by former Clinton administration appointee Eric

---

65 "Firedoll Foundation," InfluenceWatch, https://www.influencewatch.org/non-profit/firedoll-foundation/; "Sparkplug Foundation," InfluenceWatch, https://www.influencewatch.org/non-profit/sparkplug-foundation/.

66 Park MacDougald, "The People Setting America on Fire," *Tablet*, May 6, 2024, https://www.tabletmag.com/sections/news/articles/people-setting-america-on-fire-soros-tides-wespac; Joseph Simonson, "Is This Suburban New York Charity a Terrorist Front Group?," *Washington Free Beacon*, May 20, 2024, https://freebeacon.com/national-security/is-this-suburban-new-york-charity-a-terrorist-front-group/.

67 "The NGO Network Orchestrating Antisemitic Incitement."

68 Josh Meyer, "American Muslims for Palestine Helped Drive Campus Protests over Gaza. Who Are They?" *USA Today*, May 22, 2024, https://www.usatoday.com/story/news/investigations/2024/05/22/gaza-student-protests-american-muslims-for-palestine/73775372007/.

Kessler, which controls a network of funders including the New Venture Fund, the Hopewell Fund, and the Sixteen Thirty Fund, which together have more than $3 billion in assets and hundreds of subsidiary organizations.[69] Among the key funders of Arabella Advisors are Democratic Party mainstays George Soros and Pierre Omidyar.

Arabella Advisors manages and provides support for both Democratic super-PACs and lobbying organizations, and a complex array of left-wing organizations, often in violation of IRS regulations regarding non-profits involved in political activities.[70] The latter included the Alliance for Global Justice, which was revealed to be fundraising for the PFLP and which also housed Samidoun and the US Campaign for the Academic and Cultural Boycott of Israel. Both utilized the Democratic Party's online funding portal ActBlue until the connections were exposed by lawsuits.[71] ActBlue was recently exposed as having illegally accepted foreign donations for US political campaigns.[72] Other Arabella activities such as the New Venture Fund channeled Ford Foundation money to the black communist magazine Hammer & Hope, which offered strong endorsement of Hamas and the October 7 massacre.[73]

National and local government support for protest groups through seemingly unrelated vectors is a newly-documented dimension of the anti-Israel movement. One example is the $50 million awarded by the Biden administration's

---

69 Hayden Ludwig, "The For-Profit D.C. Firm Staging America's 'Grassroots' Movements," *Tablet*, September 14, 2022, https://www.tabletmag.com/sections/news/articles/for-profit-dc-firm-staging-americas-grassroots-movements-arabella-advisors.
70 Andrew Kerr and Joseph Simonson, "Top Democratic Operatives Were Quietly Pulling the Strings at a Voting Rights Group. Lawyers Say They May Have Broken the Law," *Washington Free Beacon*, July 10, 2023, https://freebeacon.com/democrats/top-democratic-operatives-were-quietly-pulling-the-strings-at-a-voting-rights-group-lawyers-say-they-may-have-broken-the-law/.
71 Ibid.; Gabe Kaminsky, "Democratic Behemoth ActBlue Boots Anti-Israel Group Accused of Terror Ties Off Platform," *Washington Examiner*, September 7, 2023, https://www.washingtonexaminer.com/news/2585296/democratic-behemoth-actblue-boots-anti-israel-group-accused-of-terror-ties-off-platform/; Andrew Kerr and Joseph Simonson, "Documents Provide Rare Glimpse Into How Arabella Advisors Exerts Centralized Control Over a Vast Left-Wing Advocacy Network," *Washington Free Beacon*, July 10, 2023, https://freebeacon.com/elections/documents-provide-rare-glimpse-into-how-arabella-advisors-exerts-centralized-control-over-a-vast-left-wing-advocacy-network/.
72 Gabe Kaminsky, "House Republicans Press ActBlue on Donation Fraud and Protection Services," *Washington Examiner*, February 8, 2024, https://www.washingtonexaminer.com/news/house/3255905/house-republicans-letter-actblue-donation-fraud-protection-services/.
73 "Arabella Advisors: Dark Money Group Behind Black Communist Solidarity Magazine Boosting Hamas," *Gazette*, October 12, 2023, https://gazette.com/news/wex/arabella-advisors-dark-money-group-behind-black-communist-solidarity-magazine-boosting-hamas/article_57885be7-30ea-568e-a894-b9fda7465e79.html.

Environmental Protection Agency under terms of the "Inflation Reduction Act" to the Climate Justice Alliance.[74] This umbrella group of some 80 organizations includes the Grassroots Global Justice Alliance which organized an anti Israel protest at the US Capitol at which over fifty activists were arrested.

The foundations and individuals funding protests thus connect both the Biden administration (through Federal agencies) and former members of the Obama administration who lead various NGOs and protest groups.[75] The obsessive anti-Israel focus manufactured on campus and in street protests was designed in part to support an Obama policy goal, relegating Israel and other traditional American allies in the Middle East as part of a "realignment" that recognizes Iranian hegemony.[76]

At the local level discretionary funds distributed by individual members of the New York City Council provided millions of dollars to various organizations such as the Muslim Community Network, CAIR, and Jews for Racial and Economic Justice, which then organized anti-Israel protests.[77] Linda Sarsour's Arab American Association of New York, which along with Within Our Lifetime organized a "Flood Brooklyn for Palestine Protest," received almost $7 million, with individual city council members providing hundreds of thousands of dollars in grants.[78]

A much larger structural example is more than $1 billion in Department of Education grants to K–12 schools, districts, and consultants to promote "diversity, equity, and inclusion."[79] These promote a general ideology of anti-capitalism, anti-settler-colonialism, and racial separatism and grievance in the name of "anti-racism." Israel and Jews as the supreme examples of "settler-colonialism" and "white privilege" are routine features of "antiracist pedagogy," particularly since

---

74 "Inflation Reduction Act Funds Climate Group That Blames U.S. for Hamas War," *Wall Street Journal*, February 8, 2024, https://www.wsj.com/articles/inflation-reduction-act-climate-justice-alliance-taxpayer-dollars-epa-palestine-4c345171.
75 Sean Cooper, 'The People Setting America on Fire," *Tablet*, February 7, 2024, https://www.tabletmag.com/sections/news/articles/people-setting-america-on-fire-soros-tides-wespac.
76 Michael Doran and Tony Badran, "The Realignment," *Tablet*, May 10, 2021, https://www.tabletmag.com/sections/israel-middle-east/articles/realignment-iran-biden-obama-michael-doran-tony-badran.
77 "Anti-Israel Campus Protest Backers Got $2.7M in NYC Council Pork," *New York Post*, May 4, 2024, https://nypost.com/2024/05/04/us-news/anti-israel-campus-protest-backers-got-2-7m-in-nyc-council-pork/.
78 "Pro-Palestine Rally Sponsors Raked in $9M in City Funds," *New York Post*, November 4, 2023, https://nypost.com/2023/11/04/metro/pro-palestine-rally-sponsors-raked-in-9m-in-city-funds/.
79 "Granted," Parents Defending Education, https://defendinged.org/investigations/granted/.

the emphasis on transgenderism has faltered under scrutiny.[80] "Ethnic studies" and its even more radical offshoot "liberated ethnic studies"[81] have also become a vector for government funds to be channeled through schools and districts to consultants, many of whom are university faculty members, and to pay the same for curriculums that target Israel and Jews, in addition to the United States, as examples of unmitigated evils.

Conclusions

Antisemitism has frequently been called the "world's oldest hatred," but this anodyne formula obscures how ideas are recycled with innovations to fit the times, then transmitted, and supported. The political economy of anti-Israel bias and antisemitism in America, which has only been sketched here, provides a portrait of how individual beliefs and movement-scale ideologies are reproduced and disseminated. Though "timeless" in the sense of Jews being the perennial target of shifting forms of hatred, there is nothing organic about antisemitism.

Beliefs are backed up by money, not least of all provided by or acquiesced to, by taxpayers. Regulations regarding charitable deductions, tax-exempt foundations and organizations, direct government funding, and oversight by law enforcement are all ultimately political decisions made, one hopes, in a democratic context. Tolerating foreign funding of American institutions along with hundreds of thousands of foreign students is both a foreign policy and thus national security decision and an economic decision. And building antisemitism into school curriculums and then tolerating street violence are explicit decisions to target Jews. In structural terms, the twenty-first-century allegation that Jews are the singularly demonic examples of white supremacy and settler-colonialism is similar to the thirteenth-century allegation that Jews desecrate the Host.

The Hamas massacres of October 7, the Gaza War, the destruction of Hamas, and the end of the Assad regime in Syria have all relegated many policy goals to the ash heaps, while the anti-Israel street protests and antisemitic violence in America helped propel the reelection of Donald Trump. At least parts of the political economy of anti-Israel hatred and antisemitism will now face unprecedented scrutiny and enforcement. Antisemitism will not disappear but will mutate, as

---

80 Leor Sapir, "The Kinderfada Revolution," Manhattan Institute, February 7, 2024, https://manhattan.institute/article/the-kinderfada-revolution.
81 Erec Smith, "Crack Down on Anti-Semitic K–12 Curricula," *City Journal*, February 7, 2024, https://www.city-journal.org/article/crack-down-on-anti-semitic-k-12-curricula.

it always does. Understanding its political economy, however, offers the opportunity of exposing its mechanisms as well as social and ideological foundations.

Addendum

Since this piece was submitted for publication in December 2024, revelations have expanded regarding US-government funding of entities connected to the BDS movement and antisemitism worldwide. USAID grants to the Tides Foundation, Rockefeller Brothers Fund, and other left-wing organizations that fund the BDS movement within the US were complemented by funding of Palestinian "civil society" groups, some of which were connected to Hamas and the PFLP. Some $198 million was also awarded by USAID to "miscellaneous foreign awardees" in the West Bank and Gaza during 2024 alone. An unknown number of Palestinian NGOs have been funded by USAID through the National Endowment for Democracy, International Republican Institute, and other intermediary organizations under such rubrics as "democracy assistance" and "promoting civil society." Unknown amounts of US money were then used to support BDS activities as well as terrorism.

In addition, USAID funding went to a global network of thousands of media groups through Internews Network and other organizations. Internews Network, which also received funding from BDS supporting entities such as the Open Society Foundation and the Macarthur Foundation, is closely connected to the USAID funded World Economic Forum. After 2016, Internews Network added internet censorship ("information integrity") to its purported areas of expertise. Internews Network has been active as late as 2024 in Gaza on issues such as "media consumption" where, almost by definition, it engaged with Hamas and its supporters. Here, too, an unknown amount of US money was used to fund additional information operations and possibly terrorism.

Finally, a growing number of reports also suggest that USAID staff members displayed severe hostility towards Israel, over and against the policies of the Biden administration. This was despite evidence of funds being diverted to terrorist groups and coercion of aid workers.

It thus appears that elements of the US government acting outside of Congressional appropriations or Executive oversight have contributed an outsized share of the funding behind foreign and domestic antisemitism and anti Israel bias.

CHAPTER 11

Fruit of the Land

Aviya Cammy and Justin Cammy

Our local synagogue in progressive Western Massachusetts did not install any signage on its property in the aftermath of the events of October 7, not even a "Bring Them Home"[1] sign, though until mid-fall 2024 it displayed a larger banner on its facade stating that "Reproductive Rights are a Jewish Value." Throughout the year, the synagogue was rocked by several incidents, which leadership did their best to keep out of the public eye: a daycare worker in the synagogue preschool showed up with a Palestinian flag painted on their fingernails, and a worker in the employment of the same synagogue preschool was caught on security camera vandalizing an Israeli-owned café in town. When a group of congregants placed small Israeli flags and a photo of a hostage near cookies baked for Sabbath lunch as part of the Tastes Like Home project,[2] organizers were advised that this was divisive. A candidate brought in to interview for head rabbi position was a member of the avowedly antizionist Jewish Voice for Peace and If Not Now and had stood next to Representative Rashida Tlaib and other rabbis on Capitol Hill calling for a ceasefire only weeks into Israel's campaign to

---

1 "In North America, the phrase 'Bring Them Home' has often been used in contexts that do not differentiate between support for the hostages and support for the actions of the Israeli government. As such, the phrase has sometimes been rejected as not leaving room for acknowledging the tremendous loss of innocent life in Gaza that has been a consequence of this war. This humane and moral issue then becomes political, regardless of intent." See "What We Stand For," Congregation B'nai Israel, Northampton, MA, December 6, 2024, https://www.cbinorthampton.org/blog?post_id=1608683.

2 A project begun by a small group of synagogue members dismayed at the lack of acknowledgement and advocacy for those murdered and kidnapped, "Tastes like Home," asserts that "Nothing describes home and family better than food. Each Israeli held captive by Hamas is a whole world, with family and friends waiting for them. With hobbies and dreams, and their favorite cookie. . . . By making their favorite cookie and sending it, along with their personal story to your friends and family, we will spread their light and their story further." "About," Tastes Like Home, https://tasteslikehome.co.il/about-en/.

capture or eliminate the perpetrators of October 7. Several congregants showed up to services—including on Yom Kippur—wearing keffiyehs over, or in lieu of, their prayer shawls, causing distress to those whose loved ones were directly impacted by the crimes of October 7 and consternation to those whose prayer in a Jewish sacred space was interrupted by a gesture designed to be provocative. Bemused by these happenings, during one visit to the synagogue we noticed a fellow congregant wearing an artfully knit kippah featuring a watermelon. "Do they also come in avocado?" Justin inquired.

Since October 7, the watermelon has become a ubiquitous political symbol. Watermelons are deployed both by those advocating for an immediate ceasefire (mostly without mention of the release of the hostages) *and* by those supporting resistance "by any means necessary." This makes the watermelon an especially slippery signifier, allowing both those who exhibit it and those who observe it to variously interpret its meaning in public spaces, both tangible and virtual. In November 2023, an Al-Jazeera information sheet suggested that the watermelon is "the most iconic fruit to represent Palestine,"[3] eclipsing the olive, which has long stood as a symbol of Palestinian rootedness and steadfastness.[4] This politicization of local fruit is, of course, part of the larger struggle over native claims and indigenous rights.[5]

As with many things involving the conflict between Israel and Palestinians, the watermelon has a much longer visual history than most Palestinians and their supporters are aware of when they deploy it to convey their political commitments. Though the initiation of the watermelon as a symbol of Palestinian nationalism emerges from a case of censorship in the 1980s, the fruit features extensively in Israeli art, from the earliest days of Zionist visual culture to the present. What does an understanding of the watermelon's history in the visual

---

3   Mohammed Haddad, Konstantinos Antonopoulos, and Marium Ali, "Symbols of Palestine," Al Jazeera, November 20, 2023, https://www.aljazeera.com/news/longform/2023/11/20/palestine-symbols-keffiyeh-olive-branch-watermelon.
4   The orange is yet another fruit that was once associated with Palestine. Citrus amounted to around three-quarters of all exports from British Mandate Palestine, making it synonymous with the country. As Jews increasingly purchased private Palestinian land and as more Arab land was lost in the 1948 war, Palestinians came to consider the branding of the "Jaffa" orange a symbol of their displacement.
5   The matter is further complicated by the ubiquity of the watermelon in both Israeli and Palestinian culinary traditions, making it an item that is claimed by both sides to assert their rootedness in the land. Watermelon salad with mint, traditional white cheese, and sometimes date or pomegranate syrup is a common Palestinian dish, often served with pita, olive oil, zaatar spice. In southern Gaza, roasted watermelon salad (*fatit ajir*) is another beloved dish. In Israel, chilled watermelon (often served with salty white cheese) is a summer staple in supermarkets, at family barbecues, and at the beach.

repertoire of Israeli and Palestinian political art reveal, and how must its recent visibility as a symbol of solidarity with Palestinians be more deeply understood in relation to its emblematic role in Israeli art? Put differently, if the watermelon is now a symbol for the broader struggle over the Land, a more nuanced appreciation of its overlapping and competing meanings in Zionist, Israeli, and Palestinian art is critical.

Why the Watermelon

When the green skin of a watermelon is sliced open, black seeds, red flesh, and a white rind are exposed to reveal the colors of the Palestinian flag, which itself draws inspiration from the flag of the Arab revolt against Ottoman rule during the First World War (1916–1918).[6] Used by Palestinian artists and their supporters since the 1980s, the watermelon proved especially useful at moments when flying the Palestinian flag in protest was restricted.[7] In the wake of global protests in the aftermath of October 7, the watermelon emerged as a popular expression of solidarity with Palestinians and their struggle, featured in everything from emojis to protest signs. On social media, the watermelon was used instead of the Palestinian flag due to accusations of platforms "shadow banning" content supportive of Palestinians.[8]

The watermelon is a member of the gourd family or "cucurbits" that have long grown in the Eastern Mediterranean.[9] In the book of Numbers, the Israelites cry out in the desert: "We remember the fish that we used to eat free in Egypt, the

---

6   The Palestinian flag has white in the middle, where the flag of the Arab Revolt had white on the bottom.
7   These include attempts in France and Britain in October 2023 to ban displays of the Palestinian flag for fear mass protests might be calling for the elimination of Israel and in support of terror; see Astha Rajvanshi, "In Europe, Free Speech Is under Threat for Pro-Palestine Protesters," *Time*, October 20, 2023, https://time.com/6326360/europe-palestine-protests-free-speech/.
8   See "Meta's Broken Promises," Human Rights Watch, December 21, 2023, https://www.hrw.org/report/2023/12/21/metas-broken-promises/systemic-censorship-palestine-content-instagram-and; Adele Walton, "Social Media Users Are Bypassing Censorship on Palestine," *New Internationalist*, January 21, 2024, https://newint.org/social-media-censorship-palestine.
9   The oldest remains of the wild watermelon are more than 5,000 years old and found in Libya. See Krystyna Wasylikowa and Marijke van der Veen, "An Archaeobotanical Contribution to the History of Watermelon, Citrullus Lanatus (Thunb.) Matsum. & Nakai (Syn. C. Vulgaris Schrad.)," *Vegetation History and Archaeobotany* 13, no. 4 (2004): 213–217, http://www.jstor.org/stable/23419585.

cucumbers, the [water]melons [avati☐ ☐h☐ ☐ ☐ ☐im], the leeks, the onions, and the garlics!"¹⁰ As its coupling with onions and garlic suggests, the watermelon of the biblical era was not sweet, a point supported by historians of agriculture. These biblical verses shaped associations of the watermelon with food of the poor and exploited.[11] Zionists some two millennia later looked to the Bible as evidence of Jewish indigeneity in the region. The Bible also served as a source of inspiration for Zionist artists in the nineteenth century, celebrating renewed contact with the nature of the Land of Israel.[12] The presence of the watermelon in the Bible makes its appearance in Israeli art part of the broader history of the modern revival of an ancient people and cements it as a symbol of organic belonging to the Land of Israel.

A Hebrew codex from the second century CE lists watermelons along with grapes, figs, and pomegranates, suggesting that by that time they had become sweet.[13] Beautiful and ornamental, cultivated cucurbits with their many seeds accrued associations with abundance, vitality, and fertility.[14] Cucurbits (like cucumbers and zucchinis) are often phallic in shape, though as it evolved the watermelon began to evoke a pregnant belly more than a phallus. It is therefore telling of a long association of cucurbits with sex that cucumbers and watermelons appear alongside one another in the Bible to elicit a life-force that transcended the experience of Hebrew slavery. To underscore the sexual connotations of the watermelon, its consumption requires penetration of a hard protective shell in order to partake of its juicy red flesh. The curator Shira Naftali observes that "its rounded uterine form endows it with feminine qualities . . .

---

10   Numbers 11:5 (JPS). The Hebrew words of the verse say *kishu'im* and *avatihim*. Those words in Modern Hebrew refer specifically to zucchini and watermelon, yet in the JPS translation, we are given cucumbers and melons.
11   The watermelon came to amass symbolic importance in American culture in the nineteenth century for its association with African Americans. The stereotype was prevalent in popular imagery of the late nineteenth and early twentieth centuries, especially in postcards and print media. Historian William Black examines the racial implications of the association between African Americans and watermelons and places the origins of the racist watermelon stereotype in post-Emancipation America. He notes that Europeans already had racialized the watermelon by the eighteenth century, though they associated it with the Near East and Mediterranean in Orientalist discourse. See William R. Black, "How Watermelons Became Black: Emancipation and the Origins of a Racist Trope," *Journal of the Civil War Era* 8, no. 1 (2018): 64–86, https://www.jstor.org/stable/26381503.
12   Dalia Manor, *Art in Zion: The Genesis of Modern National Art in Jewish Palestine* (London: Routledge, 2005), 54.
13   Harry S. Paris, "Overview of the Origins and History of the Five Major Cucurbit Crops: Issues for Ancient DNA Analysis of Archaeological Specimens," *Vegetation History and Archaeobotany* 25, no. 4 (2016): 408.
14   Ibid., 405.

yet the process of choosing, carrying, and cutting the watermelon ... produces an erotic encounter."[15] One must add that, though the process of "opening up" a watermelon can be experienced as an intimate act, it can also be experienced as a form of violence.

The Watermelon in Hebrew and Israeli Art

Yearned for in the Bible, and later exoticized in early modern European art,[16] the watermelon would be reclaimed by early Zionist and then Israeli artists. The roots of Israeli art begin with the desire for a national art to accompany the emerging Jewish national home in the Land of Israel. The institutional landscape of Israeli art is the direct result of the vision of Boris Schatz (1866–1932) who, at the beginning of the twentieth century, sought to develop a new visual language to represent and interpret the Jewish national project. In 1902, Schatz proposed the establishment of an art academy to Theodore Herzl, the founder of political Zionism. Approved by the Seventh Zionist Congress, Schatz established the first Jewish art academy in Ottoman Palestine, the Bezalel Academy of Arts and Crafts, in 1906.[17] The Academy was named after the biblical figure Bezalel Ben Uri (Exodus 31:1–5), the builder of the Tabernacle in the desert, who is mythologized as the first Jewish artist.

---

15   Shira Naftali, "The Watermelon Man," in *Watermelons*, ed. Carmela Rubin, Shira Naftali, and Edna Erde, trans. Talya Halkin (Tel Aviv: The Rubin Museum, 2009), 87. Naftali co-curated the only focused exhibition and study of the watermelon in Israeli art at the Rubin Museum in Tel Aviv in 2009. For more on the exhibition, see Carl Hoffman, "A Mouthwatering Exhibition," *Jerusalem Post*, January 18, 2010, https://www.jpost.com/local-israel/tel-aviv-and-center/a-mouthwatering-exhibition. For the prevalence of the watermelon in Israeli culture, see Shany Littman, "Watermelon, Fruit of the Land (and of Art)," *Haaretz*, August 14, 2014, https://www.haaretz.com/israel-news/culture/2014-08-14/ty-article/.premium/watermelon-fruit-of-the-land-and-of-art/0000017f-e627-df5f-a17f-ffffb0d80000.
16   Watermelons became present in Mediterranean parts of Europe around the fifth century. Their illustration in European art can be traced to fourteenth-century Italian and French botanical and herbal manuscripts. Watermelons were depicted frequently by seventeenth-century Dutch, Italian, and Spanish painters. In these still lives they are almost always cut (penetrated), as in Giovanni Stanchi's still life of an array of fruit and Abraham Breughel's similar painting. In both paintings, the watermelon is the only open fruit, other than the small cracks in the squash and figs. Albert Eckhout's painting of "Brazilian fruits" is an example of the usage of the watermelon as a symbol for the abundant power of the Dutch colonial enterprise, transposing the watermelon to the Americas to suggest their success in introducing new crops. See Harry Berger, *Caterpillage: Reflections on Seventeenth-Century Dutch Still Life Painting* (New York: Fordham University Press, 2011).
17   Margaret Rose Olin, "Defining Jewish Art," in *The Nation Without Art: Examining Modern Discourses on Jewish Art* (Lincoln, NE: University of Nebraska Press, 2001), 36.

Schatz's vision of an art academy was a conscious measure to rehabilitate and uplift the Jewish people (Jews had not been allowed in most of the great European art academies until their emancipation in the nineteenth century). Support of the arts was seen by Schatz and others, such as philosopher Martin Buber,[18] as part of the healing and rebirth of the Jewish nation who understood the cultivation of a national culture to be critical in the nation-building project. The Bezalel School was stylistically influenced by art nouveau and is best characterized as a fusion of old and new, East and West. Bezalel looked to biblical history, to Judaica, and to prevailing European artistic trends to develop a contemporary Hebrew art that would contribute to a Jewish national renaissance. The next generation of immigrant artists expanded this by looking to the natural world of flora and fauna in the Land of Israel to develop an artistic idiom distinct from diasporic Jewish experience, laying the foundation for artists to recuperate the watermelon as a metaphor of return to the ancient homeland.[19]

Reuben Rubin (1893–1974) and Nahum Gutman (1898–1980), two foundational figures in Israeli art, both studied for a period at Bezalel, recognizing that Zionism was not only a political revolution but an opportunity for cultural revival. They are associated with the Land of Israel School, which was more interested in painting, especially landscapes, than Bezalel's earlier focus on decorative arts. The watermelon was an ideal motif to lend itself to the cultural imagining of the "new Hebrew" in this landscape of return. It had no history of representation in European Jewish art, so it was suited to Zionism's aspirational negation of the Diaspora.[20] As a fruit that was already present in local life, it was both rediscovered and celebrated as part of an intimate return to the Land in which Jewish immigrants would "build and [thus would the land and the people] be rebuilt."

Reuben Rubin emerged as one of the leaders of the Land of Israel style, which shifted the cultural center of Zionist art from Jerusalem (home to Bezalel) to the more recently established Hebrew city of Tel Aviv.[21] His painting romanticized an attachment to the land and its peoples that was inspired by Zionist ethos and stylistically shaped by his formal training at Bezalel and at Paris's Ecole des Beaux-Arts.[22] Rubin includes the watermelon in several of his most recognizable

---

18 Ibid., 40.
19 Ibid., 48.
20 Manor, *Art in Zion*, 72.
21 Gideon Ofrat, *One Hundred Years of Art in Israel*, trans. Peretz Kidron (Boulder, CO: Westview Press, 1998), 51.
22 Manor, *Art in Zion*, 80.

early works, including *Meal of the Poor* (1922),[23] *First Fruits* (1923),[24] and *Arab Barber at Jaffa Gate* (1924).[25] Both *Meal of the Poor* and *Arab Barber* locate the watermelon as readily accessible local produce. Its presence in scenes of everyday life, inspired by Primitivist naïveté, created an obvious link between the fruit and vernacular experience. While in *Meal of the Poor* it is being consumed by those who appear to be recent Jewish immigrants (based on their European clothing), in *Arab Barber at Jaffa Gate* watermelon is fed by an Arab customer to his donkey, suggesting its lowly status.

This association was transformed by the monumental triptych *First Fruits*, which featured the watermelon in its central panel, held by a shirtless, tanned man in one hand, as he carries a bunch of bananas in the other.[26] In this work, the watermelon is transformed into a Zionist symbol, associated with the healthy new Hebrew nurtured by the Levantine sun. The shirtless man holding the watermelon and bananas is accompanied by a young woman, examining an orange with her breasts exposed. This couple is meant to embody pioneering spirit and vitality, in contrast to the more traditional Jews of the Old *Yishuv*[27] embodied by the Yemeni couple which stands beside them holding their baby and a pomegranate (another symbol of fertility). The couples are in tension by virtue of the fact that the pomegranate has sacred connotations as one of the seven species of first fruits mentioned in the Bible that were brought by the ancient Israelites to Jerusalem to be received by the Temple priests.[28] The watermelon is used by Rubin because it represents a break from the first fruits associated with a cultic past. It is Zionism itself that endows the watermelon, banana, and oranges—first fruits of a modern agricultural economy—with sacred

---

23 Reuven Rubin, *Meal of the Poor*, 1922, oil on canvas, 90 × 72.5 cm, private collection. Image source: Carmela Rubin, Shira Naftali, and Edna Erde, eds., *Watermelons*, trans. Talya Halkin (Tel Aviv: Rubin Museum, 2009), 51, https://www.rubinmuseum.org.il/en/company/art/main/?ContentID=881.

24 Reuven Rubin, *First Fruits*, 1923, oil on canvas, 188 × 406 cm, Rubin Museum, Tel Aviv, currently loaned and displayed at the Israel Museum, Jerusalem, no. L-B10.0011, https://www.imj.org.il/en/collections/403452-0.

25 Reuven Rubin, *Arab Barber at Jaffa Gate*, 1924, oil on canvas, 55 × 66 cm, private collection. Image source: Rubin, Naftali, and Erde, *Watermelons*, 43, https://www.rubinmuseum.org.il/en/company/art/main/?ContentID=878.

26 The triptych format, and the large size of the piece, shows how Rubin intended for his art to be viewed publicly, and as national art. Manor, *Art in Zion*, 95.

27 The pre-State Jewish community in Palestine. The Old *Yishuv* consisted of those Jews who were already established in the Land of Israel prior to the first wave of Zionist immigration in the late nineteenth century.

28 Alec Mishory, *Secularizing the Sacred: Aspects of Israeli Visual Culture* (Leiden: Brill, 2019), 247. The seven species of first fruits and grain mentioned in Deuteronomy 8:8 as special products of the Land of Israel are wheat, barley, grapes, figs, pomegranate, olives, and date palms.

national, rather than religious meaning. The title of the triptych celebrates the renaissance of Hebrew culture in the land as a physical and organic, informed by but not reliant on the broader Middle Eastern environment in which it exists, as evidenced by the presence of an Arab man napping alongside his camel on the right panel and a lute-playing shepherd on the other.[29] Moreover, aside from the woman with her breasts exposed, all of the Jewish figures have darker skin, suggesting a mixing together of Yemenite Jews and the idealized tanned laborer of the Zionist *Yishuv*. These Gaugin-like Primitivist and Orientalist images suggest a rural Arab population on the margins of where the real action is in the central panel, where Jews from East and West reunite on the Land.[30] *First Fruits* was displayed in the Association of Jewish Artists Tower of David exhibition in Jerusalem (1924) and was deemed so monumental and emblematic that it was considered for purchase by the National Library.[31]

Nahum Gutman, too, took up the watermelon motif early in his career. *Resting at Noon* (1926)[32] represents two laborers, male and female, taking a break in the hot desert sun. The majority of the landscape's barren rolling hills are an ochre, yellow, capturing the light and heat of the environment. These are interrupted in the distance by fields of green, meant to represent the new Hebrew farming communities which were designed to "make the desert bloom," a popular Zionist motif. Two yellow haystacks suggest rounded breasts, connecting the female body with nature through codes of rebirth. The watermelon within the composition is sliced open; the knife left inserted into its rind evoking conquest. The male figure napping in the midday heat is dressed in blue wide trousers that narrow at the bottom paired with a red belt and silk top. This clothing is more characteristic of Arab city dwellers than with Arab rural farmers, making this a misplaced representation of an Arab archetype.[33] The woman wears a blue dress with a scarf that does not provide full coverage of her hair. The couple seem at one with the landscape due to the way the curvature of their own bodies interacts with the curves of the landscape. However, they stand in contrast to the

---

29   Ofrat, *One Hundred Years of Art in Israel*, 53.
30   Rubin was compared to Gaugin in a 1928 newspaper article and is known to have been impacted by the Gaugin pieces he saw in New York exhibitions in the 1920s. See Manor, *Art in Zion*, 103. It was a common idea that local, rural Arab villagers were the offspring of the Jews who evaded Roman deportation, and that Arab village life as identical to Jewish village life was one of idyllic coexistence of humans and nature. Ofrat, *One Hundred Years of Art in Israel*, 56.
31   Manor, *Art in Zion*, 92.
32   Nahum Gutman, *Resting at Noon*, 1926, oil on canvas, 93.5 × 107.5 cm, Tel Aviv Museum of Art.
33   Manor, *Art in Zion*, 146.

idealized image of the muscular new Hebrew in their inactivity. The presence of the watermelon beside them reminds us of the ways in which the artistic deployment of the watermelon relied on both a romantic perception and grotesque portrayal of local Arab life.[34]

The various usages of the watermelon by artists of the 1920s are underlaid with Orientalist attitudes.[35] The romanticization of the land and its Arab inhabitants can be seen as a form of romanticism that aligns with Orientalist stereotypes, which idealize and exoticize the "other" as less developed and uncorrupted by modern times. As opposed to the tradition of Orientalist art which abided by academic artistic conventions, Primitivism indicated a stylistic break with the past. To classify Gutman and Rubin's works as Primitivist as opposed to just Orientalist serves to create a modern national art that "reflects the beauty of the biblical age and the fantasy of the Orient,"[36] and asserts the modernism of Israeli artists in their conscious combination of old and new, East and West, Arab and Jew. The intended mission of this art was not to exoticize or denigrate local Arabs, but to connect with Levantine culture and use it to forge a model for a new Hebrew identity rooted to place. The Orientalist ideas of early Zionists, and Primitivist artists especially, imagined people of the Middle East (whether local Arabs or non-Ashkenazi Jewish communities like Yemenis or Bukharians) to more closely resemble ancient Israelites, and thus represented them as such.[37]

The Arab Riots of 1929, in which the non-Jewish population of Mandate Palestine violently resisted the growing Jewish population, led local Jewish artists to abandon the idealization of the Arab as a model for the new Jew.[38] Nahum Gutman's *The Watermelon Vendor* (1965)[39] is a case in point. He again uses the watermelon to imagine the "primitive" qualities of the local Arab population, but here the watermelon vendor is a grotesque caricature of an Arab, his mustache prominent, and teeth bared. He is rendered holding a dagger in one hand and reaching toward his pile of sliced melons. The figure seems bloodthirsty, and perhaps hypersexual, as he makes his way through the pile of yonic melons.

---

34   With a composition inspired perhaps by Van Gogh's *Afternoon Rest* (1890) or Picasso's *Sleeping Peasants* (1919), the rendering of the figures is not particularly sympathetic: their bare feet and the open mouth of the sleeping man border on the grotesque.
35   Edward Said, *Orientalism* (New York: Vintage Books, 1978), 4.
36   Olin, "Defining Jewish Art," 44.
37   Naftali, *Watermelons*, 82.
38   Ofrat, *One Hundred Years of Art in Israel*, 59.
39   Nahum Gutman, *The Watermelon Vendor*, 1965, gouache and watercolor on paper, 50 × 70 cm. Image source: Rubin, Naftali, and Erde, *Watermelons*, 52.

Gutman's portrayal of the Arab here is no longer the ideal model for the new Jew, but rather an example of that which is potentially threatening after decades of violent struggle between Arab and Jew.

The Demotic Watermelon

Watermelon imagery simultaneously proliferated in less elite, more demotic Hebrew media. From the 1920s, it appears as a Zionist symbol in mass print when it was featured in Arieh El-Hanani's poster for the Third International Near East Fair of 1926[40] and Eliyahu Sigard's poster for the Fourth Palestine and Near East Exhibition of 1929.[41] In the former, a barefooted, handsome man dressed all in white with a white summer fedora holds a watermelon and grapes against an abstract landscape of undulating hills, while opposite him we find portrayals of the Hebrew agricultural and urban build landscape (an orchard of orange trees, a water tower, Middle-Eastern inspired architecture, modern steamships approaching the shore).

The watermelon was also prominent in posters for the Totzeret Ha'aretz (Product of the Land of Israel) campaign. The campaign began at the end of the 1920s to encourage Jews of the *Yishuv* to buy products made or grown by local Jews in order to support the fledgling Jewish agricultural economy. The movement was initiated by the Department of Commerce and Industry of the Zionist Administration, and in 1936 the Union for Totzeret Ha'aretz started operating as an initiative of the Jewish Agency, the National Committee, the United Industry Owners, and the Hebrew Workers Union.[42] Because Arab labor was cheaper, Arab-grown products were cheaper, but Zionists envisioned a Jewish state that did not rely on non-Jewish labor and encouraged the Jewish population to support Jewish farmers by commissioning posters from the graphic designer Otte

---

40   Arieh El-Hanani (Sapozhnikov), *Third International Near East Fair Poster*, 1926, lithograph, 70 × 95 cm, Central Zionist Archives, Jerusalem, KRA\513, http://www.zionistarchives.org.il/en/Pages/ArchiveItem.aspx?oi=09001e15806faf02&ot=cza_poster.

41   Eliyahu Sigard, *The Fourth Palestine and Near East Exhibition Fair Poster*, 1929, print, 68.6 × 49.5 cm, Swann Galleries, https://catalogue.swanngalleries.com/Lots/auction-lot/ELIYAHU-SIGARD-(1901-1975)-THE-IV---TH-PALESTINE--NEAR-EAST-?saleno=2267&lotNo=111&refNo=635558.

42   Yael Raviv, "Patriotic Distribution: The 'Hebrew' Watermelon," in Yael Raviv, *Falafel Nation: Cuisine and the Making of National Identity in Israel* (Lincoln, NE: University of Nebraska Press, 2015), 53–55.

Wallisch (1906–1977).[43] In one of the posters he designed for the Totzeret Ha'aretz campaign from 1939, the text urges people with a big red arrow to buy watermelons "only with this stamp" referring to stamp affixed to the watermelon that reads "Union for Produce of the Land / Hebrew Watermelon / Agriculture Produce."[44] Not only the poster experiments with bold Hebrew typescript, but the green and red colors of the watermelon draw the reader into the image. This campaign suggested that, through one's purchases, one could directly contribute to the fate of the Hebrew nation and the establishment of an independent economy. The Zionist movement sought to establish itself as self-sufficient through turning foodstuffs into an avenue to express patriotism and solidify the economy. The consumption of "Hebrew" food was therefore a conscious political statement, and a way of "performing the new or renewed Hebrew nation."[45] In another watermelon poster designed by Wallisch in 1935, the fruit appears alongside a yellow melon in an advertisement to introduce shoppers to the Product of the Land stamps on produce.[46] Every watermelon grown by Hebrew labor was marked with a union stamp in Hebrew reading "Product of the Land," advising consumers to be sure to "identify every watermelon and melon from a Hebrew farm." In this way, the watermelon emerged as a symbol endowed with deep Zionist significance.

More Recent Representations of the Watermelon in Post-Zionist Israeli Art

Sigalit Landau (b. 1969), a contemporary multidisciplinary artist known for engaging with the Dead Sea, features the watermelon in many of her sculptural and video works. She often connects the watermelon to themes of corporeality, the feminine condition, and resilience. The monumental video work *DeadSee*

---

43 Wallisch was Czech, trained at the Vienna Art Academy, and was an established graphic designer working with Zionist themes even before his immigration to the Land of Israel in 1934. He is best known for designing the first stamps issued by the Israel Post, for his design of the parchment scroll and font for the Declaration of Independence of the State of Israel, and for his posters.
44 Otte Wallisch, *Hebrew Watermelon Poster*, 1939, for the Association for Products of Eretz Israel, Shenkar Design Research Center, no. G-Wa0-Pos-163, https://designarchive.shenkar.ac.il/items/146769.
45 Raviv, "Patriotic Distribution," 53.
46 Otte Wallisch, *Hebrew Melons Poster*, 1935, for the Association for Products of Eretz Israel, Shenkar Design Research Center, no. G-Wa0-Pos-066, https://designarchive.shenkar.ac.il/items/146672.

(2005) inserts Landau's naked body into a spiral of 500 floating watermelons slowly unfurling in the buoyant water.[47] One arm reaches out towards a cluster of open watermelons, revealing their red flesh. By intertwining her own body with ripened watermelons, she points to the reciprocal relationship of humans with their immediate environment.[48] Landau sees the watermelon's associations with fertility as a perfect contrast to the Dead Sea, which is inhospitable to life. She recalls coming across research on desert agriculture that found that saline water was able to grow watermelons that are sweeter than average, compensating for the salt by producing more sugar. She reads the diabetic watermelon as a "metaphor for homeostasis: equilibrium is achieved through a process of adaptation to less-than optimal conditions."[49] In this way, Landau uses the resilient watermelon for the "exploration of the individual and collective body's relationship to a fraught landscape."[50] By posing naked in the water without any markers of ethnicity or national affiliation, Landau seeks to transcend the watermelon as a symbol for either Israelis or Palestinians, and instead points to it as a symbol for what must be encountered together.

By contrast, David Reeb's (b. 1952) *Watermelons* (2008) do not root the watermelon in any recognizable local landscape.[51] Its red slices float in a light blue space in a wallpaper-like pattern. Though on its own there may be nothing post-Zionist about the painting, in light of Reeb's known ideological affinities, this painting must be read as a challenge to earlier Zionist metanarratives, and a liberation of the watermelon into a post-nationalist milieu. Reeb was one of the few Israeli artists in the 1980s to be overtly political in his work, so this 2008 painting cannot be read as anything but influenced by the first instances

---

47   Sigalit Landau, *DeadSee*, 2005, video, 11:39, available at artist's website: https://www.sigalit-landau.com/deadsee-video-2005.
48   Nuit Banai, "On Sigalit Landau, *DeadSee* (2005)," in *Critical Landscapes: Art, Space, Politics*, ed. Emily Eliza Scott and Kirsten Swenson (Oakland, CA: University of California Press, 2015), 123.
49   Sigalit Landau, *The Burning Sea*, interview Amitai Mendelsohn, trans. Anna Barber (Jerusalem: The Israel Museum, 2022). Landau was aware of the plurality of symbolic connotations of the watermelon: evoking the pregnant belly, flesh, its usage as a Zionist symbol, its resemblance to the Palestinian flag, and more. In an interview for her 2022 exhibition *The Burning Sea*, she reveals that apart from its symbolic associations, its name in Hebrew is a pun. *Avatiaḥ* evokes both *ha'av shehivtiaḥ* (the father who promised) and *ke'ev shebatiaḥ* (the pain that is in the walls). It should also be noted that the Hebrew *avatiaḥ* and the Arabic *batikh* share the three letter semitic root b-t-kh, which, in Hebrew, also yields words relating to safety and security, evoking the hard shell of the watermelon protecting the precious fruit inside.
50   Banai, "On Sigalit Landau," 122.
51   David Reeb, *Watermelons*, 2008, acrylic on canvas, 160 × 140 cm, collection of the artist. Image source: Rubin, Naftali, and Erde, *Watermelons*, 48.

of Palestinian artists taking up the watermelon as a visual motif. His rendition leaves out the color white (in the rind of the melon) so as to resist any reading of his watermelon as co-opting the Palestinian flag.[52]

The Watermelon in Palestinian Art

The watermelon's currency in demotic visual culture saw a resurgence in the 1980s when it was recharged with overt political meaning. It was at that time that the watermelon began to be seen as a Palestinian national symbol by Israelis, transcending its earlier use as a Zionist symbol. The origin of this practice is said to date to 1980. The story cited in most newspaper and magazine articles about how the watermelon became a stand-in for the Palestinian flag is attributed to the Palestinian artist Sliman Mansour (b. 1947), who studied at Jerusalem's Bezalel Academy of Art and Design. After the 1967 war and until the Oslo Accords of 1993, an Israeli military order prohibited the public display of Palestinian national symbols.[53] In 1980, the Israeli military shut down Gallery 79 in Ramallah and detained three artists—Sliman Mansour, Nabil Anani, and Isam Bader—for incorporating the colors of the Palestinian flag into their artworks. In an interview with Al Jazeera in 2021, Mansour recounts that they were told by the Israeli military they could not use the colors in combination at all, with an officer volunteering that "even if you do a watermelon, it will be confiscated."[54] Mansour concludes that the emergence of the watermelon as a symbol of Palestinian resistance has its origins in this episode. The story, which is now legendary, is also apocryphal. In a 2021 interview with the *National*, Mansour admits to not recalling Palestinian artists after this episode rushing to incorporate the watermelon as a political motif in their work,[55] nor did Mansour himself use the watermelon in his art for political purposes, with the exception of its inclusion in a book of Palestinian stories that he illustrated.[56] By contrast,

---

52   Ofrat, *One Hundred Years of Art in Israel*, 330.
53   Alexandra Chaves, "How the Watermelon Became a Symbol of Palestinian Resistance," *National*, May 30, 2021, https://www.thenationalnews.com/arts/how-the-watermelon-became-a-symbol-of-palestinian-resistance-1.1230806.
54   "How the Watermelon Became a Palestinian Symbol of Resistance," Al Jazeera, YouTube, June 9, 2021, https://www.youtube.com/watch?v=VzWe0A-DMaA&ab_channel=AJ%2B.
55   Chaves, "How the Watermelon Became a Symbol of Palestinian Resistance."
56   Callie Holtermann, "Images of Watermelons Signal Support for Palestinians," *New York Times*, December 27, 2023, https://www.nytimes.com/2023/12/27/style/watermelon-emoji-palestine.html?smid=nytcore-ios-share.

it is in Israeli art of this period where the watermelon is more frequently redeployed politically, often by post-Zionist Jewish artists.

Mansour's story suggests that, since the 1980s, Israelis have understood watermelons to have potent symbolic and political connotations for the Palestinian people. No longer claimed as an exclusive Zionist symbol for the return of Jews to their homeland, the watermelon that appeared in late twentieth-century works by Israeli artists in conversation with its embrace by Palestinians. The watermelon's journey from Orientalist to Zionist to post-Zionist symbol in Jewish-Israeli art would be forced to undergo transformation yet again.

Critically, the first example of the watermelon used by a Palestinian artist other than Sliman Mansour is Khaled Hourani (b. 1965). He heard a version of Mansour's story and created an image of a watermelon slice for the Subjective Atlas of Palestine project in 2007,[57] responding to a prompt to create an alternative Palestinian flag.[58] This developed into a silkscreen print series titled *The Story of the Watermelon* that appeared in several exhibitions around the world. Hourani is the former Director of Fine Arts for the Palestinian Ministry of Culture and a central figure in Palestine's art discourse.[59] On Hourani's Instagram, he retells Mansour's story of censorship and says, "I borrowed from this [Israeli military] officer the idea for this artistic project, not to admire his ill imagination, but to commemorate his prohibition."[60]

Since Hourani's use of the watermelon as a stand-in for the flag in 2007, the use of the watermelon and as a Palestinian national symbol has proliferated, especially on social media and during times of increased tension. In 2021, artists such as the Abu-Dhabi based Sarah Hatahet (b. 1986) and the Palestinian Jordanian Beesan Arafat were inspired by Hourani to create their own images of the watermelon, which were published and circulated on Instagram. Hatahet's

---

57 Khaled Hourani (@khaledhourani6), *The Story of the Watermelon*, 2007, silkscreen, Instagram, May 23, 2021, https://www.instagram.com/p/CPNiXl0NhoL/?utm_source=ig_embed&ig_rid=118cd32d-e084-4a9d-baea-21f0283564da.
58 Chaves, "How the Watermelon Became a Symbol of Palestinian Resistance."
59 Mansour is known as an artist of the First Intifada, during which he led a movement called New Visions, which saw Palestinian artists boycotting Israeli art products and turning to natural materials, in accordance with the philosophy of the First Intifada that sought to boycott Israel in all ways and become self-reliant. Mansour's figurative work is also a rejection of the abstract expressionism popular in Israeli art of the time, including his Bezalel instructors. See Sarah Judith Hofmann, "Palestinian Artist Sliman Mansour Will Not Leave Israel," Deutsche Welle, May 5, 2018, https://www.dw.com/en/palestinian-artist-sliman-mansour-will-not-leave-israel-despite-not-feeling-free/a-43782048.
60 Khaled Hourani (@khaledhourani6), Instagram, May 23, 2021, https://www.instagram.com/p/CPNiXl0NhoL/?utm_source=ig_embed&ig_rid=118cd32d-e084-4a9d-baea-21f0283564da.

Watermelon of Resistance (2021) features a teary, wide-eyed figure gazing into the distance while holding a slice of the fruit with fingers sprawled open, perhaps lamenting a lack of freedom.[61] Watermelon slices float in the background, reminiscent of the wallpaper in Reeb's earlier image. Arafat's *Watermelon on Hebron Plate* (2021) features a slice of the fruit on a piece of traditional Palestinian ceramic work common in the city of Hebron. The blue and white floral patterns of the plate combined with the watermelon both assert Palestinian rootedness to place.[62]

At the beginning of 2023, Israeli Security Minister Itamar Ben Gvir equated displays of the Palestinian flag to support for terror, and proposed several bills to formally ban the display of the flag in public places[63] even though the Israeli police and military have always retained the ability to confiscate the Palestinian flag when deemed a threat to public safety.[64] Actions to protest this included demonstrations in which Jewish and Palestinian-Israelis bore the Palestinian flag, and the subversive display of the watermelon. In June 2023, the Jewish and Arab community action movement Zazim (On the Move) launched a campaign[65] in which large images of watermelons were plastered onto sixteen shared taxis in Tel Aviv, with the accompanying English text "this is not a Palestinian flag."[66] The organization This Is Not An Ulpan, which teaches both Hebrew and

---

61 Sarah Hatahet (@sarahhatahet), *Watermelon of Resistance*, 2021, digital illustration, Instagram, May 19, 2021, https://www.instagram.com/p/CPDCsFlsVr3/.
62 Beesan Arafat (@beesan.arafat), *Watermelon on Hebron Plate*, 2021, Instagram, May 18, 2021, https://www.instagram.com/p/CPBmN_BMCCV/.
63 Jeremy Sharon, "Activists Use Images of Watermelons to Protest Police Crackdown on Palestinian Flags," *Times of Israel*, June 22, 2023, https://www.timesofisrael.com/activists-use-images-of-watermelons-to-protest-police-crackdown-on-palestinian-flags/.
64 Jennifer Hassan and Miriam Berger, "Why the Watermelon is a Symbol for the Palestinian Cause," *Washington Post*, November 16, 2023, https://www.washingtonpost.com/world/2023/11/16/watermelon-emoji-palestine-meaning-symbol/. This is the same reason some European countries preemptively restricted Palestinian protests, as it can be difficult to distinguish nationalist pride from valorization and encouragement of violent resistance. See Rajvanshi, "In Europe, Free Speech Is under Threat for Pro-Palestine Protesters." See also Armani Syed, "How the Watermelon Became a Symbol of Palestinian Solidarity," *Time*, October 2023, https://time.com/6326312/watermelon-palestinian-symbol-solidarity/.
65 See the photograph of a taxi adorned with the watermelon from the Zazim campaign, photographed on June 21, 2023, courtesy of Zazim, published in Jeremy Sharon, "Activists Use Images of Watermelons to Protest Police Crackdown on Palestinian Flags," *Times of Israel*, June 22, 2023, https://www.timesofisrael.com/activists-use-images-of-watermelons-to-protest-police-crackdown-on-palestinian-flags/.
66 Zazim, whose website claims more than 400,000 members, advocates for democracy, equality, and peace with Palestinians. In a note accompanying this action, the movement added that "We'll always find a way to bypass any absurd ban and we won't stop struggling for freedom of expression and democracy...." See the movement's website: www.zazim.org.il.

Arabic also printed shirts[67] in English, Arabic, and Hebrew featuring a watermelon and the statement "this is not a watermelon" for sale on its website.[68] These campaigns by two social activist groups evoke Rene Magritte's surrealist painting *The Treachery of Images* (1929) and underline the watermelon as an increasingly unfixed and contested symbol.

The Watermelon in Time of War

Since October 7, 2023, watermelons have become ubiquitous at anti-Israel protests and as pro-Palestinian emojis. The fruit has become synonymous with the Palestinian cause, eclipsing its earlier history as a Zionist symbol. As Israeli military efforts to root out Hamas grew more intense, the direct association of the watermelon with the fate of Palestinians intensified through such statements as: "When you bomb a watermelon it spreads its seeds."[69] Here, the smashing of a watermelon is compared to the Israeli military campaign against Hamas in Gaza, with the warning that Israel's response is sowing the seeds for the next generation of Palestinian fighters. Almost overnight, the symbolic meaning of the watermelon transcended the borders of the Middle East to become a global political signifier.

Even if we were to limit our case study to public displays of the watermelon among activists in remote Western Massachusetts, we see how visually prominent it has become. For more than a year, the Western Massachusetts chapter of Jewish Voice for Peace has centered the watermelon in its weekly Instagram post urging "Jews and Friends" to gather at a well-traveled local roundabout to advocate for "An Arms Embargo: Not in Our Name! Stop the Genocide! End the Occupation."[70] Here, the watermelon is a stand-in for the word Palestine, which allows passers-by to focus on the group's specific demands without getting bogged down in contested discourse about the what and where of Palestine itself.

In fact, the watermelon image is the least controversial part of this e-poster, inviting the reader in through its non-threatening familiarity as balance to its

---

67 "This is Not a Watermelon" T-shirt for sale by This is Not an Ulpan, https://www.thisisnotanulpan.com/product-page/t-shirt-this-is-not-a-watermelon-1.
68 "This is Not a Watermelon," This is Not an Ulpan, March 2023, https://www.thisisnotanulpan.com/blog.
69 A statement frequently posted to Facebook, Instagram, and other social media. See, for instance, Palestine Online (@OnlinePalEng), X (formerly Twitter), July 26, 2024, https://x.com/OnlinePalEng/status/1816921477494841800.
70 Jewish Voice for Peace of Western Massachusetts (@jvpwesternmass), Instagram, December 1, 2024, https://www.instagram.com/p/DDA16oXPHH3/.

rhetorical claims. For instance, since JVP has long insisted that antizionism is not the same as antisemitism, and that Jews and Israelis are not the same, why do its advocates feel the need to insist that the war in the Middle East is not being conducted "in our name?" Ironically, the poster itself does the work of assuming a conflation of Jews and Israelis that the organization has long claimed does not exist. The poster's demand to "stop the genocide" echoes the broader activist deployment of the term as a way to isolate and delegitimize Israel by accusing it of committing the worst of all crimes, ignoring the challenge of fighting a terrorist group with explicit genocidal intentions. Hamas's own leadership has bragged that its war strategy is designed to invite maximal Palestinian civilian deaths in order to encourage global rage against Israel.[71] The turn to lawfare and politicide through the uninterrogated use of the word "genocide" is part of a moral inversion in which, through the help of sympathetic international human rights groups, UN agencies, and readily available antizionist Jews, the crimes of Hamas and its sponsors are deflected and projected onto Israel. In short, the visual image of the watermelon on this poster is deliberately consumed by its verbal claims.[72]

In a different poster for a festival at a neighboring town, we find the watermelon featured in a poster for QueerCore Fest 2024 "in solidarity with the people of Gaza," with proceeds going to the Palestinian Children's Relief Fund.[73] Here, we see the ways in which intersectional resistance functions, with the history of victimization and resistance within the Queer community directly mapped on to an international conflict with little understanding of the lack of tolerance for Queer expression within traditional Palestinian culture. This "collective of artists and organizers featuring DIY punk music that centers bipoc, queer, trans, gender-diverse and femme voices, community, and joy" has nothing to say about the murder, rape, and abduction of fellow-music lovers—some of whom would have identified as Queer—perpetrated by Palestinians associated with the Queer-hating Hamas and Islamic Jihad at an Israeli music festival. Apparently, these Queer punk musicians anticipate a more welcoming audience for them in Gaza City than they would have received at the Nova music festival near Kibbutz Re'im, where more than 350 people were slaughtered.

---

71 Summer Said and Rory Jones, "Civilian Bloodshed Will Help Hamas," *Wall Street Journal*, June 10, 2024.
72 Linda Kinstler, "The Bitter Fight over the Meaning of Genocide," *New York Times Magazine*, Aug 20, 2024.
73 Queercore Collaborative poster, downtown Northampton, Massachusetts, September 2024, photographed by the authors. A different version of the poster appears in the post by Queercore Collaborative (@queercorecollaborative), Instagram, September 3, 2024, https://www.instagram.com/p/C_dLanoJRFa/?img_index=1.

When it comes to the environment on college campuses, watermelons have emerged as a symbol to invite participation in organizations such as Students for Justice in Palestine. Since many young people today are highly suspicious of state power, a watermelon can be read as less political than a flag, though we find maps of Palestine (including the entirety of Israel) shaped as a slice of watermelon). At Smith College, a professor posted on their office door an image that prominently features a watermelon at its base. A dove holding an olive branch is superimposed on top of it. Above them is a black and white band evoking a keffiyeh, whose design suggests both the fertile Mediterranean coastal plain and the mountain highlands and valleys that run from the Jordan river to the sea. A red anemone wildflower (*shaka'ek al-no'man* in Arabic, *kalanit* in Hebrew) grows out of the watermelon. The lack of any printed text invites passersby to provide their own interpretation and to make assumptions about what the professor hopes students might take from its various layers of symbolic meaning.[74] Elsewhere, the window of a common room in Shattuck Hall at Mount Holyoke College featured a white flag with a large quarter watermelon inspired by Hourani's art at its center. It overlooked the main quadrangle and the library, essentially requiring any student taking classes in the building to pass underneath it. At the nearby University of Massachusetts, a watermelon in the shape of a heart proclaimed, "We [love] the UMass 57," a reference to those arrested during the student occupation of an administrative building on campus.[75] In short, since October 7 the watermelon has become so normalized as an activist symbol that it is impossible to traverse campus spaces without encountering it.

Still others deploy the watermelon in their online communication to avoid shadow bans, which occur when one's content on a social media site is blocked when it is reported as offensive or in contravention of community standards. Though the words "Gaza" or "Palestine" can easily be located using an algorithm, blocking posts that display a watermelon becomes far more challenging. Given that sometimes a fruit is just a fruit, online forums are much less likely to block the image of a watermelon in a profile, even when almost all users today understand its political meaning. What began as a way for Palestinian artists to evade regulations banning the display of nationalist symbols has now become a

---

74 In the same way that the watermelon has meaning in both Zionist and Palestinian culture, so too does the wildflower featured in this image. In fact, the pre-State Hebrew song "Kalaniyot" made famous by Shoshana Damari, with lyrics penned by famed poet Natan Alterman, remains one of the most popular Israeli songs of all time.

75 Jack Underhill, "Faculty and Students Rally in Support of the 57 Arrested During the Whitmore Sit-In," *Massachusetts Daily Collegian*, December 12, 2023, https://dailycollegian.com/2023/12/faculty-and-students-rally-in-support-of-the-57-arrested-during-the-whitmore-sit-in/.

transnational symbol of solidarity, but one that requires the deliberate erasure of its meaning in Zionist and Israeli identity.

It is important to remember that the visual deployment of the watermelon does not exist in a vacuum. It is part of a broader culture of pro-Palestinian protest and resistance that includes other symbols (the key of return, the keffiyeh, maximalist maps of Palestine that do not leave room for an Israel living alongside it) and slogans ("Free Palestine," "From the river to the sea," "By any means necessary," "Glory to the martyrs," "Intifada Revolution," "Globalize the Intifada") that make the watermelon part of a broader rhetorical and visual narrative. It becomes impossible to disentangle it from these other symbols and statements since they all circulate in the same political ecosphere.[76]

The ubiquity of the watermelon as an activist symbol caught the attention of American rapper Kosha Dillz (born Rama Even-Esh to Israeli parents). A short while after the October 7 massacre, the rapper released his single "Bring the Family Home" in support of the hostages held in Gaza. Then, he collaborated with the Los Angeles-based, Tel Aviv-born comedian and musician Or Mash on the single "Avatiaḥ" (Watermelon). Watermelons saturate the visual idiom of its music video. Or Mash appears sporting a watermelon t-shirt, holding up a hand-drawn placard reading "From the river to the sea [watermelon] will be free." Then, at the beach, she shields herself from the sun underneath an umbrella designed as a watermelon, outrageously gyrating. The Israeli-born Or Mash complains about online virtue signaling and social policing:

> How come everywhere that I go
> All these people put the avatiaḥ in their bio?
> Met this cute guy and he said I wanna see ya
> Then he ask me: Hey, what the deal with avatiaḥ?

The chorus then rehearses the narrative battle over native claims:

> Hey, ask anyone who know me,
> I'm indigenous,

---

76 Judith Shulevitz, "Listen to What They're Chanting," *Atlantic*, May 8, 2024, https://www.theatlantic.com/books/archive/2024/05/pro-palestinian-protests-columbia-chants/678321/. The suspects arrested for the murderer of a Jewish couple outside the Capital Jewish Museum in Washington on May 21, 2025, and the attempted incineration of those rallying for the release of Israeli hostages in Colorado on June 1, 2025, are alleged to have chanted "Free Palestine!" according to witnesses, suggesting that the same phrase proclaimed by some as an expression of nonviolent protest is uttered or heard by others as legitimizing terror.

They're using this emoji
Hey F this whole chat,
if you want the Land give us our watermelon back!

The entire performance is a send-up of anti-Israel activist culture, with its performativity and sloganeering ripe for parody.

In a different mode entirely, Michael "Mysh" Rozanov, an illustrator and visual storyteller based in Tel Aviv, formulated a design that embeds a slice of watermelon within the yellow ribbon that quickly came to symbolize solidarity with the hostages kidnapped on October 7. Mysh notes on his Facebook feed that it "is not an either/or," using the combined images to invite his followers to hold room for the humanity of both Israelis and Palestinians. The online reaction from his Facebook followers ranged from appreciation to outrage, with one commentator complaining, "Horrifying—you have passed the stage of symmetry between the kidnapper and the victim, and now the kidnapper is the victim."[77]

Conclusion

At a time when examining the presence of the watermelon as a symbol in Israeli art could be read as an effort to take away from its deployment as a Palestinian symbol, we must resist presentist readings in order to investigate how symbols emerge and shift meaning in and across culture. Our goal has been to highlight the flexible nature of this symbol as one that signals indigeneity in a land claimed by two peoples. The watermelon is a fruit that has been consumed in the region for thousands of years, making it an organic part of ancient Israelite, Arab, Zionist, Israeli, and Palestinian cultures. The development of the watermelon in both Israeli and, more recently, Palestinian art traditions has depended on its presence in the other; it is mutually referential, interdependent, and intertwined. The fact that the watermelon was taken up as a Zionist symbol precisely because of its presence in biblical text and the vernacular life of Ottoman and British-Mandate Palestine is just as meaningful as the fact that Mansour and Hourani attribute the birth of the watermelon as Palestinian symbol to an Israeli warning. The watermelon, like the land itself, is contested, mutually claimed, passed back and forth, argued over. Perhaps someday two peoples will be able to enjoy the fruit of the land in peace.

---

77 Mysh Illustration and Comics (@myshillustration), Facebook, May 24, 2025.

CHAPTER 12

Locating Sexual Violence: October 7 and Its Aftermath, Historically Conceptualized

Skylar Ball

What is the difference between denial and justification? More importantly: why does it matter? In the early morning hours of October 7, 2023, the Palestinian nationalist group Hamas, which has governed the Gaza strip since 2007, launched a coordinated attack on a music festival and several surrounding villages and *kibbutzim* in Israel near the north of Gaza.[1] By the end of the attack, Hamas militants had murdered nearly 1,200 people, some of them foreign nationals or Palestinian Israelis, and taken over 250 hostages captive.[2] In the weeks and months following the attack, stories of sexual violence perpetrated by Hamas on October 7 began to come to light, and questions and skepticism arose surrounding survivor accounts. Journalists performed independent investigations, survivors shared their own testimonies, and the rest of the world reacted, selectively choosing to listen or not listen, depending on who was speaking. While responses varied within ethnic and national groups, a debate which asked two separate but distinctly interconnected questions began: did sexual violence occur, and if so, was it systematic?

---

1 Yaniv Kubovich, "The First Hours of the Israel-Hamas War: What Actually Happened?," *Haaretz*, October 17, 2023, https://www.haaretz.com/haaretz-explains/2023-10-17/ty-article-magazine/.premium/the-first-hours-of-the-israel-hamas-war-what-actually-took-place/0000018b-38bc-d0ac-a39f-b9be58df0000.
2 "Today in History: October 7, Surprise Attacks Spark Israel-Hamas War," Associated Press, October 7, 2024. https://apnews.com/today-in-history/october-7.

It is critical to locate the attacks of gender-based violence which occurred on October 7—as well as the resulting discourse—within a broader historical tradition of gender's interconnectivity with nationalism, both in comparative analysis as well as within Israeli and Palestinian cultural memory and tradition. This paper will not attempt to "prove" the occurrence of sexual violence on October 7, given that evidence and testimonies abound, but will rather be an exploration of the precedents for gender-based violence in wartime as they relate to the October 7 attacks as well as an attempt to understand and locate the significance of global responses to the sexual violence of October 7. In the case of the attacks on October 7, denying the occurrence of sexual violence fits into a long-standing historical tradition of dehumanizing the enemy in conflict, a tradition which enables the perpetuation of violence where women become victims by virtue of their gender. This denial or justification does not occur in a vacuum but instead serves specific nationalistic and political goals. This paper will analyze Israeli, Palestinian, and Western responses to sexual violence testimonies in order to better understand the significance and weight of October 7 and its aftermath.

To contextualize this event, it is firstly necessary to establish a general understanding of how gender is involved in both Israeli and Palestinian conceptions of patriotism, or nationalistic identity. Specifically in the pre-state period in Israeli history (a community known as the *Yishuv*), women who died for the nation were perceived not only as national figures but also as models of appropriate national female behavior.[3] In the case of Sarah Aaronsohn, a leader of the secret pro-British spy network also known as Nili, her suicide (which she committed upon learning that she would be transferred to a Damascus prison and interrogated by the Ottoman Turkish military) served as the first example of "an active female death with secular and national overtones."[4] Historian of memory Billie Melman describes how "Nili and Sarah Aaronsohn in particular became models of activism and revolt among both revisionists and right-wing maximalists. . . . Her activities were not only a symbol of heroism and of deeds (presented as the opposite of the passivity and sterile verbosity of the intellectuals), but also part of a messianic myth."[5] Sarah, represented as a hero of the nation in popular media and children's literature, exemplified the model of female self-sacrifice for the nation, her gender relevant to what Melman describes as "the

---

3 Billie Melman, "The Legend of Sarah: Gender Memory and National Identities (*Eretz Yisrael*/Israel, 1917–90)," *Journal of Israeli History* 21 (2002): 55–92, https://doi.org/10.1080/13531040212331295792.
4 Ibid., 58.
5 Ibid., 65.

myth of *Eretz-yisraeli*-ness."[6] Melman explains that Sarah's story deviates from a maternalistic assumption common in most nationalist understandings of gender, in which women are mothers of the nation in two senses: literally, by virtue of their reproductive capacity, and pedagogically, through their role as a conduit for the transmission of national culture. This model excludes women from what Melman describes as "the apotheosis of national liberation: blood-sacrifice for the nation and participation as combatants on the battlefield."[7] Through this framework, women are unable to literally acquire land through their own blood, something seen as critical to the embodied experience of national liberation.

Sarah, and other Jewish women of her generation, formulated a non-maternalistic understanding of women's participation in the national movement, which included descriptions emphasizing Sarah's physical prowess, her freedom of movement outside of the domestic sphere, and her mastery of weapons. Even her death, with its seeming emphasis on action rather than verbiage, and sacrifice rather than victimhood at the hands of the enemy, was an inversion of the maternalistic framework. Israeli law today manifests this history of women's role in warfare through its mandatory conscription policy which extends to women in the Israeli Defense Forces. Women were employed in full combat roles during the 1948 War of Independence and Palestinian *Nakba*, have been included in mandatory conscription since then, and have served in combat roles since 2000, thirteen years earlier than the US ban on women in combat was lifted.[8] John Gillis posits that national memory is formed in terms of specific identities: gender, class, and ethnicity.[9] It is possible to also understand role *within* gender as an identity which contributes to the formation of national memory; in the Israeli example, women's role as fighters, combatants, and agents are foregrounded both in the prevailing Legend of Sarah as well as in the actualized role of Israeli women in the IDF.

Palestinian conceptions of gender as related to nationalism are relevant notably in the Hamas covenant, the 1988 version of which decrees that "the Muslim woman has a role no less important than that of the Muslim man in the battle of liberation," citing her role as the "maker of man" as well as her job to guide and

---

6   Ibid., 66.
7   Ibid., 69.
8   Jerry Votava, "U.S. Military to Permit Women to Serve in Combat Units," JURIST Legal News & Research, January 24, 2013, http://jurist.org/paperchase/2013/01/us-military-to-permit-women-to-serve-in-combat-units.php.
9   John Gillis, "The Historic, the Legendary, and the Incredible in Invented Tradition and Collective Memory in Israel," in *Commemorations: The Politics of National Identity*, ed. John Gillis (Princeton, NJ: Princeton University Press, 1996), 105–215.

religiously educate new generations.[10] This explanation follows the maternalistic framework in which women are bearers of cultural (and, in this case, ethnonational) identity. The womb has also been a central part of both Palestinian and Israeli understandings of nationalism as it plays out on the woman's body, as it is a way to literalize a battle over demographics. Yasser Arafat, founding member of the Fatah party and Palestinian Authority president from 1996 to 2004, spoke of the "Palestinian womb" as the greatest weapon against Zionism, an exemplification of how Palestinian nationalism situates women in the creation and preservation of national culture.[11] The comparison of women's roles in Palestinian and Israeli nationalism is critical to apprehending how conflict-related sexual violence on October 7 played out, and how collective conceptions of shame and dignity impact responses to this event.

The Palestinian "maternalistic" structure as articulated by Melman plays into the ways in which sexual violence in the broader Israeli-Palestinian conflict go unreported. In 2024, Jamila al-Hissi, a Palestinian woman, reported that IDF soldiers raped women at the Al Shifa hospital complex in Gaza.[12] Hamas, as well as al-Hissi's brother, denied that women were being raped by Israeli soldiers in the Al Shifa complex. While it is plausible that "one would expect Hamas to strategically use these accusations, whether false or true, to mobilize support and further increase international outrage against the offensive in Gaza," as Palestinian feminist scholar Anwar Mhajne asserts, this incident demonstrates Palestinian cultural taboos on rape as a loss of honor, leading to a decreased likelihood of visibility regarding sexual atrocities perpetrated by IDF soldiers.[13] As the analyst Muhammad Shehadeh stated on X, "Hamas has a vested interest for domestic political reasons in denying the IDF rape of Gazan women on their watch to avoid public blame."[14] Jihad Helles, a writer and preacher from Gaza with over 198,000 followers, tweeted in Arabic, "In all my life, I have never

---

10 "Doctrine of Hamas," Wilson Center, October 20, 2023, https://www.wilsoncenter.org/article/doctrine-hamas

11 Yosef Kuperwasser and Shalom Lipner, "The Problem is Palestinian Rejectionism: Why the PA Must Recognize a Jewish State," *Foreign Affairs* 90, no. 6 (2011): 4.

12 "Al Jazeera Report Alleging IDF Rapes in Shifa Hospital Retracted," *Times of Israel*, March 25, 2024, https://www.timesofisrael.com/al-jazeera-report-alleging-idf-rapes-in-shifa-hospital-retracted/.

13 Anwar Mhajne, "Understanding Sexual Violence Debates Since 7 October: Weaponization and Denial," *Journal of Genocide Research* (2024): 16, https://www.tandfonline.com/doi/full/10.1080/14623528.2024.2359851#d1e236.

14 Muhammad Shehadeh (@muhammadshehad2), "Hamas has a vested interests for domestic political reasons in denying the IDF rape of Gazan women on their watch to avoid public blame," X (formerly Twitter), March 26, 2024, as quoted in Mhajne, "Understanding Sexual Violence Debates."

heard of a single case of rape of a woman in Gaza. That's because the women of Gaza are strong and honorable to the extent that they would prefer death a thousand times over anyone touching their dignity or honor."[15] In this case, the Palestinian cultural taboo on rape is so great that it leads to widespread silencing from within of any testimony of rape or sexual violence.

When studying October 7 and its aftermath, it is necessary to consider how this event fits into broader historical patterns of sexual violence and subsequent public recognition. In situations where sexual violence has been perpetrated en masse, a major unifying factor in these events has been dehumanization of an enemy group, a condition necessary to creating conditions in which mass rape can be inflicted. A *Haaretz* article from April 2024 locates the accounts of rape and sexual assault on October 7 as part of a larger "escalation of conflict related sexual violence globally which has systematically made women's bodies (and in some cases, the bodies of men) weapons of war."[16]

The Bosnian war, which ended in 1995, marked the first instance of mass rape being punished as a war crime by an international tribunal.[17] In "Surfacing Gender: Reconceptualizing Crimes against Women in Time of War," human rights lawyer Rhonda Copelon argued that historically the condemnation of rape in war has rarely been about the abuse of women as a gender-based crime, and has instead been treated as a grave crime because it violates the honor of the man (symbolically representing the nation), and his sexual possession of woman as property.[18] Under the Geneva Conventions, rape is treated as a crime against the honor and dignity of women, implying "the loss of station or respect," situating virginity or chastity as a precondition to honor and reinforcing a social view, internalized by women, that women who have been raped are somehow dishonorable. Copelon's argument is largely formulated against a conception of genocidal rape as a unique weapon of war:

---

15 Jihad Helles (@Jhkhelles), " ي حياتي كلها لم أسمع بقضية اغتصاب واحدة لسيدة في غزة، ذلك لأن نساء غزة قويات عفيفات لدرجة أنهن يفضلن الموت ألف مرة ولا يمس أحد عرضهن أو يتعرض لشرفهن، ويا ويل من فكر في ذلك !! فهل أدركتم حجم القهر الذي نعيشه والألم الذي نذوقه !! اللهم استر عورات نساء غزة واحفظ عليهن أعراضهن!! ," X (formerly Twitter), March 24, 2024, as quoted in Mhajne, "Understanding Sexual Violence Debates."

16 Tanya Domi, "Rwanda, Bosnia, Ukraine and Now Hamas: October 7 and Surging Wartime Sexual Violence Around the World," *Haaretz*, April 4, 2024, https://www.haaretz.com/opinion/2024-04-04/ty-article-opinion/.premium/bosnia-ukraine-now-hamas-oct-7-and-the-global-rise-in-wartime-sexual-violence/0000018e-a911-defe-a3ef-bb1d61db0000.

17 Andrew Osborn, "Mass Rape Ruled a War Crime," *Guardian*, February 22, 2001, https://www.theguardian.com/world/2001/feb/23/warcrimes.

18 Rhonda Copelon, "Surfacing Gender: Reconceptualizing Crimes Against Women in Time of War," in *Mass Rape: The War against Women in Bosnia-Herzegovina*, ed. Alexandra Stiglmayer (Lincoln, NE: University of Nebraska Press, 1994), 197–218.

> Genocidal rape often involves gang rapes, is outrageously brutal, and is done in public in front of children or partners. It involves imprisoning women in rape "camps" or raping them repetitively. These are also characteristics of the most common rape in war—rape for booty or to boost the morale of soldiers; and they are common characteristics of the use of rape as a form of torture and terror by dictatorial regimes.[19]

Israeli reports and witness testimonies described Hamas militants cutting off women's breasts and tossing them in the air, of a woman found with nails driven into her vagina.[20] The goal of rape, regardless of whether it can be classified as genocidal or not, is to "strike at a woman's power; it seeks to degrade and destroy her; its goal is domination and dehumanization."[21] In the words of Lepa Mladjenovic, psychotherapist and Serbian feminist antiwar activist, it renders the woman "homeless in her own body."[22] Since the Bosnian war, the International Criminal Tribunal has widened the scope and stated that any form of rape may be considered a grave breach, the most serious classification of war crime, regardless of genocidal intent. In order to prosecute Hamas for its October 7 attack as defined as a crime against humanity, it must be proved that the rapes were committed systematically, as outlined in the Declaration of the 1993 World Conference of Human Rights in Vienna.[23] This explains the legal significance of the debate on whether systematic sexual violence occurred on October 7.

---

19   Copelon, "Surfacing Gender," 205. See Susan Brownmiller, *Against Our Will: Men, Women, and Rape* (New York: Ballantine Books, 1993); Ximena Bunster-Burrotto, "Surviving beyond Fear: Women and Torture in Latin America," in Women and Change in Latin America, ed. June Nash (South Hadley, MA: Bergin & Garvey, 1986); *Women on the Frontline*, Amnesty International, New York, 1991.
20   Liza Rozovsky, "15 Witnesses, Three Confessions, a Pattern of Naked Dead Bodies. All the Evidence of Hamas Rape on October 7," *Haaretz*, April 18, 2024. "The photograph was taken almost a week after the massacre and is definitely of poor quality. The possibility that what is depicted is indeed nails seems reasonable, certainly in combination with his testimony, but it's impossible to determine this unequivocally."
21   Copelon, "Surfacing Gender," 202.
22   Testimony before the Global Tribunal on Violations of Women's Human Rights, part of the NGO Parallel Activities, 1993 World Conference on Human Rights, Vienna, June 15, 1993, as quoted in Copelon, "Surfacing Gender," 202.
23   The Conference agreed: "Violations of the human rights of women in situations of armed conflict are violations of the fundamental principles of international human rights and humanitarian law. All violations of this kind, including in particular murder, systematic rape, sexual slavery, and forced pregnancy, require a particularly effective response." Report of the Drafting Committee, Addendum, Final Outcome of the World Conference on Human Rights, I, June 24, 1993 (hereafter Vienna Declaration).

When the Red Army occupied Berlin after the fall of the Nazi regime, the mass rape perpetrated against German women by Soviet soldiers came to signal the total defeat of Nazi Germany, a situation in which the woman's body came to stand in for the nation itself. By the most conservative estimates, it is believed that at least one in three women living in Berlin at this time were victims of rape.[24] Diaries, memoirs, and oral histories bring to light testimonies of extremely diverse experiences that women variously named as rape, coercion, violation, prostitution, or abuse: "Some women and young girls were brutally gang-raped in public with a line of soldiers waiting for their turn. In some cases, women's bodies were slit open from stomach to anus, or they were killed afterwards."[25] This type of brutalizing and lethal sexual violence is similar to eyewitness testimonies of rape victims on October 7; there is very little survivor testimony because most of the victims were killed immediately after (or, in some cases, before) they were raped. In this way, the stunning lack of survivors comes to create a silence which has been filled in with speculation and, in some cases, denial. Forensic evidence is also minimal, largely due to the Jewish tradition of immediate burials. Relief workers report that there was less interest in proving that sexual violence occurred in the immediate aftermath of October 7, as families were scrambling to arrange burials and were still reeling from widespread devastation and loss.[26]

Historian Atina Grossmann attributes the downplaying and normalization of the ubiquitous stories of rape in postwar Berlin to a widespread demand for recognition of collective guilt for Germany's crimes.[27] "Depending on who was talking, rapes were presented as the inevitable by-product of a vicious war, or, in the 'antifascist' narrative, as understandable retribution or exaggerated anticommunist propaganda."[28] This kind of response—one which either denies or justifies the brutalization of women, the seizure of their bodily autonomy, the attempted destruction of their spirit and psyche—has abounded in response to the testimonies coming out of October 7. What I wish to argue is that this is not a new or progressive phenomenon in any way and is instead part of a longstanding historical tradition of conveniently ignoring gender-based crime to serve a political or nationalistic cause. In analyzing Israeli, Palestinian, and Western

---

24 Atina Grossmann, "Gendered Defeat: Rape, Motherhood, and Fraternization," in *Jews, Germans, and Allies: Close Encounters in Occupied Germany* (Princeton, NJ: Princeton University Press, 2009), 48–86.
25 Ibid., 53.
26 Rozovsky, "15 Witnesses, Three Confessions."
27 Grossmann, "Gendered Defeat," 57.
28 Ibid.

responses to reports of sexual violence, all of which serve a particular narrative, it is possible to understand how seemingly innocuous or unrelated response to survivor testimony on October 7 serves specific political and national goals. In the case of October 7, Hamas's sexual humiliation and torture of Israeli women is also taken as "the ultimate humiliation of the whole community," with an intention "much vaster than attacking the individual person."[29] If the intention on the opposing side, however, is to delegitimize Israel as a state, sexual violence becomes the vehicle through which this can justifiably be done, regardless of the obvious immorality of sexual violence.

In "On Three Anti-Zionisms," political theorist Shany Mor attempts to differentiate between Arab nationalist responses to Zionism and Western (generally liberal or leftist) antizionism. He argues that the antizionism of the Muslim and Arab world is based upon the total rejection of any sovereign Jewish presence in the Middle East, manifesting in methods of extreme non-recognition that include boycotts and persecution of Jews in Arab countries.[30] Ali Abunimah, a Palestinian-American journalist, claimed in a May 2024 article for the Electronic Intifada that the survivor testimonies of October 7 are "'mass rapes' atrocity propaganda" aimed at delegitimizing Hamas, scrutinizing Israeli women survivor's accounts on the basis of them not speaking up sooner.[31] Many accounts coming out of Arab media focus on denying, rather than justifying, the claims of October 7 conflict-related sexual warfare. These arguments fit into what Shany Mor terms the specific tradition of non-recognition: a complete denial of the occurrence of any sexual violence on October 7. Palestinian-Egyptian feminist Randa Abdel-Fattah responded to the New York Times investigative report which concluded that sexual violence occurred on October 7, writing that "It is urgent that we call out rape atrocity propaganda and remind that this stratagem has historically been one of the most potent weapons used by white power to discredit, demonize, diabolize, and destroy black and brown men and to deflect sympathy from those resisting oppression to the actual oppressors, and finally to justify lethal responses."[32]

---

29 Ruth Halperin-Kaddari, "Sexual Violence against Israeli Women on and after October 7th," posted by UCLA Y&S Nazarian Center for Israeli Studies, YouTube, March 22, 2024, https://www.youtube.com/watch?v=k3fOArXR-X8&rco=1.
30 Shany Mor, "On Three Anti-Zionisms," *Israel Studies* 24, no. 2 (2019): 208.
31 Ali Abunimah, "ICC Has No Evidence for 7 October Rapes, Documents Indicate," Electronic Intifada, May 21, 2024, https://electronicintifada.net/blogs/ali-abunimah/icc-has-no-evidence-7-october-rapes-documents-indicate
32 Randa Abdel-Fattah, "A Critical Look at *The New York Times*'s Weaponization of Rape in Service of Israeli Propaganda," Institute for Palestine Studies, January 14, 2024, https://www.palestine-studies.org/en/node/1655054.

There is certainly a legitimate argument to be made that violence begets more violence, and Israel's prolonged military campaign in Gaza will only create a new generation of children traumatized by the horrors of war with an increased likelihood of joining militant terror organizations. However, Abdel-Fattah's choice to indiscriminately label all survivor testimonies as "propaganda" echoes some of the responses to stories of mass rapes in Berlin, in which women's stories were doubted or ignored as a form of punishment for their nation's military behavior: a demanding of collective national guilt which pushed aside the immediacy of sexual assault survivor testimony. It seems that this, too, is part of what enables denial of sexual violence testimonies coming out of Israel: an urgent need to "hold Israel accountable" for its brutal campaign in Gaza that has resulted in the deaths of an estimated 40,000 Palestinians at the time of writing precludes the seeming importance of also recognizing the atrocity of sexual violence that occurred on October 7. Perhaps some find it too complicated to imagine that two groups of people could somehow be wronged, or be harming each other simultaneously.

Western responses, especially those on the left, fit into what Shany Mor calls the truly fascinating category of antizionism: one which asserts that Israel was created in sin and tainted in its every action with sin.[33] This ideology lends itself to a certain level of cognitive dissonance in which its proponents assert that even if sexual violence was perpetrated by Hamas militants on October 7, it is justified as a "decolonial" resistance movement. Three days after the October 7 attack, in direct reference to the events that occurred, the Stanford University chapter of the nationally funded organization Students for Justice in Palestine released an op-ed in which they asserted that "Palestinians, like all peoples, have the legitimate right to resist occupation, apartheid, and systemic injustice." Groups across the country issued similar statements. As stories of Hamas-perpetrated sexual violence began to surface, student organizations did not issue retractions of these statements but instead doubled down: the SJP chapter at the University of California, Los Angeles, shared a statement which iterated that

> the notion of a good "Israeli" settler is every bit as absurd and contradictory as the myth of the "good" slaveowner. If you[r] life and livelihood are built by the brutal dispossession of other people, nothing within that framework could ever redeem you.

---

33 Mor, "On Three Anti-Zionisms," 208.

> These systems are only ever dismantled by the application of brute force by the oppressed.[34]

This dehumanizing rhetoric situates Israeli women as justifiable targets of sexual violence as a result of their government's actions, by virtue of their national identity. What this framework fails to consider is that Palestinians constitute more than a fifth of the population of Israel proper, or that Palestinian Arabs were victims of the October 7 attacks too. This argument echoes the justification of the rapes in Berlin following the Second World War as part of an "understandable retribution" against fascism.[35] Conditions of bloodshed, brutality, and gender-based violence rely on dehumanization of the other in order to be carried out. What is interesting about some Western responses to October 7 is that groups which fall on the liberal side of the political spectrum, who claim to be invested in the well-being of women and "dispossessed peoples," contribute to mass dehumanization which enables conditions for horrific gender-based violence to occur on nationalistic grounds.

Israeli and Western pro-Israel reactions to October 7 have generally been focused on two things: proving that sexual violence occurred systematically and understanding why major global feminist and leftist organizations have not condemned the Hamas's indiscriminate killing and rape and have instead denied, condoned, or even supported the attacks. Ruth Halperin-Kaddari, an Israeli legal scholar and international women's rights advocate, told *Haaretz* that she feels "completely betrayed" by the international legal organizations that she has worked with for decades, in their failure to recognize or condemn the October 7 rapes perpetrated by Hamas.[36] Halperin-Kaddari is referring specifically to UN-affiliated groups (such as UN Women) that were founded with the intent of "protecting women from violence, to champion women's rights, and to acknowledge when harm is done to women. And now, when we Israeli women are faced with the most horrible occurrence of 'conflict-related sexual violence,' there is complete silence."[37] Halperin-Kaddari's use of the term "most horrible" is indicative of a plea to be heard. In an article published in *Haaretz*, journalist Lisa Rozovsky describes

---

34 Bella Brannon, "Opinion: UCLA SJP Post Implies Violence against All Israelis," Ha'am, June 10, 2024, https://haam.org/opinion-ucla-sjp-post-implies-violence-against-all-israelis.
35 Grossmann, "Gendered Defeat," 57.
36 Ruth Halperin Kaddari, "Why Is the Cruel Sexual Violence of the October 7 Hamas Attack Being Ignored?," *Haaretz*, November 14, 2023, https://www.haaretz.com/israel-news/podcasts/2023-11-14/ty-article-podcast/why-is-the-cruel-sexual-violence-of-the-october-7-hamas-attack-being-ignored/0000018b-cdbe-d423-affb-ffbfe0d20000.
37 Ibid.

how Israeli spokespersons "latch onto every gut-wrenching report in their efforts to persuade the world of the truth of the atrocities that were perpetrated."[38] Both *Haaretz* and the *New York Times* performed independent investigations into the reports of sexual violence on October 7, collecting survivor testimonies, reports from therapists, and video and photographic evidence. These investigations found sufficient evidence to prove that sexual assault did occur, en masse, on October 7; this evidence was not forensic (due to the lack of surviving victims and the Jewish tradition of immediate burial) but was instead circumstantial and based on testimony and from photographs and videos. Both investigations found a lack of definitive and forensic proof of explicit orders to commit sexual violence. This is in contradiction to Halperin-Kaddari's claim that many of the victim's bodies were mutilated in such a pattern that made premeditation likely if not certain.[39] This does not rule out the possibility that Hamas used systematic rape as a weapon of war, it just does not offer an indictment one way or another.

As Rhonda Copelon argues, international law's requirement that rape be proved as a systematic crime is dangerous in its implications for the victim. Systematic rape is defined as a tool for genocide and for which the burden of proof falls upon Israel in order to prosecute Hamas for the October 7 attacks. Genocide is generally recognized as "the effort to destroy a people based on its identity as a people—evokes the deepest horror and warrants the severest condemnation." Copelon asserts that rape, from the standpoint of its victims, seeks the same end goal on an individualized scale. "Rape is sexualized violence that seeks to humiliate, terrorize and destroy a woman based on her identity as a woman. Both are based on total contempt for and dehumanization of the victim, and both give rise to unspeakable brutalities. From the standpoint of these women, they are inseparable."[40]

In the months following the October 7 attack, some scholars and journalists have articulated a path forward for Israel, hoping to prevent conditions that will generate further radicalism and violence. *New York Times* columnist Ezra Klein expressed his disgust with dehumanization on all sides:

> What was so repulsive to me in some leftist commentary after Hamas's massacre of Israelis was a belief in collective guilt and collective punishment. There was no debate over whether Hamas targeted and slaughtered civilians. No, the argument was that there

---

38   Ibid.
39   Ruth Halperin Kaddari as quoted in *Screams before Silence*, dir. Anat Stalinsky (Tel Aviv: Kastina Communications, 2024).
40   Copelon, "Surfacing Gender," 198.

was no such thing as an Israeli civilian. No such thing as being an innocent in Israel. It's repugnant. But does the repugnance of that logic not go both ways? Is there no such thing as a civilian in Gaza?[41]

There is a way to articulate an argument that conditions of violence create more violence—that the cycle of dehumanization is what enables horrific massacres to occur—without relying on the rejection of truth to justify violence against women. There is a difference between forward-directed conversations, which attempt to learn from the past to build better conditions for all, and autopsies of the event that point backwards, victim-blaming Israeli women for their supposed complicity in violence while simultaneously ignoring the brutalizing, dehumanizing violence that they themselves have been made victims of. This has played out in the immediate aftermath of October 7. "Iran and Hamas are counting on Israel to attack Gaza with such ferocity that the international sympathy of the past week toward Israel, even in the Arab world, evaporates quickly and is replaced by outrage at the suffering inflicted on the two million residents of Gaza," wrote Hussein Ibish in the *Atlantic*.[42]

And perhaps this is true, that a demand for collective recognition of Israel's siege on Gaza in its war with Hamas has made it easier for people to look past the "inconvenient" truth of the brutal sexual violence that Hamas perpetrated on October 7, as was the case in Soviet-occupied Berlin. Timothy Snyder, a historian who studies fascism and the conditions that enable it, implores us to believe in truth. "If nothing is true, then no one can criticize power, because there is no basis upon which to do so. If nothing is true, then all is spectacle."[43] If reports of sexual violence against Israeli women cannot be true, simply by virtue of their nationality, then what can be true? Where do we derive meaning, history, or our morals if not for truth? When we turn our backs on truth, we enable dehumanization, and we subsequently turn our backs on humanity.

---

41   Ezra Klein, "Opinion: Israel Is Giving Hamas What It Wants," *The Ezra Klein Show*, October 18, 2023, https://www.nytimes.com/2023/10/18/opinion/ezra-klein-podcast-israel-palestine.html.
42   Hussein Ibish, "Israel Is Walking Into a Trap," *Atlantic*, October 13, 2023, https://www.theatlantic.com/international/archive/2023/10/israel-hamas-war-iran-trap/675628/.
43   Timothy Snyder, *On Tyranny: Twenty Lessons from the Twentieth Century* (New York: Crown Publishing Group, 2017), 65.

CHAPTER 13

From the Cold War to University Campuses Today: The USSR, the Third World, and Contemporary Antizionist Discourse

Izabella Tabarovsky

In November 1967, the Indian chapter of the World Peace Council, a Soviet front organization, held the International Conference in Support of the Arab Peoples in New Delhi. Gathering in the capital of India were some 150 delegates representing fifty-five countries and seventy international organizations from across the Third World, the socialist bloc, and the West. India's Prime Minister Indira Gandhi, Egypt's Gamal Abdel Nasser, Cuba's Fidel Castro, and Algeria's Houari Boumedienne—the biggest political stars of the Non-Aligned Movement—sent their greetings, as did heads of Sudan, Syria, Jordan, Algeria, Kuwait, and Mongolia. Chairing the proceedings was Krishna Menon, a firebrand leftist Indian intellectual and former Indian defense minister the KGB had actively cultivated[1] in the hopes that he would rise to be the head of state.[2]

Some 1,200 delegates and visitors attended the opening plenary, at which Herbert Aptheker, a senior member of the American Communist Party (CPUSA) and influential scholar of Marxism, argued for framing the Arab Israeli conflict

---

1 Christopher Andrew and Vasili Mitrokhin, *The World Was Going Our Way: The KGB and the Battle for the Third World* (New York: Basic Books, 2006), 314.
2 Herbert Aptheker, "In Support of the Arab Peoples," *Political Affairs* 47, no. 1 (January 1968): 38–46.

in terms of "imperialism and colonialism versus national liberation and social progress," as well as through the lens of racial oppression. Contrary to Israeli rulers' claims, he declared, the greatest threat facing Israel came not from Arabs but from Israel's own extremist right-wing government, which had turned Israel into the "handmaiden of imperialism and colonialist expansionism." He equated Israel with Nazi Germany by referring to the recent Six-Day War as a blitzkrieg, a quintessentially Soviet propaganda term meant to evoke Hitler's invasion of the USSR. Today, said Aptheker, it was Jews who were "acting out the roles of occupiers and tormentors" of the oppressed. He called on the audience to work tirelessly to unmask "the horror of the June war and its aftermath." So closely did Aptheker's speech follow the anti-Israel logic and idiom of Soviet propaganda that it may well have been written for him in Moscow.

The two documents the conference unanimously adopted—the "Appeal to the Conscience of the World" (reportedly signed by 100 members of the Indian parliament) and a "Declaration"—conveyed similar messages with even more bombast. Evoking classic antisemitic tropes, they accused Israel of having cynically violated all "standards of human decency," and declared that it had made "a mockery of all human moral values." They dubbed Palestinian terrorism—a.k.a., "resistance"—as "righteous and justified." In an attempt to make the Middle Eastern conflict more relatable, they equated it with the central cause animating the Western left at the time: the war in Vietnam. They called for all the people on the planet to resist "imperialist-Zionist propaganda" and expressed appreciation for the "progressive and peace-loving" Soviet Union and other socialist states and Non-Aligned countries that "supported the Arab cause."

The message echoed throughout the global leftist universe. The CPUSA, which was almost wholly subsidized by the Soviet Union, published Aptheker's speech and both statements in full in its theoretical journal *Political Affairs*. The *African Communist*, the Soviet-financed quarterly organ of the South African Communist Party (SACP), which was deeply intertwined with the African National Congress (ANC), ran a piece titled "Zionism and the Future of Israel," closely reflecting the language of the New Delhi conference, complete with the word *blitzkrieg*. Its author, who claimed to be a South African living in Tel Aviv, accused Zionist "fanatical zealots" of exploiting the biblical concept of Jewish chosenness to fan the flames of Jewish supremacy ("chauvinism" in the language of the day), while equating Israel with apartheid South Africa.[3]

---

3   Samuel Ben Adam, "Zionism and the Future of Israel," *The African Communist* 31 (4th quarter 1967): 66–76.

What's so interesting about this half-century-old Soviet propaganda, as conveyed at a conference in India—a leader of the ascending Non-Aligned Movement—is how precisely it mirrors the language emanating from the anti-Israel left since the Hamas massacre of October 7, 2023. Today's left, too, speaks of Israel as a racist, imperialist, and colonialist state; equates it with Nazi Germany and apartheid South Africa; disparages Jews for having turned into oppressors; and proclaims Palestinians' inalienable right to resist their colonial oppression by any means necessary.

A quick excursion into the Soviet-sponsored Third World/left-wing universe of yesteryear, helps put many things into perspective—from the disastrous "anti-racism" UN conference in Durban, South Africa, in 2001 that launched a massive new global wave of anti-Israel demonization to the current grotesque spectacle of progressives using "anti-colonialism" to justify the mass murder, rape, and kidnapping of civilians in a land where Jews have lived for more than 3,000 years of their collective history, as memorialized in the works of Greek and Roman historians; monumental inscriptions by neighboring kingdoms; such globally recognized works as the New Testament, the Quran, and the Dead Sea Scrolls; and by world-famous monuments like the Arch of Titus in Rome.

That what we are watching is less an upsurge of a new and terrifying phenomenon than the zombielike repetition of the state-sponsored propaganda of a dead empire that was hardly known for truth-telling explains why the anti-imperialist, anti-colonialist prattle of today's college students feels like déjà vu to those of us who grew up in the USSR. We've heard it all before: anti-imperialism mixed with antizionist sloganeering; anti-racism interwoven with the demonization of the Jews; incantations about "world peace" and "friendship of the peoples" intertwined with the fomenting and financing of wars in faraway lands. One example in particular stands out as an illustration of profound Soviet cynicism with regard to the Third World: While calling for the boycott of the apartheid regime in every international forum, Moscow didn't for one second stop trading diamonds with South African companies De Beers and Anglo American.[4] As perestroika got underway and Soviet foreign policy priorities began to shift, some in Moscow started reaching out to the South African regime to convince it not to surrender power to Nelson Mandela.[5]

Those who try to explain the contemporary left's anti-Israel derangement by pointing to the latest academic fashions, such as critical race theory and

---

4 Irina Filatova and Apollon Davidson, *The Hidden Thread: Russia and South Africa in the Soviet Era* (Johannesburg: Jonathan Ball Publishers, 2013), 341.
5 Ibid., 617.

intersectionality, or to specific news events of the day often miss the point that the precise language used by the anti-Israel left today to condemn the Jewish State has been a conventional part of left-wing discourse for decades. During the late 1960s and early 1970s, wrote Stephen Norwood, the American far left "repeatedly denounced Israel as a criminal regime resembling Nazi Germany and enthusiastically endorsed the Arab guerilla movement's campaign to eradicate the Jewish state."[6] Similar trends were on view in the United Kingdom. "By the early 1970s, it was generally accepted across the [British] far left that Zionism was a racist ideology and that Israel was comparable to apartheid South Africa," wrote Dave Rich in *Antisemitism on the Campus: Past and Present.*[7]

The extraordinary fidelity with which progressives reproduce the tropes and warped logic of Soviet antizionist propaganda, complete with specific fictions and terms of abuse, raises questions.[8] How is it that such a multitude of groups across the globe—from all manner of communists and Trotskyists to Non-Aligned political figures, non-communist New Left, Pan-Africanists, and Cuban revolutionaries—adopted this language so completely and simultaneously? The answer is that they followed Moscow, which targeted them all with a colossal antizionist campaign, pushing out masses of printed matter, communicating these ideas in multilingual radio broadcasts, and using media and diplomatic channels to influence opinions within countries.[9]

But the most important channel of transmission for the Soviet antizionist campaign was, undoubtedly, the Third World—more specifically, an ecosystem that formed at the intersection of the postcolonial Non-Aligned Movement; the Western left, which looked toward exotic distant lands and their guerillas as the future of the revolution and a cure for their own alienation; and the USSR, which at the same time, in the 1960s, began to view this part of the world as central to defeating the "main adversary," the United States, in the Cold War.

---

6   Stephen H. Norwood, *Antisemitism and the American Far Left* (Cambridge: Cambridge University Press, 2013), 1.
7   Dave Rich, "Campus War, 1977: The Year That Jewish Societies Were Banned," in *Antisemitism on the Campus: Past and Present*, ed. Eunice G. Pollack (Boston, MA: Academic Studies Press, 2010), 258.
8   Izabella Tabarovsky, "Soviet Anti-Zionism and Contemporary Left Antisemitism," in *Mapping the New Left Antisemitism: The Fathom Essays*, ed. Alan Johnson (London: Routledge, 2024), 108–121.
9   Izabella Tabarovsky, "Demonization Blueprints: Soviet Conspiracist Antizionism in Contemporary Left-Wing Discourse," in *The Rebirth of Antisemitism in the 21st Century: From the Academic Boycott Campaign into the Mainstream*, ed. David Hirsh (London: Routledge, 2024), 34–60.

Moscow did not control this ecosystem entirely. But it had no shortage of tools with which to shape it. One of these was the multitudes of international youth festivals, solidarity forums, women's assemblies, and nuclear disarmament congresses that Moscow sponsored in support of its foreign policy goals. "It is simply impossible to list all the conferences, campaigns, and other events, organized by various international bodies with the assistance of the Soviet Union and other socialist countries," wrote Irina Filatova and Apollon Davidson in *The Hidden Thread: Russia and South Africa in the Soviet Era*. Essop Pahad, a prominent ANC activist and member of the South African Communist Party, recalled, "You could have a conference in Ethiopia, and somebody would come from Laos and Indonesia and Malaysia and Cambodia and Vietnam. . . . Where would all these people have found the money? The Soviets and the other socialist countries paid for all of this," including "for the airplanes that were hired."[10]

It was at Soviet-sponsored conferences that the Western left got to rub shoulders with its Third World revolutionary heroes. It was here that Moscow worked to inculcate its brand of conspiracist antizionism by tying it to every progressive cause of the time, turning Palestinian terrorists into a global cause célèbre on par with anti-apartheid campaigners, French leftists, and the stars of the US antiwar movement. It was here, at these all-expenses-paid gatherings, that shared narratives and opinions formed and global peer-to-peer networks were established to carry those narratives and opinions. In this ecosystem, being antizionist and anti-Israel became as much a marker of belonging as standing against imperialism, colonialism, racism, capitalism, and apartheid.

A remarkable number of figures who have shaped anti-Israel discourse in recent years came of age politically within the Soviet-sponsored anti-colonialist ecosystem. Angela Davis is one of them. A long-term member of CPUSA and a prominent member of the Black Power movement, who owes much of her political and cultural stardom to Soviet investment in her image and career (according to CIA estimates, in 1971 Moscow devoted an estimated 5% of their propaganda efforts to Davis[11]), she first met Yasser Arafat at a 1973 World Festival of Youth and Students in Berlin and credits the "powerful force" of "communist internationalism"—"in Africa, the Middle East, Europe, Asia, South America, and the Caribbean"—with globalizing the Palestinian cause.[12] Davis remains an

---

10   Filatova and Davidson, *The Hidden Thread*, 329–330.
11   Beatrice de Graaf, *Evaluating Counterterrorism Performance: A Comparative Study* (Abingdon: Routledge, 2011), Kindle edition without page numbers. To locate the quote, see footnote 41 and the text it references.
12   Sara Benton, "Angela Davis Makes the Palestinian Struggle Hers," Jews for Justice for Palestinians, September 5, 2017, https://jfjfp.com/angela-davis-makes-the-palestinian-struggle-hers/.

icon on today's anti-Israel left, and in a recent post-October 7 talk, she spoke of the "murderous power of Zionism."

Another iconic figure of the Black Power movement, Stokely Carmichael, whose virulent antizionist quotes are frequently recalled by admirers today, was also profoundly influenced by this global ecosystem. He appears to have first entered it at a conference in Cuba in 1967. He developed a close personal relationship with Fidel Castro, embarked on a Third World pilgrimage to Vietnam and Africa, and lived for many years in Guinea and Ghana, developing close relationships with their Marxist dictators, Ahmed Sékou Touré and Kwame Nkrumah, who played an important role in the Non-Aligned Movement.[13] (It speaks to the significance of the last two for Carmichael that he borrowed parts of their names for his political sobriquet, Kwame Ture.)

Another influential American who is a product of that ecosystem—meaning, that he literally grew up in it—is President Biden's former Iran envoy Robert Malley, who is currently under an FBI investigation for potentially mishandling classified information by sharing it with Iran.[14] Malley's father, Simon, an Egyptian Jew and a communist, served Nasser, built close relationships with Arafat and Castro, and dedicated his life to the "anti-imperialist and anti-American causes of Third World national liberal movements in Asia, Africa, and Latin America," writes Hussein Aboubakr Mansour. Malley the father saw Israel as "an evil vestige of colonialism," and as an editor of the Paris-based magazine *Africasia* (later renamed *Afrique Asie*), he took radical positions that were not only "virulently" anti-American, anti-Western, and anti-Israeli, but also overtly pro-Soviet. (His support of the Soviet invasion of Afghanistan—a position that was deeply unpopular in the Non-Aligned world and typically indicative of a deeper Soviet link—is particularly notable in this regard.) Malley senior boasted several Arab and African citizenships, including an honorary Palestinian one, and took his son on "revolutionary tourism trips" across the postcolonial world, Mansour reports. As a boy, Robert played with his father's friend Arafat. As a student at Yale, he wrote articles condemning Israel.[15]

On the opposite side of the Atlantic, some of the most zealous Corbynistas, too, are products of the Soviet ecosystem. They include George Galloway, who

---

13   "Stokely Carmichael Goes to Cuba," SNCC Digital, https://snccdigital.org/events/stokely-carmichael-goes-cuba/.
14   Ben Weingarten, "Congress Digs into Scandals Surrounding Biden Iran Envoy Bob Malley," Real Clear Politics, June 11, 2024, https://www.realclearpolitics.com/articles/2024/06/11/congress_digs_into_scandals_surrounding_biden_iran_envoy_rob_malley.html.
15   Hussein Abubakr Mansour, "Robert Malley and the Call from the Third World," Emet, July 20, 2023, https://emetonline.org/robert-malley-and-the-call-from-the-third-world/.

first visited Palestine Liberation Organization (PLO) camps in Lebanon in the 1970s, has made a career out of his unhinged hatred of Israel, and dubbed the day the USSR fell as the worst day of his life[16]; Ken Livingstone, who took money from the PLO to publish a weekly newspaper *Labour Herald* (printed on Libyan-funded printing press),[17] which ran several pro-PLO articles per issue and demonized Israel as a racist, genocidal, apartheid reincarnation of Nazi Germany; and Jeremy Corbyn's former advisers, the "Stalinist" Seumas Milne, who spent his gap year in Lebanon and published a pro-Soviet and pro-PLO newspaper, *Straight Left*,[18] and Andrew Murray, a forty-year veteran of the Communist Party of Great Britain (CPGB), who for a time worked for the Soviet foreign propaganda agency Novosti.[19] Corbyn emerged on the British political scene as a young Labour activist in the 1980s, when the anti-Israel, antizionist currents within the party had already been nurtured for a decade, and joined an organization that "rejected Israel's existence and campaigned to 'eradicate Zionism' from the Labour Party," wrote Dave Rich in *The Left's Jewish Problem: Jeremy Corbyn, Israel and Antisemitism*.[20]

Some of the Latin American leaders who rushed to condemn Israel and equate it with Nazi Germany in the wake of October 7 are also products of that era. Brazil's Lula Da Silva rose through the ranks of communist-aligned trade union politics,[21] and Colombia's President Gustavo Petro was for several years a member of a Marxist guerilla group responsible for political assassinations and kidnappings.[22]

As for the ANC, the plaintiff behind the bogus International Court of Justice suit accusing Israel of genocide, it occupied pride of place in that ecosystem, both as an object of admiration for its fight against apartheid and as a group that enjoyed the closest relationship with Moscow among all other national-liberation

---

16 Christopher Hitchens, "Unmitigated Galloway," *Washington Examiner*, May 30, 2005, https://www.washingtonexaminer.com/magazine/102635/unmitigated-galloway/.
17 Dave Rich, *The Left's Jewish Problem: Jeremy Corbyn, Israel and Antisemitism*, (London: Biteback, 2018), 137.
18 Peter Wilby, "The Thin Controller," New Statesman, April 16, 2016, https://www.newstatesman.com/politics/2016/04/the-thin-controller.
19 Gavin Jacobson, "Corbyn Adviser Andrew Murrey on What's Next for the Left," New Statesman, January 22, 2020, updated August 2, 2021, https://www.newstatesman.com/politics/2020/01/corbyn-adviser-andrew-murray-what-s-next-left.
20 Rich, *The Left's Jewish Problem*, 136.
21 Oliver Pieper, "Brazil's Lula da Silva: The Communist Who Wasn't," Deutsche Welle, December 29, 2022. https://www.dw.com/en/brazils-lula-da-silva-the-communist-who-wasnt/a-64240797.
22 Jeff Wallenfeldt, "Gustavo Petro," Encyclopedia Britannica, 2024, https://www.britannica.com/biography/Gustavo-Petro.

movements the latter sponsored. The ANC turned post-apartheid South Africa into a country of where "the government is itself a sponsor of anti-Zionism," with Muslim student groups using "Soviet-style terminology" and communist slogans to attack Jewish students.[23] When ANC's Jewish veteran and former ANC intelligence minister, Ronnie Kasrils, justified Hamas's October 7 pogrom on the grounds that Israel was an oppressor,[24] he was being entirely consistent with his role in the Moscow-led radical left—as opposed to Western liberal—anti-apartheid struggle.

China's incorporation of anti-Israel propaganda into its post-Oct. 7 anti-Western agitprop[25]—and its role mediating a unity agreement between Hamas and Fatah just recently[26]—has surprised many observers, but that, too, is consistent with its rich Cold War history of supporting Palestinians and condemning Israel and Zionism as part of its attacks on the West and the United States, which were even more radical than those of the USSR.[27] And we must not, of course, forget Mahmoud Abbas, who wrote his miniature dissertation equating Zionism with Nazism at a Soviet think tank run by KGB's master-Arabist Yevgeny Primakov and charged with developing "scholarly" foundations for antizionist propaganda.[28]

***

The belief that "the Cold War could be won in the Third World" began to take hold in Moscow in the late 1950s. In 1960, Soviet Premier Nikita Khrushchev spent a month with the Soviet UN delegation in New York, where he witnessed seventeen new states join the organization, sixteen of them from Africa. "Hearing Western imperialism publicly denounced by Third World leaders in the heartland of American capitalism" left an indelible impression on the general

---

23 Gregg Rickman, "The Irony of It All: Antisemitism, Anti-Zionism, and Intimidation on South African University Campuses," in *Antisemitism on the Campus: Past & Present*, ed. Eunice G. Pollack (Boston, MA: Academic Studies Press, 2011), 279, 287.
24 David Benatar, "Denying 7 October: The Case of Former ANC Minister Ronnie Kasrils," *Fathom*, February 2024, https://fathomjournal.org/denying-7-october-the-case-of-former-anc-minister-ronnie-kasrils/.
25 Josh Rogin, "Fueling Online Antisemitism is China's New Tool against the West," *Washington Post*, January 8, 2024, https://www.washingtonpost.com/opinions/2024/01/08/china-antisemitism-online-tool-west-gaza/.
26 Tessa Wong and Raffi Berg, "China Seeks to Unite Palestinian Factions with Reconciliation Deal," BBC, July 23, 2024, https://www.bbc.com/news/articles/crgm147lzv1o.
27 John Cooley, "China and the Palestinians," *Journal of Palestine Studies* 1, no. 2 (Winter 1972): 19–34, https://www.jstor.org/stable/2535952.
28 Izabella Tabarovsky, "Mahmoud Abbas's Dissertation," *Tablet*, January 18, 2023. https://www.tabletmag.com/sections/arts-letters/articles/mahmoud-abbas-soviet-dissertation.

secretary, wrote Christopher Andrew and Vasily Mitrokhin in *The World Was Going Our Way: The KGB and the Battle for the Third World*. Khrushchev flew home convinced that the way to bring imperialism (and the United States) "to its knees" was indeed by supporting the "sacred anti-imperialist struggle of colonies and newly independent states." He gave Soviet propaganda professionals appropriate instructions. In 1961, the KGB adopted a strategy to use "national liberation movements and the forces of anti-imperialism" in an aggressive new effort against the "'Main Adversary'"—the United States—"in the Third World."[29]

Khrushchev's new strategy demanded a new international posture. Moscow duly refurbished its image, discarding commitment to ideological orthodoxy and presenting itself as both a staunch advocate for peace, progress, and development and a principled opponent of imperialism, colonialism, and racism—all issues that were top of mind among newly independent nations. Soviet periodicals, translated into even more languages, were now reaching practically every country on the planet. (Some 400 were available in Latin America alone.[30]) Stories about Soviet advancements in education, public health, housing, agriculture, fashion, science, and technology supplanted dreary texts about Marxism-Leninism. Colorful photo spreads of attractive women, children, gymnasts, ballerinas, and happy members of Asian ethnic minorities painted the USSR as a forward-looking country filled with optimistic, smiling people enjoying all the benefits of socialist industrial modernity. Third World politicians and technical specialists flocked to take Potemkin village tours of the Soviet "inner periphery" (Central Asia and the Caucasus) to learn how the great, progressive Russian people helped their backward non-white brothers leapfrog into modernity. (Few seemed to recognize these as examples of Soviet racism and imperialism.)[31]

What Moscow was now selling to these countries was not a proletarian revolution but economic aid, offered in a brotherly spirit and supposedly with no strings attached. "We do not interfere in the internal affairs of the countries that are getting our aid," proclaimed a Soviet official in Cairo in 1957.[32] The real meaning of this proposition would reveal itself a few years later, when the KGB turned the Third World into the staging ground and vehicle for active measures, penetrating in particular the Non-Aligned Movement's most influential state

---

29 Andrew and Mitrokhin, *The World*, 8–9.
30 Thobias Rupprecht, *Soviet Internationalism after Stalin: Interaction and Exchange between the USSR and Latin America during the Cold War* (Cambridge: Cambridge University Press, 2015), 36.
31 Ibid., 22–37.
32 David Kimche, *The Afro-Asian Movement: Ideology and Foreign Policy of the Third World* (Jerusalem: Universities Press, 1973), 133.

actors, such as India, Egypt, Ghana, and Cuba. Newly loosened ideological strictures and theoretical adjustments enabled Moscow to engage with every kind of Third World nationalist, leftist, Islamist, and genocidaire. So successful did this new approach to foreign policy appear that by the late 1970s, the USSR was confident "the world was going our way."[33]

Moscow also worked to divine what made the non-communist New Left tick. One insight arrived in October 1967, when 50,000 American students—mostly members of the New Left—who gathered in front of the Lincoln Memorial to protest the war in Vietnam took the opportunity to pay tribute to Che Guevara, just recently executed by US-trained Bolivian forces. The spectacle must have riveted Moscow, which had viewed Guevara as a fantasist and "brave but incompetent guerilla"; it shed few tears for him. When a poll revealed that more American students "identified with Che than with any other figure, alive or dead," the KGB knew it got a gift. In the coming years, it would incorporate Che's myth into its "active-measures campaign against American imperialism."[34] The New Left's cringeworthy hero-worship of Third World militants and despots would offer numerous such gifts.[35]

The anti-imperialist crowd Moscow had at its disposal, then, was motley, and at the many conferences, seminars, and festivals Moscow sponsored, it made sure to offer a little bit for everyone. Non-Aligned grandstanders got bright media spotlights and a bully pulpit from which to harangue American imperialism. New Leftists got to rub shoulders with their revolutionary heroes in thrillingly authentic, non-capitalist settings. Orthodox communists could partake in hard-core theoretical discussions. Spending days in exotic locations bonding with peers normalized radical perspectives, turning the most extreme views into conventional wisdom. Recognizing the complicated feelings the USSR aroused among many in this group, Moscow kept its involvement in the background, using front organizations to organize and run the shows.

By the time antizionism rose to the top of its ideological priorities in June 1967, Moscow had a ready-made ecosystem with receptive members primed to condemn anything Western, American, and imperialistic, as well as a proven method to socialize the anti-Israel new ideas among them.

---

33   Andrew and Mitrokhin, *The World*, 24.
34   Ibid., 50–51.
35   On Western leftist intellectuals' idealizing of socialist and Third World regimes and how the latter manipulated them, see Paul Hollander, *Political Pilgrims: Western Intellectuals in Search of the Good Society*, 4th ed. (New York: Routledge, 2017).

***

Moscow wasn't the first party to introduce anti-Israel demonization into Third World revolutionary discourse: Arab states started doing it the moment Israel was established. Nor did the Soviets suddenly become Zionophobic in 1967: ideological antizionism had been part of the Soviet outlook from the Bolsheviks' early days. But the crushing defeat of the Soviet Union's Arab allies in the Six Day War created a massive crisis of confidence in Moscow. As Soviet Jews began to demand the right to emigrate, and Jews around the globe joined in a campaign on their behalf, Moscow turned Zionism into a bogeyman that threatened its interests everywhere at once. In the fevered imagination of KGB's head, Yuri Andropov, Zionism was a global anti-Soviet and anti-socialist force, and the only way to defeat it was by attacking it globally.

We can get a vivid picture of Moscow's approach to solving its Zionist problem from an article titled "Anatomy of Israeli Aggression," which appeared in the *World Marxist Review*—the English edition of the Prague-based Soviet theoretical journal *Problems of Peace and Socialism*. Published in forty languages and distributed in 145 countries, the journal reached an estimated half a million of the most committed leftists around the globe. The lead author of the article, Yevgeny Yevseyev, was one of the key ideologues of the new brand of Soviet antizionism—the so-called Zionologists.

The piece reported on the "Second International Conference in Support of the Arab Peoples," which took place in Cairo in January 1969. Organized jointly by the World Peace Council and the Cairo-headquartered Afro-Asian People's Solidarity Organization (AAPSO), it enjoyed Nasser's personal patronage. As fourteen months earlier in New Delhi, stars of the Third World and Non-Aligned Movement were here, including India's Krishna Menon; the world's first female prime minister, Ceylon's Sirimavo Bandaranaike; and Isabelle Blume, an ex-head of Belgium's Communist Party and the recipient of Stalin's International Prize for Strengthening Peace among Peoples, who counted Ho Chi Minh, Mao Zedong, Indira Gandhi, and Salvador Allende among her friends.[36] Fatah were there as well.[37]

Yevseyev hailed the Cairo conference as "a powerful demonstration of the anti-imperialist forces in support of the Arab people's struggle." Delegates from seventy-four countries and fifteen international organizations, including France,

---

36 "Isabelle Blume (Baudour, 22 mai 1892–12 mars 1975)," ILHS—Institut liégeois d'histoire sociale, archived at https://web.archive.org/web/20140408233643/http://ilhs.e-monsite.com/pages/biographies/isabelle-blume-baudour-22-mai-1892-12-mars-1975.html.
37 Rich, *The Left's Jewish Problem*, 60.

Italy, Sweden, Latin America, Africa, and Asia, came together, he wrote, to discuss Zionism as an "active but skillfully concealed force" that was engaged in a "worldwide struggle against the national liberation movement, communism, and other democratic forces." Having postulated this fundamentally conspiratorial notion, Yevseyev sought to debunk the view of Israel as a "small and weak state" surrounded by hostile neighbors: In reality, he wrote, Israel was a warmongering, "aggressive force" and "source of tension" in the Middle East.

Yevseyev praised the conference for exposing Zionism "as a transmission belt of world imperialism," a "modern form of fascism," and a reactionary expression of late-stage capitalism—which naturally made Israel Hitler's fascist heir apparent: "Practical application of the Zionist doctrine in the Middle East," he explained, inevitably involved "genocide, racism, perfidy, duplicity, aggression, annexation"—in other words, "all the attributes of fascism that go back to the Hitler days." The word "genocide" appeared in the piece twice, helping solidify the link between Israel and Nazi Germany and laying the groundwork for its indiscriminate use in future anti-Israel propaganda.

Yevseyev dedicated a portion of his article to painting Zionism as the enemy of the African peoples. (Undermining the American puppet Israel's budding relationships with newly independent African states was a Soviet priority in the region.) "Zionist agents disguised as specialists" were seeking to infiltrate African countries' press, trade unions, and educational institutions, wrote Yevseyev, using one of KGB's favorite tropes. Playing on the young nations' central fears, he announced that the real objective of "Israel's Zionist policy" in Africa was "to stamp out even the first tender shoots of independence" among them. Zionist propaganda, meanwhile, sought "to set one people against another and thereby prevent genuine and lasting peace in the area."

Yevseyev then proceeded to lay out a program of action that the conference adopted. First on the agenda was establishing a commission "to investigate Israeli atrocities" and peg Israel as a platform for launching imperialist aggression against the "struggle for freedom and progress." Next was mobilizing "world public opinion" against Israel by countering "the widespread imperialist and Zionist propaganda" with "truthful and detailed information" about the conflict. It was also important to build global support for Palestinians, particularly in Europe, where said truthful information was still lacking. In-country committees were to raise funds and organize film showings, exhibitions, and radio and TV programs to keep their publics informed about the "activities of the resistance organizations," while visits of "prominent Arab political and public personalities and representatives of the Palestinian resistance movement to as many countries as possible" were to be arranged. Meanwhile, it was crucial to explain to the world that the pro-Palestinian movement was directed not against Jews but against Zionism, which represented a "constant menace" to "universal peace and security."[38]

Just how accurately Yevseyev's piece described the conference proceedings is less important than Moscow's peddling of that narrative around the globe, signaling that condemning Zionism in this way was now imperative for all progressive people. It would take a separate project to identify how closely the conference's recommendations were followed. But in at least one country whose delegates attended the event—the United Kingdom—things would soon develop in ways that would please men like Yuri Andropov.

***

It's worth dwelling for a moment on how these Soviet propaganda tradeshows were organized. From the World Peace Council to the International Union of Students to the World Federation of Trade Unions to Women's International Democratic Federation, the purported sponsors were public organizations with cumulative memberships of hundreds of millions, financed by communist countries—primarily the USSR and the Warsaw pact. Overtly designed to unify people across the globe around specific issues or interests, their true purpose was to mobilize them around Soviet foreign policy priorities, which earned them the moniker of communist fronts.[39] The World Federation of Trade Unions alone, for example, counted 140 million "highly disciplined" members and published several "magazines, bulletins and pamphlets," which were distributed in 70–125 countries.[40]

During times of international crises, wrote Israeli political scientist Baruch Hazan, all the major fronts immediately declared their unreserved support for the Soviet position on the issue. For example, when the Yom Kippur War broke out in 1973, all the fronts "denounced Israel within a period of a few days, often in exactly the same words," and demanded that "all public organizations in all countries launch a wide campaign in protest against the barbarous actions of the Israeli military." Given their reach and overtly neutral status, the fronts provided crucial infrastructure for Soviet international ideological offensives. Whatever the issue—Vietnam War, Angela Davis, the campaign to discredit

---

38 C. Unni Raja and Yevgeny Yevseyev, "Anatomy of Israeli Aggression," *World Marxist Review* 12, no. 4 (April 1969): 84–87.
39 Baruch A. Hazan, *Soviet Propaganda: A Case Study of the Middle East Conflict*, 1st ed. (New York: Routledge, 2018), 109–113.
40 Ibid., 111.

Aleksandr Solzhenitsyn—the fronts cooperated with one another and could count on "enthusiastic, friendly publicity in the entire Communist-oriented press throughout the world."[41]

When it came to coopting the Third World's political agenda, Moscow's primary tool was the Asian-African People's Solidarity Organization (AAPSO), which was born in 1957 as an offshoot of the World Peace Council. The group's main publication, the *Afro-Asian Bulletin*, consistently portrayed Israel as "a creation and tool of imperialism artificially implanted in Palestine to divide African, Arab and Asian peoples, subvert their quest for independence and penetrate their economies for Western capitalism," wrote Dave Rich.[42]

In January 1969, right before the Word Peace Council-AAPSO gathering in Cairo, the two groups jointly ran the International Conference in Support of the Peoples of the Portuguese Colonies and Southern Africa in Khartoum, Sudan. According to the *African Communist*'s coverage, it brought together 200 delegates from more than fifty countries, including India, Egypt, Cuba, Vietnam and the entire socialist bloc. Nasser, Indira Ghandi, and Kwame Nkrumah sent greetings. Leaders of all key Moscow-sponsored African liberation movements—the ANC, Mozambique's FRELIMO, Namibia's SWAPO, and Angolan MPLA—were there. So were the National Liberation Front of South Vietnam[43] and Fatah.[44]

Although the conference focused on colonialism and apartheid in Africa, the declaration it adopted included a condemnation of the "imperialist-backed Zionist aggression" against "the fraternal Arab peoples."[45] Speakers at the conference talked "of a global anti-imperialist struggle that included Palestine," and the ANC delegate accused Israel of providing direct support to the apartheid regime. Conference documents "repeatedly referenced" America's war in Vietnam, "enhancing the Soviet Union's status as the favored superpower in these circles" and associating it with the Palestinian struggle against "reactionary Zionism" and "Zionist aggressors."[46]

Among the delegates at both the Khartoum and Cairo conferences was a twenty-one-year-old British anti-apartheid activist, Peter Hellyer. A member of Young Liberals, the student wing of the British Liberal Party, which had been

---

41 Ibid., 113.
42 Rich, *The Left's Jewish Problem*, 51.
43 "Khartoum," *The African Communist* 37 (2nd quarter 1969): 13–14.
44 Rich, *The Left's Jewish Problem*, 58.
45 "Khartoum," 23.
46 Rich, *The Left's Jewish Problem*, 58.

"intimately involved in campaigning against South African apartheid,"[47] he "was enthralled by the presence of leaders from all the Southern African liberation movements."[48] It was at the Cairo conference, too, that he first established contacts with the PLO on behalf of Young Liberals.[49] After the two events, Hellyer "travelled to Lebanon and Jordan on a trip organized by the Arab League."[50] He went home convinced of the South Africa-Israel linkage and that Britain's "unthinking support for Israel" needed to be reassessed.[51] He would go on to become one of the most influential activists on the 1970s British pro-Palestinian scene, helping to turn Young Liberals into the first organization on the British left "to call for Zionists to be excluded from mainstream political structures."[52]

Another globe-trotting Brit in attendance at Khartoum was Scottish Labor MP Andrew Faulds.[53] Like Hellyer, Faulds came into the pro-Palestinian movement via anti-apartheid activism. Faulds was firmly in the British mainstream, working for the Palestinian cause as part of the Labor Committee for the Middle East, founded by another centrist (and anti-communist) Labour politician Christopher Mayhew. British scholar James Vaughan details how in the coming years Faulds teamed up with assorted leftist and Palestinian groups in London to shift the tide of British public opinion in favor of the Palestinian cause. Among other things, they attacked the BBC, which they viewed as having fallen victim to Zionist propaganda. A breakthrough came in 1976, when the BBC broadcast a program produced by Palestine Action and hosted by Faulds, with the then-chair of the Young Liberals, Peter Haine, making a guest appearance. Titled *The Right of Return*, one British newspaper described the program "the most extremist anti-Israel program ever shown on Western television." Fatah's Secretary General Farouk Kaddoumi proclaimed it "the best film he had ever seen on the Palestinian issue."[54]

They notched another success by drawing powerful British trade unions into the pro-Palestinian campaign. By the mid-1970s, high-level British labor delegations were traveling to Egypt and Lebanon.[55] (One person to go on such a trip

---

47   Rich, "Campus War, 1977," 257.
48   Rich, *The Left's Jewish Problem*, 58.
49   Rich, "Campus War, 1977," 257.
50   Rich, *The Left's Jewish Problem*, 60.
51   Ibid., 61.
52   Rich, "Campus War, 1977," 257.
53   "Khartoum," 14.
54   James Vaughan, "'Mayhew's Outcasts': Anti-Zionism and the Arab lobby in Harold Wilson's Labour Party," *Israel Affairs* 21, no. 1 (December 2014): 24–47.
55   Ibid., 9–10.

was George Galloway,[56] a Scottish politician who went on to establish and chair the Trade Union Friends of Palestine; he remains one of Britain's most vehement anti-Israel activists to date.)

It was this early 1970s mix of radicals and centrists that Vaughan credits with introducing the country to an enormously "influential" and "controversial" "new language of anti-Zionism," complete with racial themes, allegations that Israel was an apartheid state akin to South Africa, conspiracism and equations between Israel and Nazi Germany.[57] One of the people who "enthusiastically" adopted the equation between Zionists and Nazis was the future mayor of London Ken Livingstone, who filled his PLO- and Libya-supported newspaper, the *Labour Herald*, with anti-Israel demonization. In 2017 he would shock the British public by pontificating about Hitler's fondness for Zionists and otherwise creating a link between the Jewish national movement with the Nazis,[58] but these views had been part of his *Weltanschauung* since the early days of his political career.) This antizionist language would prove to be the group's legacy, but they, of course, did not invent it: They simply brought it back with them from Soviet-sponsored Third World, left-wing gatherings.

***

Within a few years, the global antizionist campaign put into motion by the Arab defeat in 1967 seemed to be unstoppable. A continuous flow of international events increasingly entrenched the idea of Zionism as the enemy of all progressive causes across the Third World/Western leftist universe.

Here are a few public events that took place in 1973 alone. That year, Soviet Zionologists—all of them associated with Soviet intelligence and state security apparatus, including Yevseyev and Mahmoud Abbas's future dissertation adviser Vladimir Kiselyov—participated in at least three "scientific" events on Zionism organized in the Middle East: two in Baghdad and one in Cairo. The first Baghdad event, which took place on March 25–30, was billed as a history conference dedicated to the exploration of Arab heritage in the Middle Ages. Yet, it included talks on "Zionism's colonialist essence" and on ways for Arabs to defeat "Israel's Zionist aggression." Its final resolution called upon Arab states to work jointly with global "forces of progress and liberation," in particular the

---

56 "The Trade Unions and Palestine," *Labour Herald*, April 30, 1982, 11.
57 Vaughan, "Mayhew's Outcasts," 14–18.
58 Paul Bogdanor, "Ken Livingstone and the Myth of Zionist 'Collaboration' with the Nazis," *Fathom*, Spring 2017, https://fathomjournal.org/ken-livingstone-and-the-myth-of-zionist-collaboration-with-the-nazis/.

socialist countries led by the Soviet Union, and to spare no effort in supporting the Palestinian revolution.

The second Baghdad conference of the year took place on April 21–26 under the title of "International Conference on the Problems of Israel and Zionism." In addition to condemning Israel, it praised the Israeli left for its "active role" in supporting "the national liberation struggle of the Arab peoples of Palestine" and its fight against imperialism, which helped undermine Israel's "Zionist ruling clique." At this conference Yevseyev delivered a talk titled "Middle East in Zionist and Imperialist Plans.[59] He delivered the same talk, in Arabic, in Cairo in June.[60]

In May of that year, Gaddafi organized an all-expenses-paid International Conference of European and Arab Youth in Tripoli, Libya. Among 200 delegates from fifty-five countries were some twenty young Brits, including members of the National Union of Students, who made contacts with London-based PLO- and Fatah-affiliated groups, marking the start of a long-term collaboration.[61]

The most consequential public antizionist Third World-ist event of 1973, though, was undoubtedly the massive, glitzy fourth Non-Aligned Summit, which met in Algiers in September. There, Israel and Zionism were condemned in anti-imperialist, anti-colonialist, anti-racist, and anti-Western terms[62] in front of fifty-four heads of state and delegates from seventy-five countries[63] representing a combined population of two billion.[64] (It was at this summit that Castro publicly, and unexpectedly, cut ties with Israel—apparently, to appease Libya's dictator Muammer Qaddafi, with whom he was having a quarrel.[65]) Among the

---

59 Galina Nikitina, "Mezhdunarodnaia konferentsiia po problemam Izrailia i sionizma" [International conference on the problems of Israel and Zionism], in *Mezhdunarodnyi sionizm: istoriia i politika* [International Zionism: History and politics], ed. V. I. Kiselev, G. S. Nikitina, and A. F. Fedchenko (Moscow: Nauka, 1977), 174–175.
60 Gennadii Kostyrchenko, *Tainaia politika: Ot Brezhneva to Gorbacheva* [Secret politics: From Brezhnev to Gorbachev], part 1: *Vlast'—Evreiskii vopros—intelligentsiia* [Power—the Jewish question—intelligentsia] (Moscow: Mezhdunarodnye otnosheniia, 2019), 513.
61 Rich, "Campus War, 1977," 256–257.
62 "4th Summit Conference of Heads of State or Government of the Non-Aligned Movement," Middlebury Institute of International Studies at Monterey, James Martin Center for Nonproliferation Studies, http://cns.miis.edu/nam/documents/Official_Document/4th_Summit_FD_Algiers_Declaration_1973_Whole.pdf.
63 Richard L. Jackson, *The Non-Aligned, the UN and the Superpowers* (London: Bloomsbury, 1987), 25–26. Note that estimates of the number of states attending vary. Robert Malley states that sixty-five states were in attendance (see next footnote).
64 Robert Malley, *The Call from Algeria: Third Worldism, Revolution, and the Turn to Islam* (Berkeley, CA: University of California Press, 1996), 144.
65 Jackson, *The Non-Aligned*, 26.

guests was also UN General Secretary Kurt Waldheim,[66] a former Nazi who had participated in the annihilation of the 2,000-year-old Jewish community of Salonica[67] and would preside, two years later, over the adoption of the UN "Zionism is racism" resolution. The summit "marked the beginning" of the Non-Aligned Movement "as a voting bloc within the United Nations and international agencies," observed a former US official. In its wake, US diplomats "lobbying among Third World delegations" for the first time found themselves "rebuffed with the explanation" that they could not go against positions they had committed to in Algiers.[68]

That fall, too, the UN General Assembly passed a resolution condemning "the unholy alliance between Portuguese colonialism, South African racism, Zionism and Israeli imperialism." Soon, more than thirty black African states had broken off relations with Israel, despite Israel's extensive track record of aid and collaborations with the Third World.[69]

And that was hardly all. At the July 1975 UN World Conference on the International Women's Year in Mexico City, a declaration "on the equality of women and their contribution to development and peace" called for the elimination of Zionism along with colonialism, neo-colonialism, apartheid, and racial discrimination.[70]

The following month, foreign ministers of Non-Aligned countries met in Lima, Peru, to denounce the United States and other "imperialists" for their support to Israel's "Zionist regime" and condemned their "deliberate intention" to use Israel as a "base of colonialism and imperialism within the Third World" and as a weapon against national-liberation movements—a policy that helped "consolidate racist regimes, threaten peace and security in the developing countries and plunder their natural resources."[71]

---

66 Ibid.
67 Bilge Ebiri, "Review: In 'The Waldheim Waltz,' a Nation Reckons with Its Nazi Past," *New York Times*, October 18, 2018, https://www.nytimes.com/2018/10/18/movies/the-waldheim-waltz-review.html.
68 Jackson, *The Non-Aligned*, 28.
69 Evelyn Sommer, "Fighting Delegitimization: The United Nations 'Zionism is Racism' Resolution, a Case Study," World Jewish Congress, https://www.worldjewishcongress.org/en/85th-anniversary/fighting-delegitimization-the-united-nations-zionism-is-racism-resolution-a-case-study.
70 Ibid.
71 "Excerpts from Communique Issued by the Lima Conference of Foreign Ministers of Nonaligned Countries," *New York Times*, April 31, 1975, https://www.nytimes.com/1975/08/31/archives/excerpts-from-communique-issued-by-the-lima-conference-of-foreign.html.

By the time the "Zionism is racism" resolution, lobbied through, shaped, and facilitated by Moscow, came up for vote at the United Nations in November 1975, two-thirds of the planet—the Third World and the socialist bloc—had turned against Israel in less than a decade.

It's reasonable to wonder what moved all these countries, with their disparate agendas and loyalties, to assume such a unified stance on Israel—a country that held zero real significance for most. Some undoubtedly did it out of ideological conviction, others out of Third World solidarity with the Arab states. But for many, purely political calculation came into play as well. The anti-Israel position proved to be a cost-free bargaining chip that could be traded for something valuable, such as Arab economic aid or Soviet support.

By the end of the decade, reflexive antizionism had become a litmus test of belonging and unity in the struggle on the global left. Meetings between Soviet and Third World officials in Moscow invariably concluded with pledges to fight "imperialism, Zionism and world reaction." At the Non-Aligned Summit in Havana in 1979, the incoming chair Fidel Castro mentioned Zionism five times, postulating it as one of the main obstacles to the aspirations of postcolonial countries and as a comprehensive enemy of peace.[72] It became a term of abuse, too, "hurled back and forth in various inter-state conflicts throughout the world." For example, during the Iran-Iraq war, Iraq's President Saddam Hussein accused Iran for having fallen victim to a "Zionist-imperialist conspiracy" which broke out in 1980, while the Iranians accused Iraq of acting on behalf and in the interests of "international Zionism" (a politically acceptable derivative of the "international Jewry" of *The Protocols of the Elders of Zion*, itself widely popularized by Soviet propaganda).[73]

***

The decline of the USSR in the end of the 1980s brought the Third World/Western left-wing ecosystem to a halt. Without Soviet money, ideological brainpower, and organizational muscle, it simply could not function. Lots of leftist publications went bankrupt, and lots of leftist careers ended or changed course right in the late 1980s–early 1990s. Robert Malley's communist father's Third World-trotting career ended in 1987. Angela Davis left CPUSA in 1991, a year

---

72 "Sixth Summit Conference of the Nonaligned Countries," Castro Speech Database, Latin American Network Information Center, University of Texas, http://lanic.utexas.edu/project/castro/db/1979/19790903.html.

73 Antony Lerman, "Fictive Anti-Zionism: Third World, Arab and Muslim Variations," in *Anti-Zionism and Anti-Semitism in Contemporary World*, ed. Robert S. Wistrich (New York: New York University Press, 1990), 130.

after Moscow cut off CPUSA's multi-million-dollar financial streams. There seems to have been little soul-searching in those quarters, however. On the contrary, many disapproved of the political changes in the USSR and waxed nostalgic about the past. And why wouldn't they? They all benefited personally and professionally from the money stolen from ordinary Soviet citizens and hardly even thought about it.

ANC's example is illustrative. In addition to comprehensive military training, the USSR provided members of the organization with scholarships to Soviet universities, treated its leaders at exclusive hospitals reserved for Kremlin honchos, and sent their children to the elite Artek summer camp in the Crimea. Ronnie Kasrils, the former leader of the ANC military wing who extolled Hamas's October 7 pogrom, admitted that it had never occurred to them that they were treated as "privileged visitors" and that ordinary Soviet people might live differently.[74] Years later, ANC's veterans still fondly recalled their Soviet experience. In their minds, the USSR had "belonged to them as much" as it had "to the Soviets themselves."[75]

Activists and intellectuals who came of age in the Soviet ecosystem parlayed their internationalist experience into successful academic, journalistic, and political careers, passing on their "anti-imperialism of idiots"[76] to the next generation of students and followers. There was never an imperative for them to rethink their ideas—and it isn't even clear that they could have, given their conditioning, nor necessarily wanted to.

Somehow, liberal America slept through all of it. Having won the Cold War, it didn't even bother to disarm and discredit the ideas it opposed, the way it had after it defeated Nazi Germany. Too many American intellectuals had been leftists or had leftist parents or had been fellow travelers with leftist causes to want to look too closely at the moral and physical rot of the empire that America defeated—a victory that moreover belonged to the archenemy of the American left, Ronald Reagan. Why give Reagan and his fellow anti-communists and troglodyte McCarthy-ites credit for having been right? Having acquired new academic positions, many went on to communicate their radical politics to the next generation: many of those who taught the next generations of students "became teachers precisely because they wanted to help form a new generation of Marxists, anti-capitalists, and anti-Americans," wrote Bruce Bauer in

---

74 Filatova and Davidson, *The Hidden Thread*, 498.
75 Filatova and Davidson, *The Hidden Thread*, 683.
76 Alan Johnson, "The Left and the Jews: Time for a Rethink," *Fathom*, Autumn 2015, https://fathomjournal.org/the-left-and-the-jews-time-for-a-rethink/.

The Victims' Revolution: The Rise of Identity Studies and the Birth of the Woke Ideology.[77] As this piece shows that brand of Marxism, anti-capitalism, and anti-Americanism had conspiracist antizionism baked into it.

That the left has held onto the Soviet language of in its antizionist pursuits, down to retaining the same stilted epithets, despite the collapse and disappearance of the Soviet Union is a testament to the disenchantment of Western liberals with what they should have remembered as a heroic and deeply meaningful struggle that rescued close to a billion people around the world from totalitarian slavery.

It also testifies to the enduring utility of antizionism as a political tool. Throughout the Cold War, this ideology helped unite political actors with agendas so different as to be virtually irreconcilable. It continues to do the same today. For the progressive left, embracing Hamas and Hezbollah has become a way to set in motion the revolution of their dreams but that would otherwise remain in the realm of their intellectual fantasy. For this generation, Hamas and Hezbollah are the equivalent of the national-liberation movements of yesteryear (Viet Cong, PLO, ANC). The mechanism that led them to romanticize and mythologize its leaders such as Yahya Sinwar is reminiscent of those that led their predecessors to romanticize Fidel, Che and Arafat.

In his classic *Political Pilgrims*, Paul Hollander asks: why did so many twentieth-century Western intellectuals fall for Stalin's USSR, Cuba, Vietnam, Nicaragua, and North Korea? How did these self-described "humanists" and "humanitarians" succeed at overlooking and excusing the "repression, corruption, social injustice" and "organized lying" staring them in the face? Like Bauer, Hollander notes, as one of the factors, the unexamined legacy of the 1960s, with its "revolutionary romanticism,"[78] "adversarial culture" vis-à-vis the West and feelings of alienation and estrangement from "American society," and "its major values and institutions."[79] But there were also plenty of personal interests and political agendas involved. The real citizens of these countries—their actual struggles, their longing for dignity and freedom—were irrelevant to this enlightened bunch, who had domestic friends and foes to impress, social ladders to climb, and new op-eds and books to publish and promote. They glommed on to

---

77 Bruce Bauer, *The Victims' Revolution: The Rise of Identity Studies and the Birth of the Woke Ideology* (New York: Bombardier Books, 2023), 68.
78 Paul Hollander, *Political Pilgrims: Western Intellectuals in Search of the Good Society* (New York: Routledge, 1997), xii.
79 Ibid., lxiv–lxxv.

totalitarian states' revolutionary rhetoric as a path toward fulfilling their professional and social ambitions.

All of these motivations undoubtedly play into today's leftist intellectuals' calculations as well. This generation of Western left is not the first to align itself with jihadists: the first signs of a budding Red-Green alliance began to form already in the last decade of the Cold War. But it is arguably the first generation of radical left that relies so fully on jihadists for its vitality and, arguably, its very future. Meanwhile, today's Iran, Hamas, and Hezbollah are just as successful at turning the left into their mouthpieces as Stalin, Castro and Arafat had done with their predecessors. In the same way as Cold War Western intellectuals "managed to ignore . . . the rising tide of revelations about the general malfunctioning" of socialist systems "and their intractable social problems,"[80] the anti-Israel left of today sweeps away revelations about Hamas's atrocities and the tyrannical and inhuman nature of its regime in the name of an anti-colonialist, anti-imperialist, anti-capitalist revolution that will finally give meaning to their lives. That these crude, immoral politics and ideology, shaped by illiberal, anti-Western, anti-democratic regimes with the blood of millions on their hands, are being presented to young Americans as the main paradigm to make sense of the world is a scandalous historical irony.

---

80 Ibid., lxxv.

Part 4

THE SOCIAL CONTRACT AND THE ELECTED GOVERNMENT

CHAPTER 14

Consensus and Polarization in the Israeli Party System in the Aftermath of October 7

Csaba Nikolenyi

Introduction

The Israeli political party system was undergoing its historically most prolonged crisis of governability when the Hamas terror group invaded, murdered over a thousand, and kidnapped hundreds of Israeli civilians and foreign nationals on October 7, 2023. The several-month-long crisis, which showed no sign of easing, stemmed from the ambitious political agenda of the right-religious coalition government that had come to power following the November 2022 general elections. Specifically, the incoming coalition government sought to change the existing balance of powers among the legislative, executive, and judicial branches of government by imposing serious checks on the authority of the latter. The attempted reforms led to a sustained large-scale popular mobilization as both opponents and proponents of the reform took to the streets in growing numbers. Notwithstanding repeated warnings by the security establishment about the broader security risks created by the societal and political malaise, the government was relentless in its determination to proceed with its reform agenda.

And then came October 7. One might have imagined that the government whose popularity had been already on a steady and deep decline over the previous months would have crumbled under the domestic and external pressures that were precipitated by Hamas's attack and its aftermath. Yet, the exact opposite transpired: not only did the coalition government manage to broaden its political base in the Knesset by forming a national emergency government but the coalition parties, and the prime minister in particular, also recovered some measure of their lost popularity as the country marked the one-year anniversary of the massacre and the war that followed. This chapter describes and analyzes the changes that took place in the Israeli party system during the first year after October 7. It argues that the right-religious coalition was able recover from its falling popularity by demonstrating unity, which involved a careful balancing between keeping coalition promises and delaying difficult decisions on issues that might have pitted the coalition partners against one another, while the opposition parties were characterized by lack of coordination as well as organizational and leadership instability. The chapter starts with a brief overview of the political background that had paved the way to the general elections of 2022. Next, it analyzes the party system and the nature of the coalition government that was formed after the polls. The third section traces the expansion of the coalition and the formation of the emergency government that lasted in office from October 2023 to June 2024. The fourth section reviews the organizational changes and leadership challenges that occurred in the opposition parties to show the contrast with the continued unity and stability of the parties in the coalition. The fifth section examines the changes in the popularity of political parties throughout the first year following October 7.

Background: Israel's Crisis of Governability, 2019–2022

One of the central functions of the party system in contemporary parliamentary democracies is to ensure the orderly formation and replacement of governments. However, between 2019 and 2021, Israeli parties failed to fulfill this function.[1] The April 2019 election resulted in a tie between Likud, the political party that formed and led every coalition government since 2009 under the leadership of its chairman Prime Minister Benjamin Netanyahu, and the Blue and White electoral alliance, led by former IDF Chief of Staff Benjamin (Benny) Gantz. The rules of Israeli government formation oblige the president of the state to consult with the newly elected Knesset party groups to determine which Knesset Member (MK) will have the most realistic chance to form a viable government and then to invite that MK to do so. Whereas Likud's leader was still

---

1 For a comprehensive overview of the elections and the state of the party system during this period, see Michal Shamir and Gideon Rahat, eds., *The Elections in Israel, 2019–2021* (New York: Routledge, 2023).

recommended by a combined majority of the party groups to form the new government, Netanyahu failed to form a coalition supported by a Knesset majority. Yet, instead of returning the government formation mandate to the president, which would have allowed Gantz to try and form an alternative government, Netanyahu convinced the Knesset majority to dissolve the legislature and order fresh elections.

While the September 2019 elections also failed to produce a new government, it took the third general election held in March 2020 at the outset of the COVID-19 pandemic for Israeli parties to form a national unity-national emergency government co-led by Netanyahu as prime minister and Gantz as alternate prime minister. According to the terms of the coalition agreement between the two sides, Netanyahu and Gantz were supposed to rotate their positions after two years.[2] However, the rotation never took place because the two leaders failed to agree on the new government's budget, leading to the collapse of the government a mere six months after its formation. The subsequent elections, held in March 2021, ushered in the formation of Israel's most complex coalition government of eight political parties co-led by Prime Minister Naftali Bennett and Alternate Prime Minister Yair Lapid. This coalition was also branded as a national unity government even though it explicitly excluded Likud, which was still able to win the most seats at the polls. The Bennett-Lapid government lasted a little more than a year in office before succumbing to the irreconcilable ideological and policy differences among its constituents, triggering yet another general election.

The Formation of Israel's Thirty-Seventh Government

The November 2022 polls seemed to bring the Israeli party system back to its pre-2019 course of normalcy. Likud formed an electoral coalition with three Jewish religious political formations (the Religious Zionist–Otzma Yehudit alliance and the ultra-Orthodox Shas and United Torah Judaism [UTJ]) that pledged to work together towards the formation of a right-religious coalition government led by Netanyahu. The four party groups won a combined majority of the Knesset seats, which made the post-election government formation a

---

2   Csaba Nikolenyi, "Government by Consensus? A Comparison of the Alignment–Likud (1984–1988) and the Likud–Blue and White (2020) National Unity Coalitions," in *Polarization and Consensus Building in Israel: The Center Cannot Hold*, ed. Elie Friedman, Michal Neubauer-Shani, and Paul Scham (New York: Routledge, 2020), 139–159.

predictable process. Indeed, Benjamin Netanyahu was tasked with the formation of the new government, which he successfully completed, allowing him to be sworn in at head of the Israel's thirty-seventh, and his own sixth, government on December 29, 2022.

In terms of its composition and size, the new government was a classic case of a minimal connected winning coalition.[3] Regarding the ideological and policy positions of the coalition members, all of Likud's partners represented Jewish religious Orthodoxy, which made the coalition extremely tight and the range of ideological views represented by its members very narrow.[4] As such, the new coalition government, which was widely claimed to be the most radical and extreme in Israel's political history, constituted a significant departure from the types of coalition governments that Prime Minister Netanyahu formed and led during his long career of political leadership. In the past, all the coalition governments led by Netanyahu were oversized majority coalitions including parties both to the left and to the right of Likud, which allowed the prime minister's party to remain the pivotal balancing player vis-à-vis its partners. The coalition that came to power after the 2022 elections, however, was different: as Table 1 shows, it was a minimum winning coalition in which each member was pivotal to the continuation of the coalition's majority status, i.e., 61 of the 120 seats in the Knesset, which in turn ensured that each coalition member had a powerful veto over government policy.

Table 1. The Composition of the Thirty-Seventh Israeli Government

Party	Number of Seats
Coalition	64
Likud	32
Shas	11
UTJ	7
Religious Zionists	8
Otzma Yehudit	6
Opposition	56
Yesh Atid	24

---

3   A minimum winning coalition is such that every member is essential to keeping coalition in a majority, i.e., winning.
4   It is important to stress that ideological proximity does not imply ideological unity. Indeed, there remain significant differences among the coalition partners on salient issues such as allowing women full participation in public life, or the military service by all young Jews, both of which the Religious Zionists embrace but the ultra-Orthodox oppose.

Party	Number of Seats
National Unity	12
Yisrael Beytenu	6
Hadash-Tal	5
Raam	5
Labor	4

The new government enjoyed only a brief political honeymoon in the eyes of the public. As early as January 2023, it rolled out its ambitious judicial reform package that sought to introduce major changes in the operation of the judicial establishment, most importantly the Supreme Court, as well as in the balance of the relationship between the legislature, the executive, and the courts.[5] More than any other question, it was the issue of the judicial reform that dominated public debate, eventually leading to weekly demonstrations of a growing number of protestors against the government's agenda and, in smaller numbers and with less frequency, in favor of it. In addition to the "Israeli street," the judicial reform debate mobilized the usually apolitical office of the head of state, as President Isaac Herzog tried to mediate between the government and the opposition, even presenting his own compromise formula that might placate the two sides.[6] The debates also spilled over into the realm of national security, as a growing number of both active and reserve duty military officers and soldiers called for refusal to serve in reaction to what they claimed to be the government's attack on the fundamentals of Israeli democracy.[7] When Yoav Gallant, then minster of defense, publicly called for the suspension of the judicial reform process in March 2023 on grounds that it was undermining national security, the prime minister fired, but quickly reinstated, him after major demonstrations.[8]

---

5 Yaniv Roznai, Rosalind Dixon, and David E. Landau, "Judicial Reform or Abusive Constitutionalism in Israel," *Israel Law Review* 56, no. 3 (2023): 292–304, https://doi.org/10.1017/S0021223723000171; Ittai Bar-Siman-Tov, "Judicial Review in Israel: Typology, Developments and the Theory and Practice of Judicial Activism," SSRN, April 3, 2024, https://ssrn.com/abstract=4782873; Joshua Segev, "The 2023 Judicial Reform That Wasn't: From Non-Decision Constitution-Making to Decision and Back," *Israel Studies Review* 39, no. 1 (2024): 38–65, https://doi.org/10.3167/isr.2024.390103.
6 "'A Golden Path': After Weeks-Long Effort, President Debuts Overhaul Compromise Offer," *Times of Israel*, March 15, 2023, https://www.timesofisrael.com/a-golden-path-after-weeks-long-effort-president-debuts-overhaul-compromise-offer/.
7 Guy Ziv, *Netanyahu vs. The Generals: The Battle for Israel's Future* (Cambridge: Cambridge University Press, 2024), 82–84.
8 Ibid., 85. Also see "Netanyahu Fires Defense Minister Gallant for Calling to Stop Judicial Overhaul," *Haaretz*, March 26, 2023, https://www.haaretz.com/israel-news/2023-03-26/

Public opinion polls consistently reflected the steady slippage of the government's popularity as the reform debates were raging. Figure 1 shows that by late February 2023 the coalition had already "lost its majority" according to the weekly public opinion polls conducted by the *Maariv* newspaper that asked Israeli respondents which party that would vote for if the general elections were on the day of the survey. The judicial reform debates were particularly damaging to Likud's popularity, as the party was gradually ceding its plurality status to National Unity, an alliance of Benny Gantz's Blue and White and former Likud stalwart Gideon Sa'ar's New Hope party, which had gradually surpassed Yesh Atid as the largest opposition party in the eyes of the respondents (see Figure 2). Interestingly, the ultra-Orthodox members of the coalition (Shas and UTJ) were able to maintain the same seat shares they won in the general election, while the Otzma Yehudit and Religious Zionist parties suffered a mild decline. The single most severe losses of popularity were incurred by the Labor Party, which was consistently projected after May 2023 not to win any seats in the Knesset. In its stead, respondents awarded projected Knesset representation to the more radical Meretz, hovering between four to five seats in the weekly polls.

Is it necessary to mention that, in the past, relatively strong political parties had enough power to rein in leaders—even prime ministers—Ben Gurion on Lavon, even Eshkol on eve of war in 1967. Countless examples exist of a strong Herut-Likud performing the same function in the past with respect to Begin. In 2023, parties on left and right had been hollowed out—for different reasons. But the legal system stood as a break—a check on political power deemed illegal. Legal reform would have weakened the only check on party coalition politics today.

National Emergency Government after the Hamas Massacre

For a brief period in the immediate aftermath of the October 7 attacks there appeared to be convergence between government and opposition regarding the enlargement of the incumbent coalition and forming a more broadly based

---

ty-article/netanyahu-fires-defense-minister-gallant-for-calling-to-stop-judicial-overhaul/00000187-1f31-d4ca-afff-1f39e2be0000. Four days later, the prime minister rescinded his decision, and Gallant remained in office.

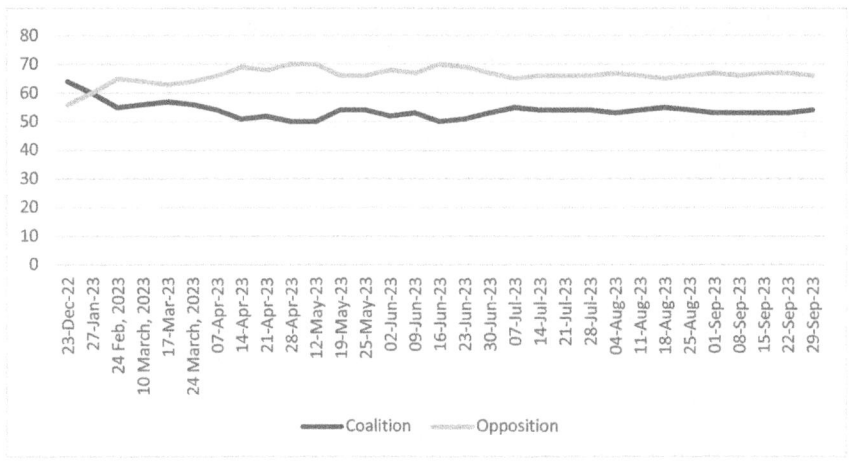

Figure 1. Projected seat shares of the coalition and the opposition, December 2022–September 2023.

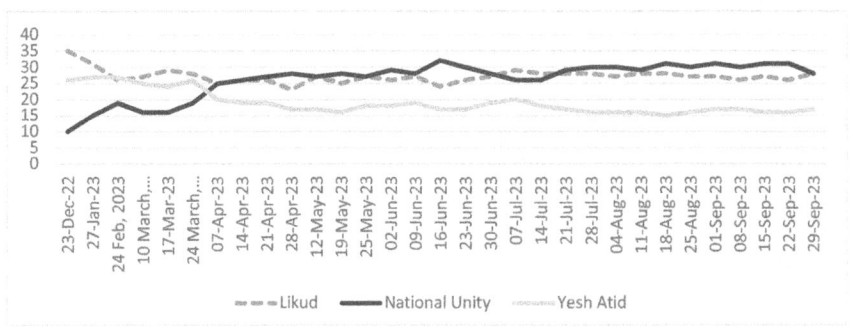

Figure 2. Projected seat shares of the three largest parties, December 2022–September 2023.

national emergency government. In a coordinated joint release, the leaders of the four Jewish opposition parties (Yesh Atid, National Unity, Yisrael Beitenu, and Labor) stated that "[w]e are all united against terror and must strike it with a firm and determined hand . . . In days like these, there is no opposition and coalition in Israel. We will give full backing to security forces to respond forcefully against terror and its proxies."[9] Indeed, the formation of such a government was especially crucial to ensure that the difficult decisions that the government

---

9   Lahav Harkov, "Israel Forms Emergency Unity Government as Netanyahu, Lapid, and Gantz Join Forces," *Jewish Insider*, October 8, 2023, https://jewishinsider.com/2023/10/israel-emergency-unity-government-netanyahu-lapid-gantz/.

would have to make conducting the war will be anchored in inter-party consensus reflecting and representing the broadest possible spectrum of the population. Yet, in the light of the heightened levels of polarization that plagued Israeli political life for the past five years, and especially so since the recently elected government embarked on its judicial reform package, it was very difficult to imagine how political parties in the opposite camps would actually overcome their deeply seated animosities and let political rivalry be replaced by compromise if not consensus. Still, in the afternoon of the attacks on October 7, the leader of the opposition, Yair Lapid, publicly stressed the urgency of forming an emergency government indicating his interest in making it happen, and Prime Minister Netanyahu duly followed up and met with the leaders of the two largest party groups in the parliamentary opposition in order to discuss the prospect of their participation in the government.

Netanyahu's position regarding the prospect of an enlarged emergency government was based on lessons from Israeli political history. His administration argued that such a government would have to follow the model of the national unity government that was formed at the time of the Six-Day War in 1967. On that occasion, Menachem Begin, who was leader of the opposition at the time, famously lent his support to Levi Eshkol's Labor-Alignment-led government, against which it had bitterly contested every single national election in the past. The replication of this precedent, however, was extremely unlikely in the context of the deeply polarized party-political landscape of 2024. At the time of the Six Day War, Begin's Gahal alliance was a new entity in the Israeli party system whose very formation indicated the gradual moderation in the political orientation of the radical right-wing Herut party.[10] Herut was seeking to move closer to the center of the Israeli party space in order to overcome its marginalization, delegitimization, and systematic exclusion from all prior coalition governments.[11] By entering the emergency government in 1967, Gahal gained important experience as being part of the nation's political leadership, and its leader, Begin, earned reputation for a statesmanship in a time of national exigency.[12]

---

10 Gahal was formed in 1965 as an electoral coalition of the right-wing Herut and the centrist Liberal Party. Eventually, it would become a single unified party under the Likud label. See Yehiam Weitz, "The Road to the Upheaval: A Capsule History of the Herut Movement, 1948–1977," *Israel Studies* 10, no. 3 (2005): 54–86.

11 Ben Gurion had famously stated that he would form a coalition with any political party, with the exception of Maki, the Communist Party, and Herut. See Ariel Levite and Sidney Tarrow, "The Legitimation of Excluded Parties in Dominant Party Systems: A Comparison of Israel and Italy," *Comparative Politics* 15, no. 3 (1983): 295–327.

12 Incidentally, it was exactly for this reason that Golda Meir feared and was steadfast opposed to including Gahal in the unity government. Weitz, "The Road to the Upheaval."

In stark contrast, the leader of the opposition in 2024 had no incentive to enter the emergency government on just any term offered. Unlike Gahal, which had won barely more than half of the seats that Mapai commanded in 1965 election, Yesh Atid was significantly stronger in relation to Likud as the party won twenty-four seats compared to Likud's thirty-two in the 2022 Knesset election. Moreover, Yesh Atid had already participated in several previous governments and its leader, Yair Lapid, even served as both alternate prime minister and subsequently interim prime minister after the 2021 elections. Due to these differences, Yesh Atid could demand significant concessions in exchange for entering an emergency government, which rendered the 1967 model inapplicable. Indeed, Yesh Atid stated that it would participate in a "reduced, professional, emergency government," which meant the exclusion of the two more radical members of the coalition, the Religious Zionist and Otzma Yehudit.[13] This demand effectively sought to give Yesh Atid a pivotal role and veto power in the emergency government, a condition that was evidently unacceptable to Likud.

Other opposition parties had different perspectives. Yisrael Beitenu's condition to enter an emergency government was driven by policy; the party asserted that the elimination of both the organization and the leadership of Hamas must be recognized as an explicit objective of the war. The Labor Party also maintained its support for the government's war effort but did not show any interest in joining the government. Finally, National Unity was the only Jewish opposition party that did not make its entry conditional either on a radical change in the composition of the government or the government's war objectives. Instead, the party asked that it should be given a genuine and credible opportunity to influence government decisions during the war, especially regarding decisions that pertained directly to the management of the war effort.

The broadening of the government's parliamentary base was also supported by the different members of the coalition. In addition to several senior lawmakers in the prime minister's Likud party, who echoed their leader's desire to expand the government, the ultra-Orthodox Shas as well as the Religious Zionists declared their unwavering support. The attitude of Otzma Yehudit to an emergency government was more lukewarm as the party publicly blamed the senior former members of the security establishment and the armed forces, including Gantz,

---

13   Carrie Keller-Lynn and Jeremy Sharon, "Lapid Urges Emergency Government, Says PM Can't Manage War with Extreme Cabinet," *Times of Israel*, October 7, 2023, https://www.timesofisrael.com/lapid-urges-emergency-government-says-pm-cant-manage-war-with-extreme-cabinet/.

the leader of National Unity, for the evident lack of preparedness in the defenses of the state on October 7.[14]

It took all but four days for an eventual agreement to be hammered out and include National Unity in a newly enlarged emergency government.[15] The agreement, which was signed on October 11, stipulated that the emergency government was not going to advance any legislation that was not related to the war effort and that it would make only such decisions and appointments that served that overall objective. This clause ensured that National Unity would not become a "fig leaf" which the religious-right coalition members could use to cover up the continued progression of their legislative programs including judicial reform. The agreement also addressed Gantz's demand that his party should be given credible opportunities to influence government decisions. Specifically, it awarded National Unity five ministerial positions, all without portfolio, in the emergency government, with four of them assuming full membership and one with observer status in the national security cabinet. The five members who represented the party in the emergency government came from the top leadership of the two constituent parties of National Unity: Benny Gantz, Gadi Eizenkot, and Hili Troper from Blue and White; and Gideon Saar and Yifat Shasha-Biton from New Hope. Furthermore, the agreement stipulated that there would be the formation of a smaller war cabinet of three members consisting of the prime minister, the minister of defense, and Benny Gantz, with two additional members (Gadi Eizenkot and Ron Dermer, the government's minister for strategic affairs) serving as observers. Finally, the parties agreed that while the inclusion of additional parties in the government would require the mutual consent of both the prime minister and Benny Gantz, a seat in the war cabinet would be left vacant for Yair Lapid, leader of opposition, without conditions, should he wish to join the government.

The formal enlargement of the government required confirmation by the Knesset, which was granted at an evening plenary session on October 12. Although the addition of the new ministers was easily passed with a sixty-six to four margin, the lack of enthusiasm on the part of the opposition parties was

---

14   Ariel Kahana, "Gormim bekhirim: 'Im ha-memshela lo timotet et Ḥamas—nifrosh" [Senior officials: "If the government doesn't topple Hamas—we will withdraw"], *Israel Hayom*, October 11, 2023, https://digital-edition.israelhayom.co.il/israel-hayom/20231011.
15   Dvir Jabara, "Me-iḥud le-shefel: Toledot memshelet ha-ḥerum me-kenisat Gantz ve-'ad ha-'aziva" [From unity to decline: The history of the emergency government from Gantz's entry to his departure], N12, https://www.mako.co.il/news-politics/2024_q2/Article-1461c7b3db7df1026.htm?Partner=searchResults.

evident. Yair Lapid specifically noted that while his party would not oppose the formation of the emergency government, three specific reasons prevented Yesh Atid from entering it: "the persistence of 'extremists' in the hardline government, a double security cabinet structure without clear lines of authority, and the presence of those at fault for the 'failure' to prevent Saturday's crushing Hamas massacre, which triggered the war."[16] The leader of the opposition further argued that Gantz was making a strategic mistake by agreeing to the conditions that formed the basis of the newly expanded government. On the one hand, Gantz and Eizenkot were in a clear minority in the war cabinet against the prime minister and his two Likud ministers. Even though the minister of defense, Yoav Galant, could be expected from time to time to side with his former military colleagues, party discipline would constrain him to toe the line set by the prime minister, his immediate superior. At the same time, Gantz's National Unity party was also in a clear minority position within both the national security cabinet and in the overall coalition.

In Lapid's view, the double minority that was imposed on National Unity clearly prevented the party and its leader from making any kind of meaningful and substantive impact om the direction of the war effort, which was the very reason for their agreement to join the emergency government. From Gantz's perspective, however, this double minority was well worth the price if he was going to be able to turn his efforts at helping direct the war into an electoral gain.

With the swearing of the National Unity ministers, the formation of the emergency government was complete and the parliamentary opposition quickly renewed its attacks against it.[17] Responding to a public sparring between Prime Minister Netanyahu and Benny Gantz about the responsibility of the security establishment for the October 7 massacre, Yair Lapid openly called to remove Netanyahu from office and to form a "national reconstruction government" led by the Likud and including National Unity, Yisrael Beitenu, and the

---

16 Carrie Keller-Lynn, "Knesset Okays War Cabinet; PM: Saturday 'most horrible day for Jews since Holocaust,'" *Times of Israel*, October 12, 2023, https://www.timesofisrael.com/knesset-okays-war-cabinet-pm-saturday-most-horrible-day-for-jews-since-holocaust/.

17 Soon thereafter, a public exchange took place between Likud and Avigdor Lieberman, with the former announcing the addition of Yisrael Beitenu to the coalition and the latter denying it. See Yehuda Shlezinger, "Ha-Likud hodi'a she-Liberman mitztaref le-memshela, yo"r Yisrael Beitenu: 'Mukhan leitztaref rak le-kabinet ha-milḥama'" [Likud announced that Lieberman joins the government; leader of Yisrael Beitenu: "I am only ready to join the war cabinet"], *Israel Hayom*, October 15, 2023, https://digital-edition.israelhayom.co.il/israel-hayom/20231015.

ultra-Orthodox parties.[18] Reiterating his central message in all the previous election campaigns since 2019, Lapid stressed that the removal of Prime Minister Netanyahu from public office was the single most important objective around which he wanted to form this alternative coalition. It was evident that even in the face of the war against Hamas, the same polarizing tendencies that had brought the party system to an impasse between 2019 and 2021 would prevail over the need for national unity and consensus.

Internal divisions within the governing coalition emerged quickly and led to particularly divisive infighting over the passage of the supplementary budget in December. While there was general agreement that the war required the addition of twenty-nine billion NIS to the government expenditures, the allocation of large sums of funds to ministries that were controlled by Likud's smaller coalition partners and had seemingly little to nothing to do with the war effort led to a deep division between an alliance of ministers from National Unity and Likud, whose departments were sidelined in the allocation of the new budgetary outlays, and the rest of the coalition. Table 2 shows the increases, and deductions, of funds which generated particularly bitter public scrutiny and debate. The main issue had to do with the diversion of public funds at the critical time of the war, whose cost were escalating by the day, to keep the ministries and projects of the coalition partners afloat. Although the supplementary budget was eventually passed with a fifty-nine to forty-five margin on December 14, it did so without the support of the National Unity members and against the abstention of two senior Likud politicians, Gila Gamliel and Yuli Edelstein.[19]

---

18 Carrie Keller-Lynn, "Lapid Calls on Netanyahu to Quit, Says Government Isn't Functioning during War," *Times of Israel*, November 15, 2023, https://www.timesofisrael.com/lapid-calls-on-netanyahu-to-quit-says-government-isnt-functioning-during-war/.

19 For a comprehensive overview of the recent budget debate, see Dvir Jabara, "Lifnei ha-ishur ba-memshela: Tza'akot be-yeshiva al ha-taktziv ha-metukan" [Before government approval: Shouting in the meeting on the amended budget], N12, November 28, 2023, https://www.mako.co.il/news-politics/2023_q4/Article-973838b6ec41c81026.htm; "Barkat heḥ'riyim et ha-hatzba'a, Gantz hitnaged—ve-ha-taktziv ha-metukan avar be-kri'a rishona" [Barkat boycotted the vote, Gantz opposed—and the amended budget passed first reading], N12, December 6, 2023, https://www.mako.co.il/news-politics/2023_q4/Article-c84c6746f5e3c81026.htm; "Ha-Knesset ishra et taktziv 2023 ha-me'udkan ha-kolel ka-5 miliard shekalim be-khassafim koalitzioni'im" [The Knesset approved the updated 2023 budget including about 5 billion shekels in coalition funds], N12, December 14, 2023, https://www.mako.co.il/news-money/2023_q4/Article-971a2ecd9b76c81026.htm; and "Following Rancorous Debate, Knesset Passes Amended Wartime Budget," *Times of Israel*, March 13, 2024, https://www.timesofisrael.com/following-rancorous-debate-knesset-passes-amended-wartime-budget/; Carrie Keller-Lynn, "NIS 29 Billion Wartime Budget Boost Passes amid Outcry over Funds for Non-War Needs," *Times of Israel*, March 14, 2024, https://www.timesofisrael.com/nis-29-billion-wartime-budget-boost-passes-amid-outcry-over-funds-for-non-war-needs/.

Table 2. Selected Details of the December 2023 Supplementary Budget

Ministry (party of minister in charge)	Previous budget (in millions of NIS)	Supplementary 2023 budget (in millions of NIS)
Ministry of Jerusalem and Tradition (UTJ)	24	68
Ministry of Heritage (JP)	74	101
Ministry of National Missions (RZ)	133	343
Ministry for the Empowerment of Women (Likud)	3.5	14
Ministry of Regional Cooperation (Likud)	22	38
Ministry of Diaspora Affairs (Likud)	56	91
Ministry of Science and Technology (Likud)	25	22

As the war unfolded, a widening gulf developed between the government and some of the opposition parties regarding the objectives that the armed forces should prioritize and pursue. At the outset, the emergency government had set two specific war objectives for the IDF: a) to destroy Hamas's military capability and b) to free and return the hostages home to their families. Although the government did not formally prioritize between these objectives, the senior leadership of the government seemed convinced that success on the former objective would bring about success on the latter. The opposition, however, was divided on this issue. The conservative Yisrael Beitenu agreed with the government's pursuit of these objectives; however, both Yesh Atid and the Labor Party argued that Israeli society needed to heal and that such a national healing was impossible unless the release of the hostage was given utmost priority no matter the price to pay. The growing frustration in the opposition benches led Labor Party leader Merav Michaeli to submit a motion of no-confidence, the first since the outbreak of the war, against the government. Michaeli argued that "[s]ince October 7th, we have refrained from this step, but it has been 108 days during which we have seen the government involving itself in everything else, in removing the national spokesman, in passing a corrupt budget, in embarrassing leaks from Cabinet meetings. Everything but the hostages. For that reason, we have decided to file a vote of no confidence today, on the grounds that the hostages have not yet been recovered."[20] The motion failed, as it attracted the support of

---

20 "Knesset Votes on No-Confidence Motion against Netanyahu," *Israel National News*, January 22, 2024, https://www.israelnationalnews.com/news/383999; Sam Sokol, "No-Confidence

only eighteen MKs, yet it was an important signal to indicate the end of a brief spell of war-time political unity.

The emergency government proved to be highly unstable and within eight months National Unity had left it entirely. The party's exit from the coalition occurred in two stages. The first occurred in March 2023, when Gideon Sa'ar took his New Hope faction from the National Unity alliance and established it as an independent Knesset party group.[21] Sa'ar claimed that his exclusion from the war cabinet prevented him and his party from having a meaningful impact on the government's war policy. Since National Unity was technically an electoral alliance of two distinct political parties, Sa'ar felt that his demand to be included in the war cabinet on equal terms with Gantz was justified and it would better reflect the partisan composition of the emergency coalition. Otherwise, New Hope was simply lending its legislative weight in support of the government without receiving anything in exchange.[22] A little over two months later, the rump National Unity followed suit. Increasingly frustrated with his inability to shape the war effort in the war cabinet, Benny Gantz issued a public ultimatum to the prime minister demanding that Netanyahu provide a clear vision for the timeline and aftermath of the war by June 8.[23] The latter's refusal to do so prompted Gantz and the remaining National Unity ministers, Eizenkot and Tropper, to resign, thus ending the emergency government.

In a surprising postscript, Gideon Sa'ar later decided to take his New Hope back into the coalition in September 2023 seemingly without any demands or preconditions. The inclusion of New Hope did not constitute another emergency government but was an ordinary expansion of the incumbent coalition. Although the prime minister reportedly offered Sa'ar the position of minister of defense, he declined and entered the government without even a coalition agreement. Thus, by the eve of the first anniversary of the massacre, Netanyahu's

---

Motion Against Netanyahu Fails in Knesset, with Only 18 Votes in Favor," *The Times of Israel*, January 22, 2024, https://www.timesofisrael.com/no-confidence-motion-against-netanyahu-fails-in-knesset-with-only-18-votes-in-favor/.

21 Carrie Keller-Lynn, "Sa'ar Splits from Gantz's National Unity Party, Demands Seat in War Cabinet," *Times of Israel*, February 1, 2024, https://www.timesofisrael.com/saar-splits-from-gantzs-national-unity-party-demands-seat-in-war-cabinet/.

22 "Gideon Sa'ar Joins Netanyahu Government as Minister Without Portfolio," *Jerusalem Post*, September 29, 2024, https://www.jpost.com/breaking-news/article-822418.

23 Sam Sokol, "Gantz Quits War Government, Says PM Preventing 'True Victory' over Hamas, Urges Elections," *Times of Israel*, June 9, 2024, https://www.timesofisrael.com/urging-elections-gantz-quits-wartime-government-accuses-pm-of-botching-war-effort/.

coalition had become larger, the opposition had become weaker and the prime minister's most radical coalition partner, Otzma Yehudit, had lost its blackmail power withing the government.

The State of the Opposition: Organizational Instability and Leadership Change

The ability of the opposition parties to apply effective pressure on the government was significantly hampered by their internal challenges and instabilities as well. The first such change was the historic leadership primaries held by Yesh Atid in March 2024. Since its foundation in 2013, the party has been led by its founding leader, Yair Lapid, who has consistently rejected demands for the establishment of internal democracy within the party by allowing its members to have a say in choosing the party leader. However, the party's stagnation in the public opinion polls not only showed its inability to capitalize on the massive security failure that had taken place on October 7 under the Likud-led government's watch, but it also revealed its leader's security deficit. In contrast to National Unity, which was led by a former IDF chief of staff, Yesh Atid's leader could not boast of any security or military credentials, which was seen as a significant liability at the time of national exigency. Lapid's challenger for party leadership was Ram Ben-Barak, former deputy director of Mossad, who came very close to defeating Lapid, but the incumbent eventually prevailed with a narrow margin of 29 votes in the party's 723-member electoral college.[24]

The leadership change in the Labor Party was much more profound. The incumbent party chairperson, Merav Michaeli, had already indicated her decision to stand down and not seek another term at the helm of the party in May 2023. Her decision to do so was driven by the party's devastating electoral performance under her leadership in the November 2022 elections as well as its inability to make any gains in the subsequent public opinion polls. Michaeli's demise was further evinced by her three colleagues' decision in the Labor Party

---

24 For details on the Yesh Atid leadership election and party regulations, see "Terms for Chairman of Yesh Atid Party," Yesh Atid, last modified March 2024, https://yeshatid.org.il/terms-chairman-yesh-atid-party; and "Candidates for the Position of Party Chairman," Yesh Atid, last modified March 2024, https://yeshatid.org.il/candidates-for-the-position-of-party-chairman.

Knesset faction to force her to share decision-making power with them.[25] In short, Michaeli had already lost effective command of the party well before the outbreak of the massacre and the war that followed.

The Labor leadership primaries were extremely unusual: although four candidates stepped forward to seek elections, none of them came from among the well-known stalwarts of the party. Three of them had no major legislative or electoral experience, and each of them secured less than 2% of the votes cast in the internal polls. The fourth candidate, Yair Golan, was well known in Israeli politics both as a former candidate for the position of IDF chief of staff in 2015 as well as an MK on behalf of the Meretz party between 2019 and 2022. Golan, however, had not been a Labor member and had to join the party specifically to seek the party leadership. Golan's central objective was the consolidation of the progressive left-of-center forces in the Israeli party system under one banner and in one party which, effectively meant the amalgamation of Labor and Meretz. It is important to stress that Michaeli specifically rejected this type of coordination with Meretz at the time of the November 2022 elections. Eventually, Golan swept the polls and won the Labor leadership with 95.15% of the votes in his favor.[26] A month later he successfully implemented the merger of the two parties under the new name The Democrats.[27]

Changes in Party Popularity during the War

As mentioned earlier, the governing coalition was already suffering from a deep decline in its popularity because of the paralyzing public debate about the judicial reform. Figure 3 shows that, by the eve of the Hamas massacre, the coalition had indeed lost its projected Knesset majority according to the weekly polls conducted by *Maariv*. With small fluctuations over the course of the next several months, the relative gains that the opposition had made vis-à-vis the coalition would remain consistent. It is interesting to note that the steepest weekly changes in both the coalition's and the opposition's projected

---

25 Shalom Yerushalmi, "Labor MKs Seek to Replace Leader Michaeli, Claim Party's Future Depends on It," *Times of Israel*, April 17, 2023, https://www.timesofisrael.com/labor-mks-seek-to-replace-leader-michaeli-claim-partys-future-depends-on-it/.
26 Hezki Baruch, "Yair Golan Wins Labor Party Leadership Primaries: We Will Advance," Israel National News, May 29, 2024, https://www.israelnationalnews.com/news/390721.
27 Hezki Baruch, "Labor and Meretz Announce a Merger; Will Be Known as the United Left," Israel National News, June 30, 2024, https://www.israelnationalnews.com/news/392341.

seats shares were registered in response to the formation of the emergency government, which, as we saw earlier, included National Unity, one of the principal opposition parties.

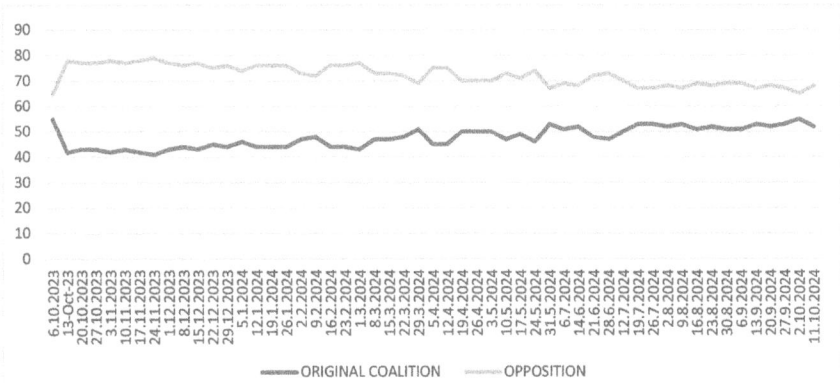

Figure 3. Poll predictions of the coalition vs opposition seat shares since the start of the Hamas War.

Figure 4 provides a more detailed comparison of the projected seat shares of the coalition members. It shows that Likud was unable to recover the loss that it suffered during the initial weeks after the massacre. Although the party remained consistently the largest member of the coalition in terms of the projected seat shares, it lost its majority within the coalition throughout the entire period. In stark contrast, the two ultra-Orthodox parties seemed almost unaffected by the national turmoil: both UTJ and Shas were able to maintain the same number of seats they won in the 2022 election in every weekly poll. The biggest changes were registered by the Religious Zionists and Otzma. Whereas the former was the larger of the two in the electoral alliance they had formed in the 2022 Knesset election, that relationship was quickly reversed in the weeks after the massacre. Not only was Otzma projected to win more seats than the Religious Zionists in every weekly poll after November 3, 2023, but the latter was actually projected to miss the electoral threshold altogether in several polls. Furthermore, Otzma also became the second largest member of the coalition, in several weekly polls it received even more seats than Shas. Considering that the Sephardi ultra-Orthodox party had entered the Knesset after the 2022 elections with almost twice as many seats (eleven) as Otzma (six), the evident increase in the latter's popularity was striking. Given the party's radical ideological outlook and policy position, it also lent growing evidence to the claim that the original coalition was moving steadily to the right as the war dragged on. In that light, the inclusion of National Unity in the emergency coalition was exactly the kind of balancing act that Netanyahu had practiced on so many occasions before in his political career.

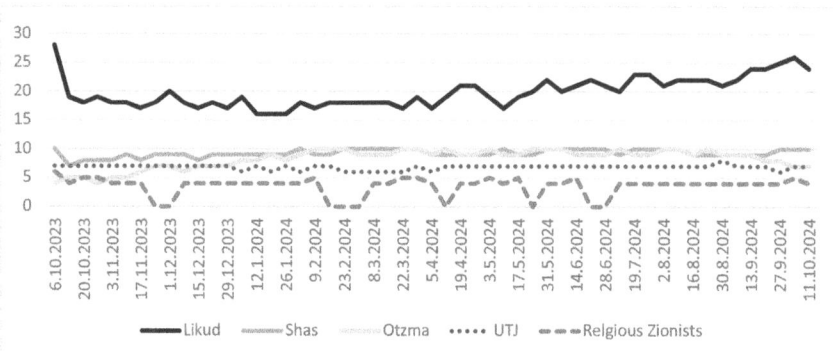

Figure 4. Poll predictions of the coalition parties' seat shares since the Hamas War.

A similarly dramatic transformation took place among the opposition parties. Although Yesh Atid started out as the largest opposition party after the general elections, it had been overtaken by National Unity as early as March 2023. The gap between the two former allies continued to grow and widen at Yesh Atid's expense in the aftermath of the war, in some weeks National Unity was even projected to win twice as many seats as Yesh Atid. A further piece of evidence showing the expected electoral slippage of Yesh Atid was the rise of Yisrael Beitenu, which was forecast to overtake it in several weekly polls towards the first anniversary of the massacre. By far the most pronounced change was the gradual decline of National Unity; after a stable projected performance until March 2024, the party went into a nosedive in March 2024 following its split and the exit of Gideon Sa'ar's New Hope party from the emergency coalition. The slippage of National Unity was further accelerated in June 2024 in the wake of Benny Gantz's decision to exit the government altogether.

Like the projected strengthening of the more radical elements within the original coalition, the opposition also underwent a process of radicalization: as the centrist National Unity and Yesh Atid were losing ground, the more radical parties of the left (Labor and Meretz) were projected to make significant gains. As mentioned earlier, one of the major challenges facing the Labor Party under Merav Michaeli's leadership was the question of cooperation with Meretz.

Although Labor's decision not to form an electoral alliance with its more radical former ally might have been part of the reason Meretz failed to cross the electoral threshold on its own, by the time of the Hamas massacre, it was Meretz and not Labor that was projected to win parliamentary representation. In fact, it was not until May 2024 that Labor was reported to have regained sufficient popularity to win the bare minimum of four seats in the Knesset and it was not until after Yair Golan's sweeping victory in the Labor leadership primaries that the newly launched Democrats emerged with a projected seat share that more than doubled what Labor had won in 2022. In short, according to the polls, left-wing voters in Israel rewarded the growing radicalization of Labor under its new leadership marked by the consolidation of its alliance with Meretz.

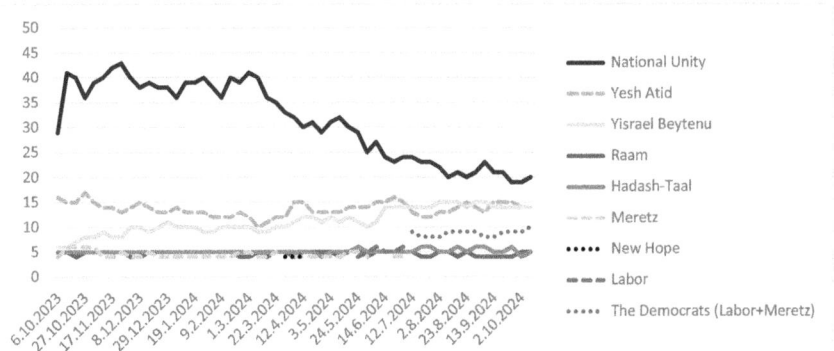

Figure 5. Poll predictions of opposition parties' seat shares since the Hamas War.

All in all, with the passage of time, Netanyahu and his coalition were gradually regaining their popularity in the eyes of the public. Figure 6 documents how Likud's projected seat shares eventually caught up with National Unity's by July 2024. Thereafter the two parties were shown in a tight neck-to-neck rivalry; however, from September onwards the large governing party consistently polled more seats than National Unity. Although Likud was never projected to win fewer seats than Yesh Atid, its advantage over the largest opposition party had grown sizably by the summer and kept growing thereafter. Likud's rebounding was further reinforced by polls that compared respondents' assessment of Prime Minister Netanyahu's suitability for being the heads of government with other leaders. In these polls, Netanyahu consistently outperformed both Yair Lapid, the leader of the opposition, and Avigdor Lieberman, the leader of Yisrael Beitenu. In the first half of September 2024, he polled less support than Naftali

Bennet; however, he quickly recovered by its edge by the end of the month. Unsurprisingly in the light of the seat projections, Netanyahu's chief rival for leadership was Benny Gantz throughout the war. However, Gantz's advantage also started to narrow after his decision to exit the government, and by the fall of 2024 it had all but disappeared.

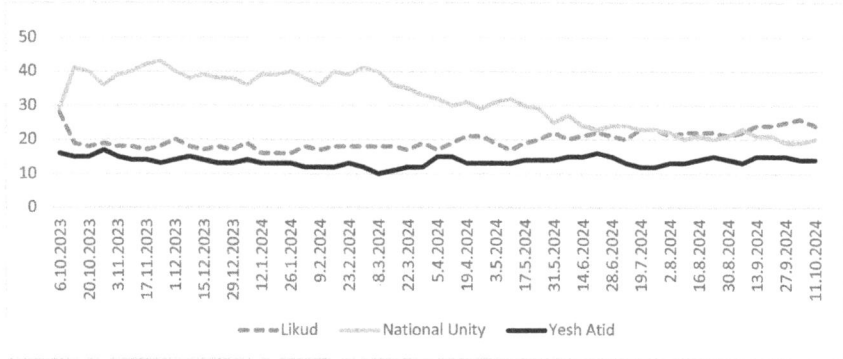

Figure 6. Poll predictions of the three largest parties' seat shares since the Hamas War.

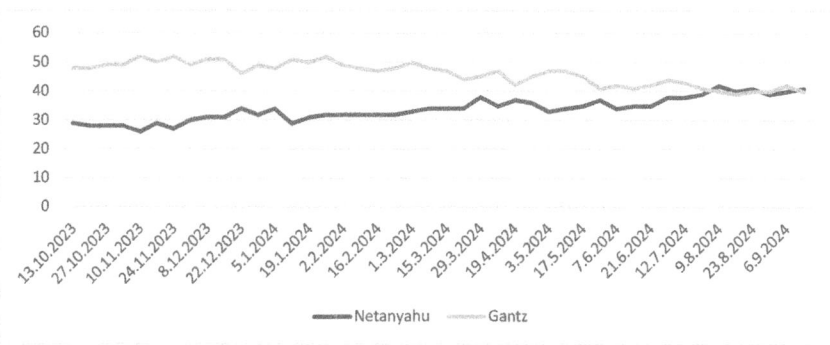

Figure 7. The suitability of Benjamin Netanyahu vs Benny Gantz for the position of prime minister.

Conclusion

The Israeli party system was in a deep state of malaise when Hamas inflicted the worst terror attack the nation had ever suffered. Although in the immediate aftermath of the massacre it seemed that the need for political national unity in the face of national existential threat would overcome political polarization, the party system quickly rebounded to its pre-war state of divisions. The emergency government proved to be short-lived, and the largest opposition party, Yesh Atid, consistently maintained its determined fight to try and remove Prime Minister Netanyahu from office. Yet, thanks to its internal cohesion and stability, the incumbent coalition has made significant gains by the eve of the first anniversary of the Hamas attack as it both enlarged its parliamentary support base and was steadily closing the gap of its popularity deficit. At the time of writing, Prime Minister Netanyahu's sixth government has turned out to be the most stable coalition since the inception of the governability crisis in 2019. This is not an insignificant achievement. Although the state of polarization has certainly not abated and Israeli society remained no less deeply divided one year into the war than it had been before, the party system seems to have restabilized and has kept the potential for government instability in check, which is a crucial asset at a time of war.

Conclusion: October 7—The Wars over Words and Deeds— Taking Stock

Donna Robinson Divine

Calendars to the contrary, if the history Francis Fukuyama's declared over was not restarted on 9/11, it was certainly resurrected on October 7. That day's savagery not only exerted a gravitational pull toward war and destruction across the Middle East; it also powered prophecies of global catastrophe. As proud of their capacity for torture as for their occupation of Israeli territory, Hamas militants spread videos of their atrocities across the internet even as they were committing them. That such an obvious rampage could be instantly converted into the well-known fable where Israel is always the aggressor and the sole cause of the region's bloodshed is extraordinary even in an age of artificial intelligence. Labeling Israel a purveyor of genocide essentially holds the country's citizens, no matter their words or their deeds, responsible for the barbaric attacks they endured at the hands of a group proudly proclaiming its right to kill off a people and obliterate its homeland. Thus, did October 7 launch fierce wars as much over words as over deeds with Hamas supporters embracing actions more akin to cultic rituals than to movements calibrated to dispense concrete political achievements.

A discourse emerged filled with so many distortions of history and of reality that it convinced the contributors to this book of the need, not only to set the record straight but, perhaps more importantly, to establish a record. What gives our project its narrative coherence is not simply the information it presents to increase the understanding of what actually happened, but also the energy it hopefully generates for the next set of questions to investigate. Surely this book matters not only because of what its several essays disclose but also because it is able to spur continuous serious inquiries. Let me take stock, then, of how well this volume has discharged this dual scholarly mission.

Part One: On the Violence and the Myths

Before it was a rampage, it was a myth: that a history gone wrong in 1948 could be reset. Turning Southern Israel into a slaughterhouse would show the world that eviscerating the Jewish state was possible and that only such bloodshed could bring its victims the redemption they deserved.

It is not unusual for wars to generate myths. The First World War is often associated with the deification of the nation-state as the structuring principle for peace despite unleashing forces that produced unprecedented scales of murder and suffering. But magical thinking about 1948 came before its enactment in the October 7 atrocities, conferring authority on what was imagined, not on what actually happened. The orgy of violence drew its emotional resonance as both a symbol of atonement for the founding of the Jewish state and as a vow to cleanse the world of its demonic force.

Such magical thinking instantly took hold of the university campus as faculty and students proclaimed Hamas's savagery the pathway to liberation. The slogans—"Palestine will be free [or, in Arabic, 'will be made Arab'] from the river to the sea"—chanted by people awash in clothing conscripted for political, not fashion, statements, soon flowed through accounts in the mainstream media.[1] Rhymed couplets professed a hallucinatory vision of extirpating the Jewish state, performances that gave off a distinct preference for fiction rather than for reality.

For October 7 was no ordinary Hamas assault on Israel. Nor was it distilled from the pattern laid down in earlier Israeli-Gaza wars—from 2008 to 2012, 2014, 2021. Past clashes were stopped by international mediation limiting casualties even as their numbers were consistently higher for Palestinians than for Israelis. October 7 was different because it was intended to change the direction of regional political developments and to return history to its proper orbit where it would deliver justice to Palestinians, the people presumably so long denied it. The carnage aimed not at echoing the past but rather at showcasing how to undo it.

Instead of considering where the October 7 depravity was likely to take Israelis and Palestinians, protests turned attention away from the present and back to

---

[1] Simon Plosker, "When the Media Battlefield and the Home Front Collide," Honest Reporting, October 6, 2024.

the trauma of 1948. No sooner had the torture, occupation of Israeli territory and military bases, the emptying out of cities and communities in the south and north been trumpeted across social media, they were retrofitted as restitution for the devastation of 1948, holding butchered Israelis accountable for the depredations perpetuated on them in 2023. This is a remarkable view of history; it never ends. Not only can history be reframed, it can also be redone.

An outlook that appears a throwback to an era associated with the irrational has been incorporated into contemporary idioms of global politics primarily because its core narrative is carried by a word—*Nakba*—that overflows with imagery. The term—linguistically associated with natural disasters—began its political odyssey when it was deployed to account for the massive defeat of Arab armies in the 1948 War. Primarily aimed at awakening Arabs to the need for modernization and for national unity, this Arabic word for catastrophe was initially reinvented to shock Arabs into addressing the serious dysfunctions across their lands.[2] The Palestine question in this reading was cited as concrete evidence of the need for radical change and as capable of being addressed only in the aftermath of regional transformation.

Linking unity and modernization brought Arab countries a future riddled with many more defeats than victories. Despite massive investments in training and weapons, the military capacities of the Arab states never matched those fielded by Israel. And, ironically, the more the ambitions for Arab national solidarity were proclaimed or even attempted, the more the violence and dislocation as aspirations for unity sucked in malign forces spewing out instability within the borders mapped by states in the Middle East.

Ensnared by trying to reach impossible goals, Arab states were also trapped by conflicting imperatives that turned their confrontations with Israel into domestic disasters spreading suffering across the Middle East. Arab state failures only deepened the dependency of Palestinians on international organizations because they were caught in the crossfire of the radically different policies of countries where they found refuge. Dependency was so pervasive that Palestinians reconfigured the definition of *Nakba* as the core element of their identity. Palestinians wanted the world to see them as a people subjugated by an oppression that imbued them with a legitimate, if not sacred right to resistance, by any means. Palestinian identity became simultaneously a trope for powerlessness and a metaphor for righteous redemption through violence.

---

2   Constantin Zureiq, *Ma'ana al-Nakba* [The meaning of catastrophe] (Beirut: n.p., 1948). See also Eugene L. Rogan and Avi Shlaim, *The War for Palestine: Rewriting the History of 1948* (Cambridge: Cambridge University Press, 2007).

This perspective ricochets through the contemporary discourse tightly coiled around Palestinians as indelibly stamped by their catastrophic defeat (*nakba*) of 1948 and by the unacknowledged persistence of its wounds—displacement, alienation, and indignity. For that reason, the Palestinian narrative focuses not on what can be done in the present but rather on what should be undone from the past, a preoccupation not only hovering over political decisions, but also imprisoning them. Even raising questions about the familiar template of Palestinians as innocents—they produced their own multimedia show of October 7 deeds—is to be condemned as complicit in their subjugation.

Viewing Israel as a source of the world's evil provides continuous inspiration for the conviction that the Jewish state can be exterminated. The horrors of October 7 are the latest graphic illustration of this outlook. What typically follows the savagery of deeds is, in fact, the savagery of words. A lexicon is quilted to signal that what was done to Jews is righteous, but what the Jewish state is doing to Palestinians constitutes "crimes against humanity."[3] Supporters of Hamas now adopt a set of memes more suitable for TikTok than for the OED saturating a scripted language with a mission akin to a secular ritual that produces experiences—a sense of the sublime—forging connections and links rather than transmitting information or deepening knowledge.

The Hamas juggernaut capturing Israeli land and subjecting communities to death and destruction radiates energy to all sorts of protest movements by showing that borders can be crossed, prominent cultural institutions disgraced, and military power broken if hostile to a sacred cause. A performative culture—waving a keffiyeh, carrying a flag—fed rounds of political mobilization against established structures of power denounced for never moving beyond their colonial, racist past and for recycling rather than erasing poverty, oppression, and violence. Organizations charged with producing knowledge, scientific research, medical cures, records of the lived experiences of the past, once taken for granted as indispensable, become disposable but not only because of some daisy-chain links to the Jewish state. After all, Christmas Church services have no obvious connection to Israel yet they have been disrupted.

The demonstrations are designed to give the impression that opposing Israel is a core sign of the times, a cosmic generational issue, which will have a seismic electoral power in the future. Embracing Hamas is now the ready-made portal

---

3   Peter Berkowitz, "Disregarding Military Necessity to Accuse Israel of War Crimes," Real Clear Politics, December 22, 2024. See also Alexander Yacobson and Azar Gat, "Reply to Michael Walzer on Israel's Pager Attack and Just War Theory," Real Clear Politics, October 13, 2024.

to enter the order combating global inequity. For the fault line dividing the old oppressive order from the new progressive just world is said to run decisively and deeply through Palestine. Israel's supporters live in the past while the future assigns liberation passports to their righteous victims, no matter the brutality spilling forth from their acts.

Palestinians have turned their confrontation with Zionism into a clash of civilizations. Repeatedly rejecting the many options put before them to build a state and forge their own national future, Palestinian leaders have chosen to enact their national struggle as a cause rather than as a battle for land and sovereignty. That decision has brought them international attention, material resources and massive suffering for those engaged in an apocalyptic war that can never be won and never ended.

Part Two: On the Global Delusions

October 7 opened a front against a global order at a time when its resources were stretched and the institutions set up for conflict resolution unstable, partly the outcome of an ongoing stalemated war on the European continent. More importantly, an infrastructure designed to reduce conflict in the twentieth century is clearly not capable of constructing a strategy effective for stopping wars in the twenty-first. It is wishful thinking on a grand scale to believe the international order is discharging its mandate to resolve disputes or even to manage them. Everywhere there is evidence of failure. Consider America's struggle to stop Houthi piracy across sea lanes vital to commerce reversing an eighty-year US Naval history of keeping trade routes to the Middle East and Europe open. Challenges to cargo shipping have reached as far as the Indo-Pacific, weakening the spine that sustains globalization.[4]

The institutions invested with the expectation to protect people from harm may actually be the breeding ground for chaos and violence. For these institutions are precariously perched on an unstable alloy of states whose power is weakening and whose interest in sustaining a shared system of rules is eroding.[5]

The international order has not been shattered this seriously since the First World War, when multi-ethnic, religiously diverse empires collapsed.

---

4   David Samuels, "Rapid-Onset Political Enlightenment," *Tablet*, December 19, 2024, https://www.tabletmag.com/sections/arts-letters/articles/rapid-onset-political-enlightenment.
5   John Spencer, "What the ICC/ICJ/UN Gets Wrong about Israel," Jewish News Syndicate, July 17, 2024, https://www.jns.org/what-the-icc-icj-un-gets-wrong-about-israel/.

Substituting the nation state for the fallen imperial realms fulfilled some but not all ambitions, and the map drawn then still projects instability and fosters violence. No better example of its contested cartography can be found than in the Middle East. The post-First World War era offer to Zionism may have given the movement its first major success, but the widespread rage and opposition it provoked in the region tainted the very idea of the state as the adequate antidote to perpetual war.

The second significant triumph for Zionism came after the Nazis had destroyed an entire European Jewish population in the Second World War. Great Britain still governed Palestine, but its last official policy statement in 1939 promised a single state that would leave Jews a minority. Because Zionism's leaders viewed such an outcome as unacceptable, they launched a strategy, combining violence and diplomacy to win Jewish independence. Perhaps because of an unstated feeling that a Jewish State might serve as some compensation for genocide or because the country was waging its struggle against what was then considered the avatar of colonialism—the British Empire—Israel found sufficient global backing for its fight for independence.

Despite Israel's many successes—a population under a million in 1948 reaching almost ten million today, a standard of living its founders could not have imagined, let alone built, men and women from all sectors of society continuing to display absolute willingness to pay the high prices exacted for preserving their citizenship—the country has never been able to disgorge the belief that the founding of a Jewish state was a historic mistake, a past gone wrong that must be—and actually can be—set right. The United Nations' decision to accept the 1947 partition resolution, typically cited as the basis for Israel's legitimacy, was, for some in today's telling, the trigger for wars, dispossession, and grotesque injustices.

Still, the intense focus on Israel's national Jewish identity as the single reason for the landscape of protests is overdrawn. For part of what motivates principled opposition to Israel is the country's embrace of the state as a just and legitimate form of political association. Many of Hamas's most fervent disciples condemn the state as a fatally flawed framework. It is undoubtedly true that the state generates and perpetuates the inequities linked to birthplace. The place and circumstances of birth have an enormous impact on life span as well as on opportunities offered and restrictions imposed. A state inevitably limits the kinds of community that can be "imagined" because its borders are drawn to divide people as much as to unite them. Globalization and the internet have added to the erosion of the idea of the state as the default setting for the world opening up a breach that movements waging battles against oppression and inequality want to fill.

On this view, the state of Israel only compounds the injustices emanating from empowering the Jewish nation.

Nothing explains the reason for the scant evidence of apostasy about the state better than the Nova Music Festival, a gathering promoting universal peace and love, now branded in the country's memory as a field of mass murder, serial rapes, and kidnappings. October 7 reminded all Israelis of the fragility of their country when state institutions go missing in action.

As the killings unfolded, the army issued its call up for reserves to report for combat. 130% responded. Hundreds of thousands of Israelis who were traveling or working in other countries made their way back to their homeland to put themselves directly in the line of fire. Groups that had spent ten months demanding an end to the government's announced plans for judicial reform instantly reoriented their focus to the people evacuated from their communities, helping them to relocate together even as government ministries stopped functioning. Every video of volunteers packing food or clothing or toys for the tens of thousands of people forced out of towns and villages in the north and south shows religious Muslims and Jews working together. Every survey counts more Israeli Arabs supporting the war, increasingly identifying firmly as citizens of Israel.[6] Every public demonstration draws Arabs and Jews. Israeli Arab citizens who were supposed to be released from prison in exchange for hostages preferred having their day in an Israeli court even at the expense of an instant release. Walking into the assembly of people calling for the hostages to be freed, several leaders of the Druze community received a prolonged standing ovation. Finally, it is important to note that, since October 7 plunged Israel into wars on seven fronts, the birth rate has skyrocketed.[7]

The stampede of violence after October 7 has also had a seismic impact on the institutions designed to consolidate the current supposedly rules-based order. The military aim to destroy Hamas forced Israel into an epic confrontation against the well-funded international infrastructure built around the Palestinians as refugees and innocent victims. To defeat Hamas required attacking UNRWA personnel and facilities, for the two had become intertwined. Some UNRWA employees participated in the October 7 savagery; others seized or held hostages. Some worked as teachers in UNRWA schools while training as Hamas

---

6   "Amid War, Poll Finds Arab Israelis' Sense of Kinship with State at a 20-Year High," *Times of Israel*, November 11, 2023, https://www.timesofisrael.com/amid-war-poll-finds-arab-israelis-sense-of-kinship-with-state-at-a-20-year-high/.

7   Rachel Fink, "Israel Sees Wartime 'Baby Boom' With 10 Percent Rise in Births in Final Months of 2024," *Haaretz*, January 10, 2025.

field soldiers. Unlike the approach adopted by the UN for refugees from other countries, which emphasized safety and rehabilitation, UNRWA was invested with the principle of encouraged Palestinians in their care to adopt a so-called right of return to their original homes and villages. Until they returned, they remained refugees, a condition that turned out to be permanent for them and a cachet for their progeny.

Unsurprisingly, their numbers keep rising as descendants of the original refugee population are incorporated into UNRWA's mandate exponentially increasing the count from 894,000 in 1950 to 5,442,947 in 2019.[8] The UN cannot afford to lose so critical a part of its structure and budget regardless of its involvement in the massacre. The Western countries funding these international agencies were uncomfortable with the disclosures of UN personnel joining the atrocities if only because of their own role in sustaining an infrastructure implicated in periodic outbursts of violence.

But the international organizations servicing Palestinian needs are still able to count on a sacred status acquired over many decades. For the countries funding them, the costs of replacing these international enterprises are too high, too complicated, and likely to provoke domestic unrest given the substantial demographic shifts in Europe.

Finally, it is important to remember that the democracies once in charge of the global order are not the only game in town. China, Russia, Iran, and North Korea provide alternatives attractive to many rulers of countries opposing the norms set up initially by democracies in Europe or America. Better to continue to cultivate ambiguity about the links between international relief charities and Hamas regardless of the facts. The response to the discovery of stocks of weapons or intelligence headquarters in subterranean locations beneath hospitals or to the battles erupting near schools and mosques serving as staging grounds for attacks is to double down on the suffering in Gaza.

To borrow from Bob Dylan, the times they are a-changing, and sometimes you do not need to be a weatherman to see just which way the wind is blowing. Gaza wars in the past have spurred international pressure on Israel to stop the bloodletting and permit the customary pay-offs to Hamas leaders in return for burying their rocket launchers until exhumed before the next round. But what may provide relief to the international order strikes fear in Israel and may be fatal to its long-term survival if not to its short-term recovery.

---

8   Adi Schwartz and Einat Wilf, *The War of Return: How Western Indulgence of the Palestinian Dream Has Obstructed the Path to Peace* (New York: St. Martin's Press, 2020).

Part Three: On the Campus Land of Make-Believe

It says something about American higher education that so many university presidents are applauded for holding graduation ceremonies despite weeks of student encampments set up to protest the Gaza War. Proclaiming the return to peace in our time at the end of the semester calendar, university heads were keen to praise the moral seriousness of students, double down on the difference between antizionism and antisemitism, emphasize the sanctity of free speech in what were called "mostly peaceful demonstrations," and to consider, if not defer, to demands to explore breaking educational, cultural, and financial ties with Israel. Accompanying algorithmically generated messages were also somber pleas for a permanent ceasefire in Gaza, sometimes—but not always—adding the return of the hostages to the entreaties.

That not one leader of what are considered the best universities and colleges across the globe demanded students gain more knowledge about the origins and evolution of the Middle East Conflict is telling. No one even dared ask student protesters to interrogate whether their demands were consistent with an accurate reading of history or politics—regional or global—or whether their appeals to "globalize the intifada" were likely to bring on more war or more peace for the very people their protests were intended to serve. Conceding to sufficient demands to enable graduation festivities effectively reduced what is supposed to be an intellectual discourse to the level of sound bites, becoming just another example of academic failure. It also catalyzed the Gaza War into the same cliches about the Israeli Palestinian conflict that not only perpetuates false assumptions but also helps sustain the ongoing violence.

Few images exert as enduring a hold on the campus political imagination as Palestinians as part of the "wretched of the earth," deprived of power to forge their own future through ordinary diplomatic negotiations. Ground down into passivity, Palestinians are supposedly confined by their own incapacity for action into either violent outbursts or into appeals to people of goodwill to become their tribunes for restitution.

For that reason, the rapists, kidnappers, and mutilators were transubstantiated by activist-scholars into icons of liberation to encourage the people across the globe to see these atrocities as models for emancipatory impulses. Not even Frantz Fanon imagined a violence of this magnitude laying the foundation for genuine post-colonial freedom.

The apocalyptic images of dead Israelis on October 7 became the prelude to "liberation" bestowing a sacred quality on Hamas's depravity. The anti-Israel crusades on campus not only degraded the study of the Jewish state, they also denied Palestinians full access to their actual historical record. It required so many inversions of language that the development of the Jewish national home is condemned now not by might or by power but rather by false analogies, misplaced modifiers, and mistakenly applied theories. Consider the word "genocide." That the Palestinian population on the West Bank and Gaza has increased fourfold since 1948, according to the Palestine Central Bureau of Statistics' 2024 assessment, should elicit an instant correction if not apology for rhetorical excess. But lack of a single shred of evidence that can corroborate an alleged Zionist genocidal impulse has done nothing to short-circuit its deployment in classrooms and lecture halls.

A chatbot-like narrative, splicing away at facts, is pitched to fit in with campus campaigns for social and racial justice as activists churn up their rhetoric to include every imaginable war crime no matter how totally unmoored from reality it might be. Think how easily the misfiring of a Palestinian Jihad missile killing scores of people in the parking lot of the Ahli Baptist hospital was marketed by major Western media outlets as an Israeli atrocity producing five hundred casualties. Hamas needed an Israeli war crime, so it invented one, and successfully retailed it to CNN, BBC, MSNBC, Associated Press, the *Washington Post*, and the *New York Times*, outlets that retained their headlines, if not their fake pictures, of the so-called depravity long after the evidence was available to debunk it.

Campus idioms became the soundtrack for protests within and without the well-groomed grounds of the university. A world divided between oppressors and oppressed comes pre-installed with free speech replacing academic freedom. It awards credit to feelings, not to thinking; it pays tribute to narrative and not to empirical evidence.

What should be happening on campuses regarding the Middle East conflict—meticulous research with a careful examination of data and events aiming for clarity—has too often been discarded for an advocacy that masquerades as scholarship with books and articles feeding each other in a cul-de-sac like an echo chamber claiming a kind of "intellectual legitimacy" through repetition rather than through a process of objective verification.

Totally lost beneath the calls for civil discourse was the core principle that should have been paramount for the academy: namely, how to offer students an education that gives them credible knowledge about the history and politics of a conflict so many embraced as a righteous cause without the faintest idea of what the slogans emblazoned on their banners or shouted out in their marches actually mean. University courses should show students how to think about the Middle East, not how to imagine this conflict aligning with how they see themselves.

That Hamas attacks did not trigger questions and discussions is a missed opportunity. What kind of liberation can Palestinians expect from people willing to unleash this kind of violence? Will Palestinians gain individual freedom from such a victory? The same experts who caution Israel to think long and hard about what will happen once Hamas is defeated militarily should also consider what is likely to follow if Hamas wins. These are critical questions particularly for social justice warriors who call to make Palestine whole from the Mediterranean to the Jordan River. If the terrible toll exacted by this more than a hundred years' war produces only shouts and slogans, then the academy, itself, is likely and rightfully to be listed as one of its casualties.

Part Four: On the Broken Social Contract

No one in Israel saw the October 7 attacks coming, but it did not take long for the country's citizens to feel snagged by a government whose sell-by date was thought to have expired on that terrible day. Nothing is the same in Israel since October 7 except the prime minister and his major coalition partners. Unlike other wars Israel has fought remembered for their Hebrew names, this one will likely continue to carry the name of "October 7" because the barbarism of that day was not only a portrait of terror but also a mirror of failure.

An October 7 massacre would rip the social contract undergirding the almost universally recognized right of any state to protect the lives and property of its citizens. Such a traumatic shattering of the fundamental commitments of a state to its citizens would also certainly have been understood as thrusting war upon any country suffering such an assault. But October 7's savagery had a deeper resonance in an Israel founded precisely to end the chain of catastrophes that cycled so repeatedly through Jewish history. No word is more evocative of October 7's rupture than *ḥatufim*,[9] the term most Israelis have adopted for hostages, particularly since others were available. *Ḥatufim* carries a deep historical resonance. It identifies an era when Jews were paid to round up young men in their villages for

---

9   Philologos, "Israelis Have Three Different Words for 'Hostages,'" *Mosaic*, September 12, 2024, https://mosaicmagazine.com/observation/israel-zionism/2024/09/israelis-have-three-different-words-for-hostages/.

long military service in accordance with quotas set by Czar Nicholas I in Russia. The word itself evokes a terror unleashed from the outside tearing apart the close, sometimes intimate, ties binding community members to one another.

Tales of October 7 horror and of uncommon acts of bravery have leached into popular discourse and will endure as stories laced with a bitter twenty-first century irony shaded with the dread of 1948 looming in the background. For the first time since Israel's War of Independence, battles raged on land within the borders mapped, however tentatively, in 1949. A titanic struggle for safety and security can no longer be said to be behind Israelis who had to evacuate homes and communities in the country's north and south and who still are unable to return.

That there is no prescribed atonement for such a cataclysmic breach of the social contract does not rule out a reckoning by the very people whose lives and futures have been put on the line by a government that had already inflicted prolonged misgovernance on the county. For, even if a massacre on this scale could not have been imagined or predicted, a hollowing-out of the state's principles had already opened sinkholes in the country in ten months of protests against the government's agenda to reform the judiciary.

In the election, returning Benjamin Netanyahu to his sixth term as prime minister, the defining issue judging by campaign rhetoric appeared to be security and political stability. But the coalition cobbled together several months after the election wrapped the government around an agreement centered on transforming the judiciary. That agenda reflected much more about what was needed to bind together political parties with disparate interests in January 2023 than about what drove the votes cast in November 2022 in one or another direction. In fact, the specific judicial overhaul pushed forward in January was purposely constructed to prevent securing any conceivable parliamentary consensus.

The alarm bells once ringing over judicial reform have been redirected onto the conduct of the war since October 7. It seems reasonable to wonder if military gains will be squandered by a coalition not only divided over goals and priorities but also about plans for a post-war Gaza. Widely reported public disputes between government ministers—and the firing of the minister of defense—cannot help but add to public unease about the judgment of those who should be held to account for a war no one anticipated and for whose devastation few in the governing coalition acknowledge as a consequence of their words or their deeds.

There is a persistent cloud following the government coalition that can be distilled down to the prime minister's unwillingness to be held accountable for Israel's security failures. Despite the emergence of a new reality, the governing coalition has been preserved, along with much of its controversial critical budgetary allocations, in this, Israel's longest and most complicated war. coalition stability seems to propel the nation toward division rather than unity. Prime Minister Netanyahu is determined to step into the legendary role of wartime leader to bring a victory to wash away any association he might have with the horrors of October 7. It is no accident that Netanyahu has appeared in Knesset debates with a copy of Plutarch's *The Rise and Fall of Athens*, a book that offers vivid descriptions of the magnificent speeches of Pericles.[10] Or that he and his personal advisor, Ron Dermer, in back-to-back long interviews in the *Wall Street Journal*, give Netanyahu almost exclusive credit for the country's military victory over Hamas and Hezbollah and even for transforming the Middle East.[11]

Notwithstanding the brilliant military achievements, the public bickering between ministers and officials overseeing defense and security services coupled with open accusations of disloyalty throw any claims of serving a common national purpose by the government into stark relief. Many ministers assume that the election empowered them to continue to conduct policies reflective of their political party wills notwithstanding the law of the land or without regard to the wisdom of altering highly volatile policies—Jewish prayer on the Temple Mount comes to mind—at a time when the country is crisscrossed by violence. Acting as if an election, no matter how free and fair, granted consent for a mandate to remake the country, stretches, if not distorts, the power conferred through suffrage.

That there has been no serious public soul searching about October 7 by those at the helm of the state compounds the sense of crisis if not the growing conviction of a leadership whose interests are inconsistent with the needs of its citizens. Nothing has done more to illustrate the unshakeable faith of the coalition in its own rectitude than its adamant refusal to authorize a state investigation of October 7 failures. Rejecting such a probe is viewed as a desperate bid to stave off a torrent of criticism likely to be directed at Prime Minister Netanyahu who was prime minister for almost all of the years Israel adopted what is now seen as a flawed strategic doctrine. In the book Netanyahu published in 2022, he wrote that "the cost in blood and treasure [of overthrowing Hamas] was not worth it," adding, "Did I really want

---

10 Yehuda Halper, "Netanyahu and the Siege of Samos," *Times of Israel*, June 18, 2024, https://blogs.timesofisrael.com/netanyahu-and-the-siege-of-samos/.

11 Barton Swaim, "How Israel Turned the Mideast Around," *Wall Street Journal*, December 13, 2024, https://www.wsj.com/opinion/how-israel-took-its-own-side-in-a-fight-middle-east-policy-war-a98838dc; Elliott Kaufman, "Benjamin Netanyahu: The Inside Story of Israel's Victory," *Wall Street Journal*, December 20, 2024, https://www.wsj.com/opinion/netanyahu-the-inside-story-of-israels-comeback-victory-middle-east-change-dad847d8.

to tie down the IDF in Gaza for years, when we had to deal with Iran and a possible Syrian front? The answer was categorically no. I had bigger fish to fry."[12]

Denying Israelis a full and fair probe into what went wrong on October 7 is a fundamental breach of Zionism's founding principles. For the essential and original Zionist claim was not that Jewish nation building was unique but rather that Jews possessed a different way of being a nation. Zionism proposed to expand the ethical claim that all were responsible for caring for their community into the core norm of obligation defining citizenship in what would become the Jewish state.

Citizenship in Israel gives priority to the idea of obligation rather than to any bill of individual rights. The commitment to guarantee individual rights, always taken for granted implicitly, has only become more explicitly delineated as the country has grown in population and in diversity. It has taken time for the idea of rights to unfold and co-exist equally with the notion of obligations. Both norms ripened a set of institutions that manage and preserve the tensions between "duties" and "rights" rather than dissolve either of them. They co-exist because they are, in fact, co-dependent. Institutional protection for individual rights drives economic growth, military power, global prestige, and international alliances while the expectation that citizens will discharge their duties sustain traditions, solidarity, and historical memory. The first increases the value of a Jewish state; the second, adds to its endurance.

Everything that has happened since the October 7 tragedy has shown that Israelis—whatever their ancestry, ethnicity, religion, or religious practice—are determined not only to investigate the reasons for this tragedy but also to preserve the state as the place they call home. While there is no prescribed atonement for the breach wrought by October 7, Israelis have shown quite decisively by running toward not away from the fire that they want not only a thorough investigation of the reasons for such massive failures but also a reckoning. An election is the only political mechanism that offers a judgment on whether a government has met the needs and demands of its citizens. Israelis deserve to be able to ask as much from their rulers as those same people making fateful decisions demand from them.

---

12   Martin Kramer, "Bibi's Evolving Hamas Story," *Sandbox*, August 11, 2024, https://martinkramer.org/2024/08/11/bibis-evolving-hamas-story/.

www.ingramcontent.com/pod-product-compliance
Ingram Content Group UK Ltd.
Pitfield, Milton Keynes, MK11 3LW, UK
UKHW020259141225
465959UK00005B/37